Automobility and the City
in Twentieth-Century Britain and Japan

SOAS Studies in Modern and Contemporary Japan

SERIES EDITOR:
Christopher Gerteis (SOAS, University of London, UK)

EDITORIAL BOARD:
Stephen Dodd (SOAS, University of London, UK)
Andrew Gerstle (SOAS, University of London, UK)
Janet Hunter (London School of Economics, UK)
Barak Kushner (University of Cambridge, UK)
Helen Macnaughtan (SOAS, University of London, UK)
Aaron W Moore (University of Edinburgh, UK)
Timon Screech (SOAS, University of London, UK)
Naoko Shimazu (NUS-Yale College, Singapore)

Published in association with the Japan Research Centre at the School of Oriental and African Studies, University of London, UK.

SOAS Studies in Modern and Contemporary Japan features scholarly books on modern and contemporary Japan, showcasing new research monographs as well as translations of scholarship not previously available in English. Its goal is to ensure that current, high-quality research on Japan, its history, politics and culture is made available to an English-speaking audience.

Published:
Women and Democracy in Cold War Japan, Jan Bardsley
Christianity and Imperialism in Modern Japan, Emily Anderson
The China Problem in Postwar Japan, Robert Hoppens
Media, Propaganda and Politics in 20th Century Japan, The Asahi Shimbun Company
(translated by Barak Kushner)
Contemporary Sino-Japanese Relations on Screen, Griseldis Kirsch
Debating Otaku in Contemporary Japan,
edited by Patrick W. Galbraith, Thiam Huat Kam and Björn-Ole Kamm
Politics and Power in 20th-Century Japan, Mikuriya Takashi and Nakamura Takafusa
(translated by Timothy S. George)
Japanese Taiwan, edited by Andrew Morris
Japan's Postwar Military and Civil Society, Tomoyuki Sasaki
The History of Japanese Psychology, Brian J. McVeigh

Postwar Emigration to South America from Japan and the Ryukyu Islands,
Pedro Iacobelli
The Uses of Literature in Modern Japan, Sari Kawana
Post-Fascist Japan, Laura Hein
Mass Media, Consumerism and National Identity in Postwar Japan,
Martyn David Smith
Japan's Occupation of Java in the Second World War, Ethan Mark
Gathering for Tea in Modern Japan, Taka Oshikiri
Engineering Asia, Hiromi Mizuno, Aaron S. Moore and John DiMoia
Automobility and the City in Twentieth-Century Britain and Japan.
Simon Gunn and Susan C. Townsend

Forthcoming:
Kenkoku University and the Experience of Pan-Asianism, Yuka Hiruma Kishida

Automobility and the City in Twentieth-Century Britain and Japan

Simon Gunn, University of Leicester, UK
and
Susan C. Townsend, University of Nottingham, UK

BLOOMSBURY ACADEMIC
LONDON • NEW YORK • OXFORD • NEW DELHI • SYDNEY

BLOOMSBURY ACADEMIC
Bloomsbury Publishing Plc
50 Bedford Square, London, WC1B 3DP, UK
1385 Broadway, New York, NY 10018, USA
29 Earlsfort Terrace, Dublin 2, Ireland

BLOOMSBURY, BLOOMSBURY ACADEMIC and the Diana logo
are trademarks of Bloomsbury Publishing Plc

First published in Great Britain 2019
Paperback edition published 2021

Copyright © Simon Gunn and Susan C. Townsend, 2019

Simon Gunn and Susan C. Townsend have asserted their right under the Copyright,
Designs and Patents Act, 1988, to be identified as Authors of this work.

Cover image © Traffic crossing under bridge at
Shibuya Station, Tokyo, Japan. (© Björn Neumann/Getty Images).

All rights reserved. No part of this publication may be reproduced or transmitted
in any form or by any means, electronic or mechanical, including photocopying,
recording, or any information storage or retrieval system, without prior
permission in writing from the publishers.

Bloomsbury Publishing Plc does not have any control over, or responsibility for,
any third-party websites referred to or in this book. All internet addresses given
in this book were correct at the time of going to press. The author and publisher
regret any inconvenience caused if addresses have changed or sites have ceased
to exist, but can accept no responsibility for any such changes.

A catalogue record for this book is available from the British Library.

A catalog record for this book is available from the Library of Congress.

ISBN:	HB:	978-1-3500-7593-1
	PB:	978-1-3502-0177-4
	ePDF:	978-1-3500-7594-8
	eBook:	978-1-3500-7595-5

Series: SOAS Studies in Modern and Contemporary Japan

Typeset by Integra Software Services Pvt. Ltd.

To find out more about our authors and books visit www.bloomsbury.com
and sign up for our newsletters.

In memory of Derek John Townsend (1934–1988)

Contents

List of Figures	xi
List of Graphs	xiii
Preface	xiv
Note on Text and Translation	xviii
Introduction: Automobility and the City between East and West	1
Japan and Britain	3
Motor cities: Nagoya and Birmingham	5
East and West	11
Objectives	12
1 Planning the Automotive City, c. 1920–1960	17
Traffic and the history of town planning	18
The emergence of the professional town planner	23
The impact of the Second World War	26
Post-war reconstruction	29
The rise of the motor industry	35
The onset of mass motorization	37
Conclusion	41
2 Civic Engineering: Roads Construction and the Urban Environment	43
The motor revolution and its consequences	46
Civic engineering	52
Traffic architecture	61
The physical environment of the motor city	67
Conclusion	70
3 Automobility and Urban Form	73
Urban form before 1945	74
Transport and urban form after 1945: Nagoya	78
Transport and urban form after 1945: Birmingham	88
Conclusion	96

4	Driving the Motor City: The Experience of Automobility	99
	The euphoria of the expressway	99
	Car ownership in the 'Motor Age'	101
	Automobility and consumerism	106
	Cultures of driving: Casualties, congestion and breakdown	111
	Driving and urban legibility	118
	Pedestrians and containment of the car	121
	Conclusion	124
5	Pollution and Protest	127
	Automobility and environmental awakening in the 1950s and 1960s	129
	Birmingham: The challenge of Spaghetti Junction	136
	The growth of protest in Birmingham	139
	Nemesis	142
	From Yokkaichi to Nagoya	144
	Crisis, compensation and adjustment 1972–1979	148
	Conclusion	151
6	*Kuruma Banare*: Turning Away from the Car?	155
	The Highbury initiative	155
	1973 and all that	157
	Rebalancing automobility	159
	The persistence of automobility	169
	Conclusion	172
Conclusion		175
	Meeting the objectives	177
Notes		184
Bibliography		222
Index		246

List of Figures

I.1	Map of cities in England and Wales	7
I.2	Map of cities in Japan	8
1.1	Personal transport before the car: Rickshaws in front of Nagoya station, *c.*1925	22
1.2	Birmingham City Engineer, Herbert Manzoni	24
1.3	Reconstructing the bomb-damaged city: Nagoya station in 1946	31
1.4	Corner of Navigation Street and Suffolk Street, Birmingham, 1952 – before the motor city	34
1.5	Hisaya Ōdōri under construction, 1946	35
2.1	The new Birmingham, 1964: Plan of the Inner Ring Road and city centre	44
2.2	Mobility and modernity Japanese-style: Hirokōji Dōri and Maruei department store, 1950s	45
2.3	The Birmingham Inner Ring Road under construction, 1959, with Bryant's sign	55
2.4	100-metre-wide road: Hisaya Ōdōri under construction at Sakae intersection at the end of the 1950s	57
2.5	Going underground: Underpass off Hurst Street, Birmingham, 1965	60
2.6	Urban neon: Ringway Centre by night, 1960	62
2.7	Smallbrook Ringway 1962 with the Albany hotel on right	66
2.8	Hisaya Ōdōri's wide vistas with the TV tower	68
2.9	Car park ramp off Moor Street Ringway, Birmingham	70
2.10	Underground street (*shitagai*) at Fushimi, Nagoya	71
3.1	Map of Nagoya wards, 1968	81
3.2	Approach to the Nagoya Station Complex (JR Central Towers) opened in 1999	82
3.3	Map of Chūbu region, Japan	83
3.4	Map of expressway system around Nagoya showing the Marusa formation at the centre	85
3.5	Map of Birmingham districts and surrounding towns in the West Midlands conurbation, *c.*1955	89
3.6	Concrete collar: Central Birmingham and the Inner Ring, 1973	92
4.1	1958 Subaru 360: The Lady Beetle	106

4.2	Artist's impression of the Bull Ring shopping centre, early 1960s	108
4.3	Manzoni Gardens, 1965, surrounded by roads	116
4.4	Pedestrians invade central Nagoya in the 'promenade', 1970	123
5.1	Aerial view of Gravelly Hill Interchange (Spaghetti Junction), 2008	137
6.1	Historic Tokyo dwarfed by the Metropolitan Expressway: The Meiji Nihonbashi Bridge	166
7.1	Space and vista: Hisaya Ōdōri seen from the TV tower	181

List of Graphs

1.1	Numbers of vehicles in Nagoya and Birmingham, 1955–1973	38
2.1	Private car ownership in Britain and Japan, 1945–2000	46
3.1	Percentage of passengers carried by mode of transport in the Chukyo transportation range, 1969–1975	86
3.2	Percentage of passengers carried by mode of transport in the Metropolitan transportation range, 1969–1975	87
4.1	Percentage of households with at least one car in Japan and Britain, 1951–2000	101
4.2	Department for Transport, Reported Traffic Accidents and Casualties, Great Britain 1950–2017 (HMSO, London, 2017)	112
4.3	Comparison of road accident injuries in Britain and Japan, 1950–2000	113
6.1	Personal transport vehicle ownership in Britain and Japan, 1945–2000	162

Preface

This book is the result of a collaboration between an urban historian of Britain (Simon Gunn) and a historian of ideas specializing in Japan (Susan Townsend). Collaborations such as this between different types of historian and across different societies have become increasingly rare. It is over fifteen years since the publication of the pioneering comparative study, *Urban Reconstruction in Britain and Japan, 1945–1955: Dreams, Plans and Realities,* co-authored by Nick Tiratsoo, Hasegawa Jun'ichi, Tony Mason and Takao Matsumura. Since then comparative history has given way to transnational and global history (themselves often construed as an extension of larger national histories of empire), while comparative studies of Japan and Britain have been almost non-existent. Partly for these reasons, our study has always had the air of an experiment, combining different approaches to historical writing – intellectual history and urban history – in a comparison of two countries – Japan and Britain – and two cities – Nagoya and Birmingham, which were, in particular respects, radically distinct and startlingly similar.

It has been a long project, starting in 2008 with the idea of comparing the history of Birmingham and Nagoya as 'motor cities'. Our departure point was the idea that Nagoya and Birmingham were, indeed, places worthy of comparison: both centrally located, second to their respective capitals, Tokyo and London, each with long histories of industrial production. In the twentieth century both cities became major centres of motor manufacturing – cars, motorbikes, vans, trucks – and began to be planned around the priorities of motor traffic. Birmingham and Nagoya, like the larger societies of which they were part, appeared a productive standpoint from which to examine a global historical process, automobility, which nevertheless exhibited distinctive cultural features in different countries and parts of the world. Our questions were specific and simple. How did mass motorization come about in Japan and Britain? How, in particular, was it integrated with cities which pre-existed the automobile age? What were its implications for the urban environment and how were its effects handled by people – politicians, planners, residents, drivers, pedestrians and others? Although straightforward, these questions had no ready answers. Automobility has only recently become an object of historical study in Britain and studies of automobility in Japan were almost all economic histories of the motor industry. There was no precedent for a comparative study of the relationship between automobility and the city in the two countries.

We were able to begin research in 2011 with the benefit of a generous grant from the Leverhulme Trust.[1] With the aid of two researchers, Matthew Parker and Mino Kōsei, sources and data were collected from a wide number of archives and libraries in Britain and Japan. As well as documentary records, such as those generated by departments of national and local government, a variety of primary sources were consulted including film, photographs, magazines, posters – and, of course, automobiles themselves. As the research progressed we became increasingly aware of the widening ramifications of the subject, from the micro-histories of local protest against roads 'blight' to the threat of global warming in which mass automobility has been a significant contributor. It also gradually became clear that our study, which originally focused on the relatively narrow period of 'high motorization' between the mid-1950s and the mid-1970s, required to be extended backwards and forwards in time. By expanding the time-period studied to extend from the 1920s to the 1990s, we highlight the long relationship between automobility and the city in places like Nagoya and Birmingham, where planning for motorization began early and the effects of automobility were long-lasting, enduring, indeed, to the present and beyond. As a consequence, our study now covers much of if not the whole of the twentieth century.

We have accumulated an unusual number of debts in the course of this study which has involved many people and institutions over the last decade. We are most grateful, firstly, to the Leverhulme Trust, whose grant made the research for this book possible. Special thanks go to Mino Kōsei and Matthew Parker, our researchers between 2012 and 2015, who not only uncovered many of the sources for us but also contributed significantly to the ideas we have elaborated in the book. We are grateful to the Centre for Advanced Studies (CAS) University of Nottingham for providing us with 'seed-corn' funding to hold a workshop in Birmingham in April 2010. Through the workshop we made contact with leading experts in the field of Japanese urban history, Paul Waley and André Sorensen, as well as in the history of urban planning in Britain and Birmingham, David Adams and Alan Wenban-Smith. At the workshop we also made contact with our Japanese colleagues Hotta Yoshihiro, an expert on the architecture of motorization, and historical geographer Mizoguchi Tsunetoshi at Nagoya University. Their generosity and support were invaluable in helping us organize a conference in Nagoya in April 2014, and we thank them and the University of Nagoya for their kind hospitality in hosting the event. We would also like to thank the librarians and archivists in the major collections used: the David Wilson Library, University of Leicester; Birmingham Central Library Archives and Local Studies; University of Birmingham Special Collections; the Media Archive for Central England, University of Lincoln; the National Archives; the British Library; Library of the Institute for Civil Engineers, London. We are grateful to the archivists and librarians in Japan in the collections used there: the National Diet Library, the Ministry of Land, Information, Transport and Tourism (MLIT) Library and the Japanese Automobile Manufacturers Association Library in Tokyo; the NHK Archives in Saitama; Nagoya City Archive, Toyota Museum of Science and Technology Library and the Nagoya Urban Institute in Nagoya.

We are most grateful to Mark Norton, who generously allowed access to the wonderful photographs of 1960s Birmingham by his father, D.J. Norton, and the related collections of Leonard Stace and Geoff Thompson. We offer our thanks to Network 2010 for allowing us to publish historic photographs from its website 'Timeline Nagoya' taken from collections held in the city's libraries and archives. Our thanks goes also to Dr Aaron Andrews, who provided invaluable assistance with maps, tables and putting the manuscript together.

Papers based on this project have been given at seminars, workshops and conferences at numerous institutions, including the universities of Leicester, Nottingham, Birmingham, Brunel, Cambridge, Manchester, Oxford and Reading; the Institute for Historical Research, London; the Nissan Institute, Oxford; the Department for Transport, London; Charles University, Prague, University of Helsinki and the Leibniz Institute for the Study of Society and Space, Erkner, Berlin; Columbia University, Yale University and the North American Conference on British Studies; the University of Talinn and the University of Nagoya. Simon Gunn and Susan Townsend are grateful to the organizers and participants in these meetings whose contributions have helped sharpen the arguments and ideas in the book. Simon Gunn is particularly grateful to the Leibniz Institute for the Study of Society and Space and the Charles University, Prague for opportunities to discuss the themes of the book with colleagues as visiting professor in 2014/5 and 2017.

Many other people have contributed directly to the project. On the Japanese side, Susan Townsend would like to thank Saho Matsumoto-Best and Anthony Best for introducing me to the city of Nagoya in 2004/5 by inviting me (and my husband Paul) to Nagoya City University (Meishidai) as visiting professor. At Nottingham, I extend special thanks to my colleagues in the Department of History, especially Sheryllynne Haggerty for encouraging me to present a paper at the AIB (Association of International Business) Conference at Reading in 2011, and then to publish it in the *Journal of Business History*. Sheryllynne also organized a workshop at Nottingham University, funded by CAS, on the theme of automobility at which I presented a paper, together with Simon Gunn and eminent expert on American transport history Maggie Walsh. Simon and I would like to thank Maggie for all her advice and for agreeing to serve as external advisor for the project, together with statistician Mike Baxter. In CAS, thanks must go to Sue Hopcroft, Sally Bowden and Lisa McCabe for their support in the process of preparing the Leverhulme bid. In the School of History, thanks goes also to Tracy Sisson in the Research Office for dealing with the complexity of the Japan-side of the finances. Finally, thanks to the anonymous engineer at the UoN Philoenic Society who, shortly before we left for Nagoya in 2004, said 'you do know don't you that Nagoya is the Birmingham of Japan,' thus planting the seed of an idea that was to grow years later into this project.

On the British side, Simon Gunn would like to thank Christoph Bernhardt, John Davis, Graeme Davison, Michael Dnes, John Gold, Erika Hanna, Peter Grimsdale, Luda Klusakova, Peter Larkham, Peter Mandler, Helen Meller, Frank Mort, Chris Otter, Gordon Pirie and Frank Trentmann for their advice and support at different points in the project. My colleagues at the Centre for Urban History, Leicester, provide a highly valued environment for research in British and global history. In particular, I should like to thank Richard Butler, Colin Hyde, Alistair Kefford and Prashant Kidambi together with recent PhD students who have worked on related topics, Richard Harrison, Sally Hartshorne and Georgina Lockton. Krista Cowman has provided perceptive comments and support over many years and I am especially grateful for the advice on the role of women in roads campaigns, drawing on her own pioneering research on women, children and the city. Otto Saumarez Smith has been a great colleague and advocate of a new urban history of later twentieth-century Britain;

the tri-annual workshops we have organized together since 2014 under the title of the Society for the Promotion of Urban Discussion have been a constant source of ideas and inspiration. A special debt is owed, too, to Guy Ortolano for his support and helpful criticism over a number of years.

Susan Townsend and Simon Gunn have both been the beneficiaries of periods of study leave to undertake the research and writing. We should like to acknowledge gratefully the support of the universities of Nottingham and Leicester in making this possible. The series editor, Christopher Gerteis, and our editors at Bloomsbury, Emma Good and Beatriz Lopez, have offered enthusiastic and helpful support throughout, which has smoothed the production process. We thank also the anonymous reader whose thoughtful comments and advice on the first manuscript have helped us to correct one or two mistakes and to improve the balance of the final manuscript. Finally, our thanks to Gabriele and Paul for putting up with us during the writing of this book. Their patience and generosity may have been tested but it has not been found wanting.

Simon Gunn
Susan C. Townsend
Leicester and Nottingham, December 2018.

Note on Text and Translation

Japanese names are cited throughout using the Japanese convention of family name first, followed by given name. In Japanese words and names macrons are used to denote the long vowels 'o' (ō) and 'u' (ū) occurring naturally in the Japanese language. Where Japanese authors have given their names using a different convention in their publications, such as Itoh (rather than Itō) or Hiroo (rather than Hirō), these usages have been retained. In common place names such as Tokyo (pronounced Tōkyō) macrons are not used. Occasionally, macrons are also used to denote long vowel sounds in English loan-words such as 'a' (ā) as in *mai-kā*, or 'e' (ē) as in *motarizēshon* where these would normally be written in *katakana*. Translations from Japanese to English are by Susan Townsend unless otherwise stated.

Introduction: Automobility and the City between East and West

In the later 1960s automobility and modern urbanism seemed to have come together in a new relationship that was reshaping the very form of the city and the possibilities of movement within it. A Japanese film from the period encapsulated this novel alliance. Suzuki Seijun's classic *Tokyo Drifter* (*Tokyo Nagaremono*) (1966) opens with a spectacular sequence of images of the 'new Tokyo'. An aerial shot of a spaghetti-like mass of railway lines along which the famous bullet-train, the shinkansen, is streaming out of a station cuts to one of traffic flowing in seemingly choreographed movements along the complex, curving and intersecting elevations of Tokyo's new expressway system. Finally, the camera comes to rest on the arching and flowing forms of Tange Kenzo's shiny, futuristic blend of modern and traditional architecture, the magnificent Yoyogi National Gymnasium built for the 1964 Olympic Games. Suzuki depicts the new Tokyo as a city of flows against a backdrop of American-style clubs, cool jazz music and women (mostly prostitutes) wearing the latest fashions. Much of the action takes place in cars; in underground concrete car parks; and, in one memorable scene, in a scrapyard where we witness a car, with a body presumed to be in it, being burned, melted and crushed.[1] It is no coincidence that the film was made in 1966, the year designated by the Japanese media as 'Year One of the My Car Era' (*Mai-kā Gannen*).

By the 1970s the cityscapes evoked by the film-maker Suzuki had become a familiar visual trope, deployed in detective series and thrillers on film and television. It was a trope that reflected how city centres across Japan and Britain – and much of the world – were becoming 'modern', recreated under the banner of urban renewal. Less often observed is how central a role automobility occupied in this new world. The modern city of the 1960s and 1970s represented in films and photography is criss-crossed by expressways which loop over and under it; traffic is omnipresent, whether in flow or jammed; the city itself is increasingly viewed from the car window, seen in motion rather than experienced on foot or from a stationary vantage point. Some fifty years earlier, in 1924, a similar vision came to a young architect in Paris as he stood watching the motor traffic flood past him. He described it as a kind of epiphany:

> On that 1st day of October, on the Champs Élysées, I was assisting at the titanic awakening of a comparatively new phenomenon, which three months of summer had calmed down a little – traffic. Motors in all directions going at all speeds. I

was overwhelmed, an enthusiastic rapture filled me ... The simple and ingenious pleasure of being in the centre of so much power, so much speed ... We have confidence in this new society, which will in the end arrive at a magnificent expression of its power.²

The young architect was Charles Édouard Jeanneret Gris, better known as Le Corbusier, the founding father (or *enfant terrible*) of modernist architecture and town planning. The idea that came to him in that moment on the Champs Élysées was the recognition that automobility, and in particular the motor car, was revolutionizing what a city was and what it might become. 'The city is crumbling, it cannot last much longer; its time is past,' he concluded. 'The torrent can no longer keep to its bed ... everything is changed, the norm of our existence is completely demolished and reversed.'³ Hyperbole notwithstanding, Corbusier understood with startling clarity that Paris, capital of the nineteenth century, would be thoroughly reshaped by the advent of the motor car in the twentieth century.

This book takes up the insights of Corbusier and Suzuki. It is about the impact of mass automobility on cities in Japan and Britain – specifically Nagoya and Birmingham – in the twentieth century, especially after 1950. This was the period in which mass car ownership took off in both countries. In Japan car ownership soared from 1 million in 1963 to over 14 million some ten years later; these years became known as the 'My Car Era' (*Mai-kā Jidai*). While in Japan in 1955 there was only around one car per thousand head of population, Britain by comparison was an old motoring country and from the 1950s a car became something British working-class families might realistically aspire to; between 1950 and 1975 the ratio of cars to head of population went from 1:22 to 1:4.⁴ By 1980 there were 15.3 million cars in Britain (0.28 cars per person) compared to 23.6 million cars in Japan (0.21 cars per person) in 1981.⁵ Yet it was not just the advent of mass car ownership that transformed cities but the infrastructure that went with them: motorway and road systems, roundabouts and gyratories, a battery of lights and signs, multi-storey car parks and drive-in shopping malls and, ultimately, car-free pedestrian zones. From the 1950s, as we shall see, cities like Nagoya and Birmingham were not being designed merely to accommodate the new 'motor society'. Instead, cars were literally driving the whole process of urban reconstruction and renewal. They radically altered cities and the lives lived in them, though for some sections of the population more than for others. How this process happened and with what consequences is the subject of this book.

Cars divide people as well as places. Some people are deeply attached to their car, treating it as an extension of their home or even of themselves. Others see it as deeply destructive, the cause of injury and death and, in the longer term, of the changes occurring to the planet's climate. Both perceptions have substance as commentators have long realized.⁶ Cars are an extraordinary aid to mobility and personal freedom; they can take you exactly where you need to go, whenever you want, and drop you at the door. At the same time, they enact 'car-nage'. More than a million people worldwide are killed in road accidents each year and automobiles are a major source of pollution, from noise to carbon emissions, which threaten planetary survival.⁷ Rather than taking sides in this debate, however, our interest is in showing historically how this dichotomy between the motor car and the environment, which we term the 'ME (motorization/environment) dilemma', took root in Britain and Japan at precisely the period we are studying.⁸ For while the advent of mass motorization in the 1960s was trumpeted as heralding the 'My Car Era' in Japan and the 'car-owning democracy' in Britain, it also invoked mounting criticism as a threat to people's safety and an environmental hazard.⁹ Our study therefore comprehends two meanings of the term 'urban environment', indicating the physical form and fabric of the city – its 'environs' – and the term in its more obviously ecological sense, denoting 'nature' (including the city and its inhabitants), especially as it is affected by human activities. An essential part of our story is to show how in Britain and Japan the meanings of 'environment' were shaped by the encounter between the car and the city in the age of mass motorization, the fears this encounter aroused among planners and populations, and the political chain of events to which they ultimately gave rise, from popular celebration to mass protest.

Japan and Britain

Why Japan and Britain? After all, the United States is commonly considered as the homeland of automobility, the place where car culture took root earliest and most deeply. The historiography of driving reflects this dominance, North America providing what is currently the largest and richest body of scholarly writing on the advent of mass automobility in the twentieth century. From the 1920s urban streets in American cities were reordered to make way for cars and trucks: pedestrians were restricted to sidewalks, streetcars were gradually phased out and engineers sought to use traffic lights and underpasses to ensure a smooth flow of motor traffic. The American city, in Peter Norton's term, was recast as 'Motordom'.¹⁰ Within cities as well as between them, the freeway became the model of travel; from 1956 a system of interstate highways was inaugurated nationwide.¹¹ In American political culture, meanwhile, the freedom to drive became closely associated with citizenship and national identity. 'In the twentieth century', Cotten Seiler has argued, 'to drive was to assume the performative contours of the generic "American"'; 'to be American is to claim automobility as one's habitat and *habitus*'.¹²

The American example was hugely influential, of course, from car advertising to traffic engineering. But there are dangers in taking the American case as the *ur*-history of automobility from which all other countries are derivatives or deviants. There were other influences, not least the examples of the German autobahn network, constructed in the 1930s, and of the reconstruction of war-ravaged European cities like Cologne where urban motorway systems were implanted after 1945.¹³ Moreover, Britain, like Germany and the United States, had enjoyed a continuous motoring tradition since the late nineteenth century. In the early 1950s Britain was the world's largest exporter of cars, chief amongst which was the Austin A40, made at Birmingham's Longbridge plant and, under agreement, by Nissan from 1952 at their plant in Yokohama, Japan.¹⁴ Japan surpassed Britain as a producer of cars in the 1970s, its exports increasing eighteen-fold between 1965 and 1975; by 1980 it had outranked the United States to become the world's largest auto manufacturer.[15] For more than a decade after 1945, however, the road infrastructure of both countries lagged well behind that of other industrial nations. A national motorway system was not initiated in Britain until 1959, when the first stretch of the M1 was opened, years or even decades after its Continental counterparts.[16] Road conditions in Japan were even worse. In 1956 only 2 per cent of the country's total road length and 19 per cent of national highways were paved. 'The roads of Japan are incredibly bad', the economist Ralph J. Watkins reported in the same year. 'No other industrial nation has so completely neglected its highway system.'[17] Consequently, the building of a national road infrastructure was a high political priority in both countries from the late 1950s.

Japan and Britain, then, were globally significant producers and – by the 1960s – consumers of automobiles. They also shared certain archaic features, most striking in the case of Japan, which meant that the infrastructure for mass automobility, notably roads, was ill-prepared for the 'motor revolution' and was only installed following major governmental investment during the 1960s and 1970s. In both countries, too, cities presented a special problem. In Japan's major industrial centres such as Nagoya and Osaka, the problem was a result of bombing raids during 1944/5, in which transport systems, including roads, were targeted as well as manufacturing and military sites. In urban Britain bombing during the Second World War was less destructive but the difficulty remained of how to engineer modern roads systems into old cities, built for horse not for motor transport.[18] Britain and Japan represent a suitable case for comparison, in short, not because their history of automobility was identical but because they shared certain features that made for parallel experiences in the second half of the twentieth century: an economy increasingly dominated by the motor industry, the expansion of mass car ownership (later but more rapid in Japan than Britain), an outdated roads infrastructure that was the object of an unprecedented programme of state investment and a problem of how to reconstruct urban areas for the incipient 'motor revolution'. They also exhibited key differences, as we shall explore, which are essential to the comparison. Most important though, the examples of Britain and Japan suggest the existence of a variety of auto-modernities, rather than the singular model that takes North America to be the vanguard and exemplar of 'motordom' as of so much else.

Comparative history in this fashion enables us to recognize the particular and the generic across different societies. It allows us to think about processes that were transnational, like automobility itself, in the same frame as the nationally and culturally specific ways in which those processes played out in particular times and places. Driving, for instance, may be a mechanical art that is everywhere the same, but who drives, what it means to drive and the codes of driving behaviour vary significantly between cultures as most people are, in fact, aware. In short, comparative history enables us to begin to make historical judgements about similarities and differences in the large-scale historical processes that are routinely referred to as 'modernization' – about what was distinctive historically in the embedding of mass automobility, a development that is so often taken for granted as a neutral, technical and ubiquitous accompaniment of modern urban life.[19]

Motor cities: Nagoya and Birmingham

Beyond the national context, this study of automobility and the urban environment focuses on two cities. Nagoya and Birmingham have good reason to claim to be the principal 'motor cities' of Japan and Britain respectively, those most strongly identified with automobility in general and the car in particular. Nagoya is well-known as the birthplace of Toyota Motor Corporation after entrepreneur Toyoda Ki'ichirō (1894–1952) developed the first 'Model A1' prototype passenger car in 1934 in a special division of his family firm. Unlike Western Europe and the United States, Japan's early motor industries developed from manufacturers who were already established in other fields but then diversified.[20] Toyoda Automatic Loom Works was a textile manufacturing firm situated to the north-west of the city centre, within a twenty-five minute walk of Nagoya Station. In 1938, one year after it was founded, Toyota Motor Co. Ltd. moved its operations to the small town of Koromo some 30 kilometres (18 miles) east of Nagoya.[21] In 1959 the town was renamed Toyota City and by 1970 had a population of 220,000. In the 1960s the whole Nagoya area was referred to as the Chūkyō Auto Region, a business term borrowed from Detroit and reflecting the concentration of automotive engineering in the four prefectures that made up the urban area (Aichi, Gifu, Mie and Shizuoka), with Nagoya as its capital.[22] By comparison with Nagoya, Birmingham's motor industry had a longer provenance. Herbert Austin bought the derelict printing works at Longbridge, some 10 miles from Birmingham city centre in 1906, and by the 1920s it was already Britain's largest car manufacturing plant.[23] While Toyota's first mass-produced vehicle rolled off the production line in 1946, Austin's first mass-produced car, the Austin Seven, was developed in 1922. Many of the elements of the later Birmingham motor industry were indeed already present by the First World War, such as Dunlop pneumatic tyres established in Erdington, an industrial suburb, in 1889, and BSA motorcycles which started production in 1910. Even before the Second World War Herbert Manzoni, Birmingham's chief town planner, liked to refer to it as the 'city of the motor car', a phrase that acknowledged its pre-eminence, along with neighbouring Coventry, in a variety of types of motor-related production.[24]

Yet the appellation 'motor city' always meant more than just a place of motor production. Taken narrowly, of course, the title applied most accurately to single industry towns like the *autostadt* of Wolfsburg, home to Volkswagen and built around the works from 1938; the firm still employed almost two-thirds of the urban workforce in 1998.[25] Detroit, the original motor city, was effectively a one-industry town from the 1920s, which partly accounted for its dizzying descent into bankruptcy when the auto industry first suburbanized from the 1950s, then collapsed. But by the 1960s its status as a motor city related also to Detroit's elaborate expressways, its authorities' commitment to the car over all other forms of urban transportation and its global projection through a highly successful local music label, Tamla Motown.[26] It was not Nagoya but Toyota City that identified itself most strongly as a motor city because of the almost total dominance of the motor manufacturer. Indeed, unlike Manzoni in Birmingham, Nagoya's chief reconstruction planner, Tabuchi Jurō (1890–1978), rarely mentioned the automobile in his autobiography.[27] Nevertheless, in 1959 Nagoya was twinned with Los Angeles and in 2005 with Turin, the centre of motor manufacturing in Italy.

In Nagoya and Birmingham too, there were other reasons than car production for aligning with or adopting the title of motor city, notably both cities' commitment to new types of traffic engineering and plans for ambitious programmes of road building. It was Herbert Manzoni's desire to publicize new roads engineering developments, including the early one-way system, his 'cog-wheel' method of traffic circulation and, above all, the pioneering proposal for an Inner Ring Road, that lay behind his publicizing Birmingham as the 'city for the motor car'.[28] Similarly, Nagoya's post-war reputation as designed around the car was epitomized by its celebrated 100-metre-wide boulevards, Hisaya Ōdōri and Wakamiya Ōdōri, originally conceived as two of a total of sixteen such super-highways to be built in Japanese cities.[29] While our research has revealed that the main intention behind their construction was as a refuge in times of disaster, Nagoya was nevertheless 'one of the few major Japanese cities to have comprehensively restructured its road network into a planned system of major arterials, secondary arterials and local streets' according to the urban historian André Sorensen.[30] In this book we argue that it was not so much the large-scale presence of motor manufacturing in post-war Nagoya and Birmingham as their design around the needs of motor traffic that marked them out in the eyes of contemporaries as 'motor cities'. In this respect they were distinguished from other cities in twentieth-century Japan and Britain and to some extent exceptional. Yet the policies and processes of mass motorization we analyse in relation to these two cities were far from unique. While they stand out, they also throw into relief much of what was happening with regard to roads, traffic and urban renewal in other cities and places.

As cities, Birmingham and Nagoya had much in common as well as some obvious differences. Geographically, both cities occupy a roughly central location nationally, Birmingham in the Midland plain and Nagoya in the Nobi plain, though unlike land-locked Birmingham, Nagoya has a major seaport. Both were also part of what by the 1970s had been identified as new 'megalopolitan' areas, simultaneously dispersed and linked up by the existence of mass automobility. The French geographer, Jean Gottman, is credited with being the first to use the term 'megalopolis' in 1961 to describe the north-eastern seaboard of the United States. But by the 1970s others such as Peter Hall were identifying the industrial heartlands of England, encompassing Birmingham, the Midlands and the north-west, and the Tokyo-Nagoya-Osaka urban belt in Japan as 'megalopolitan' regions.[31] Located on the Pacific Ocean, Nagoya has long been susceptible to natural disaster, including typhoons, earthquakes and a major tsunami in 1959, all of which affected how planners and others thought about its urban design. Lack of significant natural features as well as the urban 'sprawl' evident in both cities by the mid-twentieth century meant that road systems were increasingly important as a means to urban identification. From the 1930s planners divided Birmingham into inner, middle and outer rings which from the 1960s were defined by the major ring roads that acted as their boundaries.[32] Nagoya and Birmingham lay between their national capitals and other major manufacturing cities (Tokyo and Osaka, and London and Manchester, respectively), making them important transportation hubs by road, rail and air. In the 1960s Birmingham was regarded by central government as a central pivot in the emergent national motorway system, and the first expressway in Japan was centred on Nagoya. The two cities were

Figure I.1 Map of cities in England and Wales.

also capitals of much larger metropolitan areas. Nagoya, which received official city status in 1889,[33] lies at the centre of what is now known as the Chūkyō Metropolitan Area[34] and Birmingham is the capital of the Metropolitan County of the West Midlands, created under local government reform in 1974. At the 1951 census the city of Birmingham had a population of 1,113,000, a total which had changed very little by 1991. By comparison, Nagoya city had a population of 1,353,000 in 1942, swelling to 2 million by 1969, almost double that of Birmingham, and remained at roughly that level over the next twenty years.[35] A key factor for planning – and, in part, an outcome of the historical processes we investigate in relation to urban form in Chapter 3 – was the fact that by the later twentieth century Birmingham itself had half the population density of Nagoya.[36]

Economically, too, there are points of comparison. Birmingham has long been known as Britain's 'second city' and while Nagoya is officially Japan's fourth largest city in population, the Chūkyō Metropolitan Area is one of the three most important economically (see Figures 1.1 and 1.2).[37] Both were traditionally centres of manufacturing industry, the complement to the financial capitals of London and Tokyo, respectively. Historically, though, their economic paths were rather different. Birmingham is the older city, settled in the Anglo-Saxon period and mentioned in the Domesday Book of 1086.[38] From the sixteenth century it developed as a major centre for manufacturing, especially for metal goods. By the Industrial Revolution of the nineteenth century it was known as the 'city of a thousand trades' in tribute to its myriad workshops producing all types of goods: toys, jewellery, guns, tools, locks, nails, bolts, buttons, railway engines and gas fittings. With industrial expansion came rapid demographic growth, Birmingham's population increasing from 31,000 in 1770 to 523,000 in 1901.[39] If modern Birmingham was 'made' by nineteenth-century industrialization, the nineteenth century bequeathed a two-fold legacy

Figure I.2 Map of cities in Japan.

to the twentieth. First were the tracts of Victorian housing which occupied much of the central area and 'middle ring' to which an 'outer ring' of twentieth-century housing was added in the 1920s and 1930s under pressure from the city's population which had doubled again to 1 million by 1939.[40] Second was the inherited industrial structure of small workshops which remained substantially intact into the second half of the twentieth century and onto which the expanding automobile industry was grafted. Apart from a few industrial 'giants' – Austin at Longbridge, Joseph Lucas at Hockley, BSA motorcycles at Small Heath – boasting a workforce of thousands, the great majority of firms remained small; figures show that as late as 1971, 80 per cent of Birmingham's manufacturing firms employed fewer than eleven workers.[41]

Nagoya, sometimes anecdotally termed the 'Birmingham of Japan' for its apparent post-war planning around the car, may have been less ancient than its British counterpart, but in the Tokugawa or early modern period it was a substantial urban centre with a population of 50,000 in 1613 swelling only gradually to 75,000 by 1750. It too early developed a mixed manufacturing economy, including ceramics, artisan goods and food-processing. In the later nineteenth century workshop-based engineering and textile manufacturing were added to the mix.[42] For much of the early twentieth century the population of Nagoya and Birmingham grew in step, the former to 1 million in the 1930s; it was only in the 1950s and 1960s, when Birmingham's population remained static, that Nagoya outstripped it demographically.[43] The combination of textiles and engineering was the basis for the growth of twentieth-century Nagoya and its hinterland as a region of automotive manufacture. Unlike Western Europe and the United States, Japan's early motor industries developed from well-established manufacturing concerns, as we have seen, which then diversified into automotive production. Toyoda Ki'ichirō developed his prototype passenger car in 1934 at the Toyoda Automatic Loom Works and started to manufacture it from 1937 when the motor firm was formally established. Yet from the early 1930s Nagoya's heavy industry was geared to war; rather than cars, its engineering works were turned to production of military aircraft. Nagoya effectively became an 'arsenal city', contributing massively to the war effort in China after 1937 and in the Pacific and Southeast Asia after 1941.[44] One consequence was that, unlike Birmingham, Nagoya's emergence as an 'auto-region' was not accomplished till the 1950s and only officially recognized as such – in imitation of the Detroit Auto Region – a decade later.[45]

Politically also, Nagoya and Birmingham had a history of relatively autonomous local government and experience of city planning from the 1920s, which partly accounts for the unusually comprehensive nature of their post-war redevelopment. In Nagoya, Ishikawa Hideaki (1893–1955), who was in the Ministry for Home Affairs but assigned to the Aichi Regional Commission on Town Planning in Nagoya in 1920, helped to lay the foundations of the modern form of land readjustment, the most important legal tool for urban planning in Japan. While Ishikawa was in residence from the 1920s until the mid-1930s, Nagoya became, in the words of the planning historian Carola Hein, the 'centre of, and the engine that drove, urban planning in Japan'.[46] In 1926 a master plan was prepared which concentrated on infrastructure and the separation of the city's functions. Trade and office activity would dominate the centre of the city, industry would concentrate around the harbour, while housing was confined to the outlying districts. The whole city, including several new parks, was to be connected through a planned system of streets and canals.[47] Thanks to the experience of land readjustment[48] and the existence of earlier plans, a coherent vision of city planning was realized to a remarkably large extent. Birmingham too was deemed a national leader in town planning from the early twentieth century. The late Victorian tradition of municipal socialism associated with Joseph Chamberlain was carried over into the inter-war years in the spheres of housing, roads construction and green space, including one of Britain's earliest 'green belt' policies.[49] As Anthony Sutcliffe and Roger Smith aptly remarked, 'the hallmark of Birmingham's [inter-war] planning was spaciousness'. This applied in particular to the inter-war outer suburban ring, less so to the city's central areas which were characterized by a tightly confined shopping and office district, surrounded by a great expanse of slum housing intermixed with small factories and industrial works. If planning did not yet encompass all aspects of Nagoya and Birmingham, a comprehensive planning vision for each city was already in place before the Second World War.

The effects of war, notably those caused by bombing, intensified the urgency of planned reconstruction and the priority given to it by local and central government. Like much of urban Japan, Nagoya suffered major destruction of people and property from air raids between December 1944 and July 1945. By the end of the Second World War much of the population had been evacuated, leaving fewer than 670,000 people in the city, half the number in 1943.[50] It is estimated that between one-quarter and one-third of Nagoya's area was flattened and the heart of the city almost completely destroyed, including Nagoya Castle and most of Atsuta Shrine, the city's religious centre to the south of the city.[51] As with Nagoya, Birmingham's industrial capacity was vital for the war effort, its motor and engineering works commandeered from 1939 as 'shadow factories' specializing in the production of airplane engines, airframes and munitions.[52] Only London was more heavily bombed and, outside London, only in Liverpool were more people killed.[53] Yet if damage to life and property was considerable, Birmingham did not suffer wartime devastation on anything like the scale of Nagoya or industrial conurbations such as the Ruhr in Germany.[54]

Overall, then, there were significant historical and geographical parallels between the two cities. They included similarities in location (e.g. central/midland and situated between their respective capital cities and other large manufacturing centres), economic and administrative importance (e.g. capitals of large metropolitan areas competing with rival centres) and industrial and manufacturing profile (e.g. automotive industry, workshop-based engineering). Since the turn of the twentieth century, the two cities faced similar challenges in planning for growth, reconstruction and technological change, never more so than in the period immediately after the Second World War. These parallels make Birmingham and Nagoya particularly well suited to a comparative analysis of the part played by automobility in transforming urban environments in the twentieth century. They allow us to examine, at a local level and in a measurable way, the effects of the advent of mass motorization on different parts of the world.

East and West

Together with city and nation, one further geographical dimension requires elucidation: East and West. It is a dimension, of course, that has loomed large in recent theory and historiography. Global and postcolonial history have taught us to be wary of large-scale generalizations about East and West, 'Orient' and 'Occident', and the kinds of easy assumptions about cultural difference that go with them.[55] At the same time, postcolonial theory in particular has given heightened attention to the notion of 'difference' itself, not least in undertaking comparative analysis across cultures.[56] The tension between similarity and difference, universalism and particularism, is very apparent in the historiography of Japan, itself largely written by Westerners or by Japanese scholars utilizing Western categories of social science, including those of history. Studies of Japanese urban development have tended towards exceptionalism, represented by the concept of *Nihonjinron* (debates about the Japanese) predicated on national cultural uniqueness.[57] According to Japan specialist Conrad Totman, narratives of exceptionalism in the recent historiography of Japan prioritize nationalism and ethnic identity, and Japan's position in a global hierarchy of 'developing' or developed economies (particularly evident in accounts of Japan's 'economic miracle'). In so doing they have placed Japanese urban and industrial history not only outside the broader experience of industrializing societies, but also outside broader notions of the changing human relationship to the environment globally. Such tendencies are exacerbated by researchers who regard themselves as 'Japan specialists', leading them to search for what is special in 'their' chosen country or region.[58]

On the other hand, Henry Smith suggested in relation to urban thought, that it is hard to avoid comparing Western and Japanese ideas of the city because of the enormous influence of Western ideas since the opening of the country following the Meiji Restoration in 1868. A comparative approach is further complicated by the survival of Japanese traditions within Japan's Westernizing processes.[59] Indeed, the imbrication of traditional Japanese philosophy, socio-cultural forces and Western technology, some historians have argued, has contributed to the relative success of many of Japan's larger cities, thus providing an inviting model and inspiration for urban designers in the West.[60]

In *Provincialising Europe*, Dipesh Chakrabarty offers helpful ways of thinking about these hybrid processes and, in particular, how to move beyond the intellectual double-bind involved in using the knowledge of Western (or European) social science to study non-Western subjects. For Chakrabarty, 'The point is not to reject social science categories but to release into the space occupied by particular European histories sedimented in them other normative and theoretical thought enshrined in other existing life practices and their archives.'[61] In studying, historically, the interlinking categories of automobility, urbanism and environment across Britain and Japan, this is a line we have tried to tread. While we have sought to avoid essentializing Nagoya and Birmingham as representative of Japanese or British society, we have been attentive to the differences between them, often related to larger national frameworks of planning, culture and politics. In fact, in many instances ideas about automobility, urbanism and environment had no unique national belonging; they were part of a complex transnational circulation of expert knowledge and practice that was especially intense in the post-war decades across 'developed' and 'developing' nations.[62]

In part because of the global and transnational 'turns' in historical writing, comparative East–West urban histories are in fact rare for the modern period.[63] For Britain and Japan the work by Nicholas Tiratsoo, Hasegawa Jun'ichi, Tony Mason and Matsumura Takao, *Urban Reconstruction in Britain and Japan, 1945–1955*, is an exception, but as the dates suggest, it is tightly focused on the legacy of wartime damage in cities in both countries. No study has yet been attempted to compare two specifically industrial cities in Britain and Japan during the twentieth century. In this sense, by bringing together the urban history of modern Nagoya and Birmingham around the theme of automobility and environment, our study remains experimental. It involves the challenge not only of working with two different cultures and historiographies but also of researching in different sets of national (and local) archives. Whether the comparative analysis is worthwhile can only be judged by the quality of the critical insights generated about the histories of Britain and Japan, understood separately and together, as they unfolded in the course of the twentieth century.

Objectives

In researching and writing this book we have been guided by three interrelated objectives. The first is to compare the relationship between motor vehicles, the urban environment and planning in two major centres of automotive production by analysing their reconstruction as 'motor cities' in the mid-twentieth century. Between 1955 and 1990 it is clear mass motorization played an important role in the planned (and sometime unplanned) reshaping of Nagoya and Birmingham. Just how important, though, is not always self-evident. Were roads and the infrastructure of automobility a by-product of post-war urban reconstruction, defined by the building of mass housing and the remaking of city centres in the international image of high-rise office blocks and shopping malls? This is the orthodox view of architectural and urban historians.[64] Alternatively, was it the need to cope with mass motorization itself that literally drove post-war urban redevelopment, especially in industrial cities like Nagoya and Birmingham where the car was king? Such is the implication of infrastructure studies, epitomized by Stephen Graham and Simon Marvin's classic work, *Splintering Urbanism*.[65] It is also the logic of sociological notions of the 'car system', a socio-technical complex composed, in the words of Kingsley Dennis and John Urry, of 'humans (drivers, passengers, pedestrians), machines, materials, fuel, roads, buildings and cultures'. In this view, post-war cities were remade in order to enable the embedding of the 'car system' at the behest of governments, oil and motor industries and consumer desire.[66] There are, then, large issues at stake in how one understands the place of automobility in post-war urbanism.

The second objective is to explore historically the contradiction between the promise of freedom and mobility afforded by widening car ownership and contemporary concerns about the impact of the car on the environment and quality of life of crowded cities. Our hypothesis here is that the period between the early 1960s and the mid-1970s saw the emergence of the 'ME (motorization/environment) dilemma'. The publication of the Buchanan report *Traffic in Towns* in 1963 was an international landmark in this respect, simultaneously seeking to re-engineer cities to accommodate rising volumes of traffic while restricting motor access to central and residential areas of the city in the name of 'civilized life'; to reconcile, in other words, mass automobility with quality of urban living.[67] In Japan and Britain, however, the celebration of the car as a symbol of affluence and personal freedom was accompanied – and to some extent overtaken – by concerns about its deleterious consequences for congestion, pollution and community cohesion, the tipping point between these positions occurring around 1970. Our study thus also explores the 'ME dilemma' at the point of its emergence as a significant societal question in Japan and Britain.

Our third objective is to establish a comparative framework through which to analyse the philosophical and cultural understandings of the urban environment and 'nature' implicit in the adaptation of cities like Nagoya and Birmingham to mass car ownership and use. Were there substantive cultural differences between East and West that silently shaped post-war urban environmental policy in general and planning for the car in particular? Japanese society, informed by Buddhist and Confucian ethics and an essentially non-dualistic view of self and nature, is assumed to have had a fundamentally different view of nature (*shizen*) from Christian or Western societies predicated on Cartesian dualism. This distinction has informed a generally positive view of Japan as an eco-centric society in which the urban environment represents 'an indigenous part of the natural environment' and which, among other things, is used to explain the swift Japanese response to the problems associated with vehicle emissions and pollution control by comparison with Western governments.[68] However, like Britain, the impetus for change in Japan initially came from the United States largely because car manufacturers such as Honda Soichirō were responding to vehicle emissions that were emerging as a major issue of public health in Los Angeles, the firm's American base.[69] But the Japanese government also responded to well-publicized incidents of photochemical smog appearing over Japanese cities in 1969 and 1970 by pre-empting American laws on exhaust emissions. Nor were environmental concerns all on the Japanese side; there was a distinct conservationist thrust to *Traffic in Towns*, which infused urban policy more widely with the introduction of protected or 'conservation areas' in British cities following the Civic Amenities Act of 1967.[70] As we see in Chapter 5, democratic processes, including mass protest and electoral pressure, played a significant part in both countries in determining environmental policy and the responses of the automobile industry to pollution control.[71] In other respects, too, our study suggests that the Japanese experience of urban modernity was less singular than is often assumed by scholars. This applies not only to planning for the car and the attitudes to the urban environment that informed it, but also to stereotypes of the Japanese as group-oriented, duty-bound and hostile or indifferent to the ideals of individual freedom identified with consumer cultures in Western societies. Just as planners in Japan and Britain may have shared certain assumptions about how cities should be moulded to fit the new automobility, so Nagoya motorists in the 'My Car Era' may have had more in common with their Birmingham counterparts than popular – and scholarly – perception has allowed.

Through these three interlinking objectives the book tackles a series of overlapping dimensions of automobility and the city in twentieth-century Japan and Britain. It is organized in the following way. In the first two chapters we examine the planned reconstruction of Birmingham and Nagoya as motor cities before and after the Second World War. What assumptions about motor transport in general and the car in particular guided the approaches of planners? How was mass automobility to be fitted into old cities, which, in Britain at least, were already suffering congestion before 1939? How were the imperatives of highway construction integrated with other planning priorities, such as prevention of natural disaster (especially in the case of Nagoya), housing, business and industry? We also examine similarities and differences between the two cities in the design of roads and 'traffic architecture', including the surroundings to roads, from the planting of verges to the building of garages and car parks. This analysis of planning processes leads to the question of urban form, addressed in Chapter 3, in which we examine the effects of automobility on urban 'sprawl'. To what extent was urban morphology by the 1950s and 1960s actually driven by mass motorization, by public fixed-rail and bus transport as well as the private car, and to what extent did planners try to encourage or contain it? In all these domains the comparative dimension is to the fore. When looking at planning, space and form, in effect, we may be able to discern different conceptual approaches to the relationship between traffic and the city. Behind these comparisons lies the larger question of whether we can speak of a Japanese 'way' to mass automobility distinct from the British (or even Western) 'model' suggested by Birmingham.

In the later chapters of the book, we move away from questions of planning and expertise to the issue of how mass automobility shaped experiences of the city. As the quintessential consumer commodity and marker of 'affluence' in the 1960s, the car was not only linked to new types of urban experience – commuting, shopping, holidays and leisure – but also to the new forms and sights of the modern city – high rise living, elevated expressway, shopping mall. In motor cities such as Nagoya and Birmingham this connection was explicit: the car and the city were welded together as spectacle as well as engineering. There is a familiar assumption that modernist living produces standardized experiences, but examining automobility through advertising, film and other media points towards significant differences in the ways commodities like cars were appropriated in different national and cultural settings, from vehicle design to driving etiquette.

Automobility was also – and increasingly – experienced negatively. From the later 1960s, in both Japan and Britain, opposition to motor vehicles began to emanate from a range of social interests, including pedestrians, residents' associations, women's groups and environmentalists. In the final two chapters of the book, we explore how even in those cities most committed to the car, protest began to surface about pollution, destruction and 'blight' caused by mass motorization. The 'oil shock' of 1973, when petrol prices rose rapidly and exponentially, provided a further external impetus to question the supremacy of the car and a way of life which appeared environmentally wasteful and increasingly unsustainable. By the 1980s, we argue, the notion of the 'motor city' as an ideal-type city of the future was over. What remained in both Britain and Japan was a lingering addiction to private automobility alongside a growing recognition that this addiction constituted a threat to people's health, to the quality of urban life and, ultimately, to the planet itself. In its ramifications, therefore, this study – like the car itself – takes us from the most intimate spaces of people's everyday lives to the largest questions of environmental survival.

1

Planning the Automotive City, c. 1920–1960

Outside North America the history of the car can justifiably be studied separately from the history of the city before 1930; thereafter their histories become increasingly inseparable. On the one side the car emerged as the essential accoutrement of modern urban living in the mid-twentieth century. On the other, the problem of how to squeeze automotive traffic into already densely packed townscapes loomed ever larger until, by the 1960s, it dwarfed all other physical considerations. As a review of Birmingham's redevelopment put it in 1959: 'The motor car is becoming the fundamental consideration of modern urban life' – not least for city planners.[1] Yet there was a paradox here. For a while the problem of mass automobility seemed urgent – even terrifyingly immediate – in Japanese and British cities in the 1960s and 1970s, the solutions to those problems in the form of road planning and techniques of traffic control were already half a century old. In both Nagoya and Birmingham major schemes for reorganizing the city around the priorities of motor, or 'mixed', traffic had existed from the 1920s.

In this chapter we examine the pre-history of the automotive city in Nagoya and Birmingham from the First World War. After the First World War both cities had developed plans for urban remodelling that included major road systems. In Nagoya in the 1920s, town planner Ishikawa Hideaki envisaged connecting the whole city, including several new parks, through a planned system of streets, many of them widened to accommodate motor traffic.[2] For Birmingham, the City Engineer Henry Stilgoe suggested a series of ring roads – inner, middle and outer – as early as 1918, ostensibly inspired by a visit to Vienna with its famous *Ringstrasse*.[3] Thereafter the planning history of the two cities is suggestive of the long gestation of major civil engineering works: Nagoya's civil engineering showpiece, the 100-metre-wide roads, was completed by 1963. However, Birmingham's Inner Ring Road was not formally completed until 1971, while the first section of Nagoya's Urban Expressway did not open until 1979.

This chapter starts with planning for automobility in Nagoya and Birmingham in the 1920s and 1930s and the significant intervention in those histories represented by the Asia-Pacific War (1931–45) and the Second World War, in particular the consequences of strategic bombing for their subsequent reconstruction after 1945. The persistence of earlier plans into the post-war period is then examined in some detail, not least the question of how civil engineering projects associated with major road construction should be financed in the climate of post-war austerity experienced by both countries. Urban roads were designed not simply or primarily for the private car before the 1950s but had to accommodate a 'mixed economy' of traffic, including buses, trams and light vehicles. In the case of Japan, defeat and occupation caused a more radical break with the past than occurred in Britain, but Nagoya was unusual in resurrecting plans originally drawn up in the 1920s.[4] In all this the national contexts – political, legal, fiscal – and the inherited infrastructure of automobility, from motor industry to road network, require exploring since these shaped the process of mass motorization and governmental responses to it from the later 1950s onwards. But we start with the early history of town planning in Japan and Britain, which first brought automobility and the city into relationship.

Traffic and the history of town planning

From the beginning of the twentieth century the movement in favour of town planning reflected concerns with the problem of motor traffic. In Britain, the Roads Improvement Association lobbied consistently to enhance the network and quality of the nation's roads, first for bicyclists, then for motorists, resulting in the foundation by government of the Roads Board in 1908.[5] In 1903 the novelist H.G. Wells wrote of the 'necessity for adapting our roads to accommodate an increasing new traffic of soft-tyred mechanical vehicles'.[6] The adaptation deemed necessary was not only to road surfaces, caked with mud and dust, but also to traffic itself, the dangerous mixing of machines, animals and people all legitimately using the roads. It was London's circulation that was earliest – and most consistently – deemed to require remedial intervention. The first 'Town Planning and Housing' supplement of the *Architectural Review* in 1910 included an article by David Barclay Niven that proposed the development of a ring road encircling the capital and the same idea was echoed by the early planner G.L. Pepler in his call for a 'girdle round London' at the international town planning conference organized by the Royal Institute of British Architects (RIBA) in 1910.[7] As well as promoting traffic flow, the concept of the ring road in this earliest phase intersected with British planners' desire to contain urban sprawl while simultaneously encouraging green spaces in the manner of the garden city.

Although the concept of the ring road was less well-known in Japan, in 1907 news of Ebenezer Howard's Garden City Movement, from the first example at Letchworth (1903), spread among Japanese intellectuals and policymakers. British ideas about town planning, and the Garden City Movement in particular, inspired Shibusawa Ei'ichi, the entrepreneur and developer of Den'enchōfu, the most notable 'garden city' suburb near Tokyo. As in Britain, the capital initially led the way in city planning, with the Tokyo City Improvement Ordinance (TCIO) passed into law in 1888. Described as 'Japan's first planning law',[8] the TCIO authorized the government to rearrange the city streets 'in view of the permanent advantages to be gained in the municipal administration of commerce, public health, fire prevention, and transportation throughout the entire urban area.'[9] Large-scale urban planning in Japan in the early Meiji Period reflected Western influences brought back by a group of elite Japanese samurai engaged in the Iwakura Embassy to the United States, Britain and Europe between 1871 and 1873.

These young men were greatly impressed not only by the grand vistas of Paris but also by the French capital's role as a commercial and economic centre. The mission's chronicler, Kume Kunitake, noted that an efficient transportation system was vital to prosperity and well-built, good-quality roads and streets were an indicator of a city's commercial and economic vitality. The mission also recorded details about the construction techniques of road building, from the use of stone paving in Europe to tarmacadam in Washington as well as measuring road-widths and noting the use of trees to provide shade. TCIO planning included measures specifically designed to alleviate traffic congestion through introducing more uniformity to streets and eliminating bottle-necks, especially near bridges. Such was the link between roads and streets as an index of civilization and modernity that street improvement became a corner stone of Japan's urban construction policies in its colonies, in cities such as Seoul.[10]

A subsequent generation of Japanese modernizers and social reformers, many of them influenced by Western liberalism and socialist ideas, insisted that only technology and practical education could meet the challenges that modern cities posed.[11] However, unlike Haussmann's Paris, Japanese planners at home and in the colonies adopted a gradualist approach to street and road improvement. Rather than flattening existing urban areas to make room for roads, they were content with making incremental improvements over time which were not only less expensive but also less likely to incite opposition. This approach was particularly important in the colonies where planners adapted idealized plans to reflect local demands as well as different topographical conditions.[12]

In Nagoya during the 1920s it was the engineer Ishikawa Hideaki who led the way in re-conceptualizing the relationship between roads and green spaces after he was seconded to the city from the Ministry for Home Affairs. Ishikawa is regarded as one of the very few 'visionary' Japanese planners, along with the architect Tange Kenzō who was associated with Hiroshima's reconstruction planning and a futuristic plan for a motorized Tokyo in 1960.[13] Like many other young social reformers and city planners, Ishikawa was a man of the Taishō[14] generation: those born in the 1890s who were most exposed to the radical influences of Western liberalism and socialism, often to the dismay of their Meiji generation peers who were born in the 1860s and 1870s. Ishikawa's genius lay in combining both the monumental aspects of the early Meiji period and the modernizing impulses of the 1920s and 1930s. He was also unusual in applying a comprehensive plan to what was then a relatively unimportant regional city. During his posting to Nagoya, Ishikawa travelled extensively, visiting China in 1921 and Europe between 1923 and 1924 where he met Raymond Unwin and discussed his master plan for Nagoya based on the separation of the city's functions.[15] On his return, he drew up a plan envisaging a network of forty roads in 1924. His 1926 plan also included the creation of twenty-four parks covering an area of over 5.5 square kilometres, highlighting the importance of green spaces to the well-being of townspeople in terms of health, recreation and sanitation.[16]

These ideas reflected the prevailing spirit of Western-influenced Taishō liberalism and democracy. The movement went hand-in-hand with an emphasis on the creation of gardens and parks for the sake of hygiene and health. The ideas were promoted by government-sponsored organizations such as the Cultural Life Research Group (Bunka

Seikatsu Kenkyūkai) and the Alliance for Lifestyle Improvement (Seikatsu Kaizen Dōmeikai), both founded in 1920.[17] Ishikawa also articulated a concept of 'scenic beauty' in plans to protect areas of natural and historical interest, and his designs for new residential areas to the east of the city incorporated open land and forest.[18] A 1924 committee within the Alliance for Lifestyle Improvement recommended: 'Public Housing (apartment houses) and garden city facilities should be constructed in accordance with the circumstances of the metropolis' and called for unified planning for houses and roads along the lines of the Garden City.[19] The incorporation of green spaces into road design was one of Ishikawa's most important legacies to Nagoya's post-war reconstruction planning. His idea of publicizing plans widely in order to garner public support was also ahead of his time. He was active in the new Society for Urban Creativity (Toshi Sōsaku Kai) inaugurated in April 1925 to serve as a forum for discussing ideas about the urban environment, housing, green spaces and road construction; in this view roads were an aid to environmental improvement and public health, not antithetical to them. To support these ideas a journal, *Toshi Sōsaku* (Urban Creativity), was published from September 1925 until April 1930.[20] In this way Ishikawa acted as a conduit for introducing Western ideas about city planning into Japan.[21]

As with Nagoya, Birmingham did not lag behind London in the movement to planning or to rings. The City Corporation established a Town Planning Committee in 1911 and two years later a plan for the districts of Quinton, Harborne and Edgbaston in the south-west of the city, designed to limit suburban development on what was then Birmingham's fringe, was the first such scheme nationally to be approved by the Local Government Board.[22] In contrast to Nagoya, ring roads were an integral part of the early planning vision; an outer ring for Birmingham had been proposed as early as 1908 and in 1918 the City Engineer Henry Stilgoe suggested an 'inner ring' or 'kind of loop' around the city centre, linking together the existing arterial roads. Here was the origin of the Inner Ring Road, Birmingham's major civic engineering achievement and Britain's first urban motorway, whose route was to remain largely unchanged when it was finally opened half a century later.[23] As Birmingham steadily expanded its city boundaries to the north, east and south through the first three decades of the twentieth century, so arterial and ring roads became increasingly important in circumscribing and connecting the urban form.[24]

By contrast, the concept of transportation rings or loops was limited to the building of intra-city railways in Tokyo, where railways arrived in 1872 and the electric tram in 1903. However, even the famous Yamanote railway loop, which encircled the city to the west of Tokyo station and Ginza, linking the main districts of Shinagawa, Shibuya, Shinjuku, Ikebukuro and Ueno, did not start out as a loop. It began from freight lines running from central Japan to the port at Yokohama at the end of the nineteenth century. Only after the final phase of the Tokyo City Improvement Project was completed in 1919 did the Yamanote line connect the various stations and subcentres.[25] Before the age of the automobile: 'The history of the Yamanote epitomizes how various separate lines of movement become entangled, forming phenomenological and symbolically powerful loops and linkages.'[26] Only in the later twentieth century did roads in Japanese cities take on the mantle of modernized connectivity and mobility.

The inherited urban form as well as changes in urban transportation added to the increase in traffic congestion in both cities between the wars, but there were differences in the nature of the traffic and the problem. In Birmingham rising levels of motor traffic were blamed in part on the siting of industrial factories in and around the central core. Birmingham City Council established a special committee on traffic congestion in 1936 to investigate the problem in the central area. The issue, however, was not so much the private car as the increased mix of traffic on the streets. What particularly concerned local authorities, in cities like Manchester and Birmingham in the 1930s, was the congestion caused by the different means of mass public transport, notably tramways, trolley buses and motor buses.[27] It was similar concerns, combined with the high rates of road casualties in the 1930s, that impelled the Metropolitan Commissioner of Police in London, Alker Tripp, to begin advocating for strict segregation of pedestrians and vehicles, a principle that would become an orthodoxy of traffic planning in Britain after 1945. Following visits to cities in the United States, Tripp was aware of the effects of rising levels of motorized traffic in urban streets, but as yet the dominance of the car was by no means assured.[28] In 1930 there were still only a million cars on Britain's roads which kept it a luxury item for the well-to-do.[29] In Birmingham several measures were taken up to deal with urban traffic, including a one-way system, introduced in 1933, but their effects were seen as necessarily short term. As a government official later noted, 'The layout of the streets in central Birmingham is in the main unchanged from that existing early last century, since when the population has increased twelvefold.' Herbert Manzoni, the City Engineer, had come to the same conclusion in 1941, predicting gridlock in central Birmingham within a decade.[30]

Still more than in Birmingham, the traffic problem in early twentieth-century Nagoya was exacerbated not so much by the number of motor vehicles but by the sheer variety of means of transport. Even in the mid-1930s there were still fewer than 2,000 automobiles in Nagoya city. However, motorized vehicles jostled for space with numerous bicycles, including 809 'automatic' bicycles (*jidōjitensha*) and no less than 26,630 carts pulled by hand. This was despite the fact that there had been a decline in the number of both *jinrikisha* (rickshaws) and carts drawn by animals, which had been important modes of urban transport in the Meiji Period (Figure 1.1).[31] Thus 'mixed traffic' moving at different speeds was squeezed into narrow, winding streets, originally used exclusively by pedestrians.

Problems of traffic stimulated governmental responses in both countries. Trams were seen as part of the problem in Britain and Japan, as in many other countries, their fixed lines inhibiting other forms of mobility.[32] Electric trams were gradually replaced by trolley buses in Nagoya and by motor buses in British cities, including Birmingham, which claimed to have the largest municipal bus fleet outside London by the 1930s.[33] Given the gravity of the traffic situation, creative new ways of dealing with it were constantly trialled. Driver licensing began in 1902 in Aichi Prefecture and Tokyo's first driving school, the Tokyo Automobile School, was instituted in 1914. By 1918 Tokyo had established a separate uniformed traffic police section, some of whom were issued with red motorcycles known as *aka-bai* (literally 'red bikes'). The first traffic lights in Japan were sited in Hibiya, central Tokyo, in 1930. In Birmingham traffic islands were instituted from 1920, automatic traffic lights in 1929,

Figure 1.1 Personal transport before the car: rickshaws in front of Nagoya station, c. 1925.
Source: Tsurumai Central Library Collection. http://timetravel.network2010.org/article/126

pedestrian crossings from 1934 and a speed limit of 30 miles per hour imposed on all city roads from 1935. In his capacity as City Engineer Herbert Manzoni personally devised a novel 'cog-wheel' system for filtering traffic within the city's new one-way system to keep it running smoothly. Inter-war Birmingham was consistently in step with or even in advance of international developments in the practice of what would later become known as traffic engineering.[34] In both countries, then, urban traffic congestion was a source of governmental concern and intervention from the 1920s. At this period it was viewed as a problem of mixed transport modalities not of automobility *per se*, but it was a problem that the growth of automobility would both alter and exacerbate.

In particular, there was one distinctive planning tool in the 1930s which was vital to ensuring the relative success of Nagoya's planners in dealing with traffic. In Japan, 'land readjustment is the mother of urban planning' was a common phrase used by town planners.[35] Indeed, the phrase was coined by a new journal *Kukaku Seiri* launched in Nagoya in 1935 under Ishikawa's former colleague, Den'ichi Kaneiwa.[36] The historic and widespread employment of land readjustment (LR) in Nagoya distinguished it from other cities in Japan. In public sector projects landowners were compulsorily involved so that ownership of land could be pooled in order to build roads, parks and other facilities. The land could then be divided into urban plots ready for exploitation.[37] Before the war and the introduction of new LR laws, landowners had to contribute a portion of their land for public use. The contribution was usually around 30 per cent, but in Nagoya it was as much as 50 per cent. Land that was not required could be sold as urban plots at the end of the project to help defray costs of project design, management and construction.[38] In 1899, an Agricultural Land Consolidation Law (*Kōchi Seiri Hō*) was passed to facilitate improvements through grouping scattered landholdings and building irrigation systems. Its modern legal form was based on a German model widely used in Frankfurt and promoted in Germany by Franz Adickes, a leader in the German urban planning movement, from the 1890s. Nagoya had a long history of using the 1899 law and, in fact, eight LR projects totalling nearly 15 square kilometres had already been realized on Nagoya's urban fringe before the passage of the first national city planning laws in 1919.[39] A modified form of LR was used to rebuild large areas of Tokyo and Yokohama following the 1923 Great Kanto Earthquake.[40] In Nagoya LR was used to an unusual extent; by 1945, more than half the city's land had been subjected to some form of LR.[41] This made it much easier for engineers and planners to use this tradition to acquire the land necessary to implement plans for road widening and road building.

The equivalent in Britain of land readjustment was the system of compulsory purchase whose origins, 'bogged down in complexity and obscurity', went back to the nineteenth century.[42] This was the basis of a mechanism to favour the interests of the community, represented by central government or local authority, over those of private or individual interests in matters related to land use. Governmental powers over land, however, were significantly boosted by the Town and Country Planning Acts of 1944 and 1947, which gave local authorities, firstly, statutory controls over war-damaged areas of the city and, subsequently in 1947, over areas designated for comprehensive redevelopment.[43] In Birmingham, as we shall see, powers deriving from wartime legislation were integral to efforts to remake the post-war city. Despite differences in the nature of the traffic 'problem', therefore, the authorities of cities like Nagoya and Birmingham were alert to the issues arising from traffic well in advance of the advent of mass motorization and had begun to experiment with remedies through planning, design and the legal infrastructure.

The emergence of the professional town planner

If town planning was well advanced in Britain and Japan by the 1930s, planning as a profession was less so. While a Town Planning Institute was established in Britain in 1914, few of those involved in the early movement had any specific training in the field. Many of the leading planners of the inter-war period had a background in architecture, including Edwin Lutyens, William Holford, Donald Gibson and Patrick Abercrombie, who succeeded S.D. Adshead as Professor of Town Planning at University College, London.[44] In Japan, it was not until 1951 that the City Planning Institute of Japan (CPIJ) was founded, by contrast with the Japan Society of Architects (Nihon Kenchiku Gakkai) which was founded as early as 1886 and succeeded by the Architectural Association (Kenchiku Gakkai). Indeed, throughout most of the twentieth century, no posts were designated 'urban planner' in central government organizations and ministries in Japan.[45]

In both countries, an alternative, but in certain respects subordinate, avenue into the profession was via civil and municipal engineering, a dimension that has been largely overlooked in the existing historiography.[46] Ishikawa, for example, was the son of a railway company employee in Obanazawa in Yamagata prefecture and studied civil engineering at Tokyo Imperial University graduating in 1918.[47] In Britain, a similar figure was Francis Forty who worked with Abercrombie on the London plans of 1943/4; another was Herbert Manzoni who held the role of City Engineer at Birmingham between 1935 and 1963. Manzoni's career was characteristic of the wider group in many respects.[48] Born in Liverpool he studied engineering at Liverpool University at the same time when Abercrombie was Professor of Civic Design there, followed by three years training ('pupillage') with an engineer in his native Birkenhead. In 1929 he was appointed Deputy City Surveyor at Birmingham and six years later, aged thirty-six, he succeeded to the post of City Engineer with responsibility for municipal housing, utilities and roads. Quickly acknowledged as a national expert in urban roads construction, and President of the Institute of Civil Engineering in 1961, Manzoni put roads at the centre of his vision for the renewal of Birmingham.[49]

Like Ishikawa, Nagoya's post-war city engineer Tabuchi Jurō also graduated as a civil engineer from Tokyo Imperial University in 1915. In 1938 he was transferred to Sendai in the north of Japan before being sent to China to work on the reconstruction of 'war-damaged areas' (inflicted, of course, by his countrymen) in Shanghai and Nanjing. He was responsible for helping to clear damage which was still in evidence after the Yellow River flooded in 1938, and went to Beijing in May 1942 where he worked as an engineer on plans for the western suburbs of the city.[50] According to the historian of technology, Aaron Moore: 'Beijing serves as a prime example of the engineers' urban planning

Figure 1.2 Birmingham City Engineer, Herbert Manzoni. Courtesy of the Institution of Civil Engineers.

ideals in north China' as well as Japanese wartime 'pan-Asian' ideology.⁵¹ In 1938 the Japanese had planned a Western Suburban New Town to the west of the city. Inspired by the Garden City and City Beautiful movements, it articulated an engineering concept of 'comprehensive technology' which grew out of the Manchukuo Civil Engineering Bureau's 1937 vision of co-ordinated technical planning primarily in relation to flood control, but which included improved transportation and communications.⁵² The aim in Beijing was to alleviate overcrowding and improve hygiene. The plan included parks and green spaces arranged throughout the city and wide squares positioned at the intersections of a number of tree-lined boulevards. Most importantly, a 100-metre-wide road was to run through the town's centre. Construction began in 1941 but, according to Moore, was fraught with difficulties, not least of which was the need to negotiate with numerous 'actors and forces beyond their control, which continuously shaped the entire project'. In the end the plans were scaled down to meeting the needs of the Japanese population of the city for housing and infrastructure.⁵³ By the time Tabuchi arrived in Beijing in May 1942, therefore, very little of the original plans were being carried out, and although he made no mention of the plan for a 100-metre-wide road in his autobiography it is possible that he knew of its existence in the original plan. After he returned to Japan in May 1945, three months before the end of the war, he was contacted by the president of Nagoya's city council, Sato Masatoshi, who invited him to help with the reconstruction of the city. There was apparently no shortage of offers from other cities, such as Osaka, seeking experienced engineers and planners. After some consideration, Tabuchi, then aged fifty-five, accepted Sato's invitation.⁵⁴

In the decades after 1945, the striking consistency of Manzoni's and Tabuchi's engineering visions contributed significantly to Birmingham's and Nagoya's recreation as 'motor cities'. Manzoni put ring roads at the heart of his planning vision and Tabuchi would let nothing get in the way of constructing the two 100-metre-wide roads. In both cities, road-building success was not just dependent on these two high-profile city engineers, of course, but they were each fortunate in being unrivalled as power brokers on their home turf. Moreover, they could depend on the backing of dynamic teams dealing with reconstruction, the Public Works Committee in Birmingham and Tabuchi's hand-picked team in Nagoya's Planning Department. At Birmingham, Manzoni had no competition as chief planner. In many British cities planning was hampered by rivalry between the offices of the City Engineer and the City Architect, but in Birmingham the latter post was only created in 1952 and its first occupant, A.G. Sheppard Fidler, had to work with schemes for roads, housing and the city centre set out by Manzoni and his team a decade or more earlier. Manzoni benefitted from cross-party support on the City Council and beyond: Labour, Conservative and Unionist politicians, as well as representatives of the Chamber of Commerce and the local Trades Council, all remained staunchly behind Birmingham's road agenda throughout his long period of office.⁵⁵ Tabuchi at Nagoya likewise benefitted from a favourable institutional context. The sociologist Yazaki Takeo pointedly argued in 1963: 'As the network of the bureaucratic system was perfected throughout the nation [after 1945], the government agencies became the integrating organs forming the nucleus of each city'.⁵⁶ In many ways Nagoya's relative neglect by an otherwise interventionist central government, compared with Tokyo and Osaka, gave Tabuchi a more-or-less free hand in reconstruction planning. He had a good relationship with former colleagues in the Home Ministry and does not appear to have been obstructed by the Supreme Commander of Allied Powers', General Douglas MacArthur's, headquarters during the Occupation.[57] In Japan as well as Britain, the figure of the chief planner was never more powerful than in the decades around mid-century and with it, a conception of the city shaped by an engineering imaginary.

The impact of the Second World War

For both Manzoni and Tabuchi, the aftermath of the war allowed them to make sweeping changes to their cities' fabric. Birmingham suffered limited damage by comparison with the devastation caused by bombing in Nagoya. It may have been one of the most badly hit of Britain's major provincial and industrial cities, but the worst of the raids were over by spring 1941 and the extensive spread of inter-war Birmingham and its industry meant that large areas of the city were little affected. In the words of the city's principal historians 'the war caused more inconvenience than injury, more decay than destruction'. Nevertheless, the figures suggest that 5,200 people were killed or injured in the bombing raids in Birmingham. By contrast, no other city apart from Tokyo was subject to as many raids as Nagoya (twenty-one raids between 13 December 1944 and 24 June 1945 according to the United States Strategic Bombing Survey (USSBS)).[58] There were over three times as many casualties as in Birmingham: 8,152 people were killed and over 10,000 were injured. Moreover, the levels of destruction in the city meant that over 519,000 people were left homeless and of these 85 per cent were forced to evacuate the city.[59] As regards property, some 2,300 factories were destroyed or damaged in Birmingham without seriously affecting production levels, whereas large tracts of Nagoya were turned into an urban wasteland of rubble and dereliction in which production was largely halted.[60]

Praised as 'a man of action and determination', Tabuchi was ruthless in making the most of the legal framework provided by Nagoya's tradition of using LR in road-building. He not only capitalized on a culture among landowners and landlords of sacrificing land for the public good, but benefitted, perhaps inadvertently, from the aftermath of mass evacuations.[61] In 1961, Tabuchi admitted that it was sometimes necessary to take decisive measures which, in hindsight, seemed to have taken advantage of the chaos and confusion of Japan's defeat. Not only had the bombings cleared vast tracts of land in the city centre but the mass evacuations meant that people were slow to return and reclaim their property. The repatriation of soldiers was also fraught with difficulty and farmers, landlords and tenants were not always in a position to protest against Tabuchi's plans. However, without such fierce resolve, he stated, town planning on such a scale would have been impossible to achieve. Like Manzoni, he relied on a powerful and resolute administration in the city's Planning Section and boasted that the success of Nagoya's urban planning had become the envy of other cities. He attributed the great achievement of the planning and construction of the 100-metre-wide roads to the total commitment of the city's administration.[62]

Inadvertently, the war also brought long-term economic benefits to the motor industry, strengthening the roads agenda from another direction. The commandeering of the large part of Birmingham's burgeoning motor industry – Austin, Lucas, BSA, Dunlop and others – by the state for war production strengthened rather than weakened it in the longer term. Not only did it encourage technology transfer within aviation, motor manufacture and engineering, but it also underlined the importance of the city and region as a centre for Britain's most dynamic industries, a point which the city's leaders were not slow to use in relation to central government after the war was over.[63] Similarly, the Nagoya region's massive contribution to the war effort, particularly the production of aircraft, including the famous Mitsubishi 'Zero' fighter, emphasized its technological and economic importance. In terms of national planning, it was one of the reasons why, in the late 1950s, Nagoya was at the centre of the creation of a national system of expressways. In different ways and at different speeds, the experience of war put roads firmly on the national agenda in Britain, Japan and, indeed, much of the developed world – plans for national motorway networks were put in place during and immediately after the war in the United States, West Germany and France, plans which would be implemented following economic recovery during the 1950s. Urban motorways like the Paris Périphérique and the infamous Cross-Bronx Expressway in New York were an integral part of post-war roads planning.[64]

In both Japan and Britain war also gave a boost to planning at regional and national levels, even as it slowed the implementation of certain planned projects. From his power base at Birmingham Manzoni quickly established himself as a leading player in planning in Britain, corresponding with the Uthwatt Committee on Compensation and Betterment in 1941/2, with an eye to the city's plans for the five central redevelopment areas, and contributing directly to the government's Advisory Panel on Redevelopment of City Centres in 1944. Consequently, Birmingham's experience and ambitions were reflected directly in the 1944 'Blitz and Blight Act', enabling local authorities to acquire, relatively easily, large amounts of land in the name of reconstruction with the promise to 'plan boldly'.[65] As Gordon Cherry argued, the powers allocated to local authorities such as Birmingham under the 1944 Act were exceptional, enabling compulsory purchase of land and property with unprecedented speed.[66] Nationally, a whole series of Acts related to land-use planning were passed in Britain between 1944 and 1947, encompassing housing, industry, city centre reconstruction and new towns, culminating in the 1947 Town and Country Planning Act, which collectively comprised what Peter Hall termed the 'planning machinery' of post-war Britain.[67] Conventionally this body of legislation is assumed to have marked a significant switch of power from the provincial cities and regions to the central government and Whitehall, specifically to the newly formed Ministry of Town and Country Planning (from 1951 the Ministry of Housing and Local Government).[68] But while the new 'planning machinery' stopped short of full-scale nationalization of the land, it vested substantial powers in the hands of local authorities to promote and arbitrate on development within their boundaries. It is worth noting that the Birmingham Corporation Act of 1946, which gave the Corporation powers to acquire the land for the Inner Ring Road and the Central Development Areas, was passed in the midst of the corpus of legislation supposedly transferring power to Whitehall.

In Japan, at a national level, wartime strategy boosted road planning. In September 1940 a 'League for the Promotion of a Plan for the Tokyo Trunk Road' was formed by the Chambers of Commerce and Industry in each of the cities involved – Tokyo, Nagoya, Kyoto and Kobe. A survey was completed in 1942 and in the following year a Nationwide Automobile Expressway Network Plan (*zenkokuteki jidōsha kokudōmō keikaku*) was created as a result. In 1944 the report of the National Road Construction Survey (*kokudō kensetsu chōsa*) made the route between Kobe and Tokyo a priority. A topographical survey map was drafted for the section between Kobe and Nagoya and got as far as the design stage. However, with the worsening war situation, the proposed construction costs of 200 million yen could not be approved and the plans were abandoned. Nevertheless, these wartime surveys formed the basis of discussions about the route of Japan's first national expressways in the 1950s. The pre-war concept of a nationwide motorway network was modelled along the lines of the *autobahn* of the Third Reich. The announcement of the Nationwide Automobile Expressway Network Plan was a response to the Railway Ministry's proposal for an express railway line, which would become the Tōkaidō Shinkansen (Tōkaidō new main line), running west from Tokyo. But it was also a theatrical gesture made in the atmosphere of militarist enthusiasm sweeping a country which had just designated the year 1940 (or Shōwa 14) the Imperial Era of 2,600 to mark the unbroken imperial line to a mythical first Emperor Jimmu (*kigen*) in 660 BCE. In this atmosphere, the terms 'Bullet Train' (*dangan ressha*) and 'Bullet Road' (*dangan dōro*) were coined by an enthusiastic and jingoistic press.[69]

For Nagoya, the long-drawn out war with China may have boosted some sectors of the economy, such as heavy industry, but it had a negative impact on regional planning. Not for nothing was the Second World War in Asia known as the 'Fifteen Years War' (actually fourteen years and eleven months) which began with the Mukden or Manchurian Incident on 18 September 1931 and ended with Japan's surrender on 15 August 1945. Numerous plans for development conceived in the 1930s were delayed or aborted by 1940 including plans for the Chūkyō region of which Nagoya was the capital. The term 'Chūkyō region' was used in business and industry circles to describe an area of around 7,000 square kilometres extending from Nagoya southwest into Mie Prefecture, north into Gifu Prefecture and east into Aichi Prefecture of which Nagoya is the capital. A 1936 plan to build a subway network of some 52 kilometres as part of comprehensive traffic planning in the Chūkyō region had to be abandoned because of the worsening economic situation when the conflict in China escalated in July 1937 into a second Sino-Japanese War. As early as 1929 Nagoya City Mayor, Oiwa Isao, announced the 'Chūkyō-Detroit Plan' intended to transform the Chūkyō region, with its growing expertise in modern machine technology, into an industrial region geared to the manufacture of automobiles. But the war in China also changed national infrastructure priorities and the plan was abandoned in the 1930s, due to insufficient finance. One of the most important plans which fell victim to poor timing was the expansion of Nagoya's port. In 1938, the inner channel of the port had been widened and dredged, opening the way for a new ten-year development plan costing 38 million yen which was approved by the Home Ministry. Aichi Prefectural authorities were instructed to begin work in 1940.[70] Financial problems were already manifest by 1939, however, and the plan was abandoned after the outbreak of the Pacific War in December 1941. Nevertheless, it was to form the basis of the Comprehensive Development Plan for the port drawn up in 1950.[71]

In fact, the war was in many ways the critical point at which both Birmingham's and Nagoya's pre-war plans were consolidated, laying the platform for the creation of the post-war 'motor city'. For Nagoya, although the Nationwide Automobile Expressway Network Plan of 1943 had to be abandoned because of the war, it proved to be a critical step which would prove foundational in the 1950s, since the original decision on the route of Japan's first expressway, between Nagoya and Kobe, was upheld. In Birmingham, most important was agreement on the plans for the building of the Inner Ring Road. Manzoni outlined a design for inner, middle and outer rings, alongside his housing plan, in 1939. In 1942 an Advisory Panel on the Inner Ring was established by the City Council, including members of the Public Works Committee and the Traffic Advisory Committee, together with representatives of the city's main architectural, shopping, trading and transport associations. The Panel laid down a series of principles which were to remain constant in the construction of the pioneering three and three-quarter mile road. They included the precepts that the ring road should not, at any point, require pedestrians to walk further than 300 yards to the shops, and that the road itself should be adapted to shops and offices, thus extending the city centre. The scheme was approved by the City Council in July 1944 and was despatched for parliamentary approval. With an estimated cost to the Council of £12 million in land value and £2.5 million in repairs to utilities such as sewers and mains, the Inner Ring Road was claimed to be the largest local authority scheme of its kind to go through Parliament.[72] Submitted in the form of a Bill it became an Act of Parliament in 1946.

Post-war reconstruction

When General Douglas MacArthur officially received the Japanese surrender on board the USS Missouri on 2 September 1945, occupied and occupiers faced the daunting task of reconstructing Japan's devastated cities.[73] Many of Japan's major cities lost up to half their populations in the last years of the war as people were evacuated into the countryside. It is estimated that between 31 per cent and 38 per cent of Nagoya's urban area was destroyed.[74] By 1951 the population in Nagoya, which had halved in the final years of the war, had almost reached its pre-war level of just above 1 million. The Occupation of Japan lasted until April 1952 and coincided with the period of reconstruction planning and much of urban rebuilding. MacArthur's Headquarters (GHQ) had little direct interest in the details of reconstruction planning, apart from curbing more ambitious plans deemed inappropriate for a defeated country, but its policies impacted on cities such as Nagoya both directly and indirectly.

The experience of the Second World War, therefore, and the effects of bombing in particular, affected the two industrial cities very differently. Housing was a top priority in both. Birmingham entered the Second World War with a clear set of planning priorities, involving slum clearance and council housing – Manzoni's *The Production of Fifty Thousand Municipal Houses* appeared in 1939. War itself served only to delay plans rather than disrupt them. Contained within the same 1946 Birmingham Act as the proposal for the Inner Ring Road were plans for slum clearance, developed before the war but also refined during wartime. They included the acquisition of housing within five central wards of the city: Gooch Street, Ladywood, Bath Row, Summer Lane, and Duddeston and Nechells, which together contained some 30,000 'slum' houses and 58 per cent of the city's Victorian back-to-backs.[75] These five Central Redevelopment Areas represented Birmingham's 'new towns', the city's response to the national programme of new towns outlined in the Barlow Report on the Distribution of Industrial Population published in 1940 and given legislative form in the New Towns Act of 1946. All five areas were situated within the circumference of the proposed Middle Ring Road, the construction of which consequently dovetailed with the slum clearance programme, enabling the City Council to take control of large swathes of land in the central area.

In Nagoya, housing policy and roads construction were complicated by directives issued to the Japanese government from GHQ. Not only was the Japanese government ordered to provide housing for bombed out and returnee Japanese citizens, but it was also required to build much larger houses for Occupation officials and their dependents, placing an enormous financial burden on a government struggling to house its own people. Already coping with a shortage of over 4 million houses for Japanese citizens, the government provided 20,000 much larger housing units for the occupiers and their families and was forced to supply building materials for another 4,000 such units in Korea. As a consequence, central government tended to prioritize housing in industrial areas outside the cities to accommodate workers. It was reluctant to take responsibility for housing within the metropolitan areas, even adopting policies to discourage an influx of returnees into war-damaged areas. The onus then fell upon local authorities, who only managed to build a fraction of the housing supply needed, until 1955 when the Japan Housing Corporation was founded. Even then house-building fell well short of the number of units required.[76]

In Nagoya more than half the residential properties in the city centre were destroyed, representing the equivalent of slum clearance, although a 'slum-like' area immediately to the west of the station notorious for its black-market activities was targeted for renewal (Figure 1.3).[77] Housing needs in 1945 were met initially by providing 3,000 prefabricated emergency shelters (*ettō jūtaku*) funded by the National Treasury. Measuring 20.7 square metres, these simply provided some protection during the first winter. By 1948 Nagoya city had built over 6,000 houses measuring around 33 square metres, constructed in wood. These were sold for around 3,500 yen each, less than £5.[78] Another 3,315 houses known as *shomin jūtaku*, meaning literally 'houses for the masses' were built through a combination of government funding, public corporations and private builders. People also took it upon themselves to build what are known in Japan as '*barakku*' or barrack-built houses, but by the mid-1950s most of the shanty houses had been replaced by low-cost housing and city housing projects. Remaining *barakku* housing had to be cleared in order to begin road construction.[79] In Nagoya, the slow progress of house building is evident in photographs taken as late as 1957 which show an enormous shanty-town development at Nishisuzaki-machi which had to be cleared to make way for the construction of the 100-metre-wide road, Wakamiya Ōdōri.[80]

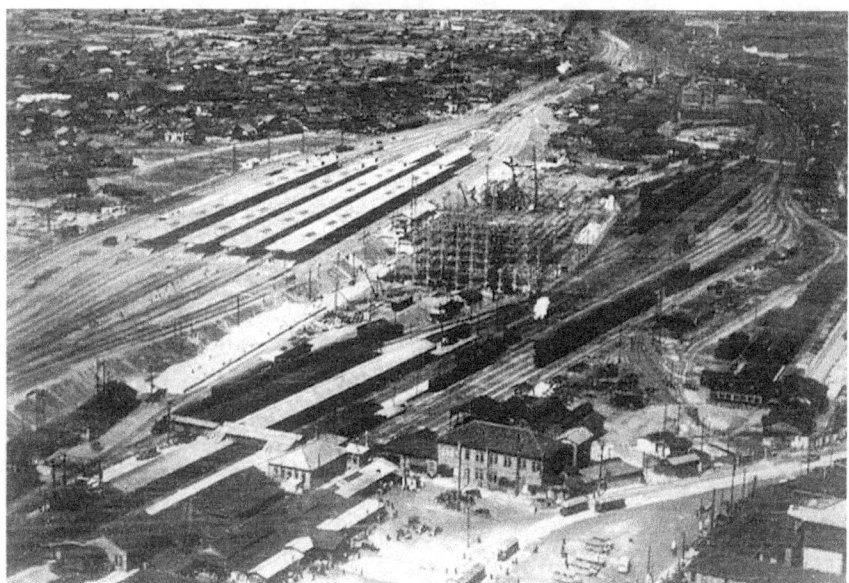

Figure 1.3 Reconstructing the bomb-damaged city: Nagoya station in 1946.
Source: Nagoya City Public Information Division. http://timetravel.network2010.org/article/129

As well as housing, Birmingham's wartime plans also envisaged the substantial reconstruction of the city centre itself around the priorities of retail, markets and offices, although the detailed plans for this remained vague before the 1950s. What is clear, however, is that the project for the Inner Ring Road was the centrepiece of a complex plan for Birmingham that linked together housing, roads development and city centre renewal in a single all-encompassing vision. As the West Midlands Road Engineer, R.J.F. Sansome, later reminded Birmingham's Town Clerk, 'the 1946 Act did not include provision for a Ring Road scheme solely as a feature to be incorporated in the development of the area but … the Ring Road was in fact the principal feature, which enabled other developments to be carried out'.[81] In effect, the Inner Ring was the hub in Birmingham's post-war plan around which other priorities would pivot.

Birmingham was also at the centre of two post-war regional plans, *Conurbation* and the *West Midlands Plan*, both produced in 1948, the former by the West Midland Group on Post-War Reconstruction and Planning including Manzoni and other Birmingham luminaries, the latter commissioned by the Ministry of Town and Country Planning and undertaken by Patrick Abercrombie and Herbert Jackson. Significantly, the attention of both plans was on projected population distribution and its immediate associated needs, and thus primarily on housing and the location of industry.[82] Though influential, neither plan was actually implemented. More important because directly affecting the city's future was the twenty-year Development Plan, approved by the Ministry of Housing and Local Government in 1952. This was the first such plan to cover the city as a whole, and allowed the nexus of the Inner Ring, the Central

Redevelopment Areas and city centre renewal to be confirmed at the heart of what would be referred to by the late 1950s as the 'new Birmingham'. What occupied most attention in the Development Plan and the public enquiry that followed, however, were questions to do with the location of industry and the shortage of land that were somewhat tangential to this planning nexus.[83] With post-war austerity there was in any case insufficient funding available, public or private, to inaugurate major development projects before the mid-1950s. The Conservative government continually stalled on committing the agreed subsidy of 75 per cent to the Inner Ring Road; 'I can see no possibility of bringing forward a scheme of this size', a civil servant in the Ministry of Transport grimly reported in July 1955.[84] This in turn slowed construction in the Central Redevelopment Areas. While compulsory purchase for the five areas identified, involving 30,000 houses and 100,000 people, was agreed in 1946, slum clearance did not start till 1948 and building not till 1952.[85] Renewal of the city centre also had to await financial recovery in the second half of the 1950s.

Urban roads were likewise part of immediate post-war planning in Japan. The reconstruction of bomb-damaged cities was guided by *The Basic Principles of Reconstruction Planning for War Damaged Areas* (*Sensaichi Fukkō Keikaku Kihon Hōshin*) issued in December 1945. This was a radical and ambitious vision of urban planning which included a target of 10 per cent of all urban areas to be allocated as green spaces, such as parks, playgrounds and broad green belts to prevent urban sprawl. The document encouraged war-damaged cities to 'create grand avenues, large boulevards ... of over 50 metres in width in large-sized cities.' The purpose of such boulevards, the document stated, was 'to establish firebreaks and to accommodate future motorization'.[86] Emboldened by this directive many cities produced ambitious plans for schemes which included the even grander notion of building 100-metre-wide roads, but it was not clear from where the idea originated. An earlier draft of *Basic Principles of Reconstruction Planning for War Damaged Areas* published in October 1945 referred to the possibility of constructing roads of between 50 and 100 metres for fire prevention or aesthetic purposes. According to planning historian Hasegawa Jun'ichi, official records held by the Ministry of Construction show that sixteen 100-metre-wide roads were officially sanctioned in Tokyo, Yokohama, Osaka, Kawasaki, Hiroshima and Nagoya. As early as 1941 an article in the journal of the Japan Road Engineering Association advocated the construction of roads with substantial widths of a minimum of 40 metres (in order to act as a barrier to fires reaching 300 degrees centigrade) for the purposes of fire prevention and as places of refuge. However, no mention was made of 100 metres. Tatsuo Matsui in the Home Ministry Planning Section claimed that the figure of 100 metres was invented by planners in Nagoya and Hiroshima, adding that the Ministry was 'overwhelmed' by the amount of local support for the proposals.[87]

Occupation GHQ allegedly opposed the construction of 100-metre-wide roads by suggesting that 'in a defeated country, grand roads are not necessary'.[88] While the exact origin of this statement is elusive, urban historians Ishida Yorifusa and Ichikawa Hiroo both refer to GHQ's view that the grander visions of early reconstruction planning, especially relating to road construction, were 'inappropriate' or 'unsuitable' for a 'defeated nation', a judgement which underlined the symbolic importance of roads among the 'victorious' Western powers.[89] For both the Japanese government and GHQ, therefore, there was considerable ambiguity surrounding road-building. While there was general recognition that transportation infrastructure was important, there was very little agreement nationally about what kinds of roads were needed. In the end, plans for 100-metre-wide roads in most cities were axed after austerity measures were ushered in by a severe financial crisis in 1949. Public enthusiasm spurred progress in Hiroshima and Nagoya, making it more difficult to halt their plans by 1949 while other cities, for various reasons, stalled or demurred.[90]

If progress was halting in the aftermath of the war, the foundations of both Nagoya's and Birmingham's emergence as motor cities from the later 1950s were nevertheless being laid. In Birmingham, public transport itself was fully motorized at this period. In 1953 the Corporation finally agreed to put an end to the tram system, parts of which had already begun to be abandoned in the later 1930s.[91] The greater expense of trams as against the motor bus was a frequently cited reason, but as in other British cities, buses were deemed to be more modern and mobile: 'Birmingham is not a tramway city', Birmingham's Transport Manager A.C. Baker roundly declared in 1949.[92] The removal of 'fixed route transport operations' (tramcars and trolley buses) opened the way to the increased dominance of the motor bus. 'No large city in the world is so dependent on the motor bus for suburban transport as is Birmingham', the Corporation proudly claimed in 1955. The tramways had never been extended into the outer ring of interwar suburbs and rail transport did not step in to fill the gap; municipal estates, such as built in the 1930s, were often 3 miles from the nearest station and the railways themselves were having branch lines incrementally cut through the post-war period, even before the wide-scale closure programme of the Beeching report of 1963.[93] Brief consideration was given by the Corporation's Public Works Committee to a tube railway after 1947 and to a rapid transit system on the American model but both were successively rejected as expensive and impractical.[94] By the mid-1950s the mixed transport landscape of the inter-war years was rapidly disappearing and there was little to stand in the way of a city redesigned for the motor vehicle.

Trams were still in existence in Nagoya until the late 1960s, but pre-war plans for a rapid-transit system were delayed due to the urgency of house-building and roads construction. In October 1945 a city plan was hastily drafted, based on an estimate of a population of 2 million, which was finally achieved in 1969. In December details of the plan were finally made public in the *Chūō Nippon Shimbun* (Central Japan Newspaper) showing the two 100-metre-wide roads, Hisaya Ōdōri and Wakamiya Ōdōri, and a lattice-work of nine 50-metre-wide roads. Designed originally as a model of civic engineering for disaster prevention, Nagoya's 100-metre-wide roads were central to a new concept of urban 'road scene' (*dōro keikan*) combining traditional aesthetics associated with the great tree-lined highways of the Tokugawa period (1600–1868) with European boulevards symbolized by the Champs Élysées, much favoured by Meiji planners. As Nagoya's planning bureau stated, 'Roads are not simply about facilitating the free movement of traffic, but are the basis of urban planning which must also consider the aesthetic views of the city and the safety and security of its citizens.'[95]

The plan was approved by the City Assembly in March 1946, and on 7 August the *Nagoya Reconstruction City Planning Land Readjustment Project*, as it became known,

Figure 1.4 Corner of Navigation Street and Suffolk Street, Birmingham, 1952 – before the motor city.

Source: D.J. Norton Collection.

was launched.[96] A Reconstruction Festival was held to publicize the plans, and on 12 October Emperor Hirohito visited the city to inspect the plans. Hisaya Ōdōri with its green central park running 1.74 kilometres from north to south and Wakamiya Ōdōri running 4.12 kilometres east to west were completed in the early 1960s. This is not to say that there was no dissent regarding the project. Indeed, Tabuchi's plans met with strong opposition from both the government, who protested against the removal of Nagoya Prison which stood on land scheduled for Hisaya Ōdōri, and the public. Also on the construction site were 279 cemeteries containing around 188,000 grave plots, together with temples, and residents protested about plans to relocate these to the new Heiwa (Peace) Park on the eastern fringe of the city. According to Tabuchi's own account, it was his 'iron belief' that persuaded his detractors to continue with the plans.[97] Twinned with the Champs-Elysées, Hisaya Ōdōri became most important symbol of Nagoya's post-war reconstruction. At its centre was the TV Tower standing 180 metres high; completed in 1954 it was the first intensive radio wave tower in Japan (Figure 1.5). Despite attracting the attention of planning historians internationally, for Birmingham's historian Anthony Sutcliffe Nagoya's 100-metre-wide boulevards remained a mystery in need of 'much more explanation'.[98] As Tabuchi himself later admitted, at a time when there were very few cars in the city, the function of the 100-metre-wide roads in moving traffic was incidental rather than deliberate.[99]

As in the Birmingham area, regional planning also ensured that, in the ten years after 1950, the total road length in the Chūkyō region expanded. Roads designated as 'national highways' almost tripled from just over 23 kilometres to 63.5 kilometres while urban roads increased from 2,681 kilometres to 3,608 kilometres. Moreover, the

Figure 1.5 Hisaya Ōdōri under construction, 1946.
Source: Nagoya City Centre Collection. http://timetravel.network2010.org/article/129

percentage of total length of road which was paved in cement or asphalt increased from around 11 per cent to nearly 14 per cent.[100] This compared favourably with national statistics which showed that, in 1956, only 2 per cent of Japan's total road length, 19 per cent of general national highways and a mere 1 per cent of roads in cities, towns and villages were paved.[101] From the vantage point of town planning, in short, the experience of war in Britain and Japan did not so much mark a turning-point as a temporary break in a developmental arc that extended from the 1920s to the 1960s.

The rise of the motor industry

If town planning was one way in which Birmingham and Nagoya were becoming motorized, the changing fortunes of their local motor industries provided a further set of complementary pressures and incentives. As peacetime motor manufacture resumed in Birmingham's works – the British Motor Corporation entirely renewed its assembly plant at Longbridge in 1950, ready for production of the A40 – so output began to recover. By 1951 vehicle production in Britain had surpassed its pre-war peak and with 44 per cent of global exports of cars and 30 per cent of commercial vehicles, it became the single largest exporter in the world.[102] Austin at Longbridge was an important part of this expansion, but much wider sections of the Birmingham economy were also tied up with the motor export trade, BSA motorcycles, Dunlop manufacturing and Lucas component parts, to name some of the best known. The *Birmingham Post* was only stating what appeared to be an obvious fact when it wrote in 1955 that 'The products of this city and the neighbouring areas make a vast contribution to Britain's success in the export markets of the world'. The monetary value of exports of road vehicles was estimated at £290 million in 1953, 11 per cent of total UK manufactured exports.[103] In the aftermath of the war, the motor industry emerged in Britain and in Birmingham as the principal manufacturing industry and an essential barometer of the national and the local economy.[104]

It was a rather different story in Japan where the future of the automobile industry was much less assured in the decade after the war. In 1950 Ichimada Hisato, Chairman of the Bank of Japan, famously argued that it was meaningless to develop a Japanese passenger car industry in the face of fierce international competition.[105] The period between the implementation of the U.S. Occupation's stabilization programme known as the Dodge Line[106] in February 1949 and the outbreak of the Korean War in June 1950 was one of severe crisis nationally. Rampant inflation, low wages, severe labour unrest and a short depression brought many companies to the brink of bankruptcy, including Toyota. A syndicate organized by the Bank of Japan rescued the company on condition that it reduced its labour force. When Toyoda Ki'ichiro had announced the layoffs, the union called a strike. After three weeks, the union was forced to agree to the layoffs, but Toyoda retired early after personally taking responsibility for the strike.[107] After 1955, a stable LDP (Liberal Democratic Party) government ushered in a period of relative calm, allowing companies like Toyota to flourish and the Nagoya region to become one of Japan's leading automotive manufacturing centres with many companies supplying auto-parts to Toyoda's plant in Koromo (Toyota City from 1959).[108]

Nagoya, therefore, was a relatively late starter in contrast to Birmingham where, by the early 1950s, motor manufacturing had become the backbone of the city's economy. Estimating the numbers dependent on the industry in Birmingham is difficult because they extended well beyond those employed directly on the assembly line to the multiple components' firms, those employed in the motor trade, such as sales and repair, in transport such as haulage firms, and in offices such as car insurance. A survey of industries in the Birmingham area in mid-1954 estimated that 100,000 workers were employed in three sectors: manufactures of motors and cycles, manufacture of parts for motor vehicles and manufacture of batteries and accumulators, representing in total one in six of insured employees.[109] Some of these, such as bicycle manufacturers, were obviously not employed in the motor industry but an unquantified number of those in other sectors enumerated, such as the metal industries and bolts, nuts, etc., would have been so employed, directly or indirectly. Writing in 1958, the best estimate of the *Times*' industrial correspondent was that between one fifth and a quarter of the city's labour and capital were tied up in motor manufacture.[110] This was an exceptionally high concentration for a city of Birmingham's size and with its old and varied industrial history. Britain's other main centres of automobile production, Coventry, Oxford and Luton, were much smaller towns. Although the numbers employed directly in vehicle manufacture in Birmingham fell marginally in the 1960s and 1970s, the motor industry remained the central pillar of the urban economy.[111]

As with Birmingham, it is difficult to state exactly how much of the Nagoya region's manufacturing depended on the auto-industry in this period. When Toyota built its first plant in 1938 some 25 kilometres to the southeast of Nagoya, Koromo had been a major centre for sericulture which had been profoundly damaged by a market collapse in 1930. It still retained a large section of the population working in the primary sector. In 1951 Koromo Town incorporated neighbouring villages and was renamed Toyota City in 1959.[112] In the early 1950s, Toyota had fewer subcontractors, as its operations were all in-house. By the late 1950s and 1960s, however, dozens of supplier firms and offices were established in Toyota City, and others were clustered along the main highway into Nagoya, one of the first paved roads outside Nagoya.[113] Toyota had a good supply of underemployed or unemployed local labour in the early 1950s when around 5,000 workers were producing between 3,000 and 5,000 units a month. The first mass-produced passenger car, the Toyopet Crown, was marketed in 1955 and proved to be a huge success. In September 1959, the company opened Motomachi, its first plant geared to the mass production of passenger cars. A total of 10,000 units were produced in December 1959; by October 1963, production had trebled.[114] Heavily unionized, Toyota's success was based on relatively harmonious industrial relations which allowed the firm to introduce the radical technological and managerial innovations which were later transferred around the globe.

By 1960 the West Midlands and the Chūkyō region had emerged as the major centres of the automotive industry in Britain and Japan, respectively. Their motor industries had also become major sources of employment. However important motor production was regionally, though, it did not appear to determine the pace or scale of urban reconstruction, including roads. There was no evidence of direct links between motor manufacturing and roads policy at the urban level. While there were undoubtedly informal links between the respective city councils and major manufacturing firms like Toyota and BMC (and later British Leyland), the 'motor city' epithet was not a product of their combined efforts. Such firms steered clear of local politics even as local authorities were laying the foundations of Birmingham and Nagoya as cities of the motor car.

The onset of mass motorization

Until the late 1960s Birmingham's economy remained buoyant, not only in its manufacturing but also in its commercial sector; the city was second only to London for speculative office and retail investment.[115] These factors contributed to high wages and incomes. Household incomes in the West Midlands in the early 1960s were some 13 per cent above the national average, according to the Family Expenditure Survey, partly explained by the relatively high – and growing – proportion of working women; in Birmingham in 1961 just under half of all married women were in paid employment compared to nearer one-third nationally.[116] If social historians have been sceptical about contemporary claims as to the extent of 'affluence' among manual working-class groups in post-war Britain, it is nevertheless clear that wider social groups than ever before began to be drawn into purchasing consumer durables, notably televisions and cars.[117] Between 1946 and 1960 the numbers of private cars licensed in Birmingham almost trebled from 43,213 to 123,513, while the numbers of motorcycles expanded at a slightly faster rate from 11,724 to 36,298, trends which mirrored growth nationally.[118] In terms of personal transport, cars and motorbikes steadily replaced bicycles, the numbers of which peaked in Britain in the late 1940s.[119]

By comparison, Nagoya lagged far behind in vehicle ownership in the 1950s, despite Toyota's survival and increasing success (see Graph 1.1). Relative to Britain, wages were much lower in Japan in the 1950s and the domestic motor industry was still in its infancy. Reliable post-war statistics for numbers of vehicles in the city began in 1955, the official end of the reconstruction period, when there were nearly 50,000 motor vehicles, including 15,229 passenger cars. However, vehicle numbers increased rapidly to reach a total of 134,166 by 1960, of which still only 20,000 were passenger cars. Total vehicle numbers include the *keijidōsha* (light vehicle) classification; small three- and four-wheel trucks, vans and passenger cars of restricted dimensions and displacement which required a licence only.[120] Notably, around one-third of motorized vehicles were rented. While there were only 1,602 motorcycles over 125cc, there were 75,000 scooters and bicycles.[121] Even at this period, transport in Nagoya was much more varied in type and mode than was the case in Birmingham.

Despite noting that the numbers of car owners remained small, the 1952 Birmingham Development Plan observed that traffic congestion was inevitable given that quarter of a million people commuted into the centre of the city for work each day. As the exponential growth of car ownership became increasingly apparent by the

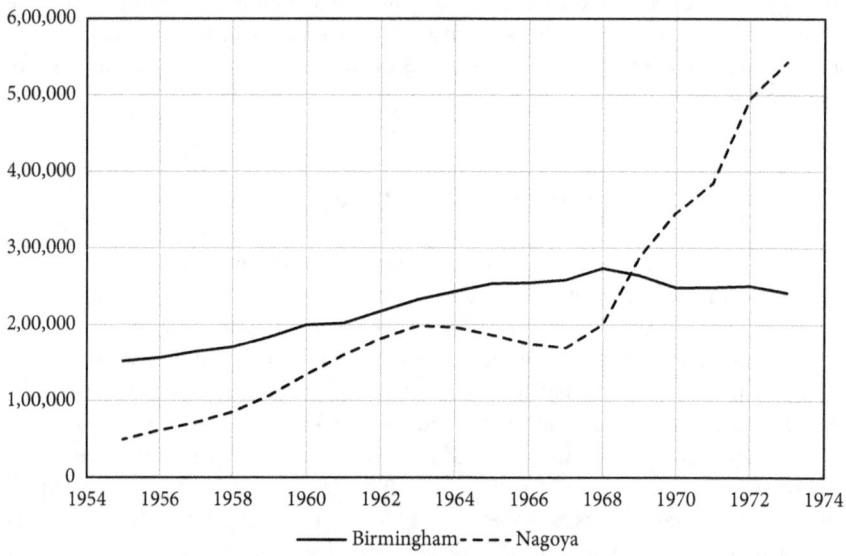

Graph 1.1 Numbers of vehicles in Nagoya and Birmingham, 1955–1973

Source: City of Birmingham Central Statistical Office, *Abstract of Statistics* (Birmingham, 1946–1973); *Nagoya-shi Hyakunen no Nenrin*, [Nagoya City, Annual of a Hundred Years] (Nagoya, 1989), 189–190.

later 1950s, so the warnings became more urgent. Urban traffic congestion will be 'one of the biggest problems with which civilization is faced in the next decade', Herbert Manzoni warned in 1959, 'liable to cause decay throughout the centre of our towns'.[122] Despite the comparatively low vehicle numbers, like other cities in Japan, Nagoya experienced severe traffic congestion in the 1950s while its new road network was being constructed. Consequently the rate of traffic accidents increased exponentially. In 1960 there were 8,913 accidents involving other vehicles in Nagoya, an astonishing five-fold increase on 1955. 'Slow-moving traffic' was cited as the major cause, indicating that congestion was held to blame. Similarly, there was a six-fold increase in the number of pedestrians involved in accidents in the same period. Rather than blaming drivers, the reason cited in the statistical report for this increase was pedestrians 'crossing in front of or behind moving traffic'.[123] These figures reflected national trends and, in the case of Nagoya, corresponded not so much to the increase in the city's population as to indices of economic growth and increasing numbers of commuters in and out of the city.[124]

Given these concerns, pressure built in both countries for governments to take action on traffic. In Britain the Roads Campaign Council was established in 1955, largely at the behest of the Royal Automobile Club (RAC), the most militant of the motoring organizations, but with the backing of the wider motor industry, notably the Society of Motor Manufacturers and Traders (SMMT) and the British Roads Federation (BRF) representing hauliers and road transport firms. This was a wealthy and powerful lobby – the SMMT, for example, organized the annual British Motor Show and represented the big four manufacturers, the British Motor Corporation (BMC), Rootes, Ford and Vauxhall.[125] It is difficult to assess the direct influence of the lobby on government but from 1956 funding for major road projects began to flow, including the construction of the Preston by-pass and the first stretch of the M1 motorway.[126]

Notable organized lobbies such as the Japan Automobile Manufacturers' Association (JAMA) and the Japan Automobile Federation (JAF) were not founded until the 1960s. But plans for new road construction found an influential champion in Prime Minister Yoshida Shigeru who was prime minister between 1946 and 1947 and again from 1948 to 1954. Travelling between Frankfurt and Rome in autumn 1954, he noted the contrast between Europe's high-quality road network and Japan's relatively primitive road structure: 'It is difficult to claim a high degree of civilization when the road network is in the condition still existing in my country.' Roads were not only a marker of civilization but poor roads directly affected industrial output and living standards in general.[127] In May 1956 a team of American specialists, led by the economist Ralph J. Watkins, was commissioned by the Ministry of Construction to investigate the potential profitability of the first part of the planned route between Kobe and Nagoya, which would become the Meishin Expressway. In November 1956, the Watkins Survey and Report Study Committee (*Watokinsu Chōsa Hōkokusho Kentō Iinkai*) reported to the Ministry beginning with the now widely quoted remark: 'The roads of Japan are incredibly bad. No other industrial nation has so completely neglected its highway system.'[128] The situation around Nagoya was found to be particularly damaging to the region's economic well-being. Of the roughly 2 million motor vehicles registered in Japan at the time, around one-quarter was circulating in the Kobe-Nagoya area. The narrow, winding main highways passed straight through the commercial and industrial centres of the towns they served and were poorly built and maintained. A 1958 report to the International Bank for Reconstruction and Development (IBRD)[129] stated:

> Congestion is all the heavier and delays are all the more prolonged because of the great variety of vehicles which use the roads. Everywhere in the area, large trucks, buses and passenger cars share the same lanes with bicycles, motorcycles, scooters, etc. This dangerous state of affairs is intensified by undisciplined driving habits and ineffective traffic policing.[130]

The construction of a national expressway to relieve congestion in the wider region was the primary concern for regional planners in the 1950s, while in Nagoya Tabuchi was occupied with overseeing the construction of the 100-metre-wide roads. It was not until 1961 that Nagoya City and Aichi Prefecture were instructed by the Ministry of Construction to conduct a Metropolitan Trunk Route Survey in preparation for planning an urban expressway.

Roads construction hardly proceeded faster in Birmingham. There was mounting concern among local officials and politicians during the 1950s at the lack of progress on the Inner Ring Road. After the passing of the Act of 1946 which gave legal endorsement to the project, a loan was received from the Treasury towards the purchase of properties along the proposed route. But no central government funding was forthcoming for the construction of the road itself, estimated in 1955 at £15 million in total with government nominally committed to providing 75 per cent of the costs.[131] The Minister of Transport, John Boyd-Carpenter was reported to have been impressed by the city's road plans when he visited for the opening of the widened arterial road at Digbeth in July 1955. A civil servant noted: 'The Birmingham Inner Ring Road is clearly a scheme of the highest importance. Birmingham is generally believed to have more serious problems of traffic congestion than any large city in the country, apart from London.'[132] Increasingly desperate to win financial support for the road from government, the Corporation sent a deputation to see the Minister in November 1955, led by Frank Price, chair of the Public Works Committee. It was accompanied by a lengthy memorandum outlining the Corporation's case, with testimonials of support from the city's Chamber of Commerce and Trades Council. What the memorandum stressed first and foremost were the industrial requirements for the road: 'The City Council would not press this Ring Road scheme at the present time were they not convinced that it is in the interests of the economic running of this city, a great producer of goods for the national export drive.' In particular, according to the report, the need arose because of the peculiar features of Birmingham's industrial structure which was characterized by a network of highly interdependent firms, as in the motor industry. 'Many Birmingham industries are arranged on a "horizontal" basis whereby a product passes through the hands of a number of firms for different processes between the raw material and the finished product.' In what was an argument neatly tailored to a government still geared to post-war economic recovery, the Inner Ring was presented as an adjunct of Birmingham's export-oriented industrial system.

It cannot be too strongly emphasised that the traffic which is being delayed for the want of a Ring Road is <u>industrial traffic</u>, the buses and cars carrying workers, the vans and lorries carrying raw materials, plant and manufactured goods ... The Ring Road should, in the Council's view, be treated for Government investment purposes in the same way as a scheme for a large conveyor installation in one of our big motor works.[133]

Despite the reluctance of the Conservative government to be drawn into supporting a scheme of this scale and duration, the pressure worked. In February 1956 the Ministry of Transport approved in principle the building of the first section of the Inner Ring Road; a grant of £731,246 was subsequently confirmed with a promise of a further instalment in 1958–1959.[134] The sums were small against a total budget for the Inner Ring Road of £15 million – the Corporation had asked for a grant of £2.7 million – and they did not commit the government to ongoing financial outlay for the completion of the project. But they enabled the project to get started. Almost forty years after the plan for a Ring had first been outlined by Henry Stilgoe, construction work on what would become Britain's first urban motorway started in March 1957. It began with a touch of farce when the new Minister of Transport, Harold Watkinson, and attendant dignitaries were showered with rubble from the overcharged detonation which was to be the symbolic highpoint of the inaugural ceremony.[135] Nevertheless, a major work of civic engineering which would take fourteen years to complete was finally underway.

Conclusion

This chapter has demonstrated strong similarities in the ways in which both cities were able to capitalize on the legacies they inherited from urban planning both before and during the Second World War, despite the destruction caused by wartime bombing. At a local level, the internationalization of town planning shortly before the First World War provided a stimulus to initiatives such as the establishment of a Town Planning Committee in Birmingham in 1911 and the Municipal Improvement Investigation Association in Nagoya in the same year. The need for coordinated local planning was prompted by rapid expansion of city boundaries in the early twentieth century. In both countries, the First World War spurred the creation and strengthening of national planning laws. In Japan, the City Planning and Urban Building Laws in 1919 comprised the first national planning legislation in Japan and the Housing and Town Planning Act of 1919 in Britain promoted the building of new housing, particularly in the state sector.

Although economically central to the war effort, Nagoya and Birmingham were far enough removed from the centres of power in their respective capitals to exercise a considerable degree of autonomy in urban planning both before and after the Second World War. Planning for transportation was already well advanced by the end of the 1920s under City Engineer Henry Stilgoe in Birmingham and Ishikawa Hideaki in Nagoya. After the war their ideas were foundational to the vision of two men, Herbert Manzoni and Tabuchi Jurō, whose leadership and strength of personality exploited, sometimes ruthlessly, the opportunities presented by the necessity and urgency of post-war reconstruction. Although Nagoya and Japan lagged behind Birmingham and Britain in car ownership numbers, it was the pressures of traffic chaos which occupied the minds of city planners rather than the growing economic dominance of the cities' car industries in the late 1950s and 1960s. In this respect, an important difference emerges in Nagoya's construction of its 100-metre-wide roads; the planning of refuges and firebreaks in the case of natural disaster. These differences are taken up more fully in the next chapter. In terms of national planning and funding, it was their position as centres of automotive manufacturing and their official commitment to automobility that ensured Nagoya and Birmingham were located, politically and geographically, at the centre of new national expressway systems.

2

Civic Engineering: Roads Construction and the Urban Environment

It was in the 1960s that Birmingham emerged as a fully fledged motor city, recognized internationally for its incarnation of automotive modernity. Nagoya's transformation into a motor city took much longer and its status was more dependent on Toyota's ascendancy as the mainstay of the Midland (*Chūbu*) automotive region of which Nagoya was the capital.[1] But in both cities roads were instrumental to a vision of urban modernity, each city implementing a flagship road project to showcase their capacity for and commitment to civic engineering. In Birmingham this was the Inner Ring Road and the Aston Expressway, the latter linking the city to the national M6 motorway that was to pass through its eastern suburbs. Unlike Birmingham, Nagoya had no urban motorway before the late 1970s. The Nagoya Urban Expressway was only started in 1967 and the first section was not opened until twelve years later. After the completion of the 100-metre-wide roads in the early 1960s, a 71 kilometre- (44 mile-) section of the Meishin Expressway (*Meishin Kōsoku Dōro*) between Osaka and Nagoya was opened in July 1963.[2] In September 1964 Ichinomiya Interchange was completed, linking Nagoya to the Meishin Expressway. The full 190 kilometre- (118 mile-) stretch was finally opened in 1965 to connect Ichinomiya to the north of Nagoya with the city of Kobe in the west.[3] Taken together, these major road projects posed enormous legal, financial and engineering challenges to underwrite the future of automobility in Japan.

Birmingham's Inner Ring Road represented a new type of road (Figure 2.1). It was Britain's first integrated urban motorway and one of the largest and most costly civil engineering projects undertaken by any British city, the mid-twentieth-century equivalent of the construction of the Victorian sewers or the London underground. It was contemporaneous with the other major civil engineering project of the period, the linked M1 and M6 motorways.[4] The initial phase of construction of Birmingham's Inner Ring in 1957 was undertaken just prior to the opening of Britain's first motorways, the Preston by-pass in 1958 and the first 55-mile stretch of the M1 north of London a year later. The first urban expressway to be built in Japan was the Tokyo Expressway, conceived in 1950 as part of the capital's reconstruction and opened to traffic in 1959. It was an integral part of the Metropolitan Expressway, a larger network centred on Tokyo to which it was later linked but, as Hasegawa Jun'ichi points out, the two were different entities.[5] The privately operated Tokyo Expressway was built well in advance of any other city, including Nagoya, and before the beginnings of the national expressway network.

In both countries, therefore, roads were central to the planner's eye-view of post-war urban reconstruction. Speaking in 1959, the year in which the programme for the 'New Birmingham' was launched, the city's chief planner, Herbert Manzoni, termed the Inner Ring Road 'the spark which set alight private development in the city centre'.[6] Massive public investment in the infrastructure would galvanize the powers of private capital to renew the city centre's outworn fabric of gaunt Victorian office-buildings, darkened warehouses and dingy shops. Birmingham's roads project exemplified the civic ambition to put the new 'motor world' at the heart of the gleaming modern city that would emerge, butterfly-like, from the chrysalis of urban renewal. These features of the 'new Birmingham' captured international attention. Henry Barnes, Traffic Commissioner for Baltimore, reported in 1959 that 'the Birmingham [Inner] Ring Road is amazing because it embodies a well-planned redevelopment for traffic, the pedestrian, and actual building'.[7] By 1960 the catalytic effect was to make the city, in the eyes of the American press, 'the biggest re-development show on earth'.[8] Praise for the design of the Inner Ring also came from Germany, home of the *autobahn*: '*Bei uns noch wunschtraum – in England schon praktiziert*', a Hannover newspaper enthusiastically affirmed; 'still a dream of the future for us – already practised in England.'[9]

The post-war transformation of Nagoya was also striking, and its model of land readjustment (LR) was well publicized. Before the war, visitors from Tokyo and Osaka spoke derisively of Nagoya as an 'overgrown farm town'. Along its historic

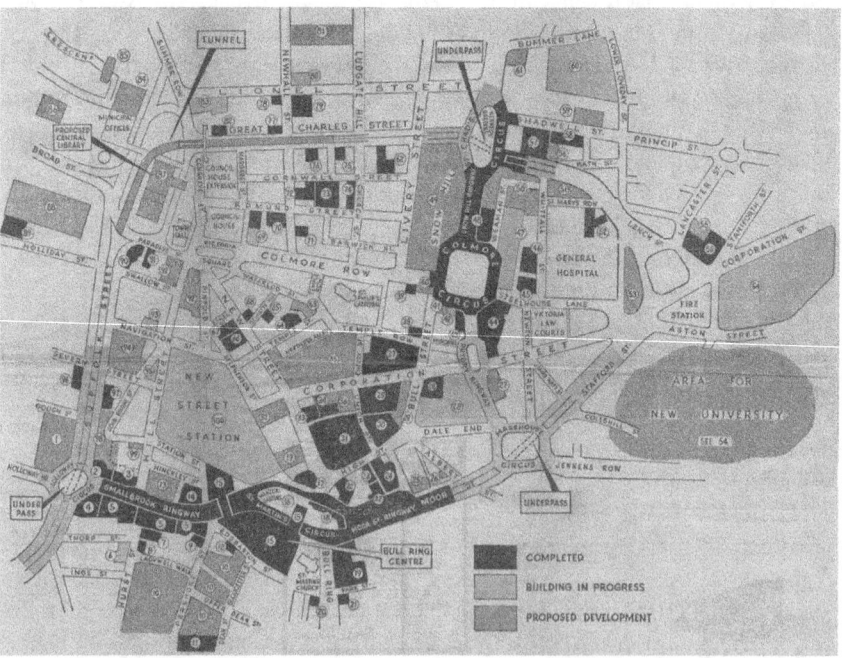

Figure 2.1 The new Birmingham, 1964: Plan of the Inner Ring Road and city centre. Source: D.J. Norton Collection.

main street, Hirokōji Dōri, there were fewer buildings more than three storeys in height. Consisting largely of small, residential workshops, they were traditional in style and built from wood. Nagoyans were stereotyped in Japan as old-fashioned in dress and taste, and lacking in cultural attainment, originality and independence.[10] But as we shall see in Chapter 3, by the 1960s Hirokōji Dōri, lined with smart, multi-storey banks and insurance offices constructed in reinforced concrete, was just one of twelve 30-metre-wide roads, opening a new vista of modern city living (Figure 2.2). Together with the two 100-metre-wide roads and nine 50-metre-wide roads, modern Nagoya offered a ground-level vison of car-dominated mobility unmatched by any other Japanese city. Nagoya's achievement was widely recognized in international circles. The British planning historian Anthony Sutcliffe referred to Nagoya's most famous 100-metre-wide road, Hisaya Ōdōri, as 'a monument of planning history.'[11] The city's civil engineer Tabuchi Jurō was proud of his achievement in the face of fierce criticism at the time, stating in his autobiography: 'As construction began, people laughed and asked jokingly whether we were building an airfield. Well, no one is laughing now.'[12] By the 1980s Nagoya's reconstruction became internationally recognized as a model of the successful use of LR which could be transferred to developing countries globally.[13] Nagoya and Birmingham were, therefore, two of the leading sites in the post-war marriage of automobility and urbanism.

This chapter tells how the long-held plans to re-engineer Nagoya and Birmingham around the priorities of roads and automobility took shape on the ground between the

Figure 2.2 Mobility and modernity Japanese-style: Hirokōji Dōri and Maruei department store, 1950s.

Source: Tsurumai Central Library Collection. http://timetravel.network2010.org/article/129

later 1950s and the early 1970s. It examines the techniques of traffic engineering and construction that created the new roads, embodying the dream of the fully motorized city and with it, a new relationship between citizen-individuals and the urban environment. One important dimension of this was the concept of 'traffic architecture', in which roads and motor vehicles were combined with modern buildings in a novel synthesis. First, though, we need to be aware of the move to mass motorization that was occurring in both countries in these years.

The motor revolution and its consequences

In statistical terms the facts of mass motorization were stark: between 1950 and 1970 the numbers of vehicles on Britain's roads more than trebled, from 4 million to over 13 million, steadily rising to 25 million by 1990. An ever-increasing proportion of these vehicles were private cars, rising from 51 per cent of the total in 1950 to 77 per cent in 1970.[14] By contrast, in 1950 the number of vehicles owned in Japan had only just crept over its pre-war figure to 414,000, one-tenth the number of vehicles on British roads.[15] However, during the next two decades Japan began to catch up and exceed the number of vehicles on Britain's roads reaching over 17.5 million by 1970 when the number of passenger cars surpassed trucks for the first time (Graph 2.1).[16]

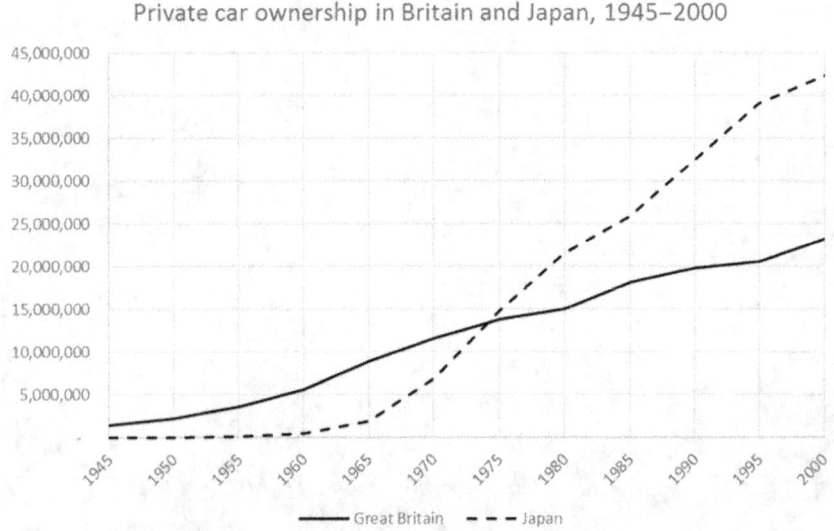

Graph 2.1 Private car ownership in Britain and Japan, 1945–2000

(Sources for Japan: Statistics Bureau, Ministry of Internal Affairs and Communications, Japan. *Historical Statistics of Japan*. Last modified, April 2012. http://www.stat.go.jp/english/data/chouki/. Sources for Britain: British Road Federation, *Basic Road Statistics* (London, 1973); Department of the Environment, *Transport Statistics: Great Britain 1964–1974* (London, 1974); Department of Transport, Transport Statistics Great Britain (London, 2015))

While the 'motor revolution' in the decades after 1950 saw an expansion in the numbers of all types of vehicle, it was the private car which led the way. For different reasons post-war governments in Japan and Britain sought to contain private consumption of automobiles. In Japan, personal consumption was suppressed in favour of saving; in Britain austerity until the mid-1950s meant that the export of cars was prioritized over the domestic market. But in neither case did this inhibit demand for cars and other types of motor vehicles.

In both countries domestic motor manufacturing powered the expansion of the automobile market. Britain produced more than a million cars a year for the first time in 1958.[17] In the same year, Japanese manufacturers produced fewer than 200,000 vehicles, of which only around one-quarter were passenger cars. But by 1967 Japanese production had escalated to 1.4 million passenger cars, reaching over 4.5 million in 1975.[18] Put in international context, Britain was the third largest automobile producer in the world in 1960, while Japan was the sixth largest. By 1970 the position had reversed, Japan now second only to the United States as a producer with Britain in fifth position.[19] Both countries, however, remained significant players in the production and export of motor vehicles through the two decades after 1950.

In response to the surge in production, car ownership rose rapidly. In Britain cars per head of population fell from one car for every twenty-two people in 1950 to one to six by 1964 and one to four by 1972, putting the country on a par with France and West Germany.[20] Japan started from a lower base rate in 1950 when there was only one car for every 2000 people. In 1964 that figure had fallen to one car for every fifty-eight people and one to nine by 1972.[21] Despite the extraordinary growth in car ownership, entering the 1970s Japan still lagged behind its Western counterparts in certain respects, although the rate of increase was to outstrip them in the last third of the century.

What these statistics cumulatively denoted was a major social shift in personal mobility and consumption, which contemporaries responded to in diverse ways. While some viewed the spread of mass motorization positively as confirmation of a new democratic age, others conjured up a nightmare vision of a country buried beneath an 'avalanche' of cars. In Japan and Britain politicians, planners and journalists concurred on two things. First, they agreed that what was happening amounted to a 'motor revolution', inevitable and irreversible. In Britain, the Labour MP Patrick Gordon Walker made the point forcefully in a speech to the House of Commons as part of a debate on road traffic in April 1960. The car, Walker announced,

> is the major dynamic factor for social change in our country today. It is doing more to change the shape of our cities, roads and countryside than any other single thing … With much greater vigour, we must rebuild our whole environment of working and living in terms of the motor car.[22]

Secondly, as Walker and many others noted, the most significant social factor behind the 'motor revolution' was the spread of car ownership to wider sections of the population than ever before, ushering in what British politicians referred to as the 'car-owning democracy'. In 1949 it was estimated that only 3 per cent of semi-skilled and unskilled workers owned a car in Britain, yet an AA survey in 1965 estimated that 60 per cent of new car owners derived from social classes C2 and DE, skilled, semi- and unskilled workers and their families.[23] As the classic study, *The Affluent Worker in the Class Structure*, put it in 1969, it seemed as if manual workers were 'invading' for the first time the hitherto middle-class preserve of car ownership.[24]

Developments were slower to take hold in Japan, although the consequences were hardly less noteworthy when they did. Despite the fact that in 1966 the Japanese media famously declared, in an imitation of the imperial reign-dating system, that 'Year One of the My-Car Era' (*mai-kā gannen*) had arrived, it was not until the mid-1970s that Japanese manual workers were also able to afford a car. While farming households were slower on the uptake, by 1970 they caught up with and then overtook non-farming households with the majority of farming households owning a car by 1975 (45 per cent owned a motorcycle or scooter). It must be pointed out here, however, that small-scale farming households existed in the suburbs of most Japanese cities to such an extent that 'farming' and 'non-farming' categories used in Japanese official statistics do not distinguish between 'rural' and 'urban'. Moreover, many predominantly farming family members held part-time jobs in local towns and cities. Consequently, car ownership in these communities also had a major effect on patterns of commuting into cities in the 1960s and 1970s. What this trend of higher car ownership among farming households indicated was not only the lack of public transport outside the cities, but also the progress of road-building, radiating out from the cities to surrounding towns and villages enabling commuting by car. The impact of road building and motorization on such communities was depicted in the classic study of the village of Shinohata by British sociologist Ronald Dore.[25] In 1955 the tarmac on the road from Sano City, the closest city to Shinohata, stopped even before it was outside the city limits. In 1965 the main trunk road from the city was metalled and in 1970 so was the branch-road leading into Shinohata allowing villagers to commute into Sano City. Dore concluded: 'No other society in history has ever been so rapidly motorized, and few societies have had such trouble adapting to the motor-car as Japan with its dense population and tightly packed settlements. Sano and its surroundings show all the signs of improvised adaptation.'[26]

The surge in the number of motor vehicles in both countries put unprecedented pressure on existing roads infrastructure both inside and outside cities which, before the late 1950s at least, remained more or less unchanged in quantity and quality from the 1930s. Britain in 1960, according to the Conservative government's own estimates, had the lowest proportion of expenditure on roads as a proportion of motor taxation of any advanced country, combined with the highest density of vehicles per road mile in the world.[27] In Japan, a 1958 survey showed that between Tokyo and Nagoya the average speed on the highway was between 40 and 45 kilometres per hour (around 25 miles per hour) for passenger cars and between 33 and 35 kilometres per hour (around 21 miles per hour) for trucks. Despite the fact that in comparative terms these average speeds were good – driving speeds in British cities, especially London, were considerably lower – planners were aware that traffic on Japanese roads was set to double in the following decade.[28] Confronted by this situation planners in Birmingham and Nagoya were not alone in their dire warnings about the effects of traffic congestion on cities and the national economy, warnings which grew more pronounced in the 1950s as we saw in Chapter 1. In Britain, in a parliamentary debate in 1959, the Labour MP Leo Strauss observed that 'it was a strange paradox that as a community became more prosperous and transport facilities increased, the more difficult it became to travel'. That, concluded Strauss, 'was what was happening in Britain', and the same was true of Japan.[29]

One consequence of poor roads infrastructure was unacceptably high roads casualties. In Britain the numbers of deaths caused by traffic accidents peaked at 7,985 in 1966 while some 384,000 people were injured. 'During all the five years of war', the new Minister of Transport, Barbara Castle, provocatively declared in the same year, 'Hitler did not manage to kill as many civilians in Britain as have been killed on our roads since the war at the hands of our own citizens'.[30] Thereafter, Britain saw a steady decline in deaths and casualties, partly due to the safety measures such as compulsory seat belts and drink-driving legislation introduced by Castle and her successors. In 1990, though, there were still 5,217 deaths and 336,000 traffic-related casualties.[31] In Japan, the number of accidents more than trebled from just over 33,000 in 1950 to 123,000 in 1956 when 6,751 people died and over 100,000 were injured on the roads.[32] The number of traffic-related deaths in Japan in 1956 was more or less equivalent to the number of deaths due to road accidents in Britain in 1961. However, considering that there were more than 10 million vehicles on Britain's roads in the 1960s compared to just over half a million vehicles in Japan in 1956, the Japanese death toll was unacceptably high making road improvement a priority. The total number of road casualties in Japan peaked in 1970 at nearly 1 million falling steadily thereafter until 1998 when the numbers began to rise again.[33]

The other serious consequence for politicians and planners in both countries was gridlock. In December 1958 traffic in central London came to a complete standstill in the Christmas rush as shoppers and cars descended on Oxford Street, Regent Street and Piccadilly. As a response, Ernest Marples, the government Minister responsible for roads, ordered the Ministry of Transport to take direct control of traffic management in the capital and to introduce traffic wardens and stiff new parking measures. For Marples, the event confirmed the need to set up a special working group which was to result – as we shall see – in the landmark Buchanan report, *Traffic in Towns*.[34] Equivalent events on Japan's roads had similar results. When Tokyo hosted the third Asian Games in the same year, 1958, the British architect J. M. Richards noted that on some occasions traffic congestion was so bad that both spectators and officials were prevented from reaching the stadium. Faced with hosting the 1964 Olympics, the Japanese government and Tokyo Metropolitan Government were determined that such a 'fiasco' would not be repeated.[35]

National concerns were echoed locally in the two cities that stood at the forefront of the 'motor revolution'. Vehicle registrations of private cars in Birmingham increased from 53,818 in 1950 to 195,120 in 1973, equalling if not exceeding the rate of growth nationally.[36] In Nagoya the rate of increase was even more remarkable: in 1955 there were just 5,229 passenger cars, of which the vast majority would have been 'officials' cars' or taxis, but by 1973 the number had increased to 271,637, most of which were for private use.[37] However, Nagoya lagged behind both Osaka and Tokyo in terms of car ownership, whereas in the late 1960s the Birmingham conurbation was only second to Greater London in terms of mass car ownership.[38] The Census of 1971 estimated that 42 per cent of households in Birmingham possessed a private car, putting the city ahead of Sheffield (39 per cent), Leeds (36 per cent), Liverpool (33 per cent), Manchester (32 per cent) and Newcastle-upon-Tyne (30 per cent).[39]

Given these levels of growth in car ownership, predictions of traffic congestion became still more dire in the early 1960s. Neville Borg, Manzoni's deputy and later successor as City Engineer, warned in 1962 that traffic in Birmingham was set to double over the coming decade and that rates of growth were plainly unsustainable.[40] Similarly, it was clear as early as 1958 that congestion threatened the whole of the economic heartland of Japan. The Kobe-Nagoya area produced 35 per cent of Japan's industrial output and export manufactures and generated 25 per cent of national income. Road traffic was already dense ranging from 3,000 to 10,000 motor vehicles a day along the route of the proposed Meishin Expressway. The volume of road traffic had increased steadily since 1945 at an average rate of between 15 and 20 per cent per annum and the region's railways were already running well beyond their original design capacity.[41]

In response to the onset of mass motorization, both central government and local authorities undertook a raft of measures, unprecedented in scope and expense, to manage the 'motor revolution' and soften what were perceived to be its most deleterious effects. In Britain, over a thousand miles (1,609 kilometres) of motorway were constructed between 1959 and 1972, linking major cities in a national network and speeding travel between them.[42] In both countries, the enthusiasm for roads was matched for the first time by expenditure in the 1960s. Between 1957 and 1970 central government roads expenditure in Britain rose annually from £49.7 million to £334.4 million. The zeal of Whitehall was matched by local authorities, whose expenditure on roads also increased exponentially from £53.2 million in 1950 to £276.5 million in 1970.[43] Road construction expenditure in Japan rose still faster from the equivalent of £179 million in 1960 to over £1.5 billion in 1970, over four times the total in Britain. These costs were distributed between central government, prefectures and metropolitan authorities. National highways and expressways were constructed as toll roads by jointly funded public highway corporations whose annual expenditure rose from the equivalent of around £35.5 million in 1960 to nearly £300 million by 1970.[44]

Birmingham's authorities were exceptional by British standards in their commitment to the roads programme, investing more than twice as much capital in highways and bridges as any other provincial city in Britain.[45] The early 1960s also saw a host of reports, commissioned by government, seeking policy and design solutions to the problem of rising traffic and congested cities. Most influential – and certainly most widely cited at the period – was the Buchanan report, *Traffic in Towns*, of 1963, which advocated a combination of urban motorways and 'environmental areas' in which motor traffic would be minimized. The Report saw no contradiction between these two ends; urban motorways would channel traffic away from imperilled city centres and enable the conditions for what its author, the civil servant Colin Buchanan, termed 'civilised urban living'. The architectural critic Terence Bendixson compared *Traffic in Towns* to the pioneering sanitary reports of the 1840s: 'Like them it exposes a social disgrace and by outlining a method of research shows that the problem can be managed.'[46] Very different in outlining a market-led approach to road pricing was the Smeed Report of 1964. Both reports were intensively debated at the Ministry of Transport-sponsored conference, *People and Cities*, held in London in December 1963, at which Birmingham's Inner Ring and broader roads programme was also showcased.[47]

Despite the warnings of traffic growth and congestion, Birmingham's planners did not share the forebodings of those critics, including Buchanan, who were anxious about the effects on cities of unfettered increase in car use. Significantly Manzoni was left out of the Study Group which produced *Traffic in Towns*. Although acknowledged as a national expert, he was considered too 'committed to ring-road ideas' by Buchanan and the Minister of Transport, Ernest Marples.[48] Yet this did not mean that Manzoni and his colleagues were unaware of or insensitive to the impact of the 'motor revolution'. Manzoni himself frequently evidenced his concerns, in 1957 comparing traffic to 'cancer', which 'in only a few years ... will strangle the country'. But he tended to optimism in his estimation of the capacity of civil engineering to cure the problem and, indeed, in his belief in the ultimate beneficence of traffic growth. Two years later Manzoni wrote:

> We are facing a revolution – a revolution which is already here – in the development of the motor car as part of our ordinary way of life. In ten years we are going to have one motor car per family. It is the aim of every family to own a motor car – and I would say the right in modern conditions of every family to own a motor car. Restriction is not the way. You have got to welcome the traffic. You have got to realise that it is an indication of a high and increasing standard of living.[49]

In stating his support for the 'motor revolution', Manzoni was merely reiterating the long-standing promise of local politicians and planners in Birmingham to recreate the city around the priorities of mass automobility.

In Japan generally, a sense of ambivalence towards motorization was always qualified by the Japanese government's commitment to economic growth. During the 1960s Japanese government policy was fixated on Prime Minister Ikeda Hayato's 1960 pledge to double national income. This ten-year plan set a target for growth in wages at 7.2 per cent per year. Described as 'the representative policy statement of the High-Speed Growth era',[50] it was based on a doubling of capital investment promoting a massive boom in investment generally. The emergence of a modern, middle-class consumer society and a broadly consensual democracy from the beginning of Liberal Democratic Party hegemony in 1955 to the oil crisis of 1973 were key features of the Japanese economic miracle of the 1960s. Equally important for the Japanese consumer was the achievement of a remarkable level of income equality not only within the urban population itself, but also between urban and rural areas.[51] Although often left out of the literature on the economic miracle, the Japanese experience of motorization during these years informs our understanding of the impact of the economic miracle on Japanese life in the post-war period, in terms of the economies of both supply and demand.[52]

Mōtarizēshon (motorization) was seen as an inevitable consequence of Japan's successful economic growth and rising standards of living. Ikeda's 'Income Doubling Plan,' as it became known, was successful beyond anyone's wildest dreams. In 1960 GNP grew by more than 13 per cent and in 1961 it was close to 12 per cent. Gross annual incomes for Japanese households grew at an average of around 9.6 per cent per annum in the 1960s, with disposable incomes increasing by 12.3 per cent. In 1960 the average monthly wage for a household in Japan (comprising on average 4 people with 1.6 earners) was just over 38,000 yen (around £37); by 1970 it was over 105,000 yen (around £122).[53] The gap between incomes and the price of a new car was closing rapidly in the 1960s.

Yet as in Britain attitudes towards the consumerism that powered automobile growth were highly ambiguous. Japanese policymakers regarded Japan as a developing country, a country of producers rather than consumers. Not only was protectionism, particularly in the motor industry, rife in the 1950s and early 1960s, but the government, following the advice of international organizations, encouraged the mobilization of personal savings in order to promote growth. In effect the government favoured a model of high saving and low consumption. Even when cheap, mass-produced Japanese cars became available in the mid-1960s, Japanese housewives, traditionally responsible for every aspect of the household budget, were exhorted to save.[54] There was no equivalent of Manzoni's idea of car ownership as a 'right' at a time when production rather than consumption was seen as the key to growth. Indeed, when in 1954 the Japanese government embarked on its ambitious programme of road-building by earmarking gasoline tax revenues solely for this purpose, it was not intended that roads be used by passenger cars. While the construction of the Meishin Expressway was deemed necessary for economic progress, when it became clear in 1964 that it was mainly being used by passenger cars, it sparked controversy and the highway authorities were forced to lower tolls for trucks and other commercial vehicles to encourage them onto the road.[55]

Despite the considerable ambiguities at both government and citizen level, though, the extraordinary expansion of car ownership in both countries was predicated on a domestic consumer revolution. This revolution was underway from the later 1950s in Britain and the early 1960s in Japan. It was fuelled by a widespread rise in disposable household income and encompassed consumer durables such as refrigerators, televisions and (in Japan) air-conditioning. But the most prized and valuable symbol of the revolution were cars.

Civic engineering

The motor city ambitions of Birmingham and Nagoya required not only the 'push' of rising car ownership but also the 'pull' factor of a legal framework for their respective authorities to acquire the land necessary for major roads and construction projects. The legal framework for the Birmingham Inner Ring Road was established with the 1946 Birmingham Corporation Act, which enabled the compulsory purchase of land along the proposed route of three and three-quarter miles. Land was acquired by the Corporation soon after the war to a depth of 80 feet (24.4 metres) on either side of the route. This so-called 'frontage land' would follow the model of the recreation of the city's Corporation Street under Joseph Chamberlain in the 1870s; such land would be leased to developers which would, in part, defray the costs of construction.[56] The purchase of land in fact was always estimated to outstrip the costs of construction. In 1963 the total cost of the road was calculated at £25 million, £11 million of which was for road construction, some £14 million for land and property acquisition; but the final cost of the Inner Ring Road in 1971 was close to £35 million. For financing, the Corporation was reliant on a grant from central government of 75 per cent of the actual cost of road building, the first portion of which was only forthcoming in 1957. Thereafter, although government considered Birmingham's Inner Ring a high priority, funding was only for one stretch of road at a time, for which the Corporation had to bid to the Ministry of Transport and the Treasury. Consequently, the financing of the project was piecemeal and, like other urban infrastructure projects of the period, subject to the vagaries of the British government's 'stop-go' policy. Throughout, however, the Corporation was insistent that its financial model for the Inner Ring made sound economic sense, claiming that the road would raise land values in the city centre and predicting that through leases and rents it would provide the Corporation with an income of £1.5 million per annum by 1969.[57]

It was the system of LR that provided planners in Nagoya with an equivalent legal and fiscal framework and a powerful tool for acquiring land for road building. In Nagoya, by 1930 already nearly 38 square kilometres had been covered by thirty-one LR projects, 95 per cent of which was in urban areas.[58] The 1946 Special City Planning Act (*Tokubetsu Toshi Keikaku Hō*) allowed local governments to carry out LR projects without having to gain the consent of landowners and required that 15 per cent of land should be allocated to such projects without compensation.[59] In 1954 a new Land Readjustment Law was enacted allowing five main groups to execute projects: private bodies, associations, local public bodies such as prefectures and municipalities, administrative agencies and public corporations.[60] Leaseholders had the right to participate in the project, but local public corporations were allowed more scope to implement and review projects. National government was empowered to subsidize local government-initiated projects from funds drawn from the Road Improvement Special Account, which collected revenues from gasoline tax.[61]

After reconstruction, 29 per cent of the planned area was covered by roads, more than double the 13.6 per cent existing before the new plans. In the city centre, the increase in road area was even more marked, rising from just over 17 per cent to nearly 41 per cent of the Nagoya City planning area.[62] Beginning in 1946, the Nagoya reconstruction project would take thirty-six years to complete, ending officially on 19 September 1982. The budget for the reconstruction plan over the life of the project totalled nearly 77 billion yen, of which around 24.5 million yen, came from the National Treasury, 1 million yen from Aichi Prefecture, 16.5 million yen from Nagoya City with the rest, around 35 million yen, made up from the disposal of financial reserves in the region. The budget for roads, (total project cost, including compensation, administration and construction) was almost 14 million yen and for parks, around 4 million yen.[63]

The construction of the Nagoya Urban Expressway did not begin until Birmingham's Inner Ring Road was almost complete. The Regional Highways Public Corporation Law was promulgated in May 1970 and the Nagoya Expressway Corporation (NEC), the first regional corporation to be established under the Law, was founded in the following September using the model of the Tokyo Metropolitan Expressway Corporation. The NEC's aims included promoting the maintenance of provincial highways in the region, collecting road tolls in the Nagoya City area and undertaking improvements and repairs. Finally, it aimed to improve transport as a whole, 'thereby contributing to the promotion of the welfare of residents and industrial and economic development'. On 25 September 1970, the day after the NEC was founded, the Governor of Aichi Prefecture approved the plans for the expressway ring road and three spurs: the Number One Kusunoki Line running north, the Number Two Higashiyama Line running east and the Number Three Odaka Line running south. Surveys and initial preparation work for construction finally began on the Odaka Line section in early spring 1971.[64]

At the time the NEC was founded, the total length of the planned urban expressway was 57.5 kilometres, and the total project cost estimated at 133 billion yen. With regard to the financing of the project cost, 60 per cent of funding came from the national government and regional public bodies. Loans were also taken out, but in accordance with the basic idea of the Corporation Law, the NEC was directed actively to seek funding (40 per cent) from the private sector. Consideration of the ratio of contributions from central government, prefectural (regional) and city was preordained by its predecessors, the Metropolitan Urban Expressway and Hanshin Expressway Public Corporations. The NEC's first budget for both income and spending was 587 million yen in 1970. Aichi Prefecture and Nagoya City contributed 23 million yen each, with the rest made up of interest-free government loans authorized by the National Road Maintenance Special Measures Law, as well as bonds. Related costs for establishing street facilities and improvements contributed by the city and prefecture came to nearly 64 million yen.[65] By contrast with the British system of funding, bonds would be redeemed and maintenance costs met through the imposition of toll charges.

As well as legal mechanisms, city planning on this scale in Birmingham and Nagoya also required new techniques of 'surgical' intervention in the urban fabric. Constructed between 1957 and 1971 Birmingham's Inner Ring Road was a pioneering piece of civil engineering, the mid-twentieth-century equivalent of the great slicing of railways through the dense growth of mid-nineteenth-century cities. Other British cities were to build urban motorways around their city centres – Leeds, Glasgow, Nottingham and Oxford among them – but Birmingham was the first and the most significant. 'No other British city', the *Birmingham Mail* boasted in advance of the inauguration of the Inner Ring by the Queen in April 1971, 'has built anything like it of such magnitude, and only two or three Continental [European] cities have done so'.[66]

The pioneering significance of Birmingham's Inner Ring Road rested heavily on its reputation as a new kind of road. Manzoni described the most innovative section – Smallbrook Ringway – in downbeat, technical terms as 'a modern type of town street which caters for pedestrians' use and continuous traffic at limited speed'.[67] But the promotional film for the 'new Birmingham' depicted it as a much bolder breakthrough, bringing together shopping and automobility in a novel hybrid mix.[68] The *Guardian*'s architectural critic, Terence Bendixson, clarified the concept in an article in 1969:

> There is a strange coming together of an American 'strip' and an English high street in the middle of Brum. In this urban hybrid the ring road is the 'strip', that unique American phenomenon of the stretched-out shopping street lined by car parks and buildings and tricked out in advertisements designed to catch the eye of the automobile citizen.[69]

The Inner Ring Road sought to integrate traffic flow with urban life – shopping, office work, leisure, entertainment – in a synthesis that at least partly owed its conception to North American models of urbanism. However, its potency as a symbolic stretch of road also drew on what the Buchanan group acknowledged was the 'peculiar magic' attached at the period to the idea of the 'urban motorway'.[70] As such, the chief purpose of the Inner Ring Road was to maintain a continuous flow of traffic. In the words of Manzoni's successor, Neville Borg, it represented a '"channel" with a number of arterials' filtering in to it', whose aim was 'uniform traffic flow' for 95,000 vehicles per hour during the evening peak.[71]

It was the Tokyo Expressway that pioneered the integration of traffic flow with shops, offices, restaurants, bars and leisure facilities in Japan. The elevated expressway was designed to link a number of two-storey buildings comprising shops and offices. Unlike Birmingham's Inner Ring Road, the carriageways were on the roofs of these buildings. Yet similar to Birmingham revenue raised from leasing highly valuable retail

Figure 2.3 The Birmingham Inner Ring Road under construction, 1959.
Source: D.J. Norton Collection.

and office space beneath the road meant that it could be operated toll-free, in contrast to most other expressways in Japan.[72] Despite the achievement of Tabuchi in making Nagoya the only city in Japan to have successfully engineered the construction of not one, but two 100-metre-wide roads, they were not pioneering in the sense of either Birmingham's Inner Ring Road or Tokyo's Urban Expressway.

Tabuchi's reconstruction planning was expressed as four main aims: that city centre roads be radically reconstructed; that not only the burned-out areas but associated areas be included and comprehensively planned; that urban sub-centres be created; and that health, sanitation, and fire and disaster prevention should be considered a priority. Although lacking a modernist urban vision on the scale of Manzoni's, Tabuchi's plans went beyond the minimum required by national guidelines. He focused on six priorities: road building, the creation of new parks, the relocation of city-centre cemeteries to a newly created park in the east of the city, the creation of new plazas in front of Nagoya's four main stations (Nagoya, Chikusa, Tsurumai and Kanayama) and reserving railway land for the Chūō (Central) Line and the forthcoming Tōkaidō Shinkansen.[73] A unified plan was needed to cover not just the 100-metre-wide roads, but also the construction of green areas and waterways. According to Tabuchi:

> The concept of the 100-metre-wide road is a little bit different from an ordinary road since one of its special features is its function in an emergency. The basis of my way of thinking was to divide Nagoya City into four large quadrants through two 100-metre-wide roads running east-west and north-south [to prepare] for disaster prevention, and to create refuge areas. This was to be done not only through constructing the 100-metre-wide roads, but also through building roads fifteen metres above the level of the Horikawa River on both sides so that life can carry on more easily in times of disaster.[74]

Here we can see that Tabuchi's idea of the function of the 100-metre-wide road was influenced by his experiences in Japanese-occupied China at the end of the war, and the colonial Japanese engineering concept of 'comprehensive technology'. While traffic management was a consideration, so was the idea of grandeur and views based on the City Beautiful movement. Most important, however, was engineering to alleviate the devastating effects of earthquakes, which were inevitably followed by fire, and flooding which was common during the typhoon season. Indeed, in 1959, Typhoon Vera destroyed the port area and most of the southern part of the city, but repairs were very quickly put in place and the area recovered within a year.

Nagoya's civil engineering achievement lay in making space for these huge roads with the minimum amount of destruction of existing buildings (Figure 2.4). The majority of Nagoya's reconstruction budget, around 48 million yen, was taken up, not by road building itself, but by the costs of relocating buildings.[75] The city's noteworthy success in using LR was also a factor in its fame for a technique of moving buildings (*kenchikubutsu iten*), often intact, to allow road widening, which is why the majority of the reconstruction budget was for 'relocating' buildings. Just after the war it was an entirely practical solution to the acute shortage of building materials, but the method was already well established in Japan and, especially

Figure 2.4 100-metre-wide road: Hisaya Ōdōri under construction at Sakae intersection at the end of the 1950s.

Source: Nagoya City Centre Collection. http://timetravel.network2010.org/article/129

when they were constructed in wood, the technique of moving buildings on rollers was not uncommon before the war. The technique had arisen primarily to move buildings back to their original position after earthquakes or floods had caused them to slide, sometimes by several metres. Most could be moved intact through a technique known as *hikiya* and, from the 1920s, some modern buildings made from reinforced concrete and other prefabricated materials were built on concrete 'rafts' enabling them to be 'floated' several metres along specially constructed rail tracks. Other buildings were relocated by a technique known as *kyakukō,* which involved dismantling larger buildings section by section and then reassembling them. By 1987, an astonishing 41,100 buildings had been physically moved in Nagoya under LR measures.[76] Buildings moved by the end of 1950 numbered 5,695, and another 6,792 had been relocated by 1955.[77] One of the most notable examples of moving a modern building intact was that of the Nagoya branch of the Asahi Mutual Life Insurance Company. Formerly requisitioned by the United States during the Occupation to be used as a dance hall and entertainment venue for American troops, it was handed back to the city in 1955. Made from reinforced concrete, this four-storey building of around 160 square metres also had a basement. The building was cut off at the basement, rotated 90 degrees and then pulled on rails 200 metres from the middle of the Hisaya Ōdōri construction site to the east side of Hirokōji Dōri. The widening of Hirokōji Dōri also involved moving several large buildings made of reinforced concrete, this being one of the reasons why they had earlier survived the firestorms of Allied bombing raids.[78] The success of this technique in Nagoya was demonstrated by the fact that even after the shortage of materials had been overcome, buildings continued to be moved in the 1970s and 1980s. Road construction and widening thus had a significant impact on the built environment of Nagoya and other Japanese cities.

While some transport infrastructure techniques in Japan and Britain had their roots in older practices which were used for new purposes after the war, ring roads, expressways and interchanges were also the products of the new science of traffic engineering and the technologies which, by the 1960s, were associated with it. In Britain, from the mid-1950s older volumetric studies of traffic were overtaken by approaches emanating from North America and Continental Europe that sought to link automobility with land-use, hence the significance of the assertion in the 1963 Buchanan report that traffic was a function of buildings (especially those in the city centre), not of towns in general as previously assumed.[79] Likewise, construction of the Tokyo Expressway began in the late 1950s, just after 'traffic engineering' as a separate division of civil engineering was introduced with the importation in 1955 of two American manuals, the *Traffic Engineering Handbook*[80] and the *Highway Capacity Manual*,[81] both published in 1950. The American handbooks gave Japanese planners new techniques of assessing the particular characteristics of traffic, establishing modern traffic operations and training in the principles of geometric design as well as general advice about traffic planning and administration.[82]

At Birmingham Manzoni was attracted to traffic engineering as a specialist branch of engineering, offering pithy maxims such as 'the capacity of any street system is the capacity of its junctions'.[83] Birmingham was early recognized as a leading centre for traffic engineering in Britain. A Department of Highway and Traffic Engineering was established at Birmingham University in 1959 and the Corporation was eager to experiment with new technologies such as closed-circuit television and computerized analysis of traffic flow.[84] To maintain constant movement on the Inner Ring there would be no pedestrian crossings or traffic lights; instead traffic would flow through tunnels and underpasses, on flyovers and around roundabouts, filtering onto the Inner Ring via multi-lane slip roads. Experimentation continued on the Aston Expressway, opened in April 1972 at a cost of £13.2 million, linking the Inner Ring with the national motorway network, the M6, M5 and – further afield – the M1. The Aston Expressway was the 'ultimate in Britain's drive towards computer controlled urban motorways', operating a tidal system in central lanes that allowed movement of traffic in either direction depending on weight of flow, regulated by electronic overhead signs. At the end of the Aston Expressway stood Gravelly Hill Interchange, popularly known as Spaghetti Junction, described by the local press as 'awe-inspiring in its complexity', requiring new techniques of driving, 'filtering, merging, turning left to go right, and so on'.[85]

The American influence in Japan was more marked than in Britain since Japan's first expressways were constructed with funding from the International Bank for Reconstruction and Development (later the World Bank), giving American civil engineers a golden opportunity to influence their design and construction. In March 1956 a bill was passed to establish the Japan Highway Public Corporation (JHC) (*Nihon*

Dōro Kōdan) which was charged with managing toll road projects and planning the Meishin Expressway which began in 1957.[86] However, Japan's distinctive geography and high population density, together with its notoriously poor roads, generally meant that modifications had to be made to the guidelines in the *Highway Capacity Manual*. Given the increasing density of traffic, the notion of 'capacity' itself had to be revised upwards from 2,000 to 2,500 vehicles per hour per lane. Similarly, the high cost of land acquisition led to scaling down in terms of area, and several innovations were made to the way in which traffic was funnelled in order to facilitate toll collection.[87] The Meishin Expressway was a laboratory for conducting surveys, planning and setting design standards as well as testing and adapting new technologies and materials to Japanese conditions. Engineers visited the United States and Europe to examine road alignments and road surfaces, deciding that asphalt should be used instead of concrete because it was quick to install and easy to repair. The architect Tange Kenzō advised the Japanese Cabinet on the main principles of modern road design and bridge construction, emphasizing elegance in form and design (*fūchi setsukei*) and, in particular, the use of S-shaped curves using clothoids, a new design principle governing the transition between curved and straight line road sections which was gaining international recognition.[88] In contrast to Birmingham, tunnels were avoided wherever possible and bridges were constructed using continuous girders to avoid bumpy joins which might affect car handling. The inclusion of interchanges and 'rest' or 'service' areas was completely new to Japan and searches were made to find and adapt suitable European and American models appropriate to Japanese climate and scenery.[89]

Birmingham's Inner Ring similarly utilized the latest materials in its construction. In Britain there had been debate since the early 1900s about road surfacing and trials involving the use of bitumen and the production of 'tarmacadam', to solve the problem of dust in particular.[90] The surface of the Inner Ring was finished in red asphalt to promote a smooth ride and to distinguish it as Birmingham's 'great red road', pre-cast concrete slabs were used for tunnels and flyovers, and arc lighting specially designed by the General Electric Company (GEC) gave 'a higher intensity of illumination than any other roadway in Britain'.[91] With this attention to the material qualities of the road went ambitious features designed to ease traffic flow. Subways were inserted to ensure total segregation of traffic from pedestrians; car parks were built alongside the Ring and a parking meter scheme introduced in 1962[92]; offices, shops, residential apartments, markets and green spaces were planned to be set along parts of the road's length (Figure 2.5). Unlike Coventry, pedestrianization of the city centre was not seen as desirable. On the contrary, Manzoni, Frank Price and the Public Works Committee repeatedly stressed the role of the Inner Ring in drawing traffic into the central area.[93] Most important throughout the construction of the Inner Ring Road, which was opened in sections from 1960, was its identification with the idea of movement. This was not merely a function of automobility and traffic; the construction of the road was also agreed from the outset to offer the opportunity for the renewal of utilities and infrastructure: water pipes, sewers, gas mains, electricity cables and telecommunications.[94] Flows of vehicles were thus accompanied in the post-war city by flows of water, energy and information.

Figure 2.5 Going underground: Underpass off Hurst Street, Birmingham, 1965.
Source: Leonard Stace Collection.

Japan's new national expressways set precedents for urban roads which, in the long term, proved to be problematic. The ability to raise revenue from tolls meant that the Meishin Expressway was cost-effective, recovering 31 per cent of its construction costs in the first year of operation. Financially, the Tōmei Expressway was even more successful, recovering 38 per cent of costs in an equivalent period when it opened to traffic in 1969. It is not surprising, therefore, that expressways were considered to be the solution to traffic problems in urban areas. However, according to Black and Rimmer 'by transferring a rural design philosophy of expressways to the cities, urban *road* planning failed to recognise the vital inter-relationship between land use, traffic and transport, and the need to plan for all transport modes'. Urban transport planning, in short, required a much greater degree of intervention and the City Planning Bureau in the Ministry of Construction was eager to adopt methodologies which would enable planners to understand patterns of transportation use and be able to predict growth in the future.[95]

In response Japanese authorities turned to American methods of transport planning and urban land use, notably the Chicago Area Transportation Study (CATS). Rather like Japan itself, Chicago, with only around 21 miles of expressway, lagged well behind other American cities in the 1950s. In 1956 the city's corporation embarked on the largest transportation survey ever conducted; published in 1962, it was based on data from interviews as well as land-use and flow-area surveys. In Japan, 1963 was the first year that a person-trip survey was carried out in the Fukuyama and Takaoka areas and another was carried out in Hiroshima in 1967. From 1969 comprehensive data based on CATS began to be collected in Tokyo and in the Hanshin (Kobe and Osaka) and Nagoya areas.[96] Between 1967 and 1978, land-use transportation studies took place in twenty-three cities and, on this basis, master plans were devised for new traffic circulation systems involving road and rail. A characteristic of transportation studies in Japan was the cooperation between government, with the Ministry of Construction bearing one-third of the costs, the prefecture, which gave final approval to all road plans, and the city.[97]

In both Japan and Britain, therefore, civic engineering and traffic engineering became interwoven to connect new national motorway and expressway networks to cities as seamlessly as possible in order to cope with rapidly increasing vehicle numbers. Within the cities themselves new legal frameworks, some local, such as the 1946 Birmingham Corporation Act and others national such as the 1954 Land Readjustment Law used in Nagoya, acquired land necessary for road building. Cities looked to internationally recognized methodologies such as the Chicago Area Transportation Study to help understand current, and thereby predict future, traffic flows and intensities. Most importantly, it emerged that new interventions were required to integrate different transportation modes – expressways, urban roads, residential roads and, in Nagoya, rapid transit subway lines. The most obvious contrast between Britain and Japan lay in the financing of such large-scale engineering which included toll charges on national expressways and most urban expressways in Japan. By the 1970s civic engineering around automobility had transformed British and Japanese cities, with flyovers, underpasses, pedestrian bridges and crossings, flurries of new signs, signals and road markings. Underlying these new visible structures were the often 'invisible' structures through which water, effluent and energy flowed. In particular Birmingham's pioneering Inner Ring was a space of flows representing a visual modernity which was less obvious in Nagoya, until the completion of the first section of the elevated Nagoya Urban Expressway in 1979.

Traffic architecture

As an essential feature of its modernity, Birmingham's Inner Ring sought to fuse the road with its surroundings in a new synthesis that Colin Buchanan was to call 'traffic architecture'. In *Traffic in Towns* (1963) Buchanan proposed that 'if buildings and access ways are thought of *together*, as constituting the basic material of cities, then they can be moulded and combined in a variety of ways many of which are more advantageous than the conventional street.'[98] Split-level structures and sunken roads were just some of the ways to reconcile mass automobility with what Buchanan referred to as 'civilized urban living'. The pioneering quality of the Inner Ring had much to do with its multipurpose character that blended and integrated different elements of the built environment.

The Inner Ring Road was designed not only to speed motor traffic but also to act as the trigger for the redevelopment of Birmingham's city centre. The 1952 *Development Plan* was explicit on this score:

Figure 2.6 Urban neon: Ringway Centre by night, 1960.
Source: D.J. Norton Collection.

> The construction of the Inner Ring Road ... will encompass the rebuilding of much old and unsuitable property, create precincts for shopping, commerce, etc., and providing sites for car parking whilst achieving the relief of shopping congestion by spreading and increasing the area of the City centre.[99]

There was to be no deviating from this aim over the next twenty years: the construction of the Inner Ring literally drove city centre redevelopment in a process aptly described as the 'triumph of infrastructure over architecture'.[100] In fact, as part of its vision for the 'new Birmingham', the city's planners had already begun to implement elements of Buchanan's ideas of 'traffic architecture' by the time of his writing. Smallbrook Ringway, an early completed length of the Ring opened in 1962, combined a long, curved frontage of five-storey shops and offices with a four-lane 'motor road' and additional 'waiting lanes' to the side (Figure 2.6). This was the stretch of road that Bendixson compared to the American 'strip', bringing together shopping, commerce and automobility in a new mix that contravened central government's earlier insistence that these functions should be kept separate.[101] While commentators like Bendixson saw the Ringway as 'a marvellous kind of jewellery for the reach-me-down commercial architecture of our times', and generating 'shoppers awheel',[102] Manzoni and the Public Works Committee viewed it more prosaically as a means of expanding the size of the central shopping area. The result for the latter would be a virtuous circle of development:

> It is expected that by the provision of the Ring Road new properties will be erected along the line of the Ring attracting increased rateable value and the life of the

centre of Birmingham will be revitalised, and this will result in further business and commerce being drawn to the City, increasing its prosperity.[103]

In Japan, too, the coming of mass automobility brought with it new kinds of functionality to the street. Hisaya Ōdōri's green open space was flanked originally by two four-lane carriageways at ground level, later reduced to three lanes when waiting lanes were introduced. Above and below road level, it incorporated split-level structures with sunken park areas leading to underground streets and pedestrian bridges spanning the four-lane roads to connect the park to neighbouring roads and department stores. In contrast to Birmingham, Hisaya Ōdōri and other parts of the city were integrated with Nagoya's high-speed underground railway, or 'rapid transit line' which also connected an expanding network of underground shopping malls and streets (*shōtengai*) which were to become a major feature of Nagoya and some other Japanese cities. The Nagoya Underground Mall Co. Ltd. was founded in 1953 with capital of 4 million yen by Sugiyama Toranosuke, former President of Central Japan Newspaper Co. The Board of Directors also included personnel from Toyota Corporation, Mainichi Newspapers and the privately owned Meitetsu Railway Company. The prospectus for the company stated that it would make use of an existing underground road from Nagoya Station as far as the tram stop at Sasashima (around half a mile to the south of the station), to construct one grand, luxurious shopping mall and amusement centre, free from the traffic confusion above ground in the busy, commercial heart of the city. Not only would the scheme revitalize the environs, notably the station area, around the heart of the mall, but also prevent further traffic congestion and accidents.[104]

In the 1950s, therefore, the first mall-type construction in Japan was centred on public transport, specifically rail and tram. On 15 October 1965, the first 1.5 kilometre section of the second rapid transit line running beneath Hisaya Ōdōri between Shiyakusho [Nagoya City Hall] and Sakae was inaugurated; the following day Nagoya's first privately funded underground car park, Sakae Park, was opened to provide 370 parking spaces. The first municipal underground car park with a capacity for 510 vehicles was unveiled in November 1966 under Hisaya Ōdōri and another seven underground car parks were built to plan by 1978. More underground pedestrian areas were built to connect subway stations to Hisaya Ōdōri and the basements of multi-storied department stores such as Mitsukoshi in Sakae. By 1969, not only were Nagoya's commercial, retail and administrative districts connected by rapid transit lines, so were two of Nagoya's great parks, Higashiyama Park in the east and Nakamura Park some 12 kilometres to the west.[105] In contrast to Birmingham, therefore, by the 1970s Nagoya already had an extensive network of rapid-transit railways which would eventually form the Nagoya Municipal Subway system.

The drive towards integration of systems and synthesis of functions in Nagoya was very similar to Birmingham's, but the means of achieving this integration included other modes of public transport to a far greater extent than in the British city. In architectural terms its subterranean nature meant that Nagoya's city-scape lacked the visual drama of Birmingham where the integration of shopping and automobility in the new 'traffic architecture' took the form of 'megastructures' – large, highly visible multi-functional built complexes – directly imbricated with the Inner Ring.[106] An early start had been made with a plan for a service tunnel linking the Inner Ring with the Big Top, Birmingham's first shopping mall, instigated by the property speculators Jack Cotton and Ravenseft in 1955 and opened in 1959. The idea of Manzoni and the Public Works Committee was that commercial traffic serving the Big Top would be funnelled off the Inner Ring by means of a service tunnel underneath the city and mall, thus easing ground-level traffic flow in the vicinity. Manzoni considered the plan, which was realized in the early 1960s, as a showpiece for how traffic congestion could be prevented by multi-level construction.

The Big Top paved the way for the still more ambitious 'traffic architecture' of the Bull Ring, 'a pioneer of its species', a vast mall spread over six floors incorporating 141 shops, offices, market stalls, restaurants, multi-storey car park and a capacious bus station.[107] As an advance on the Big Top, the Bull Ring was directly connected to the Inner Ring Road and integrated with it: shoppers were brought in by special buses while car drivers entered straight from the Ringway and had their car parked for them by a valet.[108] A further mega-structure, Paradise Circus, was built directly over the Inner Ring between 1969 and 1973; indeed central government funding for the development was dependent on this linkage, since roads remained a governmental priority at a time of reduced public expenditure on other domains. At Paradise Circus the road was tunnelled underneath a new, multi-level Central Library, the mega-structure following Buchanan's prescriptions by separating vehicles and pedestrians by levels. The architects, Alan Maudslay and John Madin, explained the principles of movement or 'circulation' for the site in a 1966 report:

> Provision has been made for this circulation [of pedestrians] by raising the buildings above pedestrian level and by providing secondary circulation at an upper level ... the main pedestrian level will be a paved concrete deck covering the 'bus interchange area and service area. Stops and ramps from Chamberlain Place will span the road and provide a continuous pedestrian paved area between the Library, Council House, and Town Hall. Escalators will carry people direct from the buses to the deck under the Reference Library block.[109]

The Inner Ring Road as well as Nagoya's subterranean city of subways and underground malls thus embraced 'traffic architecture' in diverse forms, each of which sought to provide a novel solution to the problem of integrating automobility with other dimensions of urban life. One important dimension common to both was obviously shopping. A promotional TV commercial for Nagoya Underground City featured a song and a mascot, *Mogura no Chika-chan* (Little Subway Mole). With its catchy American-style big-band sound, Chika-chan extolled the virtues of Nagoya's 'number-one' (*nambā wan*) shopping experience where shops and children were everywhere among the neon lights, enjoying shopping come rain or shine.[110] The Birmingham Inner Ring, according to a promotional film of 1965, was a 'road designed for shopping'; the mega-structures engineered were presented as part of a new 'drive-in' world.[111] Yet the road was also intended to open outwards to new types of urban experience. Subways were built to take pedestrians underneath the urban motorway, but their purpose was not merely functional; they were designed to 'create the feeling of an underground street rather than a corridor', containing kiosks, telephones, public lavatories, advertising and tiled murals.[112] Rather than representing a liminal non-place, subways were intended to connect the driver or bus passenger – now a pedestrian – with the city centre streets. Similarly, the Inner Ring created new interstices between motorway and city as the iconoclastic architectural critic, Ian Nairn, observed. Visiting the new Birmingham in 1966, he described the multi-level junction at Colmore Circus as a 'notable example of traffic amenity as well as traffic engineering', arguing that 'this urban motorway has actually improved the environment.'[113]

> In summer, it is a shady place to stop for a rest, all the more effective because of the bustle around; on a foggy day in winter, with the time on the *Birmingham Post* building glimmering through the murk, it seems to be one of the very few new places in Britain which is genuinely atmospheric. And at any time it is a splendid place for children, safe yet more exciting than an adventure playground because it is actually part of the city.[114]

Similarly Nagoya Underground City, which would later become known as *San Rōdo* (Sun Road), offered shelter from the Nobi Plain's notoriously harsh winter wind, summer's enervating humidity and the torrential downpours of the autumn typhoon season. In 1954, the Meitetsu railway company opened a department store and, later, an hotel over the rail terminal, close to its competitor Kintetsu railway company's department store. In 1957 a multi-storey Matsuzakaya department store opened with its basement connected to the mall. All were integrated with the mall so that shoppers would not have to brave either the weather or the traffic. In 1970 another underground shopping mall, Unimall, opened. Running for around half a kilometre from Nagoya Station beneath Sakura Dōri as far as what is now Kokusai Centā (International Centre), it became well-known for women's fashions, beauty salons, cafes and restaurants. This was followed in 1971 by ESCA, the 'Doorway to Nagoya', its luxurious underground space welcoming both Japanese and international visitors as they alighted from the shinkansen, the ultimate symbol of Japanese modernity. With the opening of the Central Park mall running underneath Hisaya Ōdōri in 1978, Nagoya would come to have around 78,000 square metres of underground malls, running for around 8 kilometres (5 miles) underground, the most extensive in Japan, after Osaka and Tokyo.[115] Rather ironically, while the building of the first underground street in 1954 was a reaction to the congestion and dangers of automobile traffic circulating in the station area, according to geographer Todokora Takashi, housing the automobile in vast underground car parks close to the malls was the key to the development of the new underground city.[116]

What 'traffic architecture' helped to create in central Birmingham and Nagoya was a form of mediated nature. It was this that constituted, for contemporaries at least, the modernity of the environments constructed alongside the Inner Ring and beneath Nagoya's wide roads. Like Nagoya's underground streets, Birmingham's Bull Ring Centre provided a new sensory experience of shopping. While muzak filled the air, a floor of black rubber tiling promoted a noiseless environment. The temperature of the

Figure 2.7 Smallbrook Ringway 1962 with the Albany hotel on right.
Source: D.J. Norton Collection.

centre was kept even throughout the year, protecting the shopper from the weather and enabling her (the shopper was routinely identified as female) to be kept 'warm, dry and painlessly shopping'. Here, as the promotional film promised, was 'shopping free from traffic'.[117]

On Smallbrook Ringway, the Albany hotel, the first luxury hotel opened outside London by the Strand group, boasted bedrooms with individual temperature control and an all-weather terrace with orange trees, bringing an 'atmosphere of the sunny Mediterranean to central Birmingham' (Figure 2.7).[118] In 1965 the BBC reported a plan for a giant boiler which would provide heating for the whole city centre from a single plant, together with proposals for a water garden, landscaped canals and a winter garden which would be iced over for winter skating.[119] Few of these proposals came to fruition, but they were indicative of the ambition of civic leaders to create a new synthetic environment around and within the Inner Ring. Collectively they represented a form of artificial nature: a regulated, constant sensory environment that alternated between the determinedly exotic and the merely soothing. It was an environment that was predicated on a horizon of boundless low-cost energy. A Shell-Mex advertisement for oil-fired heating in 1962 smugly captured the point: 'Of course, everyone knows that no-one but Mrs 1970 has oil-fired central heating yet. But then there are still people around who think the automobile won't oust the horse.'[120] In 1960s Birmingham and 1970s Nagoya the promise of a modern utopia was founded on a potent admixture of mass automobility, mass consumerism and the artificial control of the urban environment, underwritten by the ceaseless flow of cheap oil.

The physical environment of the motor city

When the editor of the British *Architectural Review* J.M. Richards visited Nagoya in the early 1960s, he was not impressed by its physical environment. Wartime destruction had created a novel but inchoate townscape: 'All is therefore new, with wide main streets but [also] the brashness and incoherence that at the present stage seems inseparable from Japanese city development.' He was even less impressed by the 100-metre-wide 'boulevards' which at the time were still under construction finding Hisaya Ōdōri:

> A bold enterprise, though seemingly somewhat primitive as a technique of traffic planning. In spite of its wide main streets, traffic congestion is nearly as much a problem in Nagoya as elsewhere because side streets are narrow and overbuilt.[121]

At the construction stage the multi-functional and multi-dimensional nature of the roads would not have been apparent to Richards, but in some ways he was correct. By the 1970s Wakamiya Ōdōri was overshadowed by the towering structure of the Nagoya Urban Expressway, and seemed to be little more than a token gesture to the great reconstruction idea of building 100-metre-wide roads. Remembered for its 'barakku town' it soon became a haven for the homeless finding shelter under the carriageways. Of the two roads, Hisaya Ōdōri was positioned so that it could more readily integrate traffic flow with urban life largely because it intersected with both the historic Hirokōji Dōri frequented by strollers and Sakae-machi, the bustling main shopping area with its department stores and shops. The 66-metre-wide park in the centre of Hisaya Ōdōri with its TV Tower became a focal point for market stalls, entertainment, including music, and general relaxation under the shade of its trees. On either side of the park the four-lane carriageways ran alongside wide, tree-lined pavements, unusual in Japanese cities. As Tabuchi put it:

> Within this road we have established a green belt right in the centre of the city and have also attempted the creation of a pedestrian zone providing beautiful views of the city corresponding to the Champs-Élysées in France.[122]

The emphasis on 'views' or 'scene' was, at the time, an important aspect of the culture of Japanese traffic engineering. Although Nagoya's grid-like street plan appears to reflect American concepts of time and space, there is a key difference, as town planner and Japanese garden design expert, Günter Nitschke, pointed out: 'America's greatest contributions of human ingenuity have been in the realm of time problems – the speed of and accommodation for movement of objects, people and information.' While time is most valuable to people living in a large country such as the United States with relatively fewer people, Nitschke argued, space is more appreciated in Japan, a small country with a relatively large population.[123] Wide roads, wide pavements, wide vistas; it was space, rather than facilitating the rapid flow of automobile traffic, that was the essence of Tabuchi's vision of Hisaya Ōdōri (Figure 2.8).

Figure 2.8 Hisaya Ōdōri's wide vistas with the TV tower. Photo by Susan Townsend.

In Britain, such roads tended to be celebrated as an achievement of national and urban renewal. The highpoint of Birmingham's civic engineering came with the opening of the Inner Ring Road by Queen Elizabeth II on 8 April 1971. Pride in the achievement had been suitably stimulated by the local media leading up to the inauguration. 'Birmingham people can be proud of the great red road that has been driven through densely massed property', trumpeted the *Birmingham Mail*, 'providing the spur for much needed redevelopment of the city centre itself'.[124] The inauguration was an appropriately civic occasion, the Queen's presence bestowing the royal blessing on the civic project in a ritual encounter between monarch and urban representatives familiar since the mid-nineteenth century.[125] Speeches by the Mayor, the Queen and the Conservative Minister for the Environment Peter Walker were followed by the presentation by the chair of the Public Works Committee, Councillor Harold Edwards, to Her Majesty of a commemorative medal of the Inner Ring. The royal party then embarked on a ceremonial drive round the road itself.[126]

The year 1971 also saw a special visit of a different kind, this time by Sir Colin Buchanan, author of the celebrated report *Traffic in Towns* and acknowledged to be Britain's foremost planning expert. Initially, his response to the new Birmingham appeared positive. The Inner Ring Road he declared 'a tremendous achievement. For drive, energy and the ability to find resources, it is an example to other towns'. For the most part, though, Buchanan's tone was considerably more critical. 'Birmingham's plan', he observed, 'was conceived within an engineering tradition, with an engineer's vision. Ever since, the city has been struggling to build in some environmental gains'. The environment of the city centre, in particular, he found 'terribly disappointing', lamenting the volume and noise of traffic on the central streets. 'If there is really a diminution of traffic, as the planners claim', Buchanan concluded, 'heaven knows what it was like before'.[127]

At its triumphant opening in 1971, then, Birmingham's Inner Ring was already under critical scrutiny, even if, as Buchanan acknowledged, it had set the pace for other cities. From 1964 Leeds, Newcastle upon Tyne and Glasgow began building their own Inner Rings, while a smaller version – Mancunian Way – was initiated in Manchester in 1967. Yet commentators as diverse as Buchanan and Ian Nairn were agreed that Birmingham's transformation was exceptional. 'Birmingham', Nairn declared in 1967, 'is almost a new city'. For Colin Buchanan writing in 1971, modern Birmingham had been developed 'like a monster Lego-set. When one part of the city has served its time, it has simply been demolished and rebuilt'.[128] Buchanan's observation was telling. According to Manzoni buildings had a 'built-in redundancy'; their shelf-life should be no more than 15–20 years. As early as 1954 he predicted, 'Most of our buildings put up in the last hundred years are finished ... throughout most of the country we shall see complete rebuilding of our cities and towns'.[129] Three years later he reiterated the point with reference to Birmingham:

> I have never been very certain as to the value of tangible links with the past. They are often more sentimental than valuable ... As to Birmingham's buildings, there is little of real worth in our architecture. Its replacement should be an improvement.[130]

Manzoni was no conservationist, and entirely unsentimental about Birmingham's inherited urban fabric. In these attitudes he was at odds with many of his peers elsewhere such as Konrad Smigielski, Leicester's chief city planner, or Wilfred Burns in Newcastle upon Tyne, both of whom saw historic parts of their respective cities as requiring preservation and indeed protection from the 'motor revolution' in the 1960s.[131] Manzoni was also no proponent of the walking city. According to Peter Walker, who worked in the City Architect's department in the 1950s, Manzoni 'hated pedestrians'.[132] Birmingham's obsession with automobility to the exclusion of other ways of getting about the city attracted criticism at the time: 'The pedestrian is treated like a second-class citizen', one planner complained, 'driven down steps and ramps into subterranean passages'.[133] A trickle of complaints in the early 1960s had turned into a torrent of criticism a decade later. A letter to the *Birmingham Mail* in 1969 from a 46-year-old resident of Erdington, Audrey Wilkin, complained that shopping in the city centre was exhausting, particularly for mothers with push-chairs and those without cars; women should have been consulted in the redesigning of the city centre. 'Birmingham has been built by the car for the car', a market trader complained in 1971. 'People feel insignificant'.[134]

The same ambiguity surrounds impressions of Nagoya as a drab city dominated by wide, but traffic-clogged roads. Because of the general success of its reconstruction plans, there was little criticism of Nagoya in the 1970s, unlike Birmingham. Only later did critics – mostly Western, often urban historians – begin to criticize Tabuchi's

Figure 2.9 Car park ramp off Moor Street Ringway, Birmingham.
Source: Leonard Stace Collection.

planning vision. The planning historian Carola Hein, for example, acknowledged the city's post-war planning achievement but also argued that to 'contemporary eyes, Nagoya's wide avenues appear to be over-dimensioned and cater too much to automobile traffic.'[135] Edward Seidensticker, in his well-known book on Tokyo, compared Nagoya unfavourably to Tokyo which he found 'warmer and cosier than Nagoya', because of the erasure of Nagoya's ancient street patterns and, with them, a sense of its history.[136] As automobile traffic grew, the roads in the centre of Nagoya became more hostile to pedestrians, so much so that they became known as the *waito rōdo*, 'white roads' eerily devoid of people.[137] Leaving the streets to the car, it was in the underground city that a more vibrant, but also very modern, street life went on, as John Eyre found:

> In addition to removing the main pedestrian flow from crowded thoroughfares and providing pleasant shopping in a controlled physical environment (air-conditioned in summer and heated in winter), the underground streets enable more shops to be built in prime areas of highest land values. They are one more ingredient in the continuing economic viability of the city.[138]

Conclusion

During the 1960s, then, Nagoya and Birmingham began to emerge as modern, motorized cities, both in terms of mobilities and built form. In the case of Nagoya modernity did not preclude continuity. Pradyumna Karan has stressed, by contrast with Seidensticker, that modern Nagoya allowed an older street pattern to persist, if hidden (Figure 2.10). Using the example of Nagoya's Unimall, he argued that:

> Below the ground, the historical street type – varied in architectural scale and texture, and free of vehicles – continues to exist in a transmogrified form. Within the underground shopping complex, urban life and transactions have returned to the personal level, urban life with an emphasis on the pedestrian and the fabric of small shops that - above ground - has been disappearing from Japan since the 1990s.[139]

While Nagoya's historic street patterns above ground may have been erased, the Tokugawa period grid pattern below the castle was still evident, and some of its 1920s and 1930s architecture was preserved. Hirokōji Dōri, although widened by Tabuchi, retained some of the character of the boulevards of Baudelaire's *flâneur* as pedestrians strolled over its fine Meiji bridge spanning the historic Horikawa Canal. The traditional shopping arcades of Ōsu, close to the Ōsu Kannon Temple, were also preserved and regained their popularity in the 1990s after a period of decline when the area was bypassed by the subway network. Criticisms of Western observers about central Nagoya

Figure 2.10 Underground street (*shitagai*) at Fushimi, Nagoya.

Source: Wikipedia Commons. https://upload.wikimedia.org/wikipedia/commons/5/52/Fushimi_Underground_Shopping_Street_West_Entrance.jpg?uselang=ja

carry a certain cultural freight. Richards may have been right to point to the failure of the 100-metre-wide roads as a means of traffic management, but as this chapter has shown, this was not what Tabuchi primarily intended them for. To see roads merely as failures of traffic management is to ignore the spaces between them. As Günter Nitschke pointed out, space is not so much determined by its physical dimensions, but by our concrete experience of the quantity and quality of the events contained in it.[140] In this respect Tabuchi's engineering was a success, albeit a qualified one.

The new Birmingham also was more than a concrete – and asphalt – jungle. Green spaces were introduced alongside the new: attempts were made to landscape the city centre by Sheppard Fidler, the City Architect, from 1958 and an interest in environmental planning steadily expanded among planners, especially after Manzoni's retirement in 1963.[141] As Ian Nairn noted in 1967, places for recreation and rest existed at the very heart of the city and in more formal municipal style at Manzoni Gardens, lodged between the Bull Ring and the Inner Ring Road. Play streets were introduced in the former slum area of Duddeston in 1969, enabling children to play outside free from traffic.[142] In practice, moreover, Birmingham's makeover was slow and partial; it was not achieved all at once. Describing a 'city in convulsion' in 1963, the journalist Norman Shrapnel shrewdly noted how much of the city had not changed: the 'soured landscape figured with black spires and veined with black canals, the waste dumps, and the willow herb, the sprawling factories and the sulky red sea of terraced houses'.[143] Victorian Birmingham lived on, often jarring with the new. If the heroic phase of roads engineering was coming to a close by the late 1970s, in both Nagoya and Birmingham, it was nevertheless to prove impossible to efface the traces of the past in either city – or to predict the contingencies and externalities the building of the 'motor city' would, all too swiftly, bring with it.

3

Automobility and Urban Form

It is commonly assumed that the form of the modern city, characterized by extensive suburbia and 'sprawl', has been shaped by the motor car. 'Under the present suburban regime', wrote the American scholar Lewis Mumford in 1961, 'every urban function follows the example of the motor road … scattering the fragments of a city at random over a whole region'.[1] Mumford was a stern critic of unfettered automobility but even its apologists shared the view that the form of the modern city had been radically altered by the advent of mass motorization. Indeed, flying into cities today the passenger can see clearly from above the effects of automobility on urban morphology, the road system following – and even in some cases leading – the cities' inexorable outward movement, the mosaic of suburbs and the skein of highways at the central core.

Yet as Mumford and subsequent urban historians were well aware, even modern American cities were not shaped in the first instance by automobiles. Early American suburbs after 1850 were connected to the central city by the railway and, from the late nineteenth century, by the tramway and streetcar.[2] In English cities suburbs developed still earlier from the late eighteenth century along carriage routes that transported the wealthy from semi-rural mansions to their places of work and pleasure. Edgbaston, south-west of Birmingham city centre, developed from the 1820s as a suburb for the city's substantial middle class on land owned by the aristocratic Calthorpe family; it was only connected to Birmingham by rail in 1854 when a local station was opened.[3] Suburbanization in most Japanese cities was accelerated by the economic boom of the First World War, especially in Tokyo where the suburban population increased from 420,000 in 1905 to 1,180,000 in 1920.[4] Initially, much of this growth took place towards the periphery of the capital's twenty-three existing wards, but the so-called 'outer suburbs' (*santama*) of Saitama, Chiba and Kanagawa began to emerge along railway and tram routes in the early 1920s.[5] In Nagoya sub-centres such as Ōsu and Kanayama evolved to challenge the dominance of the city centre, and suburban development began in the green hills of Yagoto and Higashiyama to the east of the city in the 1920s facilitated by electric tram routes running along new roads. The first horse-drawn streetcar in Japan appeared in Kyoto in 1898, but in May the same year a private railway company, Nagoya Denki Tetsudō, opened the Hirokōji Dōri streetcar line running just over 2 kilometres to Nagoya station. By 1921 the company was running an extensive network of electric tram lines of 42.5 kilometres connecting the suburbs to the city centre. Buses appeared in 1923 and were competing with trams by the 1930s.[6] The

American model of suburbanization, therefore, was not universal among cities in the developed world. A comparative study of American and Japanese suburbanization conducted in the 1990s argued that while most American post-war suburbs originated as automobile-oriented settlements, suburbs in Japan grew on a pedestrian scale, and only much later began to develop 'automobile-oriented landscapes'.[7]

But if the physical layout of cities like Birmingham and Nagoya was a product of earlier transport phases, automobility nevertheless made a deep impression on their form in the decades after the Second World War. This chapter examines how the advent of mass motorization and the road systems that accompanied it altered urban morphology in Nagoya and Birmingham, and in Japan and Britain more widely. In the process we shall consider new towns and residential estates, industry and the problem of commuting, and the consequences for public transport of the dominance of the private car. While the outcomes of these developments might have been obvious in some instances, in others they were not. In Birmingham, urban form was affected by unintended consequences such as 'blight' – the decay of urban neighbourhoods bordering new roads – as well as by planned ones such as the division of the city into central, middle and outer 'rings'. Land readjustment (LR) was the single most important influence on urban form in Nagoya before the 1960s and the growth in automobility. After 1945, Occupation reforms had a direct impact on housing policy and influenced new LR laws, but American General Head Quarter's (GHQ's) requisition of land, property and facilities also had unintended consequences for road building. We need to start, however, with the physical layout of Birmingham and Nagoya before the coming of mass automobility, since this enables us to pinpoint more exactly the impact of the car system on the post-war urban landscape.

Urban form before 1945

In Birmingham and most cities in England the private car mapped onto an urban form that was already shaped by successive transport systems based on rail, trams and above all the motor bus. By 1930, indeed, Birmingham's transport routes formed the lineaments of an urban configuration whose contours would remain little changed for the next half-century. Other factors, though, played a more decisive role in shaping Birmingham's physical form in the earlier twentieth century. The most direct impulse was the Corporation's relentless drive to extend the city's boundaries in all directions. In Birmingham old independent communities such as Aston and Kings Norton were incorporated. This was achieved through successive parliamentary acts in 1911 and 1931, encompassing an urban area totalling some 80 square miles. By 1938 four out of seven of Birmingham's inhabitants lived in the outer, suburban ring.[8]

The Birmingham Corporation's drive for expansion lay in demand from manufacturing enterprises for more land but also, and more important in terms of scale of land use, the demand for suburban housing in the form of council estates such as Kingstanding and Lee Hall in the 1920s and 1930s. In total, 100,000 houses were built in Birmingham between 1920 and 1939, half of which were council housing; of this new housing some 90 per cent was located in the suburbs. For the most part these new residential estates, accommodating over 10,000 people each, were not connected to the existing railway network. In the case of Kingstanding, for instance, the nearest rail stations were 2–3 miles away at Perry Bar and Erdington. From their inception, therefore, suburban estates were almost wholly dependent on motor transport, notably the Corporation's bus service; in 1949 only 3 per cent of semi- and unskilled workers in Britain owned a car. By extension, in Birmingham as in Britain more generally, fewer houses constructed in the suburbs (and even fewer on suburban council estates) between the wars were built with garages.[9] The expansion of the city's boundaries thus served to underpin the civic commitment to roads construction for bus transport as much as for the private car. From his appointment as City Engineer in 1936, Manzoni's vision of Birmingham as a 'motor city' connected municipal housing with roads in a powerful symbiosis which built on earlier developments.

The same expansionist impulses were observed in Japanese cities leading to similar patterns of population dispersal dictated by suburbanization along railway lines, tram and trolley routes and, to a lesser extent, bus routes. In 1922 the Nagoya Planning Area expanded from just 13 square kilometres (5 square miles) in 1889 to 162 square kilometres (62½ square miles) by incorporating five towns and villages.[10] As the city industrialized in the 1930s, the movement of wealthy upper classes (formerly the samurai class) and merchants into pleasant rolling country side to the east of the city fuelled demand for suburban housing as residential properties which once occupied the town below the castle (*jōkamachi*) gave way to business and commercial premises. New factories were concentrated in the south and northeast of the city forcing the former lower-class townsmen or *chōnin* out of the central area into lower-lying districts in the south and east, close to new sources of employment. By 1935 commercial and business interests occupied just over 22 square kilometres mostly in the city centre, while heavy industry and manufacturing occupied almost 60 square kilometres. Residential areas, however, now accounted for nearly half the city area, just over 80 square kilometres.[11]

This changing pattern of land use in Nagoya was led by the siting of commercial and industrial premises on the fringes of the city with ribbon development of scattered residential housing taking place alongside electric tramways connected to railway stations. With the population at nearly 1 million by 1930, most of the fields between the old city boundaries and the new residential areas were built over or turned into parks, after a 1938 plan designated open spaces in an attempt to create a green belt in the hills to the east. The containment of urban sprawl, therefore, was already becoming an issue for Nagoya's planners in the 1930s. The first attempt at planned suburbanization was revealed in a September 1940 plan which designated ten new residential areas in Nabeya-ueno in the eastern hills (now in Chikusa-ku), covering around 7 square kilometres, and six smaller residential areas in the Yagoto Hills covering just over 1 square kilometre. These were privately developed, clearly defined housing estates.[12]

The Asia-Pacific War also began to affect urban form in the 1940s. In 1942, after the outbreak of the Pacific War, the threat of bombing increased concerns about the high concentration of population and built-up areas leading to a plan for the preservation of 34 per cent of all land in the Nagoya Planning Area as open space to provide refuges or fire breaks.[13] The economic strain of the conflict in China prompted the beginning of government intervention in housing in 1941 when the private sector began to falter due to shortages of materials. Some houses were built through aid granted to the private sector under the Rented Building Association Law, but the newly formed Housing Corporation (*Jūtaku Eidan*) failed to deliver on its five-year plan to construct 300,000 housing units by 1945.[14] By comparison with the pressures from industry and housing, the automobile had little impact on urban form in Japanese cities before 1945. Quite apart from the strains of war, road widening and building, planning policy in the 1930s went hand-in-hand with disaster prevention which included the designation of green spaces to function as refuges.

Nagoya lagged well behind Birmingham, therefore, which was already developing a model of urbanism that combined low density with automobility, even if this was not initially associated with the private car.[15] The Birmingham model of urbanism went with two further features that would prove important after 1945. Unlike Greater London, Birmingham had no official green belt policy, but the fact that the Corporation owned large amounts of land on the suburban fringe meant that it could operate such a policy informally from the 1930s.[16] While an unofficial green belt did not prevent post-war building or further attempted incursions into rural land, it did mean that the contours of urban form remained relatively stable over time. Secondly, it was intended that decentralization of work and employment would follow the steady exodus of residential population to the outer, suburban ring, especially to the new municipal estates planned and, in many cases, built from the 1930s. In line with the Barlow Committee on the Distribution of the Industrial Population, set up by government in 1937, decentralization was integral to the Corporation's vision for the future city, encapsulated in the 1952 Birmingham *Development Plan* as well its influential predecessors, the Patrick Abercrombie-led *West Midlands Plan* and the study *Conurbation*, both published in 1948.[17] But contrary to Barlow, Birmingham's civic leadership saw decentralization occurring within the boundaries of the city not beyond them; unlike London, new towns at a distance from the city were not seriously countenanced before the later 1960s. As Alderman Watton, leader of the Council, put it in 1960: 'Birmingham people were entitled to remain in Birmingham if they wished.'[18] Likewise, manufacturing firms proved consistently reluctant to move outwards from their principal location around the central core. From the 1930s new industrial estates were built at Tyseley to the south-east and Tame Valley to the north-east but a more even regional spread of industry was not achieved.[19] As a result, employment in the post-1945 decades was to become if anything more concentrated in the offices and shops of the central core and the industrial districts that had traditionally surrounded it. This disjuncture between workplace and residence was to have major implications for traffic planning in Birmingham during the 1950s and 1960s, with more than quarter of a million people from the middle and outer rings descending daily on the central area.

Rather than concentrating manufacturing in the centre of the city, the 1930s in Nagoya was characterized by the movement of manufacturing out of the city centre to cheaper land in the surrounding area. Toyota's decision to move to Koromo in 1938 was just one example. Decentralization characterized Japanese cities generally after the development of the railways in the 1870s, as did polycentrism, the development of several sub-centres connected by railway. Polycentrism was a feature of Nagoya's urban and suburban development which would prove even more important after the war. Nagoya had nine sub-centres which served major segments of the city. They often had their own characteristics even though they shared common features such as banks, shops and entertainment areas.[20] The largest of these sub-centres were Ōzone, the main shopping centre for the northeast of Nagoya, Imaike in the east and Kanayama in the south.

Ōzone was the oldest entry point for goods from the interior and it was connected to Nagoya by rail and trolley bus before the war. After 1945, the development of the subway and a number of arterial roads made it a commuter hub between central Nagoya and the north-eastern suburbs. Imaike began as a small local shopping centre in open countryside until the 1920s when trolley lines linked it to new residential developments in the east. During the Occupation it became Nagoya's premier centre for the black market. Sitting at the convergence of Nagoya's main thoroughfare Hirokōji Dōri and Japan National Railways' Chūō (Central) Line, it expanded still further as residential areas spread more rapidly. In the 1960s subway linkages to Sakae and Nagoya Station turned Imaike into a major regional shopping and service centre, becoming a popular commuter hub with numerous bars and eating places. Kanayama likewise grew from a local service centre for traffic passing through its private and national stations and quickly developed in response to the southward expansion of Nagoya's business district and the arrival of the subway after the war. Like Imaike it was dominated by bars and restaurants and became popular with shoppers from the southeastern suburbs and commuters travelling to and from the city centre. Ōsu which grew in the Tokugawa period as a popular shopping area around Ōsu Kannon, a well-known Shintō shrine, lost out to the burgeoning popularity of the other large sub-centres and redevelopment of the city centre before the war. After 1945 it was by-passed by early subway building and went into decline until later in the twentieth century when its covered arcade became popular with young shoppers. Other sub-centres, Atsuta and Meikō (Nagoya Port) in the south, also functioned as transportation nodes, and Horita and Sakurayama grew in the post-war period to serve expanding residential areas to the south and southeast.[21] These centres developed in the post-war period to challenge the dominance of the city centre. Nagoya's urban form, therefore, was not as centralized or as stable as Birmingham's, but neither was its expansion constrained by the problem of high population density, in contrast to cities such as Tokyo and Osaka which had more than twice the population density of Nagoya.

Factors other than automobility thus shaped urban growth in both cities in the early and mid-twentieth century. Nevertheless, roads were important. In Nagoya, while roads were at the centre of disaster prevention, railways and electric trams were at the heart of its expansion until the growth of automobility in the 1960s. This is in contrast to Birmingham where roads were integral to the city's growth much earlier in the century. 'Most of the phases of Birmingham's growth', the city's historians wrote in 1952, 'can be studied in the bricks and mortar of main roads leading out of the city'.[22] The decades between the wars saw the incremental development of the existing radial road system, extending ever further out from the city. The authors of the study *Conurbation* noted in 1948 that the road leading out from Birmingham to Wolverhampton featured 'a string of shops [that] run continuously for four miles'. 'Ribbon development', identified in a parliamentary act of 1935 intended to contain it, was seen as a persistent threat to both the integrity of the town and the beauty of countryside, part of an ever-extending 'urban sprawl'.[23]

But as we have noted, new arterial roads were also envisaged as an essential part of the inter-war townscape, connecting the new suburban housing estates to the urban body. At Lee Hall in the mid-1930s the Corporation planned to build 3,650 new municipal houses. With the estate, Manzoni proposed a major 'town planning road', a dual carriageway 135 feet wide, which would form part of the larger system of arterial routes, providing the mobile connectors for his vision of the 'motor city'.[24] In short, many of the conditions for mass motorization were put in place in Birmingham at least two decades before the advent of the phenomenon itself. This was less the product of foresight than of the view that the city should be organized around automobility, notably the motor bus, and a model of living that prioritized low density, suburban residential housing as the natural successor to the overcrowded, insanitary 'slums'.

Automobility in Birmingham thus encouraged, if it did not initiate, further expansion into the rural hinterland, despite open space and green belt policies. In Nagoya, changes in land use, particularly the dispersal of industrial development to the edges of the city and the spread of railway lines and tram and trolley routes to the east of the city, began the process of population movement which would drastically alter its demographic form. In the next two sections we discuss the impact of transportation infrastructure in Nagoya and Birmingham during and after the Second World War.

Transport and urban form after 1945: Nagoya

The Allied Occupation affected the reconstruction of Japanese cities both directly and indirectly. First, large tracts of land were requisitioned in Japanese city centres which often acted as an obstacle to reconstruction.[25] As mentioned in Chapter 2, not only was the Nagoya branch of the Asahi Mutual Life Insurance Company acquired as an entertainment venue for American troops, but the construction site for Wakamiya Ōdōri contained at the time Amerika-mura, the headquarters of the occupying forces. The Asahi Building, which stood in the middle of the Hisaya Ōdōri construction site, was handed back in 1955, and Amerika-mura in 1958, delaying the construction of both 100-metre-wide roads.

GHQ also ruled that a clause in the new Land Readjustment Law, stating that up to 15 per cent of a property could be appropriated without compensation, was 'unconstitutional' and inserted a 'compensation for decreased value' clause into a revised 1949 Ad Hoc City Planning Act. This clause was retained in the 1954 Land Readjustment Act together with a number of other American-influenced clauses. According to planning historian Ishida Yorifusa the new act brought together 'urban redevelopment-type land readjustment projects' and 'the mechanisms for implementing land readjustment projects in suburban areas'.[26] Nagoya has been more successful in using LR for its large civic engineering projects than any other Japanese city, completing nearly 79 per cent of planned LR projects compared with just 6.8 per cent in Tokyo. Nagoya's 34.5 square kilometres developed under LR compares to Osaka and Kobe at around 22 square kilometres, Hiroshima at just under 11 square kilometres and Tokyo with less than a third of Nagoya's at 10.7 square kilometres.[27] Hayashi Kitotaka, a specialist in the history of LR, points to several characteristics of both the city and its people which made them more accepting of LR projects. Founded much later than other cities such as Tokyo and Osaka and expanding much more slowly, its historical grid-pattern of streets, characteristic of the seventeenth-century castle town, remained intact for much longer, making it easier to adapt its form to American-style automobility. Its slower development meant that agriculture still dominated until after the war, creating a strong attachment to the land. The insistence of Nagoya merchants on the equal division of assets into business capital, bank deposits and real estate meant that they were less likely to regard land in purely speculative terms. Land prices in Nagoya were, therefore, much lower than other cities and, indeed, excessive development through LR made it less attractive to speculators generally. Moreover, Nagoya's relative lack of strategic importance in comparison to its powerful competitors, Osaka and Tokyo, meant that before the war it received markedly less capital investment from central government.[28] The city, therefore, developed a greater sense of autonomy and, forced to develop urban areas at its own expense, LR was the only financially viable way to improve its urban infrastructure.[29] As car ownership grew exponentially and the city began to expand after the war, planners naturally turned to this history of using LR to achieve their aims.

By 1968 the city had reached its present-day limits of just over 326 square kilometres (126 square miles) and commuting by private car exacerbated a traffic problem that was becoming increasingly intractable. In the decade after 1963, the number of cars in Nagoya increased over six-fold to 271,637.[30] The morning commute placed particular pressure on the city's road systems. With more territory in the northeast and southeast having been annexed by the city the population more than doubled after 1950 to reach around 2 million by 1969. The eastern suburbs sprawled ever further to the east, well beyond the Kakuōzan Hills and Yagoto Hills. Residential areas covered nearly 215 square kilometres, almost two-thirds of the city area, while traditional industrial and manufacturing areas occupied roughly the same area in 1968 as in 1935, around 60 square kilometres, a slight contraction from 1963 when the sector occupied over 66 square kilometres. Business and commercial areas occupied nearly 31 square kilometres, mostly in the centre of the city.

An important feature of post-war development was the expansion of 'quasi-industrial zones' mainly occupied by light industrial and service facilities, distinguishing them from the more traditional industrial zones which developed in the late nineteenth century.[31] By 1951 around 11 square kilometres of quasi-industrial development had appeared on the city's fringes, mostly in the south, but also spreading to the east. There was also service sector and light industrial development on cheaper land on the outskirts of the city in the north and west, encouraging further suburbanization and exploiting a readily available workforce. By 1968 land use for quasi-industrial development had more than tripled in just seventeen years to over 40 square kilometres.[32] These trends demonstrate the growing importance of Nagoya's service sector and the beginnings of a long-term transition from heavy to light industry.[33] As well as contributing to increases in commuter traffic, rising employment in these areas increased the demand for new housing within the city.

On the fringes of the city, housing development was relatively dense since, in the 1950s, high-rise residential buildings provided a solution to the housing problem (*jūtaku mondai*). In the early 1960s J.M. Richards noted a 'well-designed, high density housing scheme, a group of parallel blocks with shops on the ground floor facing the street and an underground station beneath', in the eastern suburbs which had been built by the governmental Japan Housing Corporation (JHC).[34] Further out was a municipal housing scheme begun in 1949 and only just completed in 1962. Here 2,400 apartments of mostly two storeys with some four storeys, arranged in short parallel rows, housed around 10,000 people on a site of around thirteen and a half acres. They were built of reinforced concrete and the site covered bare gravelly hills with roads keeping to the valleys and steep paths or access-roads leading up to the groups of houses. The development included two primary and two secondary schools, as well as shops. Described as 'architecturally commonplace and somewhat drab' it was nevertheless the first large-scale public authority housing development of its kind in Japan.[35]

Home ownership was also on the increase. According to a 1970 housing survey, 40 per cent of homes in Nagoya were owner-occupied, 41 per cent were rented from private landlords and 9.5 per cent from public corporations (both central and local) with 9 per cent rented by employees of private firms as a 'fringe benefit'. In outlying areas, where housing was high-density and cheaper, there was often poor provision of public transport and residents relied on automobiles for commuting either into the city or to a local station at one of Nagoya's sub-centres.[36] In contrast to these high-density housing developments, the prosperous eastern suburbs of Nagoya, known locally as the 'Toyota executive belt', clung to the middle-class ideal of the detached, single-family home enclosed within a perimeter wall and accessed by a symbolic entrance gate. These homes were modelled on the urban houses of the samurai elite, rather than on American or British styles. However, despite the use of traditional styles, as Andrè Sorensen pointed out in contrast to some stereotypical views of Japanese housing: 'By far the dominant form of owner-occupied housing is the detached single-family home as in Britain and North America rather than the flattened block as in continental Europe'.[37]

These developments in the suburbs began to have an effect on the pattern of population density, as rising land prices forced newer housing out into cheaper areas. In Nagoya, although the population density remained relatively high in the 0 to 10 kilometre radius, and had even increased slightly, there was a loss of population in Nagoya's three central wards after 1955 (see map, Figure 3.1). Naka (central), Higashi (east) and Atsuta, the religious centre in the south of Nagoya, lost more than 10 per cent of their populations by 1970. The greatest increase in population density was in the 10 to 20 kilometre radius, with considerable increase in the 20 to 30 kilometre radius stretching out further into the Chūbu region and adding to commuting pressures.[38]

One reason for the increase in population density some 20 kilometres from Nagoya was the development of new towns by the government in the 1960s. One of the first was Senri Newtown near Osaka, built in 1962. In 1963 a New Residential Town Development Law was passed to encourage further developments. In 1965 Kozoji Newtown began to be built on the outskirts of Nagoya, and Tama Newtown on the outskirts of Tokyo was planned in 1965 and appeared in 1971. The idea was that these towns would foster integrated living and working, with employers moving new premises into the area. Tama Newtown was the most famous example and was heavily promoted with news and television footage of families moving excitedly into 50-square-metre apartments. It was the setting for two *anime* (animated cartoons) produced in the 1990s, *Whisperer*

Figure 3.1 Map of Nagoya wards, 1968.

Source: Adapted from derivative work: ASDFGH (talk) 政令市区画図 23100.svg: Lincun – http://en.wikipedia.org/wiki/File:Nagoya_Wards.png, CC BY-SA 3.0, https://commons.wikimedia.org/w/index.php?curid=10398265Wikimedia Commons.

of the Heart (1995) and *Pam Poko* (1994). However, most of these new towns never fulfilled their destinies. People did not flock to them, companies did not relocate there and residents ended up commuting long distances into the 'mother' towns and cities. Planned in 1960, Kozoji Newtown, 20 kilometres from Nagoya to the northeast, was the first to be developed by the Japan Housing Corporation using LR. It was scheduled for completion in 1980 when it was forecast to have a population of 80,000 people.[39] The 1963 Law was heavily criticized for creating residential areas very far from the British and American ideal: 'The planners and developers concerned did not attempt to realize the original idea of a new town in the preservation of the natural environment, fostering desirable human relations, access to jobs and so on.'[40] Enticed by cheaper housing prices and a healthier, less polluted environment, families moved to Kozoji new town only to find that it was poorly connected to other main towns and cities in the vicinity. When the expected jobs did not arrive they felt stranded and were heavily dependent on cars for work and entertainment. In recent years, as buildings began to decay many younger people were enticed back into the cities, leaving an ageing population behind. However, few people regarded new towns as permanent residences.[41]

Within Nagoya and its immediate environs, by contrast, there was continued heavy investment in transportation infrastructure after the war, particularly railways which included elevating the Chūō (Central) Line within the city and upgrading it to double track. In 1957 the first 2.6 kilometres of Nagoya's rapid transit subway was opened between the main station and the major retail district of Sakae, beginning a sustained period of subway development with new lines being added. The city also pioneered the introduction of new trolley buses to replace the old fixed-track trolley system, although they were discontinued ten years later. The area around Nagoya's central station, one of the few pre-war buildings to survive the bombing, was redeveloped into a major retail hub, second only to Sakae. The station was the convergence point of the state-owned Japan National Railways (JNR) including the Tōkaidō Shinkansen, and the private Meitetsu and Kintetsu railways. With the incorporation of rapid-transit subway stops and a bus station, the station area was the focus of major rush-hour pedestrian and surface traffic congestion.[42] Moreover, Nagoya's sub-centres, such as Imaike, Ozone and Kanayama, were also connected to Nagoya Station adding to the through-put of rail commuters (Figure 3.2).

Architect and design historian Jilly Traganou singled out Nagoya Station for a special study not only because of its central location, but because of the relationship between its road pattern and underground streets. Nagoya could be described as both the 'midland city' and as a 'corridor' or 'transit' city. With a population of around 2 million people by 1969, the city lay at the centre of the much larger Nagoya Metropolitan Area which had a rapidly expanding population of over 5 million by 1970, many of whom commuted through or into Nagoya. According to a census conducted in 1990, the rail commuting population had grown to approximately 1.69 million passengers daily.[43] But although Nagoya Station was the largest in the city, only around one-fifth of railway passengers used it, with the rest using other nodes such as Sakae, Inuyama and other sub-centre stations.[44]

Figure 3.2 Approach to the Nagoya Station Complex (JR Central Towers) opened in 1999.
Source: Photograph by Susan Townsend.

As in Britain, national planning in Japan was dominated after the 1950s by policies advocating the decentralization of economic activity away from the core industrial metropolitan areas. The 1963 New Residential District Development Act granted local authorities the powers of compulsory acquisition of large tracts of land which aimed at the dispersal of population and industry. The Chūbu Economic Sphere was established in 1966 to include nine prefectures covering central Japan from coast to coast (see Figure 3.3). As the centre of the Economic Sphere, the newly designated Chūkyō Metropolitan Area (Nagoya and parts of Aichi, Gifu and Mie prefectures) benefitted from government funding to encourage regional growth and development. The region was at the heart of planning initiatives which would impact significantly on patterns of employment, settlement and commuting. By 1966 small and medium enterprises were already moving out of the centre to more distant locations in the Chūbu Economic Sphere. However, manufacturing plants, increasingly light industry, were still found in most parts of Nagoya, including notable concentrations in the older parts of the city. Zoning within the eastern residential areas effectively halted large-scale industry in the east.[45]

Figure 3.3 Map of Chūbu region, Japan.

A key factor in the pattern of employment growth in the Chūkyō Metropolitan Area was the creation of a heavy industry zone on reclaimed land in Ise Bay south of the port which experienced massive expansion from the 1950s. Administered by the Nagoya Port Authority jointly between Nagoya City and Aichi Prefecture, the port developed into one of the largest in Japan and had a specialized handling area for automobiles. Accessibility to the port made reclaimed areas to the south attractive to industries wishing to move out of Nagoya because of soaring land prices. The effect was that the built-up area of Nagoya began to encroach into adjacent towns and cities which had attracted the outflowing population and industries. Urban sprawl tentacled southward from the port area along the west coast of the Chita Peninsula. This area contained most of the heavy industry built on reclaimed land, and within these areas land use was mixed, resulting in industrial, commercial and residential areas existing in close, and sometimes unhealthy, proximity. In manufacturing districts to the west and south of Nagoya's commercial district, growth was slowed because of poor drainage and high construction costs. These areas had a less attractive living environment and relatively poor transportation links to the port. They were a long way from the most desirable, expensive suburbs in the east which possessed superior transport links to the centre. Less skilled and poorer paid workers were increasingly forced into low-lying residential areas to the north, west and south. Often these areas were blighted by the ugliness and pollution of nearby industrial plants and poor public transportation.[46] Women, often housewives looking after children at home or with part-time jobs, were particularly affected by a move to these estates. In 1975 out of nearly 670,000 car licence holders in Nagoya less than a quarter were women.[47] The dispersal of industry at the heart of regional development, therefore, had a major impact on patterns of employment, population growth, mobility and quality of life within the region. Demographic change in the 1960s and '70s also led to a classic 'doughnut' effect and an increase in commuter traffic in and around Nagoya.[48]

After the opening of Ichinomiya Interchange in 1963, linking Nagoya to the Meishin Expressway, traffic flow into the city increased dramatically, causing massive congestion and adding to demands for an urban expressway. Nagai Takahiro, Chief of Planning for the Nagoya Urban Expressway, identified the problem as the 'sudden coming together within the city of long- and short-trip traffic', causing a rapid increase in traffic flow. His first task was to find the correspondence between measurements of these two factors and, secondly, to find a way to separate them. In particular, great importance was attached to the value of shorter journey times for commuters which were seen as necessary for the city's economic growth. The idea was to get traffic relating to Nagoya to flow in and out of the city as quickly as possible. One way of doing this was to exclude through-traffic from the city centre as well as traffic not related to the city centre districts.[49]

The resulting 'Marusa Plan' or 'Sa Plan' was less visionary and more limited in its aims than Birmingham's Inner Ring Road. The plan was named after the circle (maru) of the previously existing Nagoya Number Two Loop Road built in the 1950s (Figure 3.4). The loop-road encircled the two routes of the urban expressway's north-south line and east-west line which visually resembles the phonetic (katakana) character for 'sa'. The plan was designed to link the expressway routes with the Number Two Loop Road via six main radial roads leading off it with the aim of separating long- and short-trip traffic.[50] The 1967 plans called for the removal of trolley buses which replaced fixed trams after the war.[51] The new roads were also linked to urban regeneration schemes in bomb-damaged areas of the city. However, as we will see in Chapter 5, fierce public opposition to the plans effectively halted construction for almost ten years and the first section of the Nagoya Urban Expressway was not completed until 1979.

Figure 3.4 Map of expressway system around Nagoya showing the Marusa formation at the centre.

Source: Wikipedia Commons.

Economic growth accompanied by demographic change also had a major impact on patterns of transportation, seen most notably in the increasing dominance of the automobile, both locally and regionally. In the Chūkyō Transportation Range (defined as an area within a 40 kilometre radius of Nagoya Station) in 1969, buses, railways and private passenger cars carried roughly an equal percentage of passengers, between 27 and 29 per cent each. By 1975 this pattern had changed remarkably.[52] The percentage of passengers travelling by car increased by around 20 per cent to take a 46 per cent share, while rail passengers fell from 29 per cent in 1969 to 22 per cent in 1975. But buses appeared to be the main losers: after peaking in the mid-1960s, there was an absolute decline in the numbers of bus passengers, dropping 10 percentage points to 19 per cent (see Graph 3.1). The continued expansion of the Higashiyama and Meijo rapid transit lines into the suburbs saved the subway from decline and even increased its share of passengers from 6 to 8 per cent. By 1980, the automobile had won in the passenger stakes with 55 per cent share.[53] John Eyre, writing on Nagoya in 1980 put it forcefully: 'The auto has become the most dominant force in modifying the spatial structure of population and residential, commercial and industrial land uses within the city.'[54] By 2000 that share had increased to 71 per cent in comparison to the national percentage of 63 per cent.

The Chūkyō pattern of change is in sharp contrast to the Metropolitan Transportation Range, based on data collected within a 50-mile radius of Tokyo Station, where the railway continued to command over a 40 per cent of passenger share at the end of the twentieth century with car use being held down at around a third of all transport use (Graph 3.2). The metropolitan pattern was not dissimilar to the Keihanshin Transportation Range within a 50-mile radius of Osaka Station. Population density in these two ranges was very similar, just over 2,000 people per square kilometre in 1980, although Osaka itself had around half the population of Tokyo. Nagoya's population density, by contrast, had around half this density in 1980.[55] Population density, and

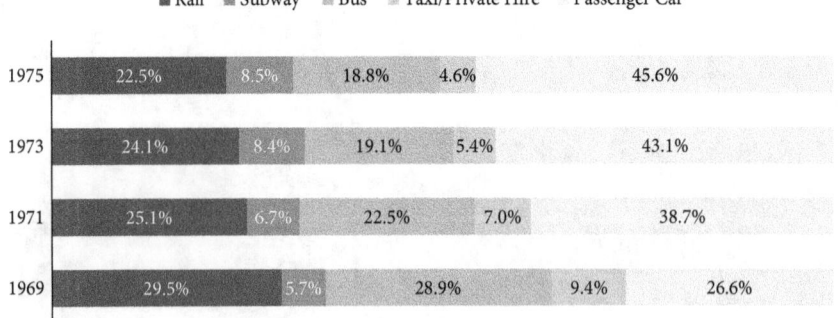

Graph 3.1 Percentage of passengers carried by mode of transport in the Chukyo transportation range, 1969–1975

Source: Historical Statistics of Japan.

Graph 3.2 Percentage of passengers carried by mode of transport in the Metropolitan transportation range, 1969–1975

Source: Historical Statistics of Japan.

difficulties or restrictions in relation to parking cars, would appear to have been a major factor in patterns of transportation use in Japanese cities. However, as recent studies of rapidly developing car-oriented, densely populated cities in China have shown, the interplay of high-density land use, the built environment and parking policies is extremely complex.[56] Factors such as the climate and topography which shaped the narrow, densely populated Tōkaidō Megalopolis must also be taken into account.[57] Scarcity of land accompanied by high land prices and speculation from the 1960s caused larger and more densely populated cities to develop multilevel characteristics such as extensive underground shopping streets and parking areas, often on two or more levels. Not only did these work to separate pedestrians from cars, as we saw in Chapter 2, but also to protect shoppers from the vagaries of Japan's sometimes-unforgiving climate.

Despite the continuing problem of congestion, Nagoya's roads appear to have coped with the flood of commuters more successfully than other large cities in Japan. Yet in the eyes of Nagoya's critics the wide roads proved to be disadvantageous in the long run both in terms of function and aesthetics. Edward Seidensticker commented that while 'in the early years after the war, praise for Nagoya and blame for Tokyo were much in fashion', some forty years later such praise seems misguided:

> Not many today think that the widening of streets can keep up with the flood of automobiles. Nagoya has its traffic jams too. Nor do wide streets seem to be among the things the Japanese are good at. They range from featureless to ugly.[58]

However, LR could yet be the answer to a more sustainable use of transport in the future. As Ishida has pointed out, the wide roads, car parks and other traffic facilities were built on publicly owned land created by the LR policy of reducing the percentage area which could be kept in private hands. Public land currently given over to automobiles could be used for new purposes, such as the widening of pavements for pedestrians, the reinstallation of tram systems, areas for outdoor cafés and roadside stalls.[59] In other words, the very mechanism responsible for building the 'white streets' may also allow Nagoya's planners to reconstruct its roads infrastructure on a more human scale.

Transport and urban form after 1945: Birmingham

We have seen that Birmingham under Manzoni's guiding influence was well-prepared for the 'motor revolution', but the rest of Britain was not. In the 1950s Britain was estimated to have a higher number of vehicles per road mile than any other developed country but its motorway network remained strikingly under-developed by comparison with Germany, Italy, France and Belgium.[60] Even in Birmingham Manzoni expressed concerns, declaring in 1959 'Urban Traffic Congestion' to be 'one of the biggest problems with which civilization is faced in the next decade', liable 'to cause decay throughout the centres of our towns, as it has done in America'. In the same year, the government's own officials at the Road Research Laboratory calculated the annual cost of congestion at some £250 million, almost five times the annual expenditure on roads.[61] The combination of rapidly mounting levels of car ownership, a rising tide of traffic and a road system that struggled to cope meant traffic would become a central issue – arguably the central issue – for town planners in Britain over the next decade, signalled by the publication of the Buchanan report, *Traffic in Towns* in 1963, with its predictions that British cities were in danger of drowning in an avalanche of cars.[62] For traffic planners the nub of the matter was the 'rush hour', the periods in the day when workers of all types, living in the suburbs or 'middle' and 'outer rings', would converge on workplaces in offices and shops based in the central area or in industrial works situated in the zones surrounding it. By the 1960s the commute to work had emerged as one of the most intractable problems of urban living.[63]

In Birmingham a number of factors made the issue of commuting particularly acute (See map of the region in Figure 3.5). First, the commitment to prioritizing roads over other modes of transport and the legacy of low-density suburban estates inherited from the inter-war years, placed special pressure on the city's roads. Car ownership levels were unsurprisingly highest in prosperous outer suburbs such as Kings Norton and Hall Green which contained a large proportion of commuter households.[64] Generally, high levels of car ownership were matched by high rates of commuting. Between 1966 and 1981 Birmingham consistently outstripped any other major British city in the proportion of its workforce commuting by car; in the latter year, the figure had reached almost 50 per cent.[65] Secondly, the target of 'decentralizing' Birmingham's industrial capacity, identified as a priority in the *Conurbation* study and *West Midlands Plan* of 1948, proved hard to achieve in practice. Both the motor and the metals industries, the backbone of Birmingham's manufacturing sector, were characterized by a high degree of interdependence; firms claimed that they needed to be located close to others in the sector for supply and sales. A report in 1967 repeated the common assertion that the 'West Midlands has a higher than average proportion of

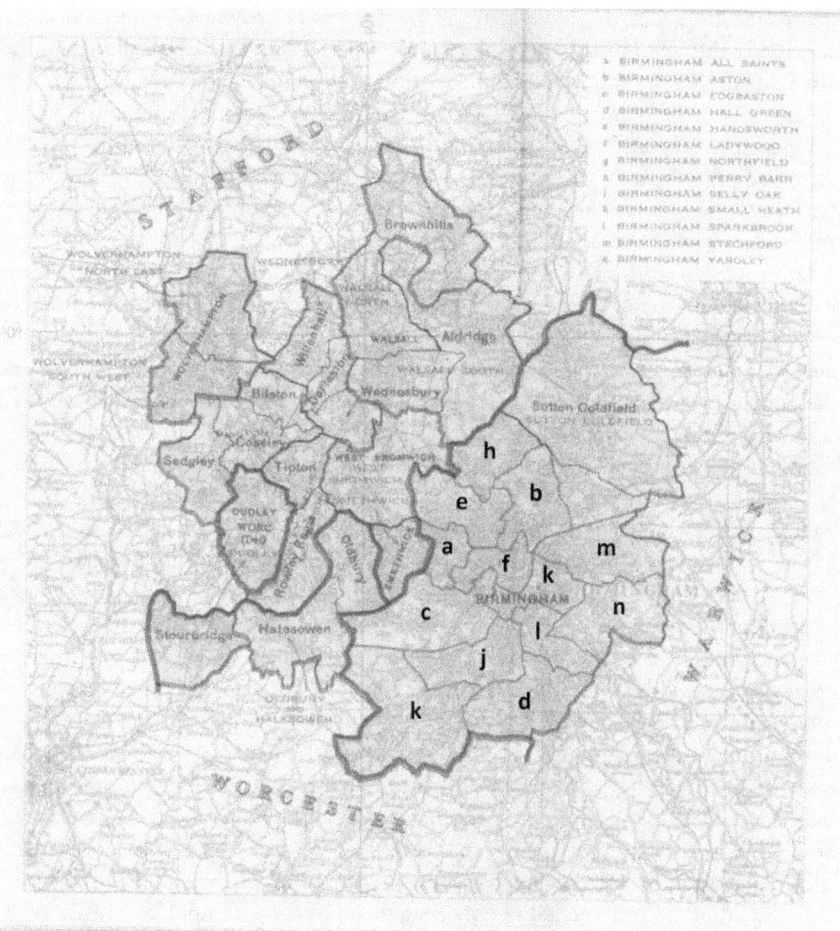

Figure 3.5 Map of Birmingham districts and surrounding towns in the West Midlands conurbation, *c.* 1955. Based on Ordnance Survey, 1955.

firms with close industrial links ... which may be most frequent in the region's metal-using industries'.[66] Birmingham's industries themselves tended to be located in the central and middle rings, both of which were losing residential population through the period. Consequently, industrial workers were forced to commute by car or bus rather than by bicycle or on foot, adding to the problem of congestion at peak times. As early as the 1930s it was reported that more than 1,000 workers at Austin's Longbridge plant were travelling over 10 miles to work.[67]

Given these pressures it was no surprise that planners and policymakers saw roads construction as a priority not only of transport but of urban policy. Expanded arterial routes from the suburbs alongside new ring roads and urban motorways were seen as the sole realistic means to meet the demands of the ever-rising tide of motor traffic. The 1952 City of Birmingham *Development Plan* envisaged three concentric ring roads, thirteen radial roads and a number of new link roads.[68] Birmingham was not alone in this respect. In Britain, local authority spending on roads increased five times between 1950 and 1970, but this expenditure was dwarfed by that of central government – responsible for all major urban roads as well as inter-city routes – which increased thirteen times over the same period.[69] Unsurprisingly, Birmingham was to the fore in roads expenditure. By 1967, the Corporation's debt in respect of highways and bridges was £22.26 per head of population, more than double the amount of any other provincial British city.[70] This not only subsidized the construction of the Inner Ring Road, the Aston Expressway and the widening and upgrading of numerous arterial routes in and out of the city, but also the creation of a Middle Ring Road, begun in 1961. Once under way, in short, mass motorization possessed its own logics, posing the conundrum of how the demographic basis of automobility might be widened without bringing movement in the city to a standstill.

While we have seen that many of the decisive features of Birmingham's urban form were determined before the onset of mass automobility, the advent of the 'motor age' inevitably had consequences for the layout of the cities and their physical fabric. As a report from the Nagoya University Hayakawa Institute pointed out in 1975, at the heart of urban planning was first the traffic problem and secondly the housing problem; the two were intimately connected.[71] In Birmingham, both slum clearance and the roads programme that went with it enabled new legal instruments of governance to be brought to bear in the form of unprecedented powers to intervene in and remodel the post-war British city. It was a process that called forth a language of medical surgery, of curettage, cauterization and incision in the urban body in the interests of collective health and welfare.[72] The most significant of these measures, as we saw in Chapter 2, was the compulsory purchase order under which both developed and undeveloped land could be summarily bought by government and local authorities for the purposes of 'reconstruction'. Birmingham Corporation, indeed, had been instrumental in obtaining the powers for compulsory purchase; in 1943 a deputation of the Corporation had argued the case to the Ministry of Town and Country Planning and Manzoni was a member of the advisory panel to the 1944 'Blitz and Blight' Act that gave local authorities the right to apply for compulsory purchase orders.[73]

Slum clearance, new housing and new communities were always considered in tandem with the roads agenda. Compulsory purchase powers were obtained by Birmingham Corporation in 1947 for its grand project of slum clearance and rebuilding in five 'central redevelopment areas' – Duddeston and Nechells, Ladywood, Gooch Street, Bath Street and Summer Lane. These areas, grouped around the central core of the city, had been identified from the late 1930s as containing 'the largest aggregations of slum housing'.[74] They would be redesigned, following Manzoni's prescriptions, as 'new towns'. But unlike the new towns surrounding London, they would be built within Birmingham rather than at a distance from it, self-contained communities based around a series of twelve-storey tower blocks surrounded by green open space.[75] In contrast to the recommendations of the Barlow report, Birmingham's post-1945 urban form would be remodelled not by extension but from within.

Compulsory purchase of large swathes of land for the central redevelopment areas enabled Manzoni to envisage them as linked by a new ring road – the Middle Ring – encircling the central area as a whole and presented as part of the 1952 *Development Plan*. This pursuit of the Middle Ring was to prove elusive but Manzoni used the areas to trial a new type of urban road, the 'parkway', a term borrowed from North America. As early as 1943 Manzoni described the parkway as a 'fast through traffic route ... throughout its length of 1,400 yards there will be no direct access on the highway from the frontage buildings, and subways will be provided at appropriate positions for the use of pedestrians who, in consequence, will have no need to cross the flow of traffic'.[76] This was to be a dual carriageway through – and connecting – the redevelopment areas while giving priority to speed and flow and contributing to the traffic system of the city as a whole. However, it was also the case that the parkways bisected the development areas, organized on conventional Radburn principles, dividing residents and amenities. Unsurprisingly the Ministry of Housing and Local Government was critical of the parkways scheme and forced a reduction in road width, although it grumblingly allowed the overall design to stay.[77] The parkways contributed to the perception of Birmingham, both official and popular, as divided into rings – centre, middle, outer – inherited from the inter-war period, but defined by social categories of age, class and 'race', the middle ring containing an increasingly elderly white working-class population in the development area tower blocks and an expanding Asian and Caribbean migrant populations in Sparkbrook and Lozells.

New Corporation estates continued to be built on the urban fringe, offering an escape from inner-area 'slums' and tower blocks alike. Lynsey Hanley grew up at Chelmsley Wood, an estate some 8 miles east of central Birmingham, built from 1966 to house over 50,000 people in a mix of flats and houses. It was close to other estates – Kingshurst, built in the 1950s and the high-rise Castle Vale, started in 1963 – but the striking characteristic of 'the Wood', as described by Hanley, was its isolation. At the edge of the city's boundaries, even the Corporation buses would not serve its inhabitants who were forced to rely on other private bus services. Hemmed in by the M6 motorway, many of its residents experienced only the roar of the traffic. 'They say it's handy for transport links: handy if you've got a car ... ', Hanley commented,

> But less if you haven't and you want to visit friends down the road on a Sunday. Neither I, my parents, nor my grandparents [who all lived on the estate] have ever owned a car; a doubly strange feat in an area whose main source of skilled employment is the motor industry.[78]

Hanley's account is shot through with the stinging disillusion with council housing that has marked much public discourse on the subject in Britain. But it also captures an experience of a particular type of urban form deriving from Birmingham's 'motor age'. As the *Birmingham Post* reflected on the Chelmsley Wood estate in 1971, 'When [the children] have grown, they will have little or no affinity to Birmingham ... the city will seem a million life-miles away.'[79] Indirectly, the effects of mass motorization were to stretch the meanings of large cities like Birmingham and to reshape how (sub) urbanism was experienced.

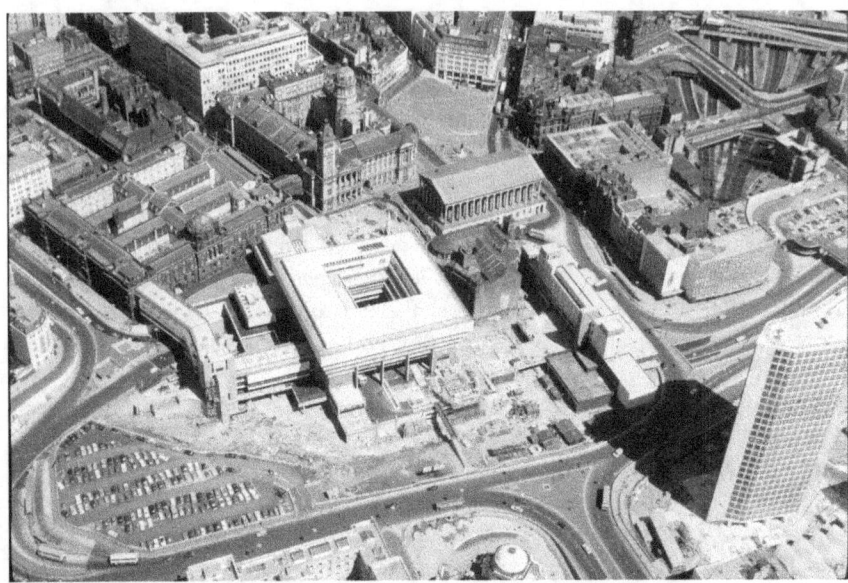

Figure 3.6 Concrete collar: Central Birmingham and the Inner Ring, 1973.
Source: Geoff Thompson Archive.

The obverse of this stretching at the margins of the city was compression at the centre. The construction of the Inner Ring Road transformed Birmingham's city centre, as we saw in Chapter 2. Not only did it raise land values, sometimes spectacularly; as contemporaries liked to point out, the Inner Ring acted as a 'concrete collar' so that Birmingham emerged from the reconstruction process with a smaller central area than that of medieval and lesser cities like York and Norwich (Figure 3.6). The construction of large urban motorways worked to push residents out of the central area, together with 'non-conforming uses' such as manufacturing industry; the building of the Inner and Middle Ring Roads was estimated to displace some 257 industrial firms and 8,000 employees for whom alternative premises had to be found.[80] Corporation policy prioritized the concentration of offices and retail shops in the central area; Birmingham's office boom from the later 1950s was actively encouraged by the Corporation, as was the policy of concentrating retail shopping in the city centre while ensuring full motor access to it. The result was to render the city as a whole more dependent than ever on its commercial core while multiplying the pressures of traffic and people. The problem of the scale of commuting to the city centre was only to grow between 1950 and 1970 when employment in office-based occupations doubled. Between 1951 and 1966 not only did Birmingham see a net growth of population of some 10 per cent, but also a net growth of employment of 13 per cent, creating significant pressures on the inner and middle rings where jobs continued to be based.[81]

Birmingham's manufacturing industries were, indeed, no more enthusiastic about decentralization – following population outwards – in the 1960s than they had been in the 1940s. The national system of Industrial Development Certificates (IDC), issued by the Board of Trade, played a part in this. In theory the purpose of the IDC system was to encourage new firms, or existing firms that considered moving, to relocate to the depressed manufacturing areas of Wales and the North. In practice fewer Birmingham-based firms wished to relocate and the IDC system recognized the argument of industrial interdependence by defining 'non-mobile' industries, including those in the Birmingham metal and motor industries, to remain in situ 'on the grounds', as Peter Hall put it, 'that links with other conurbation industry were too strong to move ... at all'.[82] Moreover, the City Corporation was reluctant to force industry out of the middle ring to the urban fringe. On the contrary, the 1952 *Development Plan* envisaged expanding the amount of land for industrial uses from 182 to 347 acres in the central redevelopment areas; like all local authorities, it feared the loss of business rates that decentralization could bring with it.[83] In the case of industry, therefore, the advent of mass motorization did not so much alter urban form or its functions as hold them in place while thousands of industrial workers would now commute with the rest of the white-collar population. In 1971, 69.1 per cent of residents in Birmingham's middle ring and 77.4 per cent of residents in the outer ring used a car or bus to travel to work, revealing the city's heavy and growing reliance on the motor vehicle for negotiating the city on a daily basis.[84]

The problem of 'blight' was one further way, largely unforeseen by planners, in which mass automobility had a direct impact on cities like Birmingham. Here again, the alteration was less to the shape of the city – its outer form – than its internal organization. Alison Ravetz has written powerfully about Hunslet, an area of Victorian terraced workers' housing in Leeds, which became cut off from the rest of the city following the construction of a series of motorways, including the M1, in the early 1970s. Hunslet became a 'twilight area', demarcated for clearance but in which a dwindling population, unable to move through old age, poverty or habit, continued to live in deteriorating conditions with fewer shops or services. The combination of delay in Corporation-led slum clearance and rehousing, on the one hand, and the onset of major roads construction and high levels of traffic on the other hand contributed to a rapidly declining quality of life and falling property values in the area. The result was what was known by the 1960s as urban 'blight'.[85]

An even earlier instance of the same phenomenon occurred in Birmingham. In 1960 Manzoni and the Public Works Committee put forward a proposal to build a 20-foot elevated 'Skyway' on the Coventry Road. The Skyway was intended to speed traffic from the middle ring to the city's boundary; according to Manzoni it would connect the city centre to Birmingham airport at Elmdon in a ten-minute car drive.[86] The Skyway would enable a 2-mile elevated route to be built, Buchanan-style, unhindered by road junctions and local traffic. But it would pass only 50 feet from the front of houses lining the Coventry Road, directly affecting 347 properties.[87] Unsurprisingly, local residents protested to the Corporation and the Ministry of Transport, citing the deleterious affect the road would have not only on living conditions in the area but also on the value of houses and property. Delay in decision-making over the scheme created the classic conditions for 'blight'. The Ministry of Transport was reluctant to give the go-ahead to the scheme and the Corporation could not reach agreement about the value of the properties or compensation to owners. Meanwhile, house prices dropped, houses became difficult to sell and the area became run-down and neglected. By 1965 Corporation officials were still discussing the Skyway with the Ministry while building societies were refusing to offer mortgages on the affected houses.[88] In 1973 the scheme, now called the 'Coventry Road Expressway', was still part of the *Structure Plan*; it was only finally scrapped by the Corporation in the mid-1970s.[89] In the intervening years, however, not only had property prices slumped but investment in the area had ground to a halt – 'blight' had set in.

Mass motorization thus had significant effects on the urban fabric along the route of major roads, altering the social and demographic composition of the areas through which major roads passed. Writing in 1971 a journalist for the *Birmingham Post* saw the cities as poised between two eras. Birmingham was a divided city, 'split between the disappearing slum properties of the Victorian era and futuristic developments which pave the way for the final emergence of Birmingham, The City of the Seventies'. At the same time, the negative externalities associated with the new motor city were all too visible along the routes of the freshly opened Aston Expressway, where hundreds of houses had been demolished. 'Here and there are pockets of houses where families wait to be rehoused, while part of a city crumbles about them. Amid the dust and decay, they are the sole witnesses.'[90] While roads and traffic were not the sole cause of changes to the physical form of the city in the post-war decades, they were integral to reshaping the spatial geography of the city in Britain. They worked to define and demarcate the 'inner city' as well as the industrial zone, the city centre and the outer suburbs.

Modifications to the urban form of Birmingham after 1945 were the product not of transport *per se*, nor even of automobility, but of the increasing dominance of the private car. Between 1952 and 1965, private car ownership in Birmingham tripled from 60,306 to 184,980.[91] Commentators at the time in Britain saw this as a phenomenon linked to growing 'affluence', particularly among working- and lower middle-class families who had not previously owned a car and who were the groups most likely to have left inner-city neighbourhoods for houses in the new estates on the urban fringe. Commenting on the new suburban estate of 'Greenleigh' (based on Debden in real life) to the east of London in the mid-1950s, the sociologists Peter Wilmott and Michael Young suggested that the car was 'beginning to move from a luxury to a necessity'. This was a stock observation of the period but Wilmott and Young went further in associating this with the distances people now had to transact between home, work, shops and relatives. These, they argued, were 'motoring distances: a car, like a telephone, can overcome geography and organize a scattered life into a more manageable whole'.[92] Wilmott and Young, like other sociologists of the period, saw cars as bound up with the spread of consumer durables – the telephone, television, refrigerator, washing machine – into working-class homes. It was part, too, of that growing 'privatization' of the working-class home noted by the researchers for the *Affluent Worker* study among others. 'Private car dominance' could thus be construed as an extension of the increased privacy of the home and the nuclear family.[93]

Aspiration and affluence, however, were only part of the story. Another equally important role was played by the central and local state in shaping transport options in mid-twentieth-century British cities like Birmingham. The key here was the steady erosion of those options over time as other forms of mobility were marginalized in favour of the private car. To begin with, the layout of the 'motor city' from the 1930s, with its low-density suburbs and significant distances between home, work and shops, militated against walking. Outside the suburbs themselves, the only part of Birmingham designed to accommodate pedestrians was the city centre. Even here, however, motorized access to the centre by cars and buses remained an article of faith for the Corporation. In 1963 Alderman Thomas, Chair of the Public Works Committee, boldly declared: 'We have not reached the conclusion in Birmingham that the motor car should be excluded from the city centre; I personally hope we never shall.'[94] By the late 1960s, though, such views came to appear idiosyncratic if not plain wrong. Critics, including many Birmingham residents, noted the problems of subways, stairs and escalators – including those in the ultra-modern Bull Ring shopping centre – for women with push-chairs, the disabled and the elderly.[95] Bicycling, like walking, was also sidelined in the new dispensation. In the 1930s and 1940s cycling was an important – in some places, the most important – means of travel to work in Britain.[96] The peak of travel by bicycle appears to have occurred in 1949 but as Rorie Parsons and Geoff Vigar have observed, it 'declined sharply until the global oil crisis of 1973' in tandem with the rise of mass automobility. As they further point out, the bicycle was more or less invisible in city development plans of the 1950s and 1960s and treated only in passing in the Buchanan report.[97] There is limited evidence of bicycling for Birmingham but what there is suggests both its limited frequency by comparison with other towns and cities, and the real difficulties associated with riding in a city organized for the car driver.[98] The steep decline of bicycling and the curtailment of walking in mid-twentieth-century Birmingham themselves amounted to an effective downgrading of the importance of the local neighbourhood in favour of a mid-range urbanism defined by 'motoring distances'.

Public transport was also downgraded over the same period. At the time of Manzoni's arrival in Birmingham in 1936, trams were the main means of vehicular transport in the city.[99] But the Corporation was increasingly antipathetic, seeing trams as costly to run and contributing to the congestion of main routes. 'Birmingham is not a tramway city' the Corporation's Transport Manager bluntly pronounced in 1949. In this Birmingham was in line with expert opinion at the period, including the authorities in similar industrial cities such as Manchester. Nationally, the Royal Commission on Transport had argued as early as 1931 that tramways were 'in a state of obsolescence' and 'a danger'; 'it will be to the advantage of the inhabitants of the towns, where they exist, to get rid of them'.[100] After 1945, this was indeed what happened in one British city after another. Trams were abandoned in 1949 in Manchester, 1952 in London, 1953 in Leeds, 1957 in Liverpool, 1960 in Sheffield and 1962 in Glasgow. Birmingham was among the earlier group, taking the decision to close the tramways in 1949, finally ceasing operations in 1953.

What replaced the trams in Birmingham as in other cities was the motor bus, invariably Corporation owned and managed. Manzoni argued that tramways could be converted to roadways relatively cheaply. Buses were generally seen as more flexible, cheaper to run and more 'modern' than trams. Travelling to school in Stockport, near

Manchester, in the late 1940s the journalist Joan Bakewell recalled preferring the tram to the bus; it was noisier and less comfortable than the bus but also more fun and – crucially – cheaper to ride. But councillors such as those in Birmingham were quick to dismiss such preferences as 'nostalgic sentiment'; trams were seen as an anachronism, 'inappropriate' to a modern city.[101] By the early 1950s the Corporation's fleet of buses represented the only significant means of urban public transport by contrast with Nagoya where rail retained its importance. Yet the bus was no less immune to competition from the car. Between 1955 and 1970, while car ownership soared, the numbers of passenger journeys by bus fell steadily from just over 500,000 to just over 300,000. Attempts to woo passengers with a park and ride scheme and express bus services in the later 1960s did not reverse the trend; privately, councillors remained sceptical about the ability of any form of public transport to persuade drivers to forsake the comforts of their car.[102]

Nor, finally, did the railways represent an alternative to motor transport. Birmingham's sprawling urban form and its low-density suburbs were considered to make rail transport and its associated infrastructure costs uneconomic. Even prior to the publication of the Beeching Report, *The Reshaping of British Railways*, in 1963, cuts were under way to suburban lines. Outside London, Beeching argued, suburban rail services could not compete for cost or efficiency with the motor bus service, or for convenience with the private car.[103] Concerns were expressed in Birmingham by MPs and councillors at local rail closures in 1962 and the lack of an integrated transport system for the city. The latter was perhaps ironic given the long-term priority afforded the private car by Birmingham's political leadership. But in this instance the Ministry of Transport, mindful of the Beeching Report to come, argued against intervening and in favour of a market-led approach based on travellers' own preferences. In this respect, one might argue, the Ministry was more Birmingham than Birmingham.[104] Following the Corporation delegation to examine urban transport planning in the United States in 1956, Manzoni had already rejected the idea of a rapid transit system as too costly to build and run. An underground or 'tube' railway, such as existed in London and Glasgow (and was to be built in Liverpool and Newcastle in the1970s), was declared to be 'hopelessly uneconomic' when it was considered by Manzoni and the Public Works Committee in 1952.[105] Instead the city authorities looked to an 'express omnibus service' which would utilize the city's future motorway system, but this, too, was to be undermined by the steady decline of bus passengers over the period. While rail and light vehicles provided alternatives to private car dominance in Nagoya before 1970, in Birmingham the private car had effectively won out over all its rivals.

Conclusion

Both Nagoya and Birmingham became car-dominated cities between 1960 and 1990 to the extent that we are justified in thinking of them as 'motor cities'. What distinguished the two cities, however, was that in contrast to Birmingham, it is difficult to overstate the importance of Nagoya Station to the life and prestige of the city. Not only was Nagoya Station many times the size of Birmingham New Street in terms of floor area and passengers carried, but there was a unique relationship in Nagoya between the station area, the car-dominated 'white streets' above ground and the many kilometres of underground streets. For this reason, the railways and the subways, although suffering some decline, were still able to offer a genuine alternative to the car.

The architect Tange Kenzo envisaged a radically engineered 'motor city' in his 1960 plan for Tokyo: 'Transportation', he argued, 'is the arterial system which preserves the life and human drive of the city, the nervous system which moves its brain. Mobility determines the structure of the city'.[106] Tange identified, and to some extent prophesied, the problems that cities such as Birmingham and Nagoya would face in the later twentieth century. Modern economic functions, he stated, necessitated mutual communication which meant those functions were drawn into the centre. At the same time, people who performed these functions spread out ever further into suburbs as housing developers sought cheaper land. Urban form thus became centripetal and radial. As more commuters travelled further out, satellite towns and cities were created which became merely 'bed towns', according to Tange, and increased the distance which commuters had to travel. Even by 1960, the result in cities such as Tokyo was 'murderous confusion' in the train stations and 'a state of paralysis' on the roads.[107] Tange's organic vision for a Tokyo completely reorganized along linear, rather than radial, lines was never realized. He was right to be sceptical about lack of political and bureaucratic will to undertake such a massive reorganization of urban form. As cities like Nagoya and Birmingham continued to expand on radial lines ever further from the city centre, the pace of motorization itself looked as if it would become unstoppable. In the half-century after Tange's plans were published, urban planners grappled with solutions that were little more than damage limitation exercises.

The coming of mass motorization in Birmingham as in many other British cities witnessed the side-lining of all other forms of transport in the two decades after 1950. To an unprecedented degree cities became organized around a single type of mobility, the 'steel-and-petroleum' car.[108] This moment was not to last. Even in motor-mad Birmingham there was a decisive attempt from late 1960s to shift policy and practice away from private car dominance to public and other modes of transport, as we shall see later. We have argued in this chapter that the major, post-war phase of mass motorization was not responsible for the urban form of Birmingham, which was effectively shaped in the 1920s and 1930s by other exigencies, notably boundary extension and house-building programmes, both 'public'- (Corporation-led) and private developer-led. In transport terms, it was an urban form that was adapted to the motor bus, which emerged between the wars as the principal form of transport over distances, gradually displacing the tram, and representing the main means of travel between the city, where employment and shopping continued to be largely located, and the new suburban estates. The rapid spread of the private car from the early 1950s as the ideal type of personalized transport was superimposed on the pre-existing road network, now cleared of trams and trolley-buses.

As such private car dominance served to consolidate rather than transform the inherited configuration of the city and, in conjunction with the informal green belt policy, to render that configuration still more rigid and 'natural'. The construction of the Inner and Middle Ring Roads, though a protracted process, served to cement an earlier, inter-war image of Birmingham as divided into central, middle and outer rings. Indeed, these road systems were integral to the redefinition of the areas themselves, the Inner Ring representing a 'moat' around the evermore constricted city centre, the parkways of the 'new towns' forming part of Manzoni's vision for the Middle Ring. Road schemes, both new and unbuilt like Skyways, changed the demographics of areas through 'blight' and dereliction. Similarly, the 'inner city' which was to be the target of so much of urban policy in Britain in the 1970s was a product of mass automobility no less than of poverty or deindustrialization; indeed, it was the causal inter-relationship of these factors that was to make the plight of the 'inner city' so intractable to policymakers. The precondition of mass automobility was the creation of 'dead public spaces' through which traffic must pass.[109] Yet traffic engineers in Japan, often thinking of the much-painted Tōkaidō of the Edo Period (1600–1868), also saw roads in a very different way: 'It is often said that roads are a part of both nature and culture and, as such, are the most important carriers of society and of life.' They looked back to a society that moved on foot and recognized that the automobile had altered such romantic views in the face of changes in the social and economic environment and technology and progress.[110] In these ways mass automobility was not an adjunct to urban modernism but an essential ingredient of it. The form and fabric of modern cities like Nagoya and Birmingham was bound up with a new and singular way of moving.

4

Driving the Motor City: The Experience of Automobility

The euphoria of the expressway

In David Lodge's novel *Changing Places*, set in Birmingham (named 'Rummidge') around 1970, the anti-hero, Morris Zapp, is presented driving along an urban motorway. Recently arrived from California, Zapp is struck by the transformation occurring in the cityscape seen from the car window.

> Morris took the newly opened section of the Inner Ring, an exhilarating complex of tunnels and flyovers ... From here you got a panorama of the whole city and the sun came out at that moment, shining like floodlighting on the pale concrete facades of the recent construction work, tower blocks and freeways, throwing them into relief against the sombre mass of nineteenth-century slums and decayed factories. Seen from this perspective it looked like the seeds of the whole twentieth-century city had been planted under the ground a long time ago and were now beginning to shoot up into the light, bursting through the caked, exhausted topsoil of Victorian architecture.[1]

Zapp's exhilaration at driving through this modernist panorama was widely shared in writing and film in the late 1960s. It was no coincidence that Zapp hailed from California (renamed 'Euphoria' in the novel) since it was home to one of the earliest and most extensive freeway systems in the world. In 1971, before the appearance of Lodge's novel, the architectural critic Reyner Banham had published *Los Angeles: The Architecture of Four Ecologies*, one of which he labelled 'Autopia', the setting for a hymn to the pleasures of driving the city's freeways. For Banham, the Los Angeles freeway represented not just a place but a 'coherent state of mind', a 'complete way of life'.[2]

'Motordom' pervaded popular culture by the late 1960s. It was at this time that the extended car chase against an urban backdrop became a dramatic highlight of Hollywood thrillers. The chase through San Francisco's streets involving Steve McQueen in *Bullitt* (from 1968) lasted a full 11 minutes, that through New York's Brooklyn in *The French Connection* (1971) some 6 minutes – a substantial slice of Hollywood films of roughly 100 minutes total. Car chases were shot from inside as well as outside the car, allowing the viewer to experience city streets and traffic at high speed and obtain panoramic views of the city as they sped past. Birmingham too was regularly selected by film producers as the setting for the car chase, as in the BBC police drama series *Gangsters*, produced at Pebble Mill between 1975 and 1978, with the curving flyovers of Gravelly Hill Interchange, better known as Spaghetti Junction, selected as the dramatic backdrop.

Birmingham's burgeoning reputation as an icon of motorized modernity was in sharp contrast to Nagoya. Apart from its two famous 100-metre-wide roads, Nagoya's cityscape remained unremarkable, noted only for its American-style gridiron plan. It was rather to Tokyo's futuristic cityscape that novelists and filmmakers turned for visual inspiration in the 1960s and early 1970s. After the feverish road construction in Tokyo for the 1964 Olympic Games, the underpasses and dramatic elevated sections of the new expressways provided fertile material for film directors, especially for the popular *yakuza,* or gangster, movies. The director Suzuki Seijun used shots of Tokyo's transportation infrastructure to spectacular effect in his 1966 cult classic *Tokyo Drifter* which opens with three carefully framed shots of modernist icons of the 'new Tokyo': the shinkansen, the new urban expressway system and Tange Kenzo's futuristic Yoyogi National Gymnasium, built for the Olympics. In effect, the opening of sections of motorway in and around cities like Los Angeles, Tokyo and Birmingham was accompanied by a discursive rhetoric that encouraged drivers and others to view and experience the new roads as a type of urban spectacle.

What we term the euphoria of driving in motor cities has been a staple of cultural criticism and theory since Banham's day.[3] But this also limits the analysis of the experience of automobility. The problem is not simply one of idealization, of a false contrast between the representation of automotive modernism and the reality of grimy, congested streets; there were times when the swooping flyovers and gleaming city centres did indeed evoke a motoring sublime, fusing machine and landscape, perception and experience. The problem is rather that the euphoric view has come to stand proxy for the richer and much more variable experience of automobility in the age of mass motorization in the 1960s and 1970s. It overlooks the messy complexity of historical actuality: the complex sociology of who 'drivers' actually were, for example, the ambivalent attitudes towards mass car ownership, the practical difficulties associated with driving and – perhaps most important – the changes that occurred in individual experience and public representation of automobility over the later twentieth century.

In this chapter we try to move beyond the view which locates automobility within the tropes of urban modernity to examine the demographics and logistics of city driving in its 'everyday' rather than 'sublime' manifestations.[4] In the first section we examine popular appropriations of driving as a new generation of motorists took to the roads; in the second we consider the relationship between automobility and consumerism; in the third section we examine the negative externalities that developed alongside mass motorization, marring the experience and curtailing the 'freedoms' of drivers; finally, we consider the effects of mass automobility on the experience of other groups, the 'no-car folk' whose interests increasingly came to the fore in the 1970s. Throughout this analysis we pay attention to the relationship of driving to the cities themselves, *urban automobility* being understood – as it was at the time – as a critically important domain of the 'motor age'.

Car ownership in the 'Motor Age'

In the 1950s and 1960s the demographics of driving altered, not only in the numbers of drivers but also in their sociological profile. The 1959 British general election seems to have been the first to have witnessed the widespread use of the phrase the 'car-owning democracy'.[5] What this signified was that manual working-class families were buying cars in significant numbers for the first time. It was estimated that between 1960 and 1964, 72 per cent of car sales were to first-time buyers, while 60 per cent of new car owners derived from social classes C2 and DE, skilled, semi-skilled and unskilled workers and their families.[6] In Britain during these years the car became an essential prop in the evolving drama of 'affluence'.[7] In reality though, car ownership was growing among all sections of the population, except the poorest, and especially fast among white-collar suburban populations. In Birmingham in 1964, some 45 per cent of households owned a car in inner-city Handsworth but the proportion rose to 74 per cent in the prosperous outer suburb of Sutton Coldfield.[8] Overall, Birmingham had the second highest percentage of car ownership per head nationally in Britain in the early 1960s, behind Coventry and just ahead of Luton, also major car-producing towns. By the late 1950s car ownership in Britain was acknowledged to be a status symbol for the aspirant white-collar and skilled working-class family. Birmingham, Herbert Manzoni

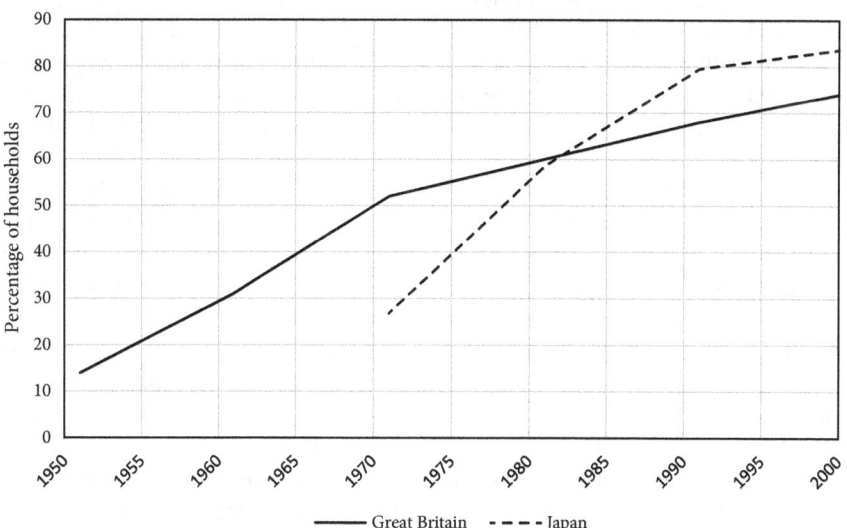

Graph 4.1 Percentage of households with at least one car in Japan and Britain, 1951–2000

(a) Comparable data is not available for Japan until 1971. Source: Department for Transport, *Transport Statistics Great Britain*. https://www.gov.uk/government/statistical-data-sets/tsgb09-vehicles (accessed 12 December 2017); Statistics Bureau, Ministry of Internal Affairs and Communications, *Historical Statistics of Japan*. http://www.stat.go.jp/english/data/chouki/12.html (accessed 9 August 2010).

announced in 1958, was a 'community which regards ownership of the family car as a symbol of achievement' and it would continue as such 'until there is a car for every family'.[9] Homes and neighbourhoods would be reorganized around the needs of the citizen motorist. 'Every dwelling and building must have a garage planned; it will be a fixture like a bathroom of telephone', Clive Bossom, Conservative MP for Leominster, urged Parliament in 1960. In future he predicted 'all shopping will be done under one roof, in supermarkets' easily accessible by car; there would be 'drive-in' cinemas and banks as in North America.[10]

Japan initially lagged behind Britain in terms of car ownership in the early 1960s (Graph 4.1). One reason was the gap between incomes and the price of cars. However, Toyota's 700cc 'Publica' took the title of the 'Car for Everyone' at the 1960 All-Japan Motor Show. It retailed at around 380,000 yen and was billed as the '1,000 dollar' car at a time when the dollar was pegged at 360 yen.[11] Most ordinary passenger cars cost around half a million yen, a little more than the annual average gross income of a worker's household of 490,000 yen.[12] Even by the end of the 1960s, in terms of national income per capita, Japan still ranked low among car-producing nations, despite the fact that incomes were increasing rapidly. By 1966 the annual average gross income of a worker's household in urban centres was a little over 855,000 yen; by 1969 it was around 1.2 million yen, more than trebling since 1960.[13] Yet various models of the Toyota Corolla 1100 cost on average between 400,000 yen and 500,000 yen. A British survey of the Japanese market noted that in 1969 Japan's national income per capita was the equivalent of approximately £536, placing Japan fifteenth in the world table. While throughout the 1960s most Japanese consumers could not afford to buy cars outright, car purchase credit schemes began in 1960 and had become very popular with consumers by 1963. By the end of the decade 75 per cent of all passenger cars were bought on instalment plans, usually 25 per cent down with the balance paid over ten to twenty-four months. Throughout the 1960s the vast majority of bank loans made to retailers selling on instalment were for car purchase.[14]

Despite the substantial rise in incomes in the 1960s and the apparent willingness of Japanese consumers to take out loans to buy high-value items such as cars, the notion of an affluent society at this time is problematic and raises questions not only about the meaning of 'affluence', but also about nature of the Japanese 'middle class'. Despite statistical indications of an 'economic miracle' in the 1960s, only in the 1980s did the notion of an affluent middle class become widely used in the media.[15] Indeed, there was a surprising continuity between pre- and post-war trends in consumerism. As the historian Andrew Gordon has pointed out, the rise of a mass consumer society was a feature of an increasingly 'mainstream' (*chūryū*), middle-class lifestyle, which had become culturally ascendant and socially prominent between 1920 and 1969, what Gordon calls the 'trans-war decades'.[16] There was much debate in the media centred on the idea of a mass society (*taishū shakai*) and its implications for Japanese national culture. A number of government surveys assessing public attitudes towards social change were carried out in the 1960s and 1970s, leading to the announcement that Japan was '90 per cent middle class' with a 'mass mainstream of 100 million people'.[17] But throughout much of the post-war period, for the vast majority of Japanese people, entry into the modern, middle-class world of consumerism remained a dream rather than a reality until the end of the 1970s. The creation of a consumer base relied on people sharing 'in the cultural imagination of modern consumer life and leisure, whether though magazines, open-air radio broadcasts, window-shopping or billboards'.[18]

Britain appeared a wealthier consumer society than Japan in the 1960s but even here the transformative effect of 'affluence' can be overstated.[19] Without a developed second-hand market in Britain before the 1970s, a car remained a significant achievement for most working-class families. The cheapest new car on the market was the Austin Mini at £500 when it was launched in 1959, which was only just less than the annual income of a semi-skilled manual worker.[20] The gap between incomes and the cheapest car, therefore, was not dissimilar to Japan at this time. The most basic family car the Ford Cortina cost £639 in 1962. Purchasing a new car was thus a major expenditure for all families financially below the comfortable middle class; as in Japan it required use of loans (or hire purchase) and was an investment for the family rather than the individual. Nevertheless, if the more extravagant claims of a 'car-owning democracy' were premature, a certain democratization of private automobility was apparent, not least in the ways cars were advertised and marketed. In the 1950s motoring was strongly associated with the middle-aged, middle-class man, depicted as a professional, business executive or more straightforwardly as a 'gentleman'. A popular manual of the early 1950s, entitled *Car Driving as an Art*, depicted driving as akin to horsemanship not as a mechanical technique. More expensive makes such as Rover and Humber were described as a 'professional man's car', an association that continued into the early 1960s.[21]

If 'affluence' did not straightforwardly underpin widening car ownership, nor was motoring automatically connected with the modern. In Japan as in Britain, driving in the 1950s was often marketed by looking backwards. Unlike the attractive modern designs of the posters for the Tokyo Motor Shows, which began in 1954, the covers of *Jidōsha Gaidobukku* (Motor Vehicles Guide Book) displayed vintage models from the very earliest years of motorization.[22] For example, the 1956 *Gaidobukku* featured a woman in Edwardian dress driving a horseless carriage marked '1900–1904', while the 1957 cover celebrated the fiftieth anniversary of Japan's first domestically made motor car, the 1907 Yoshida Takuri.[23] Yet there was no direct equivalent of the British 'gentleman driver'; it was rather the chauffeur who for a long time signalled the association between automobility and wealth in Japan. Before the war, privately owned motorcars were wholly associated with pleasure. They were used by rich Tokyo playboys to impress their geisha companions, and even taxi companies in Kyoto enticed geisha customers by lining the floors of their vermillion and black cabs with tatami matting. Indeed, many purchasers of these early cars were closely associated with the red-light and entertainment districts. Passenger cars were not considered as a practical means of increasing mobility in urban areas, but more as status symbols, the playthings of a wealthy minority.[24]

The employment of a chauffeur after the war compounded the automobile's association with wealth and status. In 1964, Isamu Koshimidzu, a pioneer advocate of off-street parking in Tokyo, wrote:

Except for the younger generation, who enjoy driving, most Japanese prefer riding in the rear seat, with chauffeurs to drive them and find parking places. The higher a person's social or business standing, the more he insists on being driven, largely for prestige reasons; from curb to building entrance is about the maximum distance he cares to walk.[25]

Around 90 per cent of automobiles circulating around the central business district of Marunouchi in Tokyo were chauffeur-driven. In some cases, companies provided all their executives and department heads with cars and chauffeurs, covering all parking charges and other maintenance costs. Both car and chauffeur were available for use both on and off-duty. As a result, private car parks were equipped with waiting rooms for chauffeurs, often air-conditioned and replete with newspapers, magazines, radios, televisions and gaming boards. Extremely high parking charges were 'no problem' for the beneficiaries since they were paid for by the company, and the costs of this provision were tax-deductible.[26]

In both Britain and Japan in the 1960s there were subtle changes, not only in the social profile of the driver – younger, more occupationally diverse, less easily class/ified – but also in the experience of driving. In Britain a new experience of the city from the car was enhanced by the design of cars, especially their interior design. As well as speed and power, car advertising in the 1960s continued to emphasize the comfort and even luxury of interiors, but it was increasingly a comfort associated with 'modern living'. Novelty and popular consumerism rather than traditionalism and craftsmanship became the watchwords of cars like Ford and Austin geared to the expanding domestic market. The use of new forms of sound insulation and synthetic fabrics for seats and carpets reduced noise and vibration, making the ride smoother and quieter. Both drivers and passengers were afforded a more contemplative view of the city seen through the car window. The advent of car radio from the later 1950s in Britain and, subsequently, taped music enhanced the sensation of what the sociologist John Urry called 'dwelling' in the private car, designed to mirror, or even function as an extension of, the suburban living room.[27] An advertisement for the 1967 Ford Corsair emphasized its 'fully reclining bucket seats', 'nylon deep-pile carpeting' and 'built-in push button radio for music wherever you go'. In 1965 the new Vanden Plas 1100 Princess with its Radiomobile was described by the manufacturers as having such advanced sound-proofing that the effect of riding in it was like an 'evening in the drawing room'; the Princess even contained a drinks cabinet and fold-down tables in the back seats for cocktails.[28] As these examples suggest car advertising in Britain often targeted the individual or the married couple with their friends, rather than the nuclear family, even if the car was often regarded as a household item. Most cars, of course, could not pretend to the style of gracious living projected by advertising. But by the 1960s the modern car interior sought to provide a kind of home in the city, an aspect of what Raymond Williams termed 'mobile privatization' that allowed the city to be experienced in a novel way.[29]

By comparison, Japanese-made cars lagged well behind the British motor industry. The interiors of Japanese cars in the 1950s and 1960s were notoriously utilitarian and the luxury end of the market was dominated by imported models, mostly from the United States. Japan also had a more diversified automobile stock than Britain. The early pattern of car ownership from the 1950s was dominated by the *keijidōsha* (light car) or 'K' car, three- and four-wheel small trucks, vans and passenger cars of restricted dimensions and displacement which initially required a licence only.[30] These cars provided a stop-gap until Japanese motor manufacturers were able to produce affordable small cars. The advent of the *keijidōsha* was reported in the international English-language motoring press in 1954, the year of the first motor show in Tokyo; the 350 cc Flying Feather produced by the Suminoe Works at Tokyo bore a remarkable similarity to the French 2CV Citroen. Doubts were expressed, however, about the willingness of Japanese consumers to buy home-produced cars, particularly in light of the continued use by government officials of American imports and an acute lack of capital in the industry.[31] Indeed, consumers were unlikely to buy Japanese-made cars even if they were available at an affordable price. Before the Pacific War, with the exception of luxury items such as silk and artisan goods such as Imari and Satsuma ceramics, lacquer-ware and hand-made paper, the label 'Made in Japan' had become synonymous with shoddy goods, both in the eyes of Japanese consumers and the rest of the world.[32]

It was the newly formed Ministry for International Trade and Industry (MITI) that campaigned against car imports and championed the Japanese car industry. In order to persuade consumers to 'Buy Japanese' the ministry even arranged a series of demonstrations in November 1951 involving Japanese and British cars being driven thousands of kilometres over five days. Having failed in previous, less strenuous demonstrations, the Japanese cars survived the test, and passenger car manufacturers began to gain support.[33] Inspired by the example of West Germany's Volkswagen Beetle, MITI's Automobile Bureau collaborated with engineering professors in Tokyo University on a plan to create a small, affordable car for the masses and, in 1955, its 'People's Car Plan' was leaked to the press. MITI produced a list of specifications in order for any proposed car to be eligible for support but, most importantly, it was to cost no more than 150,000 yen based on a production scale of 2,000 per month.[34] At the time the price tag was around half the average gross annual income of a worker's household in a major city.[35] Manufacturers, already disgruntled because they were not consulted about the plans, were unimpressed by the plan even when the price was raised to 250,000 yen, insisting that it was impossible to build such a car for the price. The plan was abandoned, but the proposal acted as a spur to manufacturers of two- and three-wheeled motor vehicles to enter the four-wheeled market.[36]

One of the most successful mini-cars was the Subaru 360 manufactured by Fuji Heavy Industries, originally an aircraft manufacturer (Figure 4.1). Nicknamed the 'Lady Beetle' for its uncanny resemblance to the Volkswagen, it retailed for 425,000 yen which, in 1958, was just above the average gross annual income for a worker's household of 416,000 yen.[37] The Subaru 360 was the star of the 1958 All-Japan Motor Show. Yet the press remained critical of the continuing failure of the industry to provide more comfortable and affordable 'ordinary' cars for the people. In the small car range, Nissan's Datsun 110 with its 860 cc engine made its debut in 1955 and was one of the first models which could claim to be 'for the people'. Its main competitor was the 1,000-dollar Toyota Publica. However, the Publica's popularity was dented by its excessively noisy engine and the Japanese motorist had to wait until the ever-popular Toyota Corolla made its debut in 1966 to take the crown of 'the car for everyone'.[38]

Figure 4.1 1958 Subaru 360: The Lady Beetle.

Source: Mytho 88, Wikipedia Commons. https://upload.wikimedia.org/wikipedia/commons/3/3c/1958_Subaru_360_01.jpg

The kinds of vehicles Japanese motorists were driving in the 1960s, then, were very different from the large, American vehicles seen on film, as well as from the saloon cars which dominated the British market. Light cars like the Subaru 360 were popular because of the introduction, after 1960, of a graduated system of taxes according to engine size which favoured cars designated 'small'. In Tokyo especially, an acute shortage of car parking space also meant that all vehicles over 360 cc had to have their own garage. Consequently, the production of larger cars over 2001 cc was very slow until after 1970. Different urban and economic conditions across countries, in short, bred different kinds of vehicles and a different experience of mass automobility.

Automobility and consumerism

Consumerism encompassed not only the ownership of a car but also the experience and purposes of driving. Indeed, the choice of personal transport was itself understood to be fuelled by consumer aspiration. 'The men, and the women, in their cars in the street, quite evidently have concluded that, if they *exist* by breathing and eating, they *live* by moving', the chair of the British Motor Corporation declared in 1969.[39] In Britain especially by the mid-1960s the car had come to be knitted into the fabric of everyday life, not just among the rich but among large swathes of ordinary women and men.

Shopping was an integral part of this; the first major sociological survey on car usage in Britain, carried out by researchers at Birmingham University in 1964, noted 'the enormous potential expansion in the use of the car for shopping'.[40] Indeed, historians have recently commented on the ubiquity of the figure of the 'shopper motorist' in visions of reconstructed city centres in Britain through the 1960s.[41] As Frank Price, chair of Birmingham Council's Public Works Committee reflected on the Inner Ring in 1965: 'Once we had started on the physical side of the road I saw quite clearly that if our vision of the New Birmingham was to take shape it was essential to make it as commercially successful as possible'.[42]

Commercial success meant enticing the 'shopper motorist' into the city centre with its array of opportunities for a modern experience of consumption; out-of-town shopping malls were not created in Britain before the mid-1970s. Price's vision of integrating motoring and shopping in Birmingham was exemplified earliest in Smallbrook Ringway, Manzoni's 'modern type of town street'.[43] Here the shop fronts were designed so that the window goods would be immediately visible to drivers passing in their cars, the 'shoppers awheel' described by Terence Bendixson a decade later. There were 'undeniable pleasures of driving around central Birmingham', Bendixson opined, with the potential for the Ring Road to become a 'festival of [neon] light that would make Piccadilly Circus look provincial'.[44] The Inner Ring was indeed a 'road designed for shopping' a promotional film proudly declared in 1965; this was an essential part of its novelty and modernity. The Bull Ring likewise was proclaimed as emblematic of Birmingham's new 'drive-in' world (Figure 4.2 below). Car drivers entered straight from the Inner Ring and had their car parked for them by a valet while buses likewise dropped passengers at the door. From the reception the shopper motorist was free 'to wander about, to cross from shop to shop, to enjoy the variety of display, and to feel part of the shopping area'. Less charitable observers found its atmosphere closer to a 'giant claustrophobic palace of multiple retailers' with an 'eerie feeling of unreality'. But whatever people's responses, the transition from car to shops was acknowledged to be seamless. With its ease of movement, piped music, air-conditioning and sound-proofed floors, the Bull Ring mirrored in important respects the experience of automobility from which the motorist and passengers had just alighted. Like the shopper, the motorist was invited to view the world with a consuming eye that was simultaneously insulated and distracted.[45]

The relationship between the Japanese and their cars was more ambiguous, especially in the city. Indeed, most cities had difficulty in accommodating the 'new craze' and 'brand new status symbol', as historian Jacques Gravereau pointed out: 'The narrow streets of the cities and villages have no pavements and are lined with poles carrying electric cabling so that cars squeeze past just centimetres from the walls of houses, it is a tragi-comedy.'[46] In Nagoya with its wide roads, the disjuncture between shopping and the car was most marked, as the proliferation of underground shopping streets testified. These subterranean labyrinths functioned as pedestrianized *sakariba*, originally meaning 'crowded places', which were closely connected to main-line and district railways, subways, as well as large underground car parks. The multifunctional and diverse nature of *sakariba* meant they were not just sites of consumption, but also 'nodal points of gathering', for eating, entertainment, amusement and temporary

Figure 4.2 Artist's impression of the Bull Ring shopping centre, early 1960s.
Source: Geoff Thompson Archive.

residence in hotels.[47] The underground streets compensated for the lack of vitality on its car-dominated, grid-pattern of streets or 'white roads' above ground. Unlike Smallbrook Ringway in Birmingham, the main overground shopping streets in Nagoya such as Hirokōji Dōri, Sakura Dōri and Hisaya Ōdōri were boulevards and very wide with pavements separated from the road by lines of trees. The trees and distance from the roadside made it difficult to see into shop windows from the car, thus distancing drivers from the window-shopping experience.

The car made its mark not only on city centres, of course, but also on the suburbs, themselves increasingly dependent on motorized transport, especially in Britain where the Beeching cuts after 1963 resulted in the closure of branch-line railways.[48] Mass automobility altered the way the suburbs were represented in popular culture. In 1964, Lew Grade, the managing director of ATV (Associated Television, Midlands), launched a new serial, *Crossroads*, located in a fictional suburb of Birmingham. The title itself was intended to gesture towards Birmingham's central location within the motoring nation. *Crossroads* was a soap opera showing every evening during the week, a Midlands rival to Granada's immensely popular *Coronation Street,* which had started four years earlier. It was set, as the title also implied, in a motel, located somewhere anonymous on Birmingham's radial road system. The series swiftly became established as the nation's second favourite soap opera after *Coronation Street* in the 1960s, despite suffering criticism for the contrived nature of its storylines and its cheap production values. *Crossroads* crystallized themes identified with the advent of mass automobility in mid-1960s Britain. The motel around which the series revolved suggested simultaneously a kind of aspirant modernity, implicit in an institution imported from North America; and a banal everydayness, signalled by its cast of characters, made up of waitresses, car mechanics and commercial travellers. *Crossroads* reflected the idea of the car and automobile culture as occupying a particular type of 'non-place'. As one critic noted, 'the motel has no real lobby and it is tied into a highway network'; it incarnated a sense of impermanence and placelessness. As Mimi Sheller and John Urry have argued, 'The motel, like the airport transit lounge or the motorway service station, represents neither arrival nor departure, but the "pause," consecrated to circulation and movement and demolishing particular senses of place and locale.'[49]

In certain respects, then, mass automobility contributed to a reorganization of urban space, rearranging the relationship between different places – home, work, shops, entertainment, school, relatives – and the temporal rhythm of the city. A classic study of suburbanization in late 1950s London noted how the spread of car ownership was transforming life in the new housing estates on the city's fringes. What had formerly been walking or bicycling distances, or dependent on public transport like the tram, now became 'motoring distances'.[50] As well as shopping, the 1964 Birmingham study of car usage noted the substantial impact widening car ownership was having on both commuting to work and on leisure, in the form of trips to the countryside at the weekend and seaside or caravanning holidays.[51] Paradoxically, though, the possession of a car also consolidated the family and home-centredness of suburban life, in Britain as much as Japan. Along with other consumer durables, like television, the car reinforced the primacy of the home over public space among all social classes, including 'affluent worker' households. Such 'innovations', the sociologist Ferdynand Zweig argued in 1961, 'strengthen the family circle, whilst actually weakening ties with mates'.[52] The latter was less true of women than of men, but the onset of mass automobility can be seen to have altered the coordinates of urban life, reinforcing the attractions of suburb and housing estate, for those able to afford a car, while simultaneously diminishing the hold of the neighbourhood and shared spaces of street and public house over individuals and social groups.[53]

The ideal of the suburb as envisaged in England never materialized in Japan on a large scale. Despite the 'income-doubling' of the 1960s, the *salariman*'s (white-collar worker) dream of a comfortable *manshon*, or condominium, apartment in a bourgeois area remained, for the most part, inaccessible.[54] Impressionistic catch phrases, largely invented by Japanese journalists and advertisers for their own purposes, purportedly reveal changes in consumerism and consumer aspirations in the three decades after 1950. In the mid-1950s the three sacred treasures of Japan's mythic imperial past – the mirror, the sword and the jewel – were transmogrified into the three S's of consumerism: *senpūki* (electric fan), *sentaku* (washing machine) and *suihanki* (rice cooker). In the mid-1960s the car made its debut in the three K's: *kaa* (car), *kūrā* (cooler, or air conditioner) and *karā terebi* (colour television). The 'internationalization' (*kokusaika*) of Japan was a major media theme in the mid-1970s and was reflected in the increasing numbers of Japanese travelling abroad, transforming the three sacred treasures into the three J's: *jettō* (overseas travel), *jūeru* (jewels) and *jūtaku* (house), the last reflecting the growing trend of home ownership. These slogans, however, have been criticized for homogenizing the Japanese and, for the most part, they do not reflect actual consumer habits during these decades.[55] Yet advertisements for houses began to show cars on their frontages, even though only a minority of urban dwellers could aspire to own houses large enough for a drive in the 1970s.[56]

Built to last only several decades, post-war suburban houses were often uniform and monotonous, with very little to differentiate the frontages of individual buildings or to distinguish one street from another. The term '*mai kā*' (my car), however, had a very specific association with the personal and individualistic nature of car ownership. Meaning specifically the 'owner-driver car', it was coined in 1961 by history of technology theorist, Hoshino Yoshiro, in his best-selling book *Mai Kā Jidai* (The My Car Era), which reviewed the advantages and dangers of modern technology.[57] The association of the private car with Western ideals was also cemented by the importation of another English 'loan word', the term '*doraibu*' or 'drive' which means going out for a drive for pleasure or sightseeing. Strictly speaking, in Japanese, the verb 'to drive' is expressed by the word *untensuru* which is confined to the mechanics of driving rather than its pleasurable aspects.

The concept of *mai kā* was also closely associated with *mai hōmu* (my home) which originated in the 1930s. In the 1960s *mai hōmu* had developed as an ideology which attempted to unite an ideal of family life with Japanese-style contemporary mass society. 'My homism' symbolized the transition from communal values, associated with the extended family often still living in the countryside, towards the more individualistic values of the nuclear family in the city.[58] In addition, the popular concept of *kokumin jūtaku* (the people's house) established the minimum unit of space required for a small family to live in, just as MITI's *kokuminsha* (the people's car) was conceived around the minimum dimensions and specifications to accommodate a family of four. The idea of *mai kā* and *mai hōmu*, though, highlighted the problem of parking; only the lucky few had access to a communal parking lot if included in the neighbourhood plan.[59] Even in more spacious residential areas, very few houses had enough land to accommodate a small frontage, let alone a garage, or 'gareji', so that accommodating the car in new homes posed an architectural challenge. Older designs of housing had wooden floors suspended well above ground level. Sometimes, the *genkan*, a small porch where people were required to take off their shoes before stepping up into the house, was on or near ground level.

The idea of houses being built with earth or 'dirt floors', *doma*, so that a space for a motorcycle or car could be incorporated into house design was a revolutionary concept introduced by architect Shinohara Kazuo in a series called *Japanese Architectural Methods* published between 1957 and 1964. His 1963 'Doma Jūtaku' (Earth-floor House) was a treatise on how bicycles, motorbikes and cars could be incorporated into modern building design in a new way, rather than in a separate garage. This concept was culturally significant, leading Bauhaus-influenced designer and architect, Yamawaki Iwao, to compare getting out of the car to taking off one's shoes before entering the house. The 'gareji' was incorporated into the building as a ground floor under piles (pilotis) or a cantilever supporting the first floor of the house, creating a space like a *genkan* beneath where shoes and car could be 'taken off'. Carports, prefabricated temporary structures introduced in the 1960s which were either free-standing or attached to the house, were, according to Yamawaki, little more than 'shoeboxes' for cars.[60]

As the possession of a parking space became more common, attention was switched to the car itself as a means of setting apart one family from others in the 'faceless' suburbs. As historian Inge Daniels observed:

In a street in the south of Kyoto, for example, all the ready-built houses were the same size and the exteriors looked alike. Still, the cars parked in front, ranging from small 'box-cars', to SUV vehicles or the latest Mercedes imported from Germany, revealed the aspirations of the inhabitants.[61]

The importance of external structures such as parking places in Japanese urban culture has been highlighted by Daniels. While individually designed houses in the post-war period tended to maintain traditional high enclosure walls and large gates, by the 1970s the typical suburban house had a much diminished exterior and often dispensed with gates altogether. As levels of car ownership rose, whether or not a house had a parking space became a significant factor in determining the purchase price. From the 1990s house designs with parking spaces became more common. Increasingly, houses built between the 1960s and 1980s were demolished and replaced with designs that could accommodate a car, even if it meant losing a room or raising an already narrow house to accommodate a car beneath, thus increasing the risk of earthquake damage.[62] Mass automobility therefore reversed traditional priorities. It had the effect of displacing the traditional emphasis on private life inside the home and directing attention instead to the public display of social status on the outside.[63]

Cultures of driving: Casualties, congestion and breakdown

In both Britain and Japan the car became an object of mass desire during the 1960s; it symbolized, perhaps more powerfully than any other commodity, status, convenience and freedom. But mass automobility also had its dark side as many contemporaries recognized. Road traffic safety had been a matter of national concern in Britain since the inter-war years; the successive road traffic acts of the 1930s sought to curb accidents through the introduction of speed limits and the Highway Code, which placed responsibility for road safety on both drivers and pedestrians. Still in 1942 the Metropolitan Commissioner of Police, Alker Tripp, could write of the 'battle-level' of road casualties, accounting for some 68,000 deaths and 2 million injured, in the years prior to the Second World War.[64] Despite successive interventions by government and police, casualty figures continued to rise. Between 1945 and the mid-1960s some 150,000 people were killed and several million injured on Britain's roads; peak annual figures for road deaths and injuries were recorded in 1965/6, reflecting the surge in motorization over the previous decade (Graph 4.2).[65] As a committedly motorized city, Birmingham witnessed more than its share of casualties: in 1974 the city had the highest rate of traffic accidents involving children of any area in Britain.[66]

Although there were fewer accidents in Japan than Britain in the early 1950s, they were more lethal. In 1952, for example, 172,000 accidents resulted in 4,706 fatalities in Britain, while in the same year in Japan just 58,000 accidents led to almost the same number of deaths, 4,696.[67] The inappropriate design of Japan's city streets for motorization was one reason given for high casualty rates, and poor driving conditions was another. When the Americans arrived in 1945, it was even unclear which side of the road they should be driving on. In 1920, Article 1 of the Roads Management

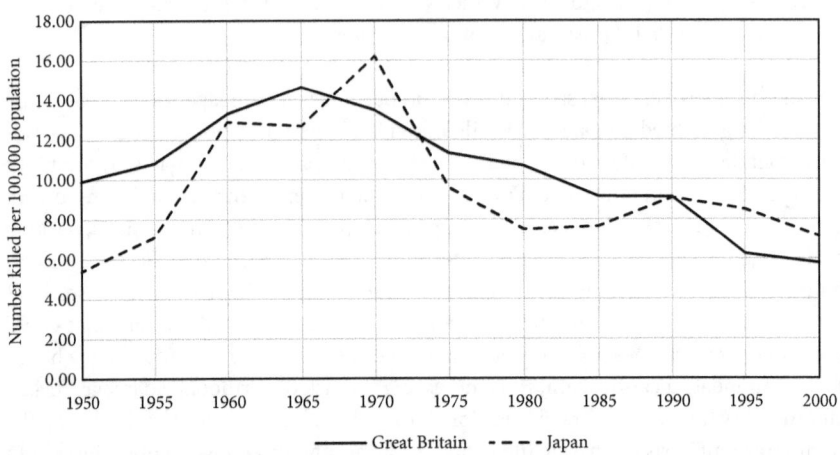

Graph 4.2 Department for Transport, Reported Traffic Accidents and Casualties, Great Britain 1950–2017 (HMSO, London, 2017)

Sources: Statistics Bureau, 'Road Traffic Accidents (1924–2005)', *Historical Statistics of Japan*, http://www.stat.go.jp/english/data/chouki/29.html. British figures from Department of the Environment, Transport Statistics: Great Britain, 1964–1974.

Ordinance reinforced the decree that all traffic in Japan, pedestrian and vehicular, should travel along the left-hand side of the road, a custom originating in the fact that British railway engineers in Japan had naturally constructed railways with the British system of left-hand traffic in mind, although not all prefectures adhered to this regulation and there was some variation.[68] The custom was also adopted by tramways, so that a general principle of driving on the left came to be adopted for vehicular traffic. U.S. military commanders, perhaps unfairly, blamed the Japanese system of driving on the left for numerous accidents, regarding it as an obstacle to the safe passage of Occupation Army vehicles. Eventually, at the end of December 1946, it seems that the Americans reflected on the wisdom of making the whole country change to driving on the right and the system of 'people left, cars left' was enforced nationally by General MacArthur's Headquarters.[69] However, in Japan as in Britain, traffic casualties continued to rise with over 4,000 deaths in the late 1940s mounting to a peak of 16,765 deaths in 1970 and nearly a million people injured. In Nagoya the number of traffic accidents peaked at 23,834 in 1963. Thereafter, the number of accidents involving other vehicles began to fall, while those involving pedestrians remained high, totalling 2,190 in 1969 before declining sharply in the early 1970s (Graph 4.3).[70]

The result in both countries was a rising chorus of concern. Some three decades after Alker Tripp had used the term 'battle-level' to describe road casualties, the Labour Minister of Transport, Barbara Castle (1965–1967), termed the continuously mounting deaths and injuries on Britain's roads a 'holocaust'.[71] The phrase 'Traffic War' was used by the Japanese media for the first time in 1963.[72] In the mid-1960s with annual casualty

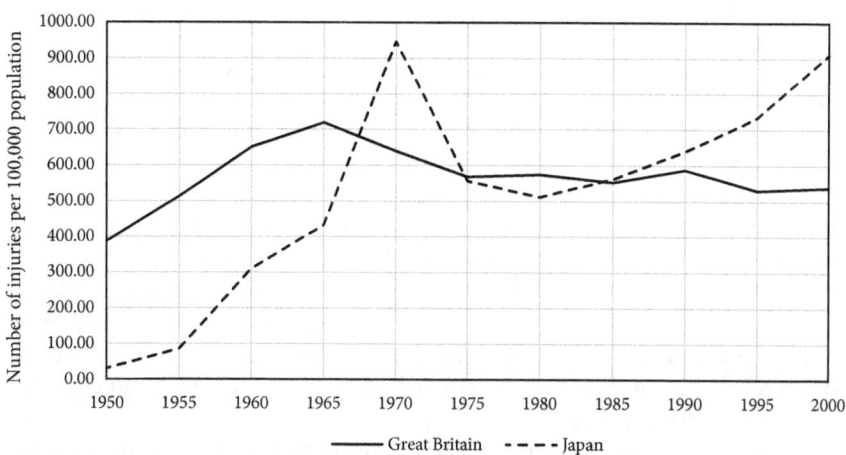

Graph 4.3 Comparison of road accident injuries in Britain and Japan, 1950–2000

Source: Statistics Bureau, 'Road Traffic Accidents (1924–2005)', *Historical Statistics of Japan*, http://www.stat.go.jp/english/data/chouki/29.html. British figures from Department for Transport, *Transport Statistics Great Britain*. https://www.gov.uk/government/statistical-data-sets/tsgb08-traffic-accidents-and-casualties (accessed 12 December 2017).

rates in Japan rising to over half a million, articles with titles such as 'Death Unlimited' began appearing in Japanese newspapers and journals. The 'slaughter on the roads' was compared to natural disasters such as typhoons and earthquakes towards which the Japanese had 'acquired the ability to be constantly aware of the threat yet to carry on without becoming unduly nervous'. The heavy toll inflicted by traffic accidents was described as 'a new and sudden plague' which was 'creeping rapidly and insidiously from the great cities to the suburbs and on to the provincial towns'.[73]

In both countries, the 1960s proved to be a tipping point in attitudes towards the car, which appeared to one Japanese journalist to be 'a kind of wild animal on wheels'.[74] Attention focused on the driver behind the wheel. In particular, the introduction of new types of roads – motorways, expressways, interchanges – raised concerns about the driver's ability to adapt to new conditions and styles of motoring. In Britain, the flamboyant Conservative Minister for Transport, Ernest Marples, articulated his fears after witnessing the opening of the first stretch of the M1 motorway in November 1959. 'I was frightened when I watched the first users', he confessed to journalists, 'I have never seen anybody going so fast and ignoring the rules and regulations … I really was appalled at the speed at which some cars were travelling'.[75] In Japan, too, there were high levels of anxiety about the impact of the car on the psychology of the Japanese. One report stated:

> It is often said that even the most sheep-like and mature person, once his hands are on the wheel, is transformed into a wolf. It is clear that the automobile touches the

deepest recesses of man's psyche, and car-craziness could usefully be the subject of extensive psychoanalysis. The magical power of the automobile has warped the psychological structure of the Japanese people in ways invisible to the eye.[76]

In Britain, commentators worried that faced with a new type of fast, straight road and no speed limit, motorists would drive irresponsibly. How would individual, untutored motorists respond to the requirement for lane discipline and regulations such as no stopping and no U-turns? As it was accident numbers were high in the opening years of the M1's existence and after several years of experiment, a speed limit of 70 mph was imposed on British motorways in 1967.[77] Speed limits on Japanese roads were generally lower. Under the 1960 Road Traffic Law, a maximum of 100 kilometres per hour (62 miles per hour) was enforced on new expressways for ordinary cars and 80 kilometres per hour (50 miles per hour) for motorcycles and light cars in 1963. Speed limits on other roads were even lower; a general limit of 60 kilometres per hour (37 miles per hour) was normal outside cities and urban areas were zoned at 40 kilometres per hour (25 miles per hour).[78]

Meanwhile, each new road development brought fresh concerns about its effects on drivers. In Birmingham the opening of Gravelly Hill Interchange and the Aston Expressway in 1972 saw anxiety levels rise. A seven-lane motorway with a novel, reversible middle lane for tidal flow, the Aston Expressway was a particular source of concern for civil servants and some road experts. J.R. Madge, a senior official in the Ministry of Transport, confessed in 1969 that the Expressway 'rather makes me shudder from the safety point of view ... We are bound to get asked [about safety testing] when the first (inevitable?) head-on crash occurs in the centre lane'.[79] The combined authority of the Royal Society for the Prevention of Accidents, the Birmingham Accident Prevention Centre, the police and the Department of the Environment was brought to bear on public education. As a spokesman put it, 'We have to teach people to drive like engine drivers and stay on the rails. They must get into the lane they require and stay there, and stop at a red light even if their road ahead is clear'. Motorists on the Aston Expressway would have to learn to obey a variety of signs determined by computer analysis of traffic flows at any given point in the day.[80] New styles of driving required motorists to suppress their instincts and obey official demands unquestioningly. In his 1971 discussion of autopia, Reyner Banham argued that driving on expressways involved obedience to instructions (such as turning left to go right) that, in sensory terms, could appear counter-intuitive. This obedience would mean that the motorist would 'hardly notice any difference when the freeways are finally fitted with computerized automatic control systems that will take charge of the car'.[81]

Such initiatives formed part of a wave of measures to control traffic, accelerated from 1967 under Barbara Castle as Minister of Transport who was depicted by Britain's motoring organizations as declaring 'total war' on drivers.[82] The arch-conservative Royal Automobile Club (RAC) in particular opposed each successive measure: the imposition of a 70 mph speed limit on motorways, procedures to prevent drink-driving, the introduction of safety belts.[83] Following Banham's example, the RAC, Automobile Association (AA) and the motoring press argued that the freedoms of the driver were being steadily whittled away by regulation. In a 1967 article set futuristically in 1998, the magazine *Autocar* depicted a dystopian motoring world in which the Ministry of Transport (renamed the 'administration of no-transport') employed psychological techniques of manipulation to habituate drivers to ever-increasing regulation. In a neo-Darwinian reversal, the article argued that all speed limits should be removed. Such limits, it argued, 'create danger by preventing fluidity'. The cry instead was to 'abandon all speed limits'. 'Drivers [should] stand on their own feet, instead of giving them the crutch of an extensive rule book. Bring back pride in skilful car control. Make roads safe but challenging …. Muscles atrophy with disuse. No wonder we have little judgement of speed.'[84]

On a day-to-day basis it became evident to commentators that once behind the wheel of a car, the much-vaunted reserve and politeness of the Japanese underwent a radical change. The public and associations representing the interests of drivers, such as the Japan Automobile Federation (JAF), the Japanese equivalent of the British RAC or AA, were concerned about the general loss of manners when driving. The monthly *JAF News* began to carry articles exhorting drivers to keep calm and show consideration to other drivers, especially in the late 1960s when the proportionate number of traffic accidents reached its height. With articles such as 'My Calm Driving' (Watashi no anshin unten) (1968), 'Let Other Cars Get By' (Tasha o hashiroseyō) (1969) and 'Let's Respect the Distance between Cars' (Shikan kyori wa otagai ni sonchō shiyō) (1969), the JAF sought to educate drivers, urging them in 1969 to sign a 'calm driving pledge' and drive in a 'heartfelt' way.[85] There were rising concerns about the number of accidents involving children, and the JAF ran campaigns on child safety, especially in urban areas, alongside regular road safety campaigns. As in Britain, children had customarily used streets as playgrounds, and most roads in residential areas close to city centres, and many in residential suburbs, had no pavements, forcing local authorities to construct dedicated play areas.[86] The provision of play areas was seen as an example of the 'harmonization of cars and humans' which became another phrase embedded within car criticism of the 1960s. As Roth explains, there was a tacit acknowledgment that 'heavy metal objects propelled at high velocities had the potential to do great damage to human flesh'. Harmonization might involve certain aspects of urban planning but the onus was on the re-education of pedestrians and the inculcation of manners in drivers.[87] In practice, such readjustments in behaviour did little to address either the enthusiasm for cars or the increasing carnage on the road.

The 1967 Tokyo Motor Show saw the creation of a 'Traffic Safety Corner' at the time when Japan had one of the highest rates of traffic accidents in the world; figures for fatal and non-fatal casualties were much higher than those for Britain.[88] Yet such was the interest in the new passenger cars on display:

> The cars themselves were almost hidden by the mass of visitors. … Not only could the visitors touch the cars, but they were allowed to sit inside, take the wheel and change gears freely. However, so great were the crowds, people had to wait an hour before they could sit in the driver's seat and savor the feeling of being an owner of a new model car.[89]

Despite warning signs put up by the Tokyo Metropolitan Police and radio announcements advising that traffic was paralyzed on the roads to the show, the public kept coming;

'ignoring', according to one report, 'with smiles on their faces, these sensible warnings, [they] continued without hesitation to swell the homicidal flow of automobiles headed towards the motor show'.[90] The obsession with the car as object, it seemed to many observers, had simply overridden all other concerns about its safety and societal impact.

Traffic congestion as well as accidents compromised the equation of motoring with personal liberty and freedom of movement. Colin Buchanan's pioneering report of 1963, *Traffic in Towns*, had warned about the imminent threats to urban life in Britain of unrestricted mass motorization. 'All the indications are that given its head the motor vehicle would wreck our towns within a decade', Buchanan predicted. Road-building itself appeared self-defeating in the view of Sir Geoffrey Crowther, writing in the report's foreword: 'Each new motorway, built to cope with existing traffic, seems to call into existence new traffic sufficient to create new congestion.' Crowther was merely repeating a truism that transport planners and government had known since the 1930s, that traffic expanded to fill new road space – the phenomenon known as 'induced traffic'.[91] While their worst fears did not appear to transpire, engineering solutions to the problem of traffic hardly offered much by way of comfort. Buchanan had largely approved of Manzoni's plans to accommodate mass automobility in the early 1960s, but a decade later he was considerably less optimistic. Standing in Manzoni Gardens in the heart of Birmingham in 1971, Buchanan observed, 'There's a hell of a noise here and the traffic seems terribly close' while he found Corporation Street 'terribly disappointing … If there really is a diminution of traffic here, as the planners claim, heaven knows what it was like before'.[92]

Figure 4.3 Manzoni Gardens, 1965, surrounded by roads. Source: Leonard Stace Collection.

In urban Japan, too, motorized traffic congestion was a major problem by the 1960s, partly attributed to the chauffeur-system in cities like Tokyo which led to increased traffic at peak time in both directions, in and out of the city. Chauffeurs used public transport to fetch their cars from the garages where they were parked overnight, drove out to a residential district to pick up their employer and then joined in the morning rush hour until reaching the drop-off point outside the company building. In the evening the process would be repeated in reverse. In the case of brief visits to destinations in the city where there was no adjacent parking, chauffeurs would continuously drive around the block until their employer appeared at the door to be picked up, exacerbating traffic congestion in the area. The Parking Facility Law of 1957 was the first attempt nationally to regulate parking in Japan's major conurbations. It permitted cities to install meters and collect fees for on-street parking in designated areas, specified minimum standards for building off-street parking facilities and required all new buildings, or additions to buildings exceeding 3,000 square meters, to provide a designated number of parking spaces. However, progress on this front, which fell mainly on private developers, was too slow to keep up with demand and failed to improve driver behaviour.[93] Koshimidzu, writing in 1964, argued that it was vital that the 'glamour' of the railway and other modes of public transport should be maintained, 'in order to keep to a minimum the menace of an uncontrollable increase in private cars'.[94] However, it was the glamour and, more importantly, the freedom associated with the car that would seduce people away from public transport, whatever the realities of road conditions.

In Japan, as in Britain, the problem of urban congestion refused to go away despite the attempts made to ameliorate it. The drive towards expressway building in the 1960s inevitably brought even more cars into the cities. The Hanshin Expressway Public Corporation opened its first section of urban toll expressway in Osaka in 1964, followed in 1967 by the expressway in Kobe City, forming the first link in a large-scale network planned for the Kobe-Osaka or Hanshin region. In 1966, with just 5,000 cars a day entering the short sections of newly built expressway, the Corporation had predicted the need for sophisticated traffic control systems. A committee drew together experts from a wide range of fields, including computing, communications engineering and economics, as well as traffic engineering. They recommended an automated traffic control system, which would allow the maximum number of cars to enter the expressway while avoiding congestion. The system came into effect in March 1970.[95]

At the time, the automated system developed by the Hanshin Expressway Public Corporation was the most advanced in Japan, and for that reason employees involved in traffic management and control for the Nagoya Urban Expressway were sent for training in traffic surveillance and accident response at Hanshin Expressway headquarters.[96] Congestion problems on the expressway toll roads were easier to resolve than on toll-free roads because the control systems were able to limit the number of cars entering the system by closing entrance ramps completely or reducing the number of open toll-booths. Once congestion was indicated on the expressway, vehicles could be forced to queue up at the relevant entrance ramps, which was considered a safer option than queuing on the expressway itself. Vehicles could also be forced off the expressway at exit ramps. These so-called 'direct' methods of control were developed at the same time as 'indirect' methods, which included providing drivers with as much information as possible, usually by radio, so that they could decide for themselves whether to exit the system.[97]

One hazard drivers had to negotiate on Japanese roads was earthquakes. The vulnerability of elevated expressways was demonstrated on the morning of 17 January 1995 when several sections of the Hanshin Expressway collapsed in the Kobe and Nishinomiya areas during the Great Hanshin Earthquake. In the 1980s, the Tokyo Metropolitan Police Department instructed drivers in the event of an earthquake to steer their cars into the nearest car park, switch off their engine leaving the keys in and continue on foot. However, as urban historian Peter Popham pointed out, in congested Tokyo, 'the plan is almost completely unworkable, as drivers, locked in burning traffic, will be unable to take their cars anywhere or do anything at all except get out and run'.[98]

More commonly, mechanical breakdown compromised the benefits of everyday automobility. Whatever the promise of speed, refinement and freedom, cars were unreliable in the 1960s and 1970s. In Britain, while roadside repair had been viewed as an intrinsic part of the 'art of motoring' in the gentlemanly era, mass motorization posed new challenges to the car owner. Drivers were encouraged to carry a toolbox in the boot in case of breakdown and the household garage was a place not simply for parking the car but for routine maintenance as well as more ambitious repairs. Over a quarter of motorists admitted to experiencing at least one breakdown per year that required AA assistance in 1965, a figure that had risen to one in two by 1970; and this was likely to be an underestimate of the real scale of car breakdown since AA members tended to own newer vehicles.[99] The second-hand car market awaits its historian but it clearly expanded in the 1960s – and these were the vehicles most prone to mechanical failure. The AA reported a breakdown every seven minutes on the opening day of the M1 in November 1959. The problem continued with the organization noting that it had attended almost 6,000 breakdowns on Britain's motorways in August 1973, blaming 'sustained high-speed motoring for exposing weak parts or skimped maintenance'. On Japan's Hanshin Expressway, the number of vehicle breakdowns rose steeply and peaked in 1970 at around 22,000 breakdowns among just under 100 million cars entering the system. Even in the late 1980s breakdowns on the Expressway were estimated to be responsible for over 90 per cent of traffic congestion.[100] With the costs of motoring also increasing, doubling in Britain in the two years following the oil hike of 1973, owning a car, in effect, could be a time-consuming, expensive and frustrating business.[101]

Driving and urban legibility

However beneficial the new urban motorway systems may have been for congestion – and the results were at best equivocal – they did not appear to make the city easier to negotiate for drivers. During the lengthy construction process of the Birmingham ring and link roads, television reports showed drivers struggling to make sense of directions. A frequent complaint was that once opened in 1959 the M1 route from London was straightforward, but it became confused as soon as drivers entered the Birmingham area; road works and demolition meant that signs were missing, while familiar landmarks had disappeared.[102] The opening of Gravelly Hill Interchange in 1972 represented a field day for news items on motorists lost or disoriented. An interview with one 'victim' of Spaghetti Junction reported that she found the whole experience 'frightening'; confused by the signs and traffic, she had been unable to identify the right exit to the roundabout and had ended up at the airport some forty minutes later, anxious the car was running out of petrol. The City Corporation arranged for taxi drivers to have a practical demonstration of the new road systems before they were opened to traffic in order to avoid costly mistakes.[103] Even the normal tendency to eulogize the experience of driving the Inner Ring after its opening in 1971 became tinged with apprehension; 'Birmingham has become the linchpin of motorway megalopolis living' pronounced the *Guardian*:

> It is a curious experience. The urban explorer dips up and down, moles underground, emerges in one covered shopping area, and is absolutely grateful when suddenly there is an open-air circus ... The cars nudge by the roof of a charming museum converted from an old hostel and now tucked down besides converging roads. They then pass within yards of the first stage of the All Saints Office Centre. [104]

A wider investigation into morphological perceptions of the new Birmingham by drivers and pedestrians suggested that spatial experiences of the city were much less coherent than civic authorities had envisaged. In 1971 researchers at Birmingham University's Centre for Urban and Regional Studies examined the mental maps of 167 residents, including motorists, in a project entitled *City Scene*. The project was based on the ideas of urban legibility of the American planner Kevin Lynch, published in 1960 as *The Image of the City*. In his influential study of Boston, Lynch had argued that a 'legible city would be one whose districts or landmarks or pathways are easily identifiable and are easily grouped into an overall pattern'.[105] By this yardstick, the *City Scene* survey suggested, motor cities like Birmingham fared poorly; they were far from legible. Among drivers, 60 per cent of respondents to the study did not have a mental map of the whole of the 3¾ mile Inner Ring Road; with the exception of Smallbrook Ringway, *City Scene* reported that 'neither the new [Inner Ring] route nor its nodal interchanges feature significantly in our maps'. As Matthew Parker aptly put it, drivers did not view Britain's first urban motorway as something unique or different; 'drivers merely saw the Inner Ring Road as *another* road'.[106]

Still more disturbing, the effect of the new road systems was to unsettle the sensory experience of pedestrians, who were forced to use the subways underneath. One respondent to the *City Scene* survey reported that 'subways are so amorphous and distorted from the above ground layout [that] one loses one's image of "above ground" in them'. In 1968 the *Birmingham Post* similarly observed that the 'distorted sounds' in subways made it hard for pedestrians 'to tell which way the traffic is going overhead, or where the next exit will bring them out'. For many drivers and pedestrians, then, the experience of the city was disrupted by mass automobility in ways that were not foreseen by town or transport planners. In general, *City Scene* concluded, Birmingham's newly developed city centre emerged as a 'confused space'. Rather than legible 'it was a city of fragments bounded by an Inner Ring Road'.[107]

Among foreigners, a journey through any Japanese city in the 1960s was equally likely to prompt a negative reaction, or at best a sense of bewilderment. According to urban historian Barrie Shelton: 'To most Western visitors, Japanese cities remain cluttered, garish, unfathomable and, seemingly, without trace of urban planning.'[108] What seemed to tourists' eyes to be the chaos of Japanese cities sometimes served to preserve ancient street patterns and characteristics, especially in the metropolitan heart of crowded Tokyo. There were parts of most Japanese cities that automobiles could not penetrate, let alone dominate. The writer Peter Popham described his experience of a short journey on foot from Aoyama Dōri, a major artery road with ten lanes of speeding traffic, to a Tokyo architect's studio. Suddenly he found himself walking 'down a snicket so narrow you might have taken it for a private drive. It was about nine feet wide'. This narrow shopping street had the characteristic white line about 18 inches from the side of the street which denoted a pedestrian area: 'In the space of a couple of yards we had passed from a place that felt like a big city to a place that had the scale of a village and the pace and activity of a small town.' As he continued his journey, the street became so narrow that there were no shops, and no vehicles could penetrate.[109] This 'conjuring trick' happened because of the failure – or reluctance – of post-war urban planners to impose a network of uniform, grid-like roads onto Tokyo. Popham memorably described this phenomenon as like a spiral or an egg: 'The image that comes to mind is that of a nut or an egg. On the outside is the high concrete of Aoyama Dōri – the hard shell,' but cradled within is 'the heart of the matter, the egg's yolk, the kernel.'[110] The Tokyo architect whom Popham was following negotiated roads and turns while reading a book. This anecdote highlights the vast difference between navigating a large Japanese city like Tokyo on foot and navigating by car where the driver is a slave to signs and directions.

The Japanese government standardized road signs in 1968 based on protocols dating back to 1934.[111] But the problem of road legibility, especially for the expressways, was literally about how well drivers would be able to read complex Chinese characters (*kanji*) through the car window. In 1961 a special sub-committee was established to consider the design of signs for the new expressways which would be legible at high speed.[112] It was decided that simplified, angular characters in a specially developed font known as '*kodan*' should be used. However, it was also clear that, especially with the 1964 Olympic Games attracting foreign visitors, an alphabetic system would have to be incorporated. The ratio of alphabetical characters to Japanese characters, the size and type of font as well as spacing and margins were tested for legibility at speed so that they could be deployed on the first section of the Meishin Expressway at its opening in 1963.[113] However, attempts to introduce bilingual signs in Tokyo in 1960 prompted scorn among the English-speaking community and embarrassment among the Japanese. Robert Trumbull, special correspondent for the *New York Times*, had obtained drawings of the new signs published by the Tokyo police authorities who were apparently holding firmly to an 'unusual version of English on new traffic signs'. One sign informed drivers that they 'May Parking and Stopping,' and another directed drivers to 'Right Turn toward Immediate Outside.' Japanese scholars condemned the signage as prime examples of 'Japlish' and the drawings were hastily withdrawn.[114]

Even bilingual signage in correct English could not temper the confusion and unease that most foreigners faced when navigating the Japanese city because of differences in the ways that streets and roads functioned. Whereas in most Western cities streets and highways work as key visual devices, underpinning a sense of order which was linear and hierarchical, in Japan, not only are fewer roads and streets named, but they exist in a patchwork: 'scattered points with no clear relationship between each other and often no clear form within themselves'.[115] Nagoya is exceptional in as much as an unusual number of roads have been named – there is even one called 'Kuruma Dōri' or 'Car Road' – making Nagoya more legible than other Japanese cities, for both motorists and pedestrians. However, in gaining legibility, it also lost many of its historic streets according to its critics.

Pedestrians and containment of the car

Criticism of the car and car culture increased at the end of the 1960s. Leading academic and commentator on modernity, Yugawa Toshikazu, is recognized as writing the first systematic criticism of the 'personal car system' in his book *Mai-kā Bōkoku-ron* (Theory of a Country Ruined by 'My Car') published in 1968. His observations were based on the processes of motorization in 'wealthy, automobile-dominated America'. The proliferation of the car created an endless cycle of roads construction which made migration to the suburbs possible. Suburbanization was essentially a low-density process which made public transport increasingly unfeasible, thus creating demand for more cars which became a necessity of life. Once the process had begun the car became impossible to contain. His book was a warning to his country to avoid such a vicious circle which had, in his view, created a kind of car-dependent 'hell' in the United States.[116] Hoshino Yoshirō, who had coined the phrase *mai-kā*, had initially welcomed the car as the ultimate symbol of freedom, but in the face of inexorably rising casualties, particularly pedestrians, began to see the car as 'barbaric'. In his 1969 book *Gijutsu to Ningen* (Technology and Man) he compared the barbarity of the car system, its pollution and road carnage, to the stupidity of launching a nuclear attack. His vision for the future was prescient in that he foresaw the development of 'car robots' – perhaps driverless cars – running on electricity. But even here, Hoshino argued, without a 'human revolution' there was no evidence that technology could prevent a major disaster.[117]

By 1970, indeed, the shortcomings of the 'motor revolution' were becoming clear. One dimension of this was the growing recognition of what were termed the 'no-car folk', the substantial proportion of households who still did not own a car. In Birmingham, commonly considered to be Britain's most 'car mad' city, over half of all households (58 per cent) were still without one in 1970.[118] In Nagoya in the same year four out of five households were without a car, and nationally, it was not until 1979 that a majority of Japanese urban households owned one.[119] Contemporary research began to reveal how the pattern of car ownership mirrored and reinforced larger patterns of inequality and disadvantage. While the numbers of private cars on roads escalated in both Britain and Japan in the 1950s and 1960s, the effect was to redraw existing lines of social difference rather than to bring about the much-heralded 'car-owning democracy' or *mai kā* era. Men were more likely to have a driving licence and travel by private car than women. In Japan just 17 per cent of women held a driving licence in 1969; in Britain the figure for women was 29 per cent in 1975/6 compared to 69 per cent of men.[120] In Nagoya by 1975, however, the number of women holding a driving licence was 21 per cent.[121] In Birmingham in 1972 two-thirds of men travelled to work by car as against one-third of women, while on the city's council estates fewer than one in ten women held a driving licence.[122]

Among men, though, social class appeared less of a determining factor: 75 per cent of foremen and skilled manual workers in Britain held a driving licence in 1972 as against 71 per cent of managerial, professional and non-manual workers. Skilled car workers were one of the groups with the highest rate of car ownership of any workers, as surveys regularly showed. The real class division was between these groups (managerial, professional and skilled men) and semi- and unskilled manual workers, of whom only a third possessed a driving licence. Age was also a factor: older women were the group least likely to own a car or to be able to drive.[123] Areas of the city which housed high numbers of Asian and Caribbean migrants, such as Handsworth, Spark Hill and Small Heath, also had relatively low levels of car ownership, at around a third of households.[124] Patterns of mobility in cities Birmingham into the 1970s thus reinforced the relative disadvantage of specific groups: the semi- and unskilled as against professional and skilled workers; the elderly as against the young and middle-aged; women as against men. Women did not begin to join the ranks of drivers in significant numbers in Japan or Britain until the 1980s.

It was consequently these groups who predominated among pedestrians and users of public transport, especially buses.[125] Despite the existence of the Pedestrians' Association since 1929, which lobbied hard to protect the rights of walkers in Britain, during the heyday of mass motorization pedestrians tended to be regarded as 'lesser citizens'.[126] In Birmingham, the local newspaper affirmed, 'it is the pedestrian who must accept inconvenience for the sake of the car and not the other way round.' Within the city centre the pedestrian was 'confined to subways and low-level circuses'.[127] By the early 1970s, however, these orthodoxies, including the idea that the city centre must be accessible to motor traffic, came into question. The levels of traffic accessing the centre began to be seen as an unwarranted nuisance. A survey conducted among shoppers in New Street – Birmingham's main shopping street – indicated that 76 per cent were in favour of pedestrianization of the central streets and only 14 per cent opposed.[128] In March 1971 city councillors undertook a 'trial walk' through the city centre, prompting strong responses. 'The whole concept [of the Inner Ring] was wrong', Alderman Florence Hammond was quoted as saying. 'Pedestrians should have been on top and the motorists underneath. The city is a place to shop, not motor through.'[129] In the face of mounting criticisms from experts, the press, shoppers, shop-owners and councillors themselves, the Corporation eventually relented. From 1 November 1972 central Birmingham was declared a traffic-free zone.

In Japan, too, the pedestrian was seen to constitute a roads problem and, as in Britain, the solution was seen as educating the pedestrian, rather than the motorist. In 1964, following a record 13,318 deaths and over 400,000 casualties,[130] the government began a series of National Road Safety Conferences presided over by the Prime Minister, Satō Eisaku. One initiative was a programme of National Road Safety campaigns held in spring and autumn annually in towns and villages. During these times traffic police were mobilized to stand at street corners as a warning to motorists, but also to caution and educate pedestrians crossing the streets. Each city, town and village had a Traffic Safety Association staffed by ordinary citizens who took up their posts on street corners bedecked in yellow hats and waving yellow flags.[131] In the meantime, other, more unorthodox, practices were adopted to reduce accidents. In Kyoto, police experimented with playing soothing music to keep drivers calm at busy intersections of the city. Elsewhere, pedestrians were harangued by loudspeakers telling them to take care and obey instructions at crossings.[132]

Efforts to separate pedestrians from motorized traffic by building footbridges simply increased a sense of inferiority, as one journalist noted: 'The reason is that the pedestrian feels he is slighted since, puny as he is compared with automobiles, he must climb up and down a series of steps to cross a road; while automobiles … sweep by over level roads with ease.' The target of such contempt was the newly introduced 'pedestrian overhead crossing', towering metal bridges often spanning up to six lanes of traffic, which proved a bane for those groups without a car. There was much sympathy for the Japanese housewife who was typically (perhaps stereotypically since the commentators were usually male) without a car. Instead of crossing a street 'in 20 steps to do her shopping the housewife must now climb 180 steps to do the same thing. As for the aged,

Figure 4.4 Pedestrians invade central Nagoya in the 'promenade', 1970. Source: Nagoya City Public Information Division. http://timetravel.network2010.org/article/129

the other side of the road is no longer a world to be visited with ease.'[133] In the 1960s the pedestrianization of streets was resisted in Japanese cities, often by store owners rather than by politicians or police. In 1969, the Tokyo Metropolitan Police Agency began to exclude cars from some shopping streets in residential areas which won huge popular support. However, a plan to pedestrianize part of the prestigious Ginza area proposed by the reforming Governor of Tokyo Minobe Ryōkichi and supported by the Chief of the Metropolitan Police was thwarted by store-owners. In September 1970, there was a nationwide 'Sunday Promenade' initiative to close a main street to traffic and hold promenades. In Nagoya, the main road from Sakae-machi, the principal shopping area, to Yabecho was closed to traffic and was thronged with people on Sundays (see Figure 4.4). However, the initiative was short-lived. Because of increasing congestion on Sundays, cars were once again allowed free-rein in the city after the Sunday Promenades were cancelled in the 1980s.[134]

Conclusion

In this chapter we began by charting the experience of automobility from Morris Zapp's euphoria of driving on the Birmingham motorway to the excitement of the Tokyo crowds as they queued and jostled to see and experience the new cars at the Tokyo Motor Show. In the same period, however, a dystopian view of automobility emerged as the promise of freedom afforded by the motor car was tempered by congestion, traffic casualties and the challenges of driving in new and unfamiliar road layouts. Increasingly evident, too, by 1970, was the exclusion of the 'no-car folk', the sections of the urban population disadvantaged and inconvenienced by the re-shaping of the city for the benefit of the car.

After the 1973 oil shock there was a more strident anti-car tone evident in the media in both Japan and Britain. The vexed issue of pollution from automobile emissions (examined in Chapter 5) strengthened the voices of an anti-car lobby and the energy crisis also marked the car out as a consumer of precious oil reserves. In Japan especially, the automobile craze was beginning to give way to the 'cycling craze,' reviving a 'practically dead' bicycle industry. In 1974 there were 30 million bicycles in Japan. Unfortunately, with them also came the attendant problem of cyclists' deaths. This included a high-profile death of avid cyclist Kurosawa Haruo, the Mayor of Sōka, a dormitory town near Tokyo, who was killed by a motorcyclist in August 1973. In this context, lack of space in Japan's cities proved even more of a menace to pedestrians, since they were now forced to share pavements with cyclists. But the brief lull in the supremacy of the car gave hope to some critics who thought the oil crisis a godsend:

> Whether we want it or not, it has given us the perfect chance to think about ourselves. And there may yet be time, if we act now before the automobile has utterly destroyed our land and our character, for the restoration of greenness to road-ravaged mountains; for the resurrection of the old villages and their gentle people.[135]

Such hopes were mostly illusory; as we shall see, the oil crisis proved to be merely a temporary truce in the traffic wars. Nevertheless, even before the crisis there was a tangible shift in public opinion which threatened the unassailable position of the automobile. Pedestrianism offers one vantage point to think about the shifting balance between the car and other forms of mobility in urban life. Mounting awareness of the pedestrian, the cyclist and the 'no-car folk' represented one indicator in Britain and Japan that mass automobility would not carry all before it. Private car dominance would give way – in certain places, under certain conditions – to plural mobilities, to walking, cycling, taking the train – and no longer to driving as the default mode of modern transportation.

5

Pollution and Protest

The problems of traffic on Japan's and Britain's roads did not cease with the building of new roads and motorways. Instead new roads merely added to growing public concern about noise and air pollution. As numbers of new drivers increased together with the volume of cars, buses and trucks, cities became ever more congested and more polluted. In the 1970s it became clear in Birmingham and Nagoya – and in many other cities in Britain and Japan – that road building and mass automobility were causing irreparable damage to the urban environment.

In May 1977 the *Sunday Times*, a leading British newspaper with a reputation for investigative journalism, published a highly critical article on Birmingham's Inner Ring Road. Based on a report conducted by an engineering consultant, Bernard Clark, the article claimed that only six years after it had been formally opened by the Queen, sections of the Inner Ring were falling apart. Water leaking into sections of the raised road structure was causing supporting beams to rust and concrete to crumble. Without expensive repairs, so the article suggested, Britain's first and most complete urban motorway would collapse within ten to fifteen years.

The *Sunday Times* report led to a major investigation into the state of the Inner Ring Road. Allegations of corruption were made involving City Council officials and the firm contracted to carry out much of the road construction work, Bryant Civil Engineering. There were accusations of a cover-up and the affair quickly became known as Birmingham's 'Watergate', a reference to the political scandal that engulfed the Nixon administration in America between 1972 and 1974.[1] It was not, however, a bolt out of the blue. The Clark report and subsequent scandal were only the last and perhaps the most symbolic act in what had become a rising tide of concern, inside and beyond Birmingham during the 1970s, about the impact of urban motorways and traffic on environment, safety and public health. From 1972, there was mounting criticism of the 'motor city' ideal which sometimes led, sometimes reflected, wider national opinion on the environmental effects of mass automobility. In Birmingham itself there were mounting protests about pollution, new roads and the effects of mass motorization on the quality of life in the city – what Colin Buchanan had earlier styled a 'civilized environment'.[2]

The early 1970s also marked a watershed in attitudes towards motorization and road construction in Nagoya, even before the city's major new motorway – the equivalent of the Inner Ring – was built. As the plan for the Nagoya Urban Expressway was given the green light in 1970, a few voices of discontent had, by the summer of

1971, become a tidal wave of opposition. A number of increasingly well-organized residents' groups demanded that construction be stopped because of environmental concerns. The Nagoya Expressway Corporation (NEC) and the City Council were forced to negotiate. Modifications issued in 1973 not only failed to satisfy protesters but also raised concerns in the City Council about the budget. Such was the furore that in March 1973 Mayor Sugito Kiyoshi froze the budget for the Expressway. The Nagoya Expressway, though, was not the sole target of protests; throughout Japan protesters were disrupting road planning.

This picture of public scandal and popular opposition mirrors wider historiographies which present the late 1960s and early 1970s as heralding a reaction against the urban modernism of the post-1945 era at the same time as the emergence of a modern environmental consciousness. The break has been seen as especially sharp in Britain. On the one hand, the late 1960s witnessed mounting criticism of expert-led town planning, following the collapse of a council-built tower block at Ronan Point, East London, in 1968 and a shift of opinion in favour of historic conservation in British towns and cities.[3] On the other, mounting concern with environmentalism was highlighted by a series of disasters such as the Torrey Canyon oil spill of 1967, intensively covered on television, radio and the press, and the beginning of roads protest with the campaign against the construction of the Westway, an elevated motorway through west London, from 1970. Official endorsement of the changing public consciousness was reflected by the formation of the Department of the Environment in 1970, bringing together the old Ministries of Transport, Housing and Local Government, and Public Building and Works.[4]

Historiographies of town planning and environmentalism have developed separately in Britain, partly due to disciplinary divisions and also because much of the new environmental history has been national and even international, rather than urban and local, in scale.[5] Equally, automobility and road protest barely register in Japanese environmental history which has concentrated on the nexus between citizen protest, NGOs and government action in dealing with well-publicized cases of industrial air and water pollution,[6] or on Japanese attitudes to 'nature' (*shizen*) in general.[7] In this chapter we bring these different histories together by focusing on two case studies. The first is of Birmingham, examining the six-year period between 1972 and 1978 when the attempt to remake Birmingham as Britain's premier 'motor city' began to unravel. The disclosure of the Inner Ring Road as fundamentally flawed in its construction was only one feature of what was to prove a swift and dramatic dénouement. Scarcely less significant was the part played by the city's motorways in the national debate about the dangerous effects of lead pollution from cars, triggered initially by Birmingham's Gravelly Hill Interchange, popularly known as Spaghetti Junction, in 1972. This was succeeded by widespread anti-car protests across the city in the years that followed, against proposed road developments, dangers from traffic and what was loosely termed 'loss of amenity'. Throughout the period the situation in Birmingham was further complicated by the effects of the oil crisis of 1973 and the concomitant economic crisis, which impaired government funding for roads and other infrastructure projects. In the case of Birmingham, in effect, we begin to see how the complex of factors encompassing urban governance, planning, mobility and environment interacted together, contributing to the dissolution of Manzoni's motor city ideal and to a wider questioning of the dominance of the private car in the urban context.

The second case study is that of Nagoya between 1967 and 1979 where protests against the construction of the Nagoya Urban Expressway effectively delayed its completion by almost ten years. In the early 1960s, the connection between automobiles, road-building and pollution was most visible in Tokyo where preparation for the 1964 Olympic Games led to a frenzy of demolition, population relocation, building and road construction. The journalist Robert Whiting was in Tokyo at the time and in a series of articles in the *Japan Times* commemorating the fiftieth anniversary of the Tokyo Olympics, he recalled what he saw:

> The transformation of Tokyo from a war-ravaged city into a major international capital, seemingly overnight, had a dark side that was rarely talked about. The games were in fact responsible for a great deal of environmental destruction and human misery in the capital and its environs, which I can attest to as one who was there.[8]

Tokyoites were not quiescent in the face of such destruction, and opposition movements increased in number and variety after 1964, often delaying or halting road construction in the capital. By the late 1960s similar opposition movements sprang up in most of Japan's major cities. While, in the 1960s and 1970s, these were usually locally oriented, taken together they were a common response to concerns about increasing motorization and plans involving large road construction projects. The newspapers of the day reveal specific health concerns such as polluting automobile emissions but also quality-of-life issues such as noise, vibration, right to sunshine, and interference with radio and television signals. The scale and breadth of local opposition was remarkable in a country recognized as having a generally poorly developed civil society. Even more remarkable was the extent to which it forced road corporations and local authorities to negotiate. Often, indeed, communities and activist groups persuaded planners to go back to the drawing board and offer alternative plans; if these later plans failed to properly address local concerns, construction was often halted, albeit temporarily.

Automobility and environmental awakening in the 1950s and 1960s

Concerns about the environmental effects of mass automobility were, of course, not new. In recognizing the significance of the case studies of Nagoya and Birmingham in the 1970s, we need to be aware of the build-up of environmental issues over the 1950s and 1960s. During this period automobility came to play a part in a wider environmental awakening in the developed world. If a modern environmental movement is often assumed to have radiated outwards from the United States, the cases of Japan and Britain suggest rather different genealogies. In both Japan and Britain air pollution from motor traffic had a leading role in the environmental drama, but it was a drama that unfolded in distinctive ways in the two countries. Understanding how automobility came to be entangled in environmental concerns in Japan and Britain at this earlier period is important in grasping the particular forms that protest against pollution and the car were to take in the 1970s in cities as wide apart as Nagoya and Birmingham.

In the early 1950s, air pollution in Japan was mostly industrial, although it was often difficult to distinguish between industrial pollution and pollution from other sources, such as motor vehicles. From the mid-1950s scientists in Japan began to publish papers on the increasing problem of air pollution, including a small number of articles on vehicle emissions.[9] In the mid-1950s air pollution began to be measured at a number of locations, mainly in the Tokyo area.[10] It was well-known that it had become more or less impossible to see Mount Fuji from Tokyo because of air pollution. In terms of cityscape this was highly significant because of the famous Thirty-Six Views of Mount Fuji, painted by Hokusai and Hiroshige in the nineteenth century. 'In the Tokyo area it was possible to observe a marked haze and decrease in visibility late on most afternoons and in the evening,' a visiting scientist reported in 1964. 'We learned that, because of this, helicopter pilots do not fly in the area after 4 pm.'[11] Although considerable research was carried out in Japan into atmospheric pollution during the 1950s and early 1960s, it was concerned primarily with measuring the concentrations of air pollutants from specific industrial sources. The first conference on air pollution research in Japan was held in 1959 which ultimately led to the formation of the Japan Society for Atmospheric Environment.[12]

Critically important to the debate on pollution from automobile emissions was the Yokkaichi asthma case which occurred in Mie Prefecture in the south of the Chūkyō region not far from Nagoya. According to the pioneering work of the environmental scholars Norie Huddle and Michael Reich, 'the history of Yokkaichi encapsulated the story of Japan's rapid development into an industrial state.'[13] In 1956 a British engineer working in Yokkaichi at the Shōwa Oil Refinery, a joint venture with British Shell, was having his lunch break. Pointing across the river towards a village called Isozu he remarked: 'Someday that little village might become unliveable.' When his remark was interpreted for a group of fishermen, they laughed in disbelief. After all they had been reading a government brochure about a master plan for the area drafted by regional development experts who spoke of the 'birth of a new industrial city with abundant sunlight and green spaces.'[14] The region was well-known for its pristine natural environment, excellent fishing waters and fertile farms; it was unimaginable that the fishermen's way of life would be altered by the planned new city. The promise of a shiny new railway station and a modern, wide expressway could only bring their markets closer. Residents took pride in being given a chance to play their part in forging the new Japan. During the Meiji Period, the area had been bypassed by the Tōkaidō railway attracting trade and commerce away from Yokkaichi to Nagoya. However, the harbour area had been extensively developed and, by the 1930s, was an important naval base with its oil refineries making it a target for Allied bombers during the war. Almost totally destroyed in the firestorms, in 1955 it was to be redeveloped as one of Japan's largest petrochemical complexes or *kombinato* in imitation of the Russian *kombinat*.[15]

In 1959 the first massive complex went into 24-hour operation. When the night lights were turned on residents in nearby towns and villages marvelled at the twinkling night scene. Visitors throughout the region came to share the 'million dollar view' as a tourist attraction. However, by spring 1960 in nearby Isozu it had become apparent to some 3,000 residents that their lives were becoming blighted, not only by constant noise but also by noxious odours. Residents asked officials politely whether something could be done about the noise and the smell. Just as politely, their requests were brushed aside on the grounds that economic development must come first. On one July day, the whole area was blanketed by fumes, forcing a primary school to close. Frightened children made their way home after being told by teachers to 'breathe as little as possible'.[16] In August 1960 the Yokkaichi City Pollution Countermeasures Council consisting of four city councillors, four industry representatives and three university professors was established to investigate the incident. In March 1961, their report confided that levels of sulphur dioxide were six times higher in Isozu than elsewhere in Yokkaichi, but the report was kept confidential. Numerous cases of asthma among children continued to be recounted by concerned mothers and a rise in respiratory problems was also noted among the elderly. Residents grew angry, held meetings and demanded to see the report. Their case was taken up by the opposition Socialist Party, but the Council still refused to publish the data. In 1963 another petrochemical complex was opened, by which time 'Yokkaichi asthma' was becoming a well-known disease.[17] In January 1964, a 62-year-old Isozu man, Furukawa Yoshiro, died in a special 'pollution-free' room in Shiohama Hospital and became the first known fatality from pollution-related disease. The case attracted media attention and protesters became increasingly well-organized. When, on 10 July 1966, an elderly, impoverished asthma victim committed suicide, Otani Kihira, a respected local leader, led a silent procession through the city carrying a framed ceremonial death picture of the victim only to find that the mayor was apparently 'too busy' to receive a deputation carrying a series of demands. One year later Otani himself committed suicide rather than suffer a lingering death from pollution-related respiratory disease.[18] As with all pollution cases in Japan at this time, only crisis, desperation and tragedy would embolden citizens and force the hand of the authorities into taking action.

Yokkaichi was the second of the so-called 'Big Four' pollution incidents. The first was a poisoning scandal caused by effluent dumped into Minamata Bay in Kumamoto Prefecture by a chemical fertilizer plant owned by the Chisso Corporation. In the 1950s hospitals in the area began admitting patients suffering from damage to the nervous system. It was discovered that it was caused through eating contaminated seafood containing methyl mercury. Tragically, the neurotoxin also crossed the placenta causing babies to be born with severe, sometimes horrific, symptoms of nerve damage. Protests in Minamata began in 1959, and the scandal made global news when the American photojournalist Eugene Smith published photographs of the victims in the 1970s.[19] At the same time, the world's press was full of photographs of traffic policemen wearing what appeared to be gas-masks in polluted cities such as Osaka and Tokyo. These images were exploited by William D. Ruckleshaus, the head of the newly established Environment Protection Agency in the United States, in his support for the Clean Air Act which eventually came into force in America in 1970. On the other side of the world, engineers in Finland designing a new petrochemical plant carefully examined the petrochemical plant in Yokkaichi.[20] The ecologist Paul Ehrlich described

Japan as the 'miner's canary', warning other nations of the dangers of unchecked pollution.[21] According to environmental historian Simon Avenell: 'Japan's ascent as a polluters' paradise and the struggles of its pollution victims propelled the country to the very forefront of a historic global environmental awakening in the 1960s.'[22] Legally, the Minamata and Yokkaichi court cases would also have enormous implications for the success of roads protests, particularly in Nagoya.

Political protest was far from unknown in Japan. In May and June 1960, when the Japanese government was about to negotiate a revised Treaty of Mutual Cooperation and Security with the United States, the country witnessed some of the largest protests in its history. Known as the 'Anpo' protests, they forced the cancellation of a planned visit to Japan by President Dwight D. Eisenhower and the resignation of Prime Minister Kishi Nobusuke. It represented 'the most significant political crisis in post-war Japan'.[23] However, security treaty revision was a high-profile national issue and the protests were centred on Tokyo, attracting huge media attention. Pollution at this time was still a local issue and Isozu a largely unknown village in the provinces.

As in the Minamata case, the development of environmental protest in Yokkaichi followed a characteristic path. Ui Jun, an environmental activist who, as a graduate student in the early 1960s, was involved in making the connection between methyl mercury and Minamata disease, wrote about the 'singularities of Japanese pollution' in 1972. The Japanese experience of pollution, especially in the post-war period, was so intense that a new word 'public hazard' (*kōgai*) had been invented to describe it.[24] 'Urban pollution', he argued:

> particularly atmospheric pollution, has been known for some long time in various cities in Europe and American, but it is only recently that the atmospheric pollution caused by fumes and exhaust gases produced by factories has come to be regarded as a problem.[25]

Significantly, even for this leader of the transnational environmental movement against pollution, exhaust gases were associated with factories, rather than automobiles. The point he was making, however, was about the emergence of a pattern of reaction and counter-reaction to pollution cases when they arose which was not specific to Japan but was being repeated globally. Pollution outbreaks went through four stages, which Ui summarized as: 'outbreak, identification, refutation and solution.'[26] After an outbreak, every effort was made to identify the cause, but, as he pointed out, there are always those who deny the truth and seek to refute some, if not all, of the findings. Surprisingly, he alleged that those seeking to refute evidence were not always the polluters or 'victimizers', but sometimes university professors.[27] There is no doubt that some academics covered up evidence. According to Simon Avenell, Ui and his colleague, both young graduates at the time, had lacked the confidence to go public with the evidence linking Minamata disease to methyl mercury, something Ui deeply regretted later.[28] Finally, a solution would be reached, but this was not always entirely to the satisfaction of the victims.

As we shall see, the roads protest movements in Japan followed a rather similar path to campaigns against industrial pollution, but they were different in one significant aspect: they were acting pre-emptively to *prevent* pollution. Their first problem was to find proof that automobile exhaust gases were a contributory factor to photochemical smog and respiratory diseases. Roads protesters were also able to cite other types of pollution such as noise, vibration, loss of light and radio and TV signals to strengthen their case. In other words, they fought for general quality of life issues. Their fight was not against polluters themselves, such as motor manufacturers, but against local politicians, the various expressway corporations and related agencies. One common feature was the realization that: 'The only deterrent force impeding the relentless progress of pollution in Japan are the citizens' movements ... launched by individuals banding together at the grass-roots level.'[29]

The Minamata and Yokkaichi pollution cases blazed a trail, largely in terms of legal settlements, but also in providing a model for citizen protest. It was the landmark Mishima-Numazu case, though, that would set a precedent to follow for anti-roads construction campaigners. From 1963 to 1964 citizens from Mishima and neighbouring Numazu in Shizuoka Prefecture, Central Japan, mounted a highly organized campaign against proposals to build a petrochemical plant in their area, and succeeded in preventing its construction. They were inspired by newspaper reports about pollution in Yokkaichi, but not only did they re-invent the terms *shimin* (citizen) and *shimin undō* (citizens' movement) to link them specifically to protests against pollution, they also shifted the focus of environmental activism from concerns about compensation to concerns about prevention.[30]

In June 1967, the first large-scale civil law suit to be brought against a polluter in Japan was filed against the Chisso Corporation, the fertilizer company at the centre of the Minamata mercury poisoning case. The Minamata case offered a potent example of legal action against pollution, and Yokkaichi's asthma sufferers were now backed by a powerful association comprising members of a number of unionized professions, including teachers and local authority workers. Supported by a team of fifty-six lawyers, nine Yokkaichi asthma victims were persuaded to file for civil damages against six companies of the Shiohama *kombinat* in September 1967.[31] The anti-pollution revolution had begun in Japan.

Like Minamata, the Yokkaichi case began to change the legal landscape of pollution litigation in Japan and the Mishima-Numazu case provided a model of activism based on prevention by 1970. As regards government action on pollution from automobiles, it is often claimed that the impetus for change came from the United States. Changes to legislation in California to reduce carbon monoxide and hydrocarbons in vehicle emissions certainly had an impact on both Japanese and British manufacturers, including the British Motor Corporation at Longbridge, since almost a third of British car exports went to the United States in the late 1950s. Toyota's main rival, the maverick Honda Soichirō, had the foresight to develop the 'clean automobile engine' in the 1960s when vehicle emissions became a major issue in Honda's Los Angeles base.[32] UK-based organizations such as the Motor Industry Research Association (MIRA) and the Warren Spring Laboratory likewise began to investigate air-based car pollution by the 1960s. For the British case, Matthew Parker argues that priorities derived from export markets rather than official concerns about public health drove research which increasingly also focused on invisible rather than visible pollutants, especially carbon monoxide.[33]

However, just as the 1970 Clean Air Act was passed in the United States, the Japanese Ministry of Transport drew up proposals on automobile emissions in 1970 for implementation in 1975. According to Phyllis Genther, it is not the case, as is often claimed, that Japanese regulation on emissions was governed by the need to export cars to the United States. Rather, the imposition of new environmental standards by the Ministry of Transport was a response to photochemical smog which appeared in a number of Japanese cities in 1970. American regulations in 1971 became an added incentive to Japanese automobile manufacturers who had already been consulted by the Ministry so that they could begin the necessary research and development to meet the new standards by 1975. In September 1971 jurisdiction for automobile emissions policy was transferred to the newly created Environment Agency which faced immense political pressure to draw up long-term automobile emissions control immediately.[34]

For Britain, industrial pollution had a long pre-history and was thus not the precursor to environmental concerns about mass automobility as in Japan. Rather, official concern in Britain focused on traffic. More specifically, the setting up of the Buchanan Study Group on *Traffic in Towns* in Britain in 1961 was prompted by fears about the consequences of the spread of automobility for the quality of urban life, fears which the ensuing Report intensified rather than dampened. 'All the indications are', the Report warned, 'that given its head the car would wreck our towns within a decade'. 'Environment' was a key term in the Buchanan report, designating the qualitative condition of the physical surroundings as well as an ecological dimension. An important recommendation of the Report was that local authority planners should seek to estimate a town's 'environmental capacity', calculated in relation to noise level, air pollution and visual blight.[35] Beyond Britain, too, there was mounting evidence of the polluting effects of cars and urban traffic. As early as 1950 a clear causal link was made between car exhaust emissions and atmospheric smog in the case of Los Angeles, which notoriously suffered from the problem. Over the decade that followed analysis of urban air pollution in the United States established a number of other damaging effects to health and environment. The American lawyer and anti-car campaigner Ralph Nader argued in 1965 that automobiles were 'pollution factories on wheels' as well as a danger to life and limb.[36] Both the Los Angeles case and Nader's critique were well-known in Britain, together with the successful campaigns of Jane Jacobs against the building of the Lower Manhattan Expressway in New York and the publication of Rachel Carson's classic exposé of the effects of DDT, *Silent Spring*, in the early 1960s.[37]

Air pollution was not the only concern; from the later 1950s noise from motor traffic also aroused considerable disquiet. In 1960 the British parliament established a Committee on the Problem of Noise under the chairmanship of Sir Alan Wilson, scientist and deputy chairman of Courtaulds, a leading company in chemicals and textiles. The Wilson Committee's final report, produced in 1963, observed that 'in London (and, no doubt, in other large towns), road traffic is, at the present time, the predominant source of annoyance from noise, and no other single noise is of comparable importance'.[38] As a result, the Committee proposed regulating vehicle noise levels, with a maximum of 85 decibels (dBA) for cars and 90 dBA for motorcycles. In Japan, likewise, traffic noise emerged as a problem and proved difficult to regulate. Nimura Tadamoto, an expert on acoustic engineering, claimed in 1984 that despite its burgeoning reputation for environmental regulation Japan 'remains the country with the worst noise pollution'. According to Sano Yoshiko, president of the 1,500-member Noise Pollution Sufferers Association, noise was associated with industrial productivity, much as smoke pollution had been in Britain at the beginning of the twentieth century: 'When Japan was rapidly developing, it was thought that the more noise there was, the greater the success.'[39] One problem was that Japanese wooden houses were particularly vulnerable to ever-increasing noise and vibration from traffic, prompting opposition to road widening in Nagoya's residential districts and demands to exclude traffic from residential areas, especially from women and the elderly.[40] The implementation of the Unit Cell Scheme in residential areas of Nagoya from 1972, as we shall see in the next chapter, was partially successful in reducing noise in some cells by around 3 dBA from an average of 59 dBA.[41]

By the later 1960s the combination of automobile and industrial pollution was so severe in urban Japan, an Organisation for Economic Co-operation and Development (OECD) report observed, that 'Tokyoites wore face masks while traffic policeman carried small oxygen cylinders during their shifts'. First aid stations were provided to treat people overcome by toxic fumes.[42] Pollution from vehicles was in large measure a product of congestion. The Basic Law for Environmental Pollution Control (*Kōgai Taisaku Kihon Ho*) enacted by the Diet in 1967 was an attempt to set standards for six kinds of pollution: air, water, noise, vibration, subsidence and offensive odours, with soil being added in 1970. According to historian Miranda Schreurs, the Basic Law for Environmental Pollution Control was among the first of its kind in the world and was important in installing pollution monitoring and setting environmental standards.[43] However, the Ministry for International Trade and Industry (MITI) insisted on modifying Article 1 of the Ministry of Welfare's draft to ensure that anti-pollution measures were 'in harmony with the healthy development of the economy', effectively drawing the teeth from the law. It was only after the Big Four pollution cases had led to a series of successful law suits, that the Diet reinstated the original wording of the law and over-ruled MITI during the so-called 'Pollution Diet' of 1970 (*kōgai kokkai*, the 64th session, November 24 to December 18, 1970).[44]

Indeed, figures for reduction in emissions of nitrogen oxides showed Japan leading the way for a time in the early 1970s. In contrast to the adversarial government-business relations in the United States, where environmental regulation was contested by industry pressure, Japan's government-business consensus allowed them to find solutions to environmental questions more quickly than elsewhere, particularly in terms of paying compensation to the automobile industry and other concessions.[45] Yet Japanese democratic processes also had a part to play. Frances Rosenbluth and Michael Thies have argued that without the unusually strong electoral pressure for environmental controls existing in the late 1960s and early 1970s, the automobile industry, among others, was quite easily able to dodge the costs of such governmental control.[46]

It was precisely in these years that government in Britain was also constituting environment as an object of intervention, as the establishment of the Department of the Environment in 1970 indicated. Here, too, air pollution from automobiles played its part in raising environmental awareness. In 1969 the British government established a Central Unit on Environmental Pollution which swiftly produced a White Paper on the subject, *The Protection of the Environment: The Fight against Pollution*. Apart from a rising concern with the subject, what this and other official reports revealed was the lack of expert consensus, particularly regarding the environmental and public health effects of mass automobility. The 1969 White Paper, *The Protection of the Environment*, for example, argued that car emissions in British towns and cities were much less acute than in the United States, that there was no evidence that carbon monoxide represented a danger to urban public health and that the lead produced from exhaust fumes was 'trivial'.[47] By contrast, the government's *Pollution: Nuisance or Nemesis* Report in 1972 took seriously the potential threat of lead pollution and criticized the absence of legislation to control vehicle emissions. It was also far-sighted, observing that personal mobility might need to be reduced in future while acknowledging that it was 'very difficult, politically, to persuade people to make sacrifices in the 1970s to avert what might be unprecedented environmental disasters in the early twenty-first century', presciently articulating the motorization/environment or 'ME dilemma'.

By the early 1970s, then, mass automobility in Japan and Britain no longer appeared as an automatic good as it had to many politicians and consumers in the 1960s. Slogans such as the 'car-owning democracy' and the 'My Car Era' came to seem glib and selfish when confronted by the series of interrelated environmental problems to which mass motorization gave rise. These costs would become all too apparent in both countries during the decade that followed. How this happened on the ground can be observed by examining successively events in Birmingham and Nagoya during the 1970s.

Birmingham: The challenge of Spaghetti Junction

Gravelly Hill Interchange, popularly called Spaghetti Junction because of its knot of intersecting over- and underpasses, was intended by its planners to be the final piece in the jigsaw of Birmingham's urban motorway system, linking the Inner Ring Road and Aston Expressway to the major national M6 and M5 motorways (Figure 5.1). When it was opened in 1972 it represented the largest free-flowing roads interchange in Europe, achieved by a series of curving flyovers, free of roundabouts and traffic lights. Within two months, though, the new Interchange was at the centre of a public row about traffic noise, environmental degradation and – soon after – potentially dangerous levels of lead pollution believed to derive from vehicle exhaust emissions. These issues, especially lead pollution, were fiercely debated and Birmingham's Gravelly Hill became an important test case in a national debate about car pollution in Britain that lasted throughout the 1970s.

When the Gravelly Hill controversy first broke in July 1972, it was at a moment of high sensitivity in Britain to issues of automobility and pollution without any consensus having been reached on their exact inter-relationship. It was noise pollution that initially provoked matters. In July 1972 Birmingham's newly appointed Air Pollution and Noise Abatement Inspector, Frank Reynolds, reported that 'the opening of the link has produced a sudden and severe deterioration in the environment of many hundreds of Birmingham citizens.'[48] Residents in the neighbourhoods adjacent to the

Figure 5.1 Aerial view of Gravelly Hill Interchange (Spaghetti Junction), 2008. Source: Highways Agency, Creative Commons.

Interchange and the Aston Expressway began to voice protest. One woman spoke of the 'brainwashing noise' from the motorway, while others spoke of barricading walls of their houses with mattresses and hardwood to try to keep the noise out. A government-funded study of noise levels in houses near to the newly opened M6 at Perry Bar found traffic from cars averaging 64 mph to create noise levels of between 74 and 67 dBA. This was within the limits set by the Wilson Committee of 1963 but did not take into account the psychological and health effects produced by continuous noise at these levels.[49]

Protest spread across the city. In December 1972 the newly formed Calthorpe Park and Lee Bank Tenants' Association, with some six hundred members, demanded to speak with the City Engineer, Neville Borg, about plans for the Middle Ring Road which was due to pass close by local housing estates. Residents pointed to the forthcoming Land Compensation Bill regarding the need to take into account compensation for noise disturbance from new motorway schemes.[50] Indeed, the problems in Birmingham featured largely in parliamentary debates during the Bill's passage. Julius Silverman, Labour MP for Aston in which Gravelly Hill was sited, was especially vituperative in his condemnation of the Interchange in a speech in November 1972. Gravelly Hill 'emits intolerable noise, fumes and dirt', he expostulated.

> As an engineering construction it is superb. As a work of art it is one of the greatest monstrosities which any Government has inflicted upon any section of this country.

Nor did the complaints recede. In 1974 a local Labour MP, Peter Snape, informed the House of Commons that his constituents 'frequently write to tell me about what they call the "living hell" on their doorsteps – the thundering traffic which makes an unbroken night's sleep a half-forgotten memory'. Some 35 per cent of the urban population of Britain was regularly exposed to 'excessive traffic noise', a survey suggested in the same year.[51]

Meanwhile, the effects of traffic at Gravelly Hill ignited a still more toxic dispute. In late 1971 Birmingham's Medical Officer of Health had instigated a study undertaken by Dr Robert Butler of Aston University into lead in the air from traffic around Gravelly Hill, some six months before the opening of the Interchange. The study was the first in Britain 'designed to look at the introduction of a motorway interchange in a city and to attempt to relate the consequent atmospheric lead levels with the blood lead levels of residents living nearby'.[52] That motorway traffic might be causing air pollution was already suspected. Days before the Interchange opened, a local Conservative MP, Sydney Chapman, addressed the Junior Minister for Environment, Eldon Griffiths in parliament: 'I will hold the dubious distinction of having a constituency [Handsworth] which is almost entirely encircled by urban motorways,' Chapman announced. 'There is genuine concern among my constituents about the level of atmospheric pollution.'[53] Expert opinion in Birmingham was divided about the effects of lead pollution in the Gravelly Hill area and the wider city. In August 1972, three months after the opening of the Interchange and the stretch of the M6 motorway to the east of the city centre, the Aston scientist Dr Butler pronounced that lead levels around Gravelly Hill had actually fallen since the previous year. By November, however, a Birmingham University chemist, Dr Robert Stephens, was reported as saying that 'children living in big cities risk brain damage from the large amounts of lead in dust' and that 'more than 90% of airborne lead came from car exhausts'.[54] Evidence was emerging from North American scientists that pollution from leaded petrol in motor vehicles was affecting the nervous system of children, the group most sensitive to it, as well as causing cardiovascular disease in adults.[55] But experts within the city could not reach agreement on the scale of the threat or its causes, partly because they were drawing on different sources, Butler on purely local studies, Stephens on international reports of lead pollution emanating from North America.

Gravelly Hill continued to be at the centre of national debate. Four hundred people lived within 100 metres of the Interchange and 4,000 within 300 hundred metres. In April 1974 it was reported to parliament that a 'drastically significant increase' of levels of lead had been found in the blood of people living in the vicinity; evidence from a sample of 100 residents showed that levels had risen by 80 per cent between 1972 and 1974.[56] In the light of the new findings, and the persistent concerns regarding the environmental effects of traffic at Spaghetti Junction, the new Minister of the Environment, Dennis Howell, himself MP for Birmingham Small Heath, established a parliamentary Joint Working Party on Lead Pollution at Gravelly Hill. Its initial report, presented in December 1974, played down fears about lead levels, arguing that 'they were in no way exceptional for urban areas' and 'there is no danger of these people developing chemical lead poisoning' while acknowledging that the long-term effects of exposure to lead from traffic were unknown.[57] Controversy and uncertainty dogged the Working Party throughout its active life. The verdict of its final report in May 1978 was no less upbeat than its first report, the press release being headlined

'No cause for concern about lead pollution at Gravelly Hill.' At the press conference, however, Dr Robert Stephens, the Birmingham University chemist who had been a long-term member of the group, broke ranks, claiming that one in five children under 13 in inner Birmingham were 'experiencing a disturbance of central nervous system functions because of elevated body burdens of lead'. New research from Germany, Canada and the United States, he argued, showed that there was a direct correlation in children between low IQ performance and high levels of lead in teeth.[58] Later the same year, scientists working at the Atomic Energy Authority at Harwell appeared to corroborate his views, suggesting that the risks from lead levels had been severely underestimated by the Gravelly Hill Working Party. On the back of this, the British Society for Responsibility in Science accused both the lead industry and government of a cover-up.[59] By late 1970 Birmingham's Environmental Health Department appeared to have conceded the case, distributing a leaflet to all households listing the dangers of lead, including those from traffic. 'Do not leave a baby in a pram near heavy traffic,' it warned. 'Discourage children from playing in or near busy streets. Keep windows facing traffic closed.'[60]

Given the vague and often contradictory findings of the experts, residents were unsurprisingly vocal in their anger. A local action committee was set up at Gravelly Hill which was consulted by Denis Howell, Minister for the Environment, prior to announcing the Working Party. The committee's vice-chairman, Reg Dawson, demanded a clear scientific statement about lead levels and radical action if they were proven to be higher than public health guidelines deemed safe. 'If the area is past that stage [i.e. above acceptable levels], then they should clear the area of people ... They've put a vast motorway system in the heart of a city. The idea was good at the time, but since then experts have said, never again anywhere else.'[61]

The City Council, too, acknowledged the problems caused by Gravelly Hill. 'If we had known what we know now', the Labour leader of the City Council, Stanley Yapp, confessed in March 1973, 'I am certain we would not now have Spaghetti Junction in its present form.'[62] While the health and environmental effects of urban motorways continued to be fiercely contested, by 1974 the balance of public and expert opinion had begun to swing away from Manzoni's vision of the modern motor city.

The growth of protest in Birmingham

In June 1972, just after the opening of the Gravelly Hill Interchange, the *Times* commented that 'unlike the fight put up by many Londoners against urban road schemes, the authorities have found little resistance to their plans in Birmingham.'[63] In reflecting on the emergence of roads protest the newspaper was alluding to the campaigns against the London Ringways scheme orchestrated from 1971 by bodies such as the London Motorway Action Group and Homes Before Roads.[64] Controversy over noise and lead pollution at Gravelly Hill Interchange altered this picture; roads protest was no longer confined to the capital. Yet Gravelly Hill itself was only part of a much wider wave of protests against motorways that overtook Birmingham from the early 1970s, adding a new layer of activism to local politics.

One aspect was local opposition to new roads, including by-passes, affecting residential areas. In Birmingham, this concerned not only the Inner Ring, which passed through 'slum' areas where the Corporation had used compulsory purchase orders to buy up and demolish large tracts of housing, but also the Middle Ring which passed through more suburban areas. One such area was Moseley and Kings Heath, neighbouring Victorian suburbs on the south side of the city. Here a by-pass had been proposed by the Corporation in May 1973, linked to the construction of the Middle Ring and a proposal for a new Midlands to Southampton motorway.[65] The by-pass, estimated to cost £8 million in 1975, threatened 324 houses which required to be demolished in the process; if built, residents claimed, south Birmingham would be divided by 'a canyon filled with motor vehicles'.[66] The leafy southern suburbs were very different socially from the predominantly working-class areas of Aston and Perry Bar that adjoined Gravelly Hill and were home to a high number of politically active professionals. Even before the Corporation's proposals for the by-pass were agreed by the Council's Public Works Committee, the Kings Heath and Moseley Motorway Action Committee (KHAMMAC) had been formed, the name echoing the London Motorway Action Group which had just successfully won its battle to halt the capital's Ringways scheme. Over the next three years, KHAMMAC evolved an imaginative repertoire of tactics to publicize its case and pressure the Council to stop the by-pass. A torchlight protest parade was held in the centre of Birmingham; city councillors were 'hijacked' in Kings Heath by mothers with babies who forced them to take a tour of the proposed route and pressed them to reopen the local railway station; and the Labour leader of the Council, Stanley Yapp, was deluged by 250 letters opposing the by-pass, delivered to his home address.[67] In response, the Council sought a compromise, including tunnelling the road under Kings Heath at a cost of £1.5 million, but to no avail. By late 1976 it was in full retreat over the road, facing widespread accusations in the local press and in parliament that delay was causing blight in the area and that the episode had become a 'farce'. In May 1977 the scheme was scrapped following a decision of the West Midlands County Council Transport and Highways Committee.[68]

Indeed, within a year of the completion of Birmingham's Inner Ring network of urban motorways, road protests were breaking out all over the city. At Colton Hackett in June 1974, residents opposed a road extension to the British Leyland Longbridge plant, claiming 'the cars are bumper to bumper ... and the place is absolutely thick with exhaust fumes'; at Nechells Parkway in November 1974 mothers blockaded the road to demand a safety barrier to protect children from traffic.[69] Women as mothers played a leading part in these protests, acting in the name of children at risk from the new road systems. In 1969 a group of women in Princip Street, a terrace of working-class housing close to the Inner Ring Road, took direct action, painting a pedestrian crossing on the street at 2 am to highlight the threat to their children from through-traffic.[70] They had good reason for their fears: it emerged in 1974 that Birmingham had the highest rate of traffic accidents involving children of any area in Britain, the numbers of such accidents having risen by 24 per cent since 1969, precisely the years when new motorways were being opened across the city.[71] Such roads were inherently dangerous and not just for children. In the first three months of 1970 alone there were 29 deaths and 1,510 people injured in traffic accidents across the city.[72] Driving home from his job as a security officer at the BBC Pebble Mill on a June evening in 1975, Peter Sayer's car collided with a concrete support pillar in St Chad's underpass on the Inner Ring. Firemen worked for half an hour to free him but by the time they reached him, he was dead. St Chad's was indeed a 'death trap'; in 1972/3 the tunnel witnessed twelve major collisions and two fatalities.[73]

Safety was also a significant worry on Birmingham's newest and most experimental road. From its inception the Aston Expressway, connecting the Inner Ring with Gravely Hill and the national motorway system, was a source of concern, particularly regarding its reversible middle lane for tidal flow. Less than a year before the opening of the road in 1972, the *Birmingham Post* published two major articles on the Expressway, arguing on the basis of a similar scheme in Montreal that serious accidents would ensue: 'On the figures available it is expected that one person will either be killed or seriously injured on the Aston Expressway every nine days.' As well as head-on collisions, there were fears of mass 'pile-ups' caused by driver confusion in the face of a barrage of overhead signals.[74] Confronted with the rising tide of damaging evidence about the effects of mass automobility, the *Birmingham Mercury* struck a doleful chord in March 1970: 'There are times when the motoring picture seems one of unrelieved gloom: more cars and more fumes (one vehicle to every twenty-four yards of road now); more accidents (an estimated one car in eight in an accident this year); more fatalities (nineteen people killed each day last year).'[75] Only the paradox that the city's motor manufacturing sector was a major contributor to this predicament seemed to escape critics' attention.

That attitudes to automobility were shifting in Birmingham were further confirmed from an altogether different direction: pedestrianization. Keeping the city centre accessible to traffic had been a cardinal tenet in the planning of the Inner Ring. Following the North American example of restricting car access would be an 'ostrich act', Herbert Manzoni pronounced in 1959, and the view persisted among the city's politicians and planners throughout the 1960s.[76] By 1970, however, pressure was growing from retail interests as well as office workers and shoppers to exclude traffic from the constricted and congested city centre. The City Corporation was forced to back down from its former position and in November 1972 streets in the central area became pedestrian only. A year later expenditure on Birmingham roads, including the extension of the Middle Ring Road, was abruptly cut short by the effects of the international oil crisis, compounding economic recession in Britain in the winter of 1973/4. In February 1974 work on all road improvement schemes in the West Midlands was put on hold for fifteen months and in October all major road programmes in Birmingham went under review.[77]

The result was that, for the first time, a public debate ensued in Birmingham and more widely about the significance and direction of the 'motor revolution' of the previous twenty years. In January 1974, with British industry on a 'three-day week' and oil prices having quadrupled in the previous two months, the *Birmingham Post* reported on a conference of transport experts at Birmingham University. Speakers, the *Post* reported, saw the oil hike as having merely intensified what was a much deeper crisis. The car had become a version of Frankenstein's monster, despoiling the environment while at the same time destroying itself, since mass automobility was outpacing the capacity of the road system to accommodate it. 'Car ownership is theoretically expanding to the nth degree,' a speaker explained, 'but land space is not and there is a limit to which we can go in polluting our atmosphere'. Janusz Kolbuszewski, Britain's first professor of traffic engineering, proposed the neologism 'slurb' to describe the way in which formerly pleasant suburbs degenerated into slums through planning blight caused by new urban expressways such as the Middle Ring. Above all, the conference emphasized the critical dilemma which a motorized society was now forced to confront: 'Mobility is threatened because we all have it.' As a result, the *Post* urged, 'government and, indeed, society as a whole need to think furiously not only about such things as passenger conveyor belts, advanced passenger trains, underground roads and so on, but about the whole concept of travel.'[78] By 1974 the contours of the ME dilemma were beginning to become clearer. Motorization and environment appeared to many transport experts as a zero-sum game; the more society had of one, the less it might have of the other.

Nemesis

With the ending of the oil shock and the establishment of the Joint Working Party on Lead Pollution at Gravelly Hill in March 1974, the immediate crisis in Birmingham over the effects of mass automobility passed. The issues did not wholly go away but rather resurfaced sporadically in protests about new roads and delays to the Middle Ring caused by compensation claims. In April 1977 the *Birmingham Mail* featured an article on a section of dual carriageway underpass, built as part of the Hockley flyover, now lying abandoned with grass and trees sprouting through the tarmac. 'Times have changed,' reflected the article, 'and there is no longer justification to complete it'; such roads seemed to be remnants of a previous era.[79] Within months of this elegy to an unloved past, however, the controversy over Birmingham's urban motorways reignited with unexpected force.

The controversy concerned the Inner Ring Road, the pioneering motorway which had so long been the symbol of the city's aspiration and status as a 'motor city'. In mid-May 1977 cracks were noticed on the Inner Ring at Masshouse Circus, causing the underpass to be temporarily closed for investigation. Worse was to come. On 29 May the *Sunday Times*, a major national newspaper and sister of the London *Times*, published an article on the state of the Inner Ring Road. Based on a report by a civil engineer, Bernard Clark, it maintained that the Ring Road was falling apart.

> Rainwater pours down supporting beams, rusting the reinforcement; chunks of concrete have crumbled away from the corners of pillars and beams holding up an underpass; and hundreds of cracks are evident in wells and staircases along much of the three and three-quarter mile road.

Without massive investment, Clark predicted, Masshouse Circus and an earlier section of the road, Smallbrook Ringway, would collapse within a decade. Corruption was also alleged in the construction of the road involving the main contractors, Bryant Civil Engineering, and officials representing Birmingham City Council.[80]

The article was swiftly taken up by the Birmingham press and the County and City Councils together launched an enquiry, soon extended to all the city's major roads, flyovers, interchanges and some car parks. While West Midlands Police began to investigate the relationship between Bryant and Sydney Pigott, who had supervised the construction of the Inner Ring on behalf of the City Council, the Director of Public Prosecutions sought to establish whether a criminal case could be mounted.[81] Those implicated in the charges issued vigorous denials. While Bryant's management declared itself gravely concerned, the company simultaneously threatened to sue the *Sunday Times* for damages.[82] The local authorities were equally bullish in defence of the Inner Ring which was still seen by many as a flagship infrastructure project. David Bevan, chair of the County Council's Transport and Highways Committee, was dismissive of the public response to the newspaper article: 'There is absolutely no need for any kind of panic action at all,' he declared in mid-June. 'This new hysteria is out of place.'[83] The Interim Report of the West Midlands County Council, with input from Birmingham's City Engineer, which appeared in mid-July was equally sanguine, declaring the Inner Ring Road structurally 'sound', while acknowledging that it suffered from poor workmanship in places, including Masshouse Circus. The cost of maintenance of the road over the next five years was estimated at £400,000, which, while substantial, was hardly on the scale conjured up by Clark's original report.[84] The views of the Labour Minister for the Environment, Bill Rodgers, followed in the same vein, although the Department voiced criticism of Birmingham City (after 1974 District) Council's maintenance procedures for the Inner Ring.[85]

However, the *Sunday Times* exposé precipitated a slew of other critical articles on the Inner Ring in the local press in the summer of 1977. A report from the City Council on the state of the subways was given wide publicity in June. On 21 June the *Birmingham Post* relayed the Council's view of the subway by the Albany – formerly the city's landmark hotel – as 'seedy' and reflecting 'a deplorable image of the city'. It was followed by a call on 24 June from the chair of the Council's Leisure Services Committee to brick up all subways in the city centre to reduce the incidence of muggings.[86] Finally, on 28 June the *Post* published a major article entitled 'The depths of despair' on the dire state of the city's subways, especially those linking the Inner Ring to the central area.

> The redevelopment of Birmingham has been a malodorous affair. The latest emission [in the form of the subways] adds another unsavoury waft to the gaseous cloud and the ratepayers are experiencing some difficulty in seeing through the murk.[87]

As this implied, the *Post* saw the official investigations into the state of the Inner Ring as to all intents and purposes a cover-up. It had become, in the paper's phrase a 'Birmingham Watergate', a charge given additional substance by the fact that Rodgers and the Labour government refused to grant an independent enquiry.

The following month, on 24 July 1977, the *Sunday Times* published further allegations that seemed to confirm the *Post*'s suspicions. They claimed that the contract for construction work on Masshouse Circus in October 1963 had gone to Bryant Civil

Engineering in preference to a lower tender from Peter Lind favoured by Manzoni's successor as City Engineer, Neville Borg. Bryant Civil Engineering had been selected despite having little experience of major roads engineering, the article implied, because of connections to the City Council, in particular Labour councillors such as Albert Shaw whose plumbing firm had previously been employed as sub-contractors by Bryant. A further Council official, the engineering supervisor Sydney Piggott, had also been involved in the firm winning the contract. Piggott, it was revealed in the May *Sunday Times* article, had resigned from Birmingham City Council in July 1974 for 'irregularities in his relationship with contractors which amounted to misconduct'. In the July article it emerged that he had accepted from Bryant's an extension to his home at Kings Heath, a box at Ascot races, use of a holiday home in Bournemouth and a trip abroad.[88] While Piggott was never charged, three directors of Bryant were convicted of corruption in April 1978 for a total of twelve years, having secured contracts worth £112 million since 1963 from the Corporation with the assistance of officials such as Piggott, Shaw and the City Architect, Alan Maudsley, who had been sent to prison after an earlier enquiry in 1974. The extent of corruption stretching back to the 1960s encouraged the judge at the Bryant's trial to label Birmingham a 'municipal Gomorrah'.[89]

This was not quite an end of the matter. In March 1978 inspectors found high alumina cement in a number of concrete beams at St Chad's Circus on the Inner Ring. Local authorities had been required to investigate the use of high alumina cement by the Department of the Environment in 1974 after it had held responsible for the collapse of a roof at a school in east London. The cement was found to become unstable when exposed to salt and water, accelerating corrosion in the structure. The international engineering firm Ove Arup reportedly warned Birmingham's City Engineer that high alumina cement was located in subway beams on the ring road but no further investigation was undertaken.[90] While questions were raised about why it had taken three and a half years to follow up the problem, a survey swiftly carried out by County Council engineers found high alumina cement in nine places on the Inner Ring. In eight of these the construction work was found to have been carried out by Bryant Civil Engineering. For Stuart Mustow, County Surveyor, this episode was the final straw. In July 1978 he proposed that Birmingham's local authority should no longer have control over the maintenance of the Inner Ring Road and that from October that year responsibility should pass to the Roads Division of the West Midlands County Council. The proposal was endorsed by the Department of the Environment, and Birmingham District Council was forced to accede.[91] Ignominiously, Birmingham's civic authority was no longer deemed fit to oversee the road that had been the centrepiece of its post-war renewal.

From Yokkaichi to Nagoya

Events surrounding air pollution in Japan and Nagoya in the years around 1970 had uncanny similarities with those occurring almost 6,000 miles away in Birmingham. They did not so much follow the pattern of Birmingham as precede it, while also taking their own particular form. In Japan the question of pollution from automobiles paralleled more closely than in Britain the issue of pollution from industrial plants. It was at the moment in the late 1960s and early 1970s when the 'Big Four' cases of industrial pollution were going through the Japanese courts that air pollution from motor emissions began to affect events in Nagoya in the form of the planned Nagoya Urban Expressway, the city's equivalent of Birmingham's Inner Ring. The Yokkaichi case, especially, was to play its own part in the escalating protest which accompanied the planning and building of the Expressway in the 1970s.

Yokkaichi was one of twelve cities within a 40-kilometre radius of Nagoya's city centre. By the late 1950s it was clear that the proximity of these cities was making increasing demands on the traffic infrastructure connecting Nagoya and the rest of the Chūkyō region. Just as the Yokkaichi City Pollution Countermeasures Council issued its report in March 1961, Aichi Prefecture and Nagoya City began an Urban Arterial Street Survey commissioned by the Ministry of Construction. With the necessity of the Nagoya Urban Expressway established, an inordinately long process of consultation, survey work and sorting out legal complications began. A draft plan, the 'Overview of the Nagoya Urban Expressway Plan', was announced in April 1967, just months before the Yokkaichi asthma victims 35 kilometres (around 21 miles) away filed their lawsuit. In June 1967 the Nagoya City Expressway Construction Promotion Alliance Association, comprising business and other political interests, vigorously campaigned for construction to begin. Nagoya City Council and Aichi Prefecture came under enormous pressure to approve the plans as quickly as possible.

With the success of the Yokkaichi victims in the courts emboldening opposition groups all over Japan in the late 1960s, the media began highlighting the pollution threat from automobiles. In January 1968 the *Asahi Shimbun* made a specific link between traffic congestion and asthma. It referred to a condition which had become known as 'kan'nana zensoku' or '"kan'nana" asthma' located around Loop Seven (kan'nana) of one of the roads constructed for the Tokyo Olympics.[92] In Nagoya, the first anti-expressway group, the Ayuchi-dōri–Kagamigaike Line (Route) Opposition Alliance, was formed in December 1968 comprising residents living along the proposed expressway route in Shōwa Ward which extended out through Nagoya's middle-class, eastern suburbs. In February 1969 another opposition alliance was formed in the Higashiyama School District, further north in neighbouring Chikusa Ward. A series of Nagoya Expressway Opposition Liaison Conferences allowed residents to meet and file petitions with the aim of influencing official policy. The Higashiyama line was planned to link the Inner Expressway Loop to the Nagoya Interchange on the Tōmei Expressway. Residents expressed concerns about compensation and the purchasing of land along the route, as well as the environmental impact of the proposed route which partly consisted of three-lane carriageways on two levels. These elevated sections raised issues of the 'right to sunlight' (*nisshōken*).[93] Even before the NEC was formed, residents were beginning to organize in protest.

The Nagoya Expressway Public Corporation was established by the Nagoya City Council in early 1970. A new Regional Highways Public Corporation Bill was drafted and the budget for the Nagoya Urban Expressway Construction Project was submitted to the National Diet and passed on 17 April 1970. On 13 May, the Nagoya edition of the *Asahi Shimbun* published the plans in a balanced editorial presenting the arguments for and against the Expressway. The article put forward the views and opinions of both the City Council representatives who emphasized its vital importance to the economic well-being of the Nagoya region, and those of the various residents' associations that naturally voiced concerns about the impact of the road on residences in the area. Local shopkeepers were worried about the impact on their businesses, especially in regard to compensation claims relating to affected premises along the route. At this stage, however, the issue of noise and air pollution was secondary to increasing anger about the lack of consultation and the fact that residents' views were seemingly being ignored.[94]

With the media becoming increasingly critical of the attitudes of government and big-business towards pollution victims as demonstrated by the Big Four pollution cases, officials could no longer simply ignore complaints. When the draft plans for the expressway were discussed in Nagoya City Council's Urban Growth and Development Promotion Committee on 25 May, they were approved subject to the imposition of the 'Three Conditions'. The first condition included a tacit recognition that 'residents whose properties face on to the urban expressway believe they will suffer harm without receiving any direct benefit.' Consequently, special attention should be paid to roadside 'victims of urban development' making sure that, where possible, due consideration was given to 'recompensing victims for their sacrifice'. The second condition was that since construction was scheduled over a ten-year period, plans would need to be kept under review to deal with changes in the future. The third condition included a commitment to draw up plans for comprehensive urban transportation networks for the 'direct convenience' of residents.[95]

The language used in Three Conditions, especially the words 'victim' and 'sacrifice' and the notion of the unbalancing of harm and benefit, sheds light on the 'GE (growth/environment) dilemma' which affected Japan in a particular way. According to Jeffrey Broadbent the GE dilemma arises in any society where economic expansion outstrips nature's capacity to absorb the waste products of productive activity. Added to the resulting 'pollution debacle' there was also the 'urban debacle' where urban growth outstrips society's capacity to provide necessary infrastructure, such as roads and sewers. In particular: 'Those for whom the costs of pollution and other disruptions exceed the benefits of industrial growth are directly afflicted with the GE dilemma'.[96] Where once the Japanese were expected to sacrifice themselves for the emperor during the war, in the 1960s and early 1970s, it was for the so-called 'Ruling Triad' of powerful government ministries, the Liberal Democratic Party, in power from 1955, and 'big business' in their relentless pursuit of economic growth. The Ruling Triad had a long track record of either ignoring complaints from victims of pollution or trying to discredit them.[97]

This is not to deny that the government acted to prevent pollution. Indeed, the Ministry for International Trade and Industry was instrumental in pressurizing industry to reduce pollutants from the mid-1960s.[98] The Air Pollution Control Law was passed in 1968 and environmental records for air pollution began with a growing number of stations set up to monitor ambient air pollution and automobile emissions. In May 1969 the government announced the first white paper on pollution. The need to monitor and control pollution from both static industrial sources and mobile sources of emissions, such as automobiles, became increasingly evident.[99] The stations measured concentrations of sulphur dioxide, nitrogen dioxide, nitrogen monoxide, carbon monoxide and suspended particles. In addition, records for the number of days on which warnings about photochemical oxidants were issued and the numbers of persons affected also began in 1970, the year of the so-called 'Pollution Diet' which would ultimately introduce some of the most stringent air quality controls in the world.[100] In Nagoya itself, sulphur dioxide monitoring began in June 1970 covering 176 locations.[101] These measures merely served to raise consciousness about air quality, thus adding more fuel to roads protests up and down the country.

Roads protest was essentially a result of the convergence of the GE dilemma and the ME dilemma. That the Nagoya residents expressed anger about the lack of consultation and demanded that their views should be taken seriously betrays an increasing weariness and suspicion in regard to officialdom. Moreover, the usual tactic of buying 'victims' off with small concessions, often relatively small compensation packages, or rewarding the 'sacrifice' with concessions such as providing public transport, was unlikely to assuage their anger and distrust, especially in the light of increasing evidence about the harm caused by vehicle emissions. Indeed, in June 1970, officials from Nagoya City Planning Bureau made little headway during a meeting held at the Chikusa Ward Office with 300 members of the Kagamigaike Route Opposition Movement. Apparently the city's planners and other officials had adopted a 'wait-and-see' attitude which the protesters condemned as 'thoughtless'.[102]

Shortly after the meeting, for the first time concrete evidence of damage to human health and plant-life by photochemical smog in the Tokyo metropolitan area was reported in the press. In July, a heat wave hit the Kansai region around Kobe and Osaka; in Toyonaka city, pupils were taken ill with the effects of smog and animals kept as pets in the school died. One newspaper reported that vehicle exhaust fumes had bleached plants and damaged the lead in lamp posts in Yanagichō in Tokyo. During one incident students at a high school collapsed and were rushed to local hospitals. Reading these reports, it seemed likely to one mother, Sasaki Kyoko, living in Osaka that if 'nothing was done to control pollution ... the Japanese archipelago would soon cease to be fit for human habitation.'[103] Articles on pollution appearing in the *Asahi Shimbun* leapt from under 300 in 1969 to over 1,600 in 1970.[104]

On 9 July 1970 a public hearing was held at Naka Ward Office in Nagoya city centre at which representatives of all Nagoya's main wards debated the expressway plans. As in Birmingham, opponents of the new road were particularly anxious about noise and increasing pollution from exhaust emissions. There was also a call for better public transportation facilities without which, participants argued, the traffic problem would not be solved. Other issues included inadequate compensation for moving homes and business premises, as well as vibration and disruption to TV and radio signals. In response, supporters of the expressway argued that with the rise in numbers of motor vehicles, the city's road network needed modernizing, while the elevated structure of the expressway was the best means of separating people and cars, thus reducing accidents and casualties. It was also argued that the expressway would eliminate congestion and boost the economy by diverting through-traffic away from the city centre. Moreover, the development of better fuel and engine technology would eventually alleviate the problem of emissions. The pro-expressway arguments seemingly made little impression on the audience. After nearly four and a half hours, a vote was taken among panel members with eighteen opposing the expressway plans and just two approving them. 'The result,' according to the *Chūnich Shimbun* 'was greeted by loud applause and cheers from everyone in the meeting'.[105]

Amidst growing opposition the NEC was given legal foundation two months later in September 1970. It was the first regional corporation to be established. But just as construction work began, photochemical smog appeared in the region for three days continuously from 18 July 1971 seriously affecting 169 victims. The incident sent shock waves through the city, increasing public concern about automobile emissions and strengthening the opposition of local residents, especially in Kagamigaike. In August a vociferous opposition campaign was launched. At Kawabashi-machi in Chikusa Ward, posters were placed along the roadside demanding that local homes and lives be protected. The protests were couched in terms of '*zettai hantai*' – 'unconditional opposition' to the construction of the Nagoya Urban Expressway.[106] By the beginning of 1972, the weight of opposition to urban road construction was increasing, and not only in Nagoya. In September 1971 protest movements began to form in the Osaka area around the construction of the Chūgoku (Central) Highway. In November, both the Fukuoka-Kitakyūshū Expressway Corporation and the Hanshin Expressway Corporation were forced to form pollution arbitration associations to counter protest.[107] All along the Megalopolis Belt, it seemed, Japanese citizens were on the offensive against roads construction.

Crisis, compensation and adjustment 1972–1979

After five years in the courts, on 25 July 1972, the judge in the Yokkaichi lawsuit awarded twelve asthma victims 88 million yen in damages to be paid jointly by six major polluting companies. It was the first successful multiple-source air pollution lawsuit and held the industries involved 'collectively responsible'. Moreover, the judgement recognized scientific and medical data linking respiratory disease and sulphur dioxide emitted by industrial plants. The firms were culpable because they had failed to conduct joint studies of the effects of their operations on the local environment and to use the most advanced pollution-monitoring systems available at the time.[108]

The case was a watershed and would have wide-ranging implications, not least for road construction opposition groups. Just as the judgement was delivered, the NEC was attempting to get approval for modifications to the original plans. On 21 March 1972, Nagoya City Council passed a supplementary resolution that, 'no stone be unturned in securing the agreement and cooperation of the residents concerned' in respect to the 'Three Conditions'. On the following day, however, the Engineering and Construction Committee of the Aichi Prefectural Assembly dropped a bombshell by supplementing 'Three Conditions' with 'Eight Clauses'. At the meeting, it was decided that the 'Three Conditions' needed further clarification to fully protect residents because the occurrence of traffic pollution by photochemical smog and other factors had exceeded forecasts. The clauses aimed at:

1. gaining the agreement and understanding of residents;
2. early construction of a public transport system (improvement of high-speed rail, bus lanes, park and ride schemes, the completion of public car parks);
3. early completion of ring-road number two (the inner ring);
4. alleviation of congestion;
5. tightening of road safety and traffic (ensuring liveable streets);
6. pollution prevention;
7. harmony with the urban environment;
8. establishment of a comprehensive transportation policy.[109]

According to Hiromi Ohno, President of the NEC, 'the period from 1971 to 1976 was the hardest period for the Corporation,' particularly in relation to the 'Three Conditions and Eight Clauses.'[110] In July 1972 Nagoya City Council passed the modifications to the Prefecture for approval. Among other changes, the Governor of Aichi Prefecture and Nagoya City Council's Clean Construction Committee demanded that measures be taken to protect the environment along the Kagamigaike route. The changes were finally approved in January 1973. Despite the best efforts of the NEC to gain the understanding and cooperation of local residents, however, many voices were raised against the potential environmental consequences. In March 1973 the Expressway construction had become the most divisive issue in Nagoya City Council's fiscal year budget deliberations. There was division between all parties involved in road construction and doubts as to whether the NEC was committed to respecting the 'Three Conditions'. In addition, there were problems in guaranteeing loans required for increased construction costs. As a consequence, the Urban Expressway budget was frozen on 22 March 1973.[111]

These events precipitated significant political changes. Shortly afterwards, on 22 April 1973 Motoyama Masao, backed by the Japan Socialist Party (*Nihon shakaitō*) and Japan Communist Party (*Nihon kyōsantō*) and running on a reform ticket, won the mayoral election and took over from Sugito Kiyoshi. Winning 48 per cent of the vote, Motoyama was formerly a professor of education at Nagoya University and was viewed by the *New York Times* as a 'Leftist' challenger to Prime Minister Tanaka's beleaguered conservative Liberal Democratic Party (LDP) which had backed Sugito.[112] Motoyama's election victory was part of a wider pattern of political change at the local level. Although the LDP maintained unbroken power in the Japanese Diet from 1955 to 1993, dissatisfaction was rife at the local level where, in 1973, non-LDP 'progressive' or 'reform' administrations were also voted into office in Tokyo, Osaka, Yokohama, Kawasaki, Kyoto and Kobe.[113] By 1975, over 20 per cent of Japan's mayors and forty-seven governors were counted as running on anti-conservative, 'progressive' or 'innovative' (*kakushin*) manifestos.[114] The most powerful of these was Minobe Ryōkichi, the governor of Tokyo elected in April 1967 and serving a second term in 1971 and again in 1975. He stood originally for greater dialogue with citizens, the 'new urbanites' who were the targets of progressive campaigns, and pledged to deal with problems such as traffic congestion and poor transport facilities. While he made advances in the provision of social security, even he was dogged by urban planning issues and unable to make much progress, and his dialogue with citizens led to a stalemate in a row over garbage disposal.[115] Similarly, Motoyama was unable to break the stalemate over roads construction in Nagoya.

Shortly after the 1973 election, opposition movements in Nagoya began concerted campaigns against the NEC's modified plans. In May another group formed in Mizuho Ward, further south along the planned Number Three Odaka Expressway, demanding that construction be stopped and, in the same month, the results of a survey conducted by the Research Institute for Environmental Engineering, attached to Aichi Industrial University, were reported in the *Chūnichi Shimbun*.[116] Under the headline 'Is the Car the Main Offender?', it suggested a strong link between Nagoya's photochemical smog and automobile exhaust gases, based on readings from eighteen sites in Nagoya in August in the previous year.[117] It was also reported that the carbon monoxide levels at busy intersections in Nagoya often exceeded the designated 10 parts per million (ppm) and that the 2.4 million daily automobile trips emitted around 680 tons of carbon monoxide and 57 tons of nitrogen oxide into the city's atmosphere each day in 1973. A study by a group of traffic engineers warned that without effective traffic policies, pollutants in the air would reach 1.8 times the 1973 level ten years hence.[118] Freelance journalist Kamata Satoshi, then working for Toyota, commented: 'Automobiles have now been proved to be the main air-pollution offenders, yet every day and every minute these offenders flow out of automobile plants and run around cities as if they owned them.'[119]

Protests escalated over the summer and were widely reported in local newspapers. When the mayor announced that road construction would go ahead, residents in fifteen wards joined together in a mass meeting and large-scale demonstration on 10 June 1973. Accusing Motoyama of 'treachery', they formed an 'influential concentration of resistance', demonstrating the growing power of well-organized citizens' groups. Once thought to be the preserve of the middle-aged and elderly people, the profile of the protesters had changed to include housewives, young workers and professionals.[120] Hayakawa Fumio noted that the residents' movements were increasingly sophisticated in their tactics, drawing on the growing influence of women as activists, the use of media, including posters and leaflets, and knowledge garnered from published academic research.[121] On 25 June Motoyama was accused of reneging on a signed deal with residents.[122] Shaken by the anger of residents directed at him, Motoyama ordered that construction on the Odaka line be temporarily halted.[123] The media responded by acknowledging the officials' 'seriousness towards residents' movement.[124] Concern mounted throughout the rest of the year, with reports of 'Exhaust Gas Hell' in the south of Nagoya, with pollutants 'five times the level of environmental standards'.[125] Residents were also active in commissioning independent surveys to gather proof that car pollution posed a threat to public health.[126]

On 16 January 1974, the budget freeze was finally lifted, but the mayor ordered a complete review of the Nagoya Urban Expressway plans. The following September the resulting special committee made twelve basic recommendations regarding air pollution, noise and other concerns. Noise was taken particularly seriously. In March 1973 residents living near the shinkansen lines in Nagoya had begun litigation against the railway company over noise and vibration. The special committee therefore recommended that compensation be made available for sound-proofing measures in homes, schools and hospitals close to the road as well as the installation of sound barriers on the road itself. In relation to the 'right to sunlight', residents would be compensated for expenses relating to costs of measures to provide a reasonable standard of lighting and heating. Schemes to reduce vibration and the introduction of night-time traffic restrictions to help counter noise were tabled. The installation of bus lanes was recommended on roads under elevated sections of the Expressway and the planting of trees in as many areas as possible, especially in residential areas.[127] Crucially, however, in relation to the suggestion that the Nagoya Expressway Corporation 'take environmental measures on automobile emissions', the committee judged that little could be done. Before September 1970 cars manufactured for domestic consumption were not fitted with the same exhaust controls as those for overseas markets. In April 1973 laws relating to pollution countermeasures forced some controls on manufacturers, although in December 1974 the Japanese Environment Agency was persuaded by the automobile industry to postpone more stringent controls for two years. Other than waiting for national laws to be implemented, the committee could merely utter the pious hope that fuel and engine technology would help decrease emissions.[128]

The final revised plan for the Nagoya Urban Expressway was passed by the Ministry of Construction on 22 November 1976. In a publicity stunt, Nagoya's citizens were invited to 'a highway walk' on the Number Three Odaka route from Takatsuji to Yobitsugi, a few months before the first 10.9 kilometres of the Urban Expressway was finally opened to traffic on 25 July 1979. The remainder of the Expressway continued to be constructed and then expanded throughout the 1980s. Yet the progress of the road did not mark a straightforward defeat for the protesters, who had forced the authorities into a series of high-profile concessions since 1970. Revisions to the earlier plans included a tunnel under the districts of Higashiyama where there had been most opposition. And when construction began again residents continued to protest at every turn right to the end of the century when an important victory was won.

Residents in the south of Nagoya, particularly those living near National Highway Route 23 which opened in 1972 to link Nagoya and Yokkaichi, suffered adverse health effects from noise, vibration and exhaust gas. In 1989 pollution victims filed a lawsuit against a number of industrial companies and government departments responsible for roads, including the Ministry of Land, Infrastructure and Transport and the Environment Ministry. As well as forcing industrial polluters to pay compensation, in 2000 the judge ordered agencies responsible for roads to acknowledge the impact on public health of automobile exhaust emissions. An injunction in 2001 ordered the Ministry of Land, Infrastructure and Transport and the Environment Ministry to take further measures to reduce air pollution and traffic volume and, with the plaintiffs, to establish a liaison group to help make improvements to the environment around the road.[129] Whereas in Birmingham the issue of air pollution had followed swiftly on completion of the Inner Ring, the Aston Expressway and Spaghetti Junction, in Nagoya it dogged every step of the planning and construction of the Urban Expressway. It represented the recalcitrant counter-stroke to the infrastructure of mass automobility.

Conclusion

Most of the accounts we have of automobility and its environmental impact in the late twentieth century are framed at a national level.[130] By contrast, this chapter has examined popular responses and protest directed towards mass automobility in two cities, Birmingham and Nagoya, at a particular moment during the late 1960s and 1970s. What it reveals is, firstly, the inter-related forces of state and social action, environment and renewal, in the unfolding politics of the 'motor city'. Inevitably, automobility was caught up in the reaction to the respective cities' modernization programmes which ran from the later 1950s through much of the 1960s and, in the case of Nagoya especially, into the 1970s. From the start of the 1970s, however, attitudes to the car were changing in both cities. Concerns with air pollution, and the effects of lead emissions on children in particular, did not wholly transform the car from its status as an instrument of consumer aspiration and mobile liberation – in Britain, above all, there was in any case a long tradition of concern about the destructive effects of mass motorization.[131] But events in Birmingham and Nagoya during the 1970s crystallized the 'ME dilemma'. They made it crystal clear that the costs in terms of public health, quality of life and a deteriorating urban environment would have to be set against any gains in mobility, convenience and freedom that the car might offer. Indeed, even these latter advantages might be in question: a British Road Federation report in 1970 claimed that traffic in the Birmingham area was moving at an average speed of 11 mph, little more than when transport was horse-drawn.[132]

The mounting reaction against the car and the related idea of the 'motor city' in Birmingham saw two peaks of activity. The first was the period between 1972 and 1974 when the effects of car pollution in terms of noise, air quality, public health and visual blight came to the fore, sparked by concerns about motorway traffic following the opening of the Gravelly Hill Interchange in May 1972. The second phase of activity followed the publication of the *Sunday Times* article on the physical deterioration of the Inner Ring between May 1977 and late 1978. Again, this was triggered by a single clear issue – the structural deficiencies of certain raised sections of the road – but it tended to attract and condense a wider set of issues about the consequences of post-war urban renewal as a whole and the efficiency and trustworthiness of Birmingham's civic government in particular. In this phase, the image of Birmingham as a 'municipal Gomorrah' came to stand in contrast – but also in significant relationship – to the Corporation's extravagant vision of the 'New Birmingham' almost twenty years earlier.

In Nagoya, protest at the environmental effects of roads construction developed in tandem with the gradual planning and construction of the Urban Expressway between 1961 and 1979. Even before the start of construction of the Expressway in 1971, residents had organized in opposition and had begun to put pressure on both the City Council and the NEC, responsible for the road. In Nagoya as in Japan more widely, groups mobilized against the effects of mass automobility on the urban environment learned from the high-profile cases of industrial pollution. Victims in cases such as Yokkaichi asthma learned to organize, reach out to allies and oppose polluting companies in the law courts. The Yokkaichi judgment highlighted the notion of corporate responsibility and strengthened the need for road builders to undertake full environmental impact assessments prior to the implementation of the large-scale urban planning projects in the 1970s. The 'Three Conditions and Eight Clauses' imposed on the NEC by Nagoya City Council and the Governor of Aichi Prefecture were a way of making sure that environmental impact assessments were carried out based on forecasts which had constantly to be revised. During the major period of urban motorway construction in Japan in the 1970s and 1980s, residents of cities like Nagoya learned not only to live with the car but to protect themselves from it – from the effects of air and noise pollution, from vibration and exhaust emissions. Through successive protests and negotiations, residents learned how to pressure authorities to modify their plans, to limit the damage from roads and traffic and, on occasion, how to enact financial reparation through the legal system.

Events in Nagoya and Birmingham were also, of course, profoundly interwoven with contemporaneous national and international developments. The successive oil crises of 1973/4 and 1978/9 made clear how the 'motor age' since the mid-1950s had been dependent on regular, cheap imports of oil from the Middle East. In Britain especially the years between 1972 and 1974 were a time of protracted national crisis – of two miners' strikes, the three-day week and power shortages – which had severe repercussions for industrial and economic activity.[133] In Birmingham they resulted in all construction work, including roads, being halted for months at a time during 1973/4.[134] Industry in the city simultaneously went into meltdown, with 200,000 jobs lost in the decade and the workforce at the Longbridge plant halved. 'In a traumatic ten years or so', commented Gordon Cherry, 'the economic landscape of the industrial heartland of the West Midlands was fundamentally altered'.[135] The motorcycle industry collapsed in Birmingham in the 1970s and the slowdown in automobile production brought into question its position at the centre of the urban economy. By 1977 the extent of poverty, unemployment and dereliction in inner Birmingham meant that it had become one of four urban areas, along with Manchester/Salford, London docklands and Lambeth, to qualify for an £11 million grant under the Labour government's Inner Cities programme.[136] The transition from the boom city of the 1960s to the 'urban crisis' of the 1970s was certainly less dramatic in Birmingham than in the motor city of Detroit but it was still swift and marked.[137]

Japan did not suffer industrial contraction in the 1970s but here also the 'oil shocks' and mounting resistance to the impact of mass automobility on the urban environment and public health made their mark on public opinion. In this respect the 1970s represented a moment of crisis, if not for automobility itself then for the idea of the 'motor city' embodied in places like Nagoya and Birmingham. What the events described in this chapter brought to the fore was not so much the harm caused by mass motorization and urban renewal independently as the damage produced through their continuous interaction. Cities like Birmingham and Nagoya promoted pollution through their motorway systems and interchanges that multiplied traffic and amplified its effects. At the same time, mass automobility was a direct contributor to the kind of widespread urban blight evidenced in Chapter 3 and to the deteriorating conditions of smog and noise which provoked intensive protest. If the 'New Birmingham' and the new Nagoya of the 1960s had automobility built into their very fabric, so the mounting critique of the car and the recognition of its deleterious consequences for urban living accompanied the dissolution of the ideal of the 'motor city' in the 1970s. Just as the motor car and the modern city were welded to each other in cities like Birmingham and Nagoya, so their fates would unravel together.

6

Kuruma Banare: Turning Away from the Car?

In 2008 an apparently unique phenomenon dubbed '*kuruma banare*' (turning away from the car) was reported in *Newsweek*. There was talk about a 'post-car society' when the late Professor Kitamura Ryūichi from the Institute of Transportation Studies suggested that the automobile no longer featured in the thinking of the younger generation. Falling sales of new cars appeared to indicate that Japan's domestic car market had reached or was nearing full capacity. A widening gap in wealth, demographic change, the growing urban population and relatively high costs of running a car were cited as reasons for its apparent loss of favour.[1] The Japan Automobile Manufacturers Association (JAMA) promptly commissioned a survey of the 'entry generation' (18–24-year-olds).[2] Both survey and long-range statistics suggest that car ownership is continuing to rise, but perceptions of the car have changed especially among the entry generation, not so much because of rising environmental awareness but because of the rising cost of living generally. Younger people were not using cars less but using them differently.

This chapter explores the differences and contradictions in car cultures across the decades of the late twentieth century. It is clear that while a critique of automobility developed in both Britain and Japan, significantly altering public attitudes and public policy towards the car, automobility appeared as embedded as ever at the start of the twenty-first century. But there is evidence of a rebalancing of the relationship between the car and the city which begins in the 1970s and we shall look at the continued expansion and changing composition of car ownership, the effects of environmentalism and the future prospects of the car. While the first oil shock of 1973 is often seen as a turning point, one can question how far either society actually 'turned away from the car' in the decades after 1973. Yet it was in Birmingham, Britain's premier post-war motor city, that there was, uniquely perhaps, a discernable 'turning away from the car' exemplified in events that took place in the late 1980s.

The Highbury initiative

Over a weekend in late March 1988 a symposium was held at Highbury, the recently restored home of Joseph Chamberlain, the man most associated with pioneering Victorian Birmingham's 'municipal socialism'. The symposium was funded at a cost of £70,000 by Birmingham City Council. It brought together experts from Britain,

Europe, Japan and North America: architects, planners, urban designers, politicians and commentators. They included among their number Ed Helfeld, director of the San Francisco Redevelopment Commission; Riek Bakker, Rotterdam's director of planning; and David Gosling, urban design advisor to London Docklands. The brief for this group of experts was to initiate a strategy to help regenerate a city – Birmingham – which was seen as suffering from a precipitous decline in its economy, social conditions and physical fabric.[3]

By the later 1980s the processes of deindustrialization, social conflict and urban decay which were so visible from the mid-1970s had become sufficiently all-pervasive for the city to be seen as undergoing a form of 'urban crisis'. There were riots in the Handsworth area of the city in 1981 and 1985 involving the black community, with police racism and high unemployment cited as causes.[4] Parts of the 'inner city' such as Aston, Digbeth and Small Heath had become bywords for urban dereliction, incorporating some of the worst pockets of poverty and deprivation in the country.[5] Underlying these problems lay the generic crisis of the regional economy, related above all to manufacturing and the motor industry. In 1961, 65 per cent of employment in Birmingham and the West Midlands was in manufacturing industry and one in five workers was employed in the motor industry. Birmingham was at the heart of Britain's booming post-war manufacturing economy, second only to London and the South-East for average income per head of population. But in the two decades after 1971 this position was swiftly reversed. Between 1965 and 1981 the region lost 370,000 manufacturing jobs; in the 1970s the motor industry alone lost 40 per cent of its workforce. By 1981 household incomes in the West Midlands were among the lowest in the country.[6] British Leyland was gradually stripped of its manufacturing components, the Austin marque ceased in 1987 and what remained of the company was sold by the government to British Aerospace in 1988. The Longbridge plant struggled on under various owners until closure in 2005. Such was the scale of destruction to Birmingham's manufacturing economy in these decades that the city was compared to Detroit, already a byword for the ravages effected by the collapse of General Motors.[7]

It was this tide of decline and decay that the international experts assembled at Highbury were called on to reverse. As part of the symposium the delegates walked around Birmingham, including the city centre. They were astonished and dismayed by what they witnessed. 'It's the most chaotic city I've ever seen', the Dutch architect and planner, Teun Koolhas, pronounced when confronted with a view of the city centre from the Inner Ring Road at Masshouse Circus. 'It's as though a child had upset a box of building bricks.' Peter Rice, a distinguished civil engineer who had worked on the Sydney Opera House and the Pompidou Centre, was equally taken aback by the sense of menace experienced walking through the underpass beneath Smallbrook Queensway. 'Visitors only need to have one experience like that to decide never to come back to Birmingham again ... Getting rid of the underpasses is not desirable – it's essential.'[8] In effect, the physical layout and fabric of Birmingham was seen by the experts as integral to the larger economic problem. Improving the urban environment was thus quickly recognized as the precondition for turning around the regional economy.

The Highbury Initiative as it became known marked a turning point in Birmingham, the start of a fresh phase in the city's regeneration, designed to counter not only the effects of economic recession but also the legacy of post-war urban renewal centred on Manzoni's vision of the fully motorized city. Thus, the first proposal agreed by the expert group was the need to 'downgrade' the Inner Ring Road, the 'concrete collar' seen as strangling the city centre. In practical terms this meant creating a breach in the road which would allow for the expansion of the central area and the diversion of through-traffic onto the still unfinished Middle Ring. This was the first step, in the experts' view, towards the regeneration of the city centre by creating a series of 'quarters' – the Jewellery Quarter, based on an important traditional small manufacturing sector, the Chinese Quarter and new 'flagship projects' such as Brindleyplace, a mix of shopping, dining, museum and cultural attractions on a restored canal-side location. As Highbury began to crystallize into urban policy in the 1990s, older sites associated with the 'motor city' such as the Bull Ring were demolished and replaced by a new postmodern shopping centre, artfully entitled 'Bullring'. In the process the private car was excluded from large areas of the city centre, now reserved for cyclists, buses and taxis with a further expanded pedestrian heart. What remained of the Inner Ring, meanwhile, was remodelled: the elevated sections that had exhilarated Morris Zapp were removed while the subways and underpasses that horrified Peter Rice were replaced by street-level pedestrian crossings.[9]

1973 and all that

The Highbury Initiative demonstrated if not a 'turning away from the car' in the truest sense of ushering in a post-car society, then a visceral disenchantment with the inhuman scale of a truly car-dominated built environment. The oil shock of 1973 may not have been a turning-point in the history of automobility *per se*, but the 'shock' of realizing that the black gold literally powering automobility was a finite and politically charged commodity followed the 'environmental awakening' in Japan and Britain.

When war broke out between Israel and a group of Middle East states, led by Egypt and Syria, leading oil-producing countries boycotted Western countries supporting Israel, including the United States, much of Western Europe and Japan. Starting in October 1973 the boycott lasted six months though the effects were felt much longer. One result was that the price of a barrel of crude oil increased more than five times between mid-1973 and late 1974.[10] In Britain it was compounded by a nationwide coal strike from November 1973, so that what started as an oil crisis snowballed into a larger crisis of politics, energy and economy. The Conservative government imposed a state of emergency, much of industry was reduced to a three-day working week and 1974 saw Labour replace the Conservatives in office following two parliamentary elections.[11] Almost devoid of domestic production of oil, Japan relied on imports for 99.7 per cent of her energy requirements, of which 43 per cent came from Arab states within the Organisation of Arab Petroleum Exporting Countries (OAPEC) and 37 per cent from Iran. The cries of 'shock' and 'crisis' from press and government merely created economic confusion and increased inflation. According to Miyoshi Shūichi, a researcher in the Japanese State Department, the 1973 shock led to a period of self-criticism and self-reflection which was 'spiritual as much as material.' Returning from the United States, he was struck by the 'calm and composed manner in which the American populace viewed the crisis, not a few calling for the institution of gasoline rationing', in contrast to the near panic experienced in Japan.[12]

In practice, though, the effects of oil shock in Japan itself were mixed. Already enduring a period of hyper-inflation since 1972 because of its trade balance with the United States, Japanese motorists were hit by price rises of 20 to 30 per cent at the pumps. But the government concentrated on demanding efficiencies in the major, energy-hungry industries, rather than targeting transport and household consumers, since these sectors were considered to be relatively unimportant as energy consumers.[13] Housewives, on the other hand, had to cope with shortages in the shops, most notably toilet paper, detergents and sugar, as prices rose and hoarding led to their disappearance from the shelves.[14] In terms of vehicle production, the number of trucks continued to increase and the production of passenger cars dipped slightly in 1974 but soon recovered.[15] However, the oil shock together with increasing concerns over air pollution caused by automobiles combined to boost the production of smaller, fuel-efficient cars in Japan for both the domestic and export markets.[16] The move towards nuclear power was the most significant change after 1973 for Japan where the supply of nuclear power grew from 0.6 per cent of total primary energy supply in 1973 to 9.4 per cent in 1990.[17]

In Britain, the oil shock had direct consequences for motoring. A speed limit of 50 miles per hour on all roads was introduced, petrol prices tripled between 1973 and 1974, and petrol rationing was threatened for the first time since the Suez Crisis of 1956. Purchase of cars in Britain fell in the aftermath of the oil shock and the costs of motoring in fuel and repairs were estimated to have doubled in the two years following.[18] Motoring in Britain would never be so cheap, nor so untroubled after 1973. Planned road construction projects were affected too, a further reason why 1973 might be held up as a turning point. In April, some six months before the oil shock, the newly elected Labour administration at the Greater London Council cancelled the large part of the Ringways scheme of the four radial roads encircling the capital. These were the two rings closest to the heart of London, which ran through heavily built-up areas. The politics of the Council's decision were complex but the retreat on roads was hailed by opponents of the Ringways scheme, notably the London Motorway Action Group, as a victory of the people over the planners. Whatever the realities – and it is clear that many planning experts also opposed the Ringways scheme – the episode was symbolically significant, indicating that new urban motorway systems could be halted anywhere.[19] More than this, the scrapping of the inner Ringways put in question the governmental roads strategy, now that the national network of inter-urban motorways had been built.

It is tempting, then, to view 1973 as the moment in which Britain, and much of the rest of the motorized world, began to question the seemingly remorseless movement towards 'car dependence', the organization of transport, urbanism and social life around private automobility. But the pivoting of this movement on the events of 1973 is problematic for a number of reasons. First, the questioning of car dominance which began before 1973 in both countries changed in substance over time between the 1970s and the 1990s. Secondly, because of its dependence on oil from Iran, Japan was also affected by a second shock in 1979, after the Iranian Revolution caused the cessation of oil exports from December 1978 until March 1979. Leaders of the OPEC countries met in Geneva and agreed the third price increase in exported oil of the year. While the 1973 oil crisis appeared to many at the time to be a temporary problem, the 1979 crisis signalled to world leaders that sudden price hikes in oil were likely to cause a chronic energy supply problem in the future.[20] In 1979, Miyoshi wrote: 'The people of the advanced countries, now painfully aware of limits to the natural resource of oil, must fundamentally change their style of living in order to preserve their civilizations, which have been constructed through the extravagant use of oil.'[21] Finally, with the exception of the Highbury Initiative which did not, in any case, take place until the late 1980s, there was little evidence of a turning away from the car after 1973, especially in Japan where car ownership more than doubled in the following decade to reach over 24 million.[22] The dramatic events of 1973/4, in effect, did not represent a moment of sudden rupture in the history of motorization. They were, rather, part of a larger and longer-term movement towards rebalancing the relationship between the automobile and the city.

Rebalancing automobility

During the later 1960s the British government initiated a series of investigations into the effects of mass automobility on cities. Following the Buchanan report of 1963 the then Minister of Transport Ernest Marples set up a further study group to complement Buchanan by looking at the potential for the problems of traffic to be eased by the redesign of vehicles. The resulting report, *Cars for Cities*, was published in 1967, recommending smaller cars, like the Mini, and alternative power sources, such as battery-driven vehicles.[23] Two years later another study group, the Urban Motorways Committee, was established to consider the environmental, legal and financial consequences of motorways in built-up areas, a recognition of their costs in falling land and property values as well as in loss of 'amenity', a new term introduced to indicate the quality or otherwise of the physical surroundings.[24] What was reflected in these reports was a growing unease about the effects of unfettered use of the car and policies which supported and even encouraged it. Peter Hall and Carmen Hass-Klau argued that the later 1960s witnessed a policy shift in Britain 'away from planning for the free use of the car and toward the promotion of public transport'.[25] By the 1970s this has hardened into something approaching a consensus. Both Labour and Conservative manifestos for the October 1974 general election contained affirmations of the need to rebalance transport priorities. 'All politicians drive on the same side', observed *The Times* newspaper, reflecting the surprising degree of unanimity.[26] Both main parties also agreed on the need to switch spending from roads to the publicly owned British Rail, confirmed in Labour's Railways Act of 1974.[27]

The national shift in public attitudes towards the automobile was repeated in Birmingham. The 1973 *Structure Plan* was the first Corporation plan to qualify the drive to motorization or what it termed 'free choice private vehicle dominance'.[28] A survey of

3,850 Birmingham residents, carried out for the *Plan*, suggested that the shift in policy chimed with public opinion, 80 per cent of those questioned agreeing that 'the use of the private car should be restrained and there should be improvements to public transport'.[29] The change envisaged by the *Structure Plan* was novel in at least two respects. First, it represented a move away from the governmental priority given to consumer choice in transport based on the 'predict and provide' model in which policy followed what were construed as the transport preferences of users.[30] Secondly, for the first time since the Beeching cuts to the railways after 1963, the City Corporation put the emphasis on rail. In Manzoni's revised *Development Plan* of 1960 the railways were only mentioned once; now they were made the cornerstone of the city's transport policy with improved suburban routes in all directions, including Sutton Coldfield to the north and Bromsgrove to the south.[31] Increased bus services were not a solution, so the *Structure Plan* argued, because they only added to road congestion. Instead, expansion of rail services was mooted as an alternative to roads, even if, as was conceded, suburban motorists might have to drive to the station in the first place.

This switch from private to public transport among planners and politicians after 1970 was predicated on recognition of the costs, financial and otherwise, of continued large-scale roads construction in Britain's cities. Birmingham was not alone either in the policy change or the shift in public opinion towards automobility that accompanied or sometimes preceded it. The Layfield enquiry into the London Ringways sat for two years and considered some 28,000 objections before it reported in early 1973. Speaking in parliament in a debate on the London Ringways in February 1973, the Labour politician Anthony Crosland could refer to the 'mounting tide of opinion against grandiose urban motorways'.[32] The same message was repeated in other British cities. In Newcastle upon Tyne an elaborate web of motorways enclosing the city centre was planned to be built in a fifteen-year period from 1972. As in London and Birmingham, this vast programme, costing some £45 million at 1972 prices, provoked opposition in the form of a campaign, SOCEM (Save Our City from Environmental Mess), and a series of public enquiries which considered noise, pollution and congestion. In fact, a large part of the network was never built, much of the funding being diverted from 1975 into the construction of the Tyne and Wear Metro.[33] Surveying the state of central areas of British cities in 1973 in a special issue of the *Guardian* newspaper, an author questioned 'whether the millions spent on urban motorways are the best use of scarce resources, including land', while noting that 'the emphasis on public transport is advancing in all cities. Rapid transport is scheduled for Manchester and Newcastle, improved rail is on the cards for Birmingham and Glasgow.'[34]

There were several reasons behind this policy change of heart, not only the financial cost at a time of economic recession and spiralling inflation. There was also the recognition that roads did not actually diminish traffic. The author of the report on Newcastle's proposed motorway programme put the matter squarely in 1974: 'A kind of Parkinson's Law operates in congested city areas; traffic expands to fill the space provided for it, and new roads may be filled to capacity within a short time of being opened'. Similar conclusions had been reached by other transport studies, pointing out that road space generated traffic and that schemes like Ringways would be counter-productive in the mid-long term.[35] Indeed, the question of 'induced traffic' – the idea that improved roads created more not less traffic – had a long history. As early as 1938 the Minister of Transport Leslie Burgin had commented that 'the experience of my Department is that the construction of a new road tends to result in a great increase in traffic, not only on the new road but also on the old one which it was intended to supersede'.[36] Awareness of 'induced traffic' was not new, therefore, but surfaced periodically during the century in expert discourse on automobility, although for the most part the Department of Transport worked on the assumption that the concept was at best unproven. Reviewing existing studies, a government committee set up to review the evidence of new roads and the generation of traffic came out flatly against the Department's orthodox view in its published report in 1994 (Graph 6.1). All the evidence, it concluded, 'tend[s] to support the existence of induced traffic … We do not feel able to endorse the Department's conclusion that the balance of this evidence is against the existence of induced traffic.'[37] New 'trunk' roads, including motorways, might actually exacerbate rather than relieve congestion.

In terms of its national and regional transportation planning, the Japanese government remained committed to extensive road development until the 1990s. However, it is important to stress that transportation policy followed the pattern of the 'High Growth Era' with roads construction running in tandem with the extension of the railway system. This is despite the fact that in the 1950s there was, according to a popular 'railway downfall theory', an assumption that railways would eventually lose out to the automobile and the aeroplane to become obsolete.[38] The legendary Tōkaidō Shinkansen, like the Meishin and Tōmei Expressways, linked Nagoya to Tokyo and Osaka and opened at around the same time. The 515-kilometre line was opened in 1964 with sixty trains per day in both directions covering the distance at a top speed of 270 kilometres per hour. By March 1999 there were eleven trains per hour and 285 trains per day. Between 1969 and 1999 passengers increased from 66 million to 130 million per year.[39] Inevitably, although the railways did not become obsolete, in terms of passengers they were rapidly overtaken by the passenger car. Both Japan Railways (Japan National Railways before privatization in 1987) and the Chūkyō region's privately run railways, Kintetsu and Meitetsu, experienced peak use in the early 1990s and then numbers began to decline, while passenger car journeys increased from just 588 million in 1969 to 3.5 billion in 1999. In comparison with the other megalopolitan regions, this trend towards the automobile was far more pronounced in the Chūkyō traffic range (within a 40-kilometre radius of Nagoya Station) than in either the Tokyo (Metropolitan) or Osaka (Kansai) ranges.[40]

As a result of increasing car use in the area, Nagoya became the focus of a government initiative to implement a pilot-scheme to restrict traffic growth within the city and in residential areas. With the construction of the Nagoya Urban Expressway temporarily halted, the city also lacked adequate roads to cope with traffic entering Nagoya from Ichinomiya Interchange on the Meishin Expressway. The result was severe congestion and rising levels of pollution on existing roads, especially on Nagoya's so-called 'inner loop-road' which was built in the 1950s and was the nearest the city had to the Birmingham Inner Ring. At peak times drivers would cut through Nagoya's residential areas to avoid congestion hot-spots, causing a huge increase in road deaths and casualties, giving the city one of the highest motor accident rates in the country,

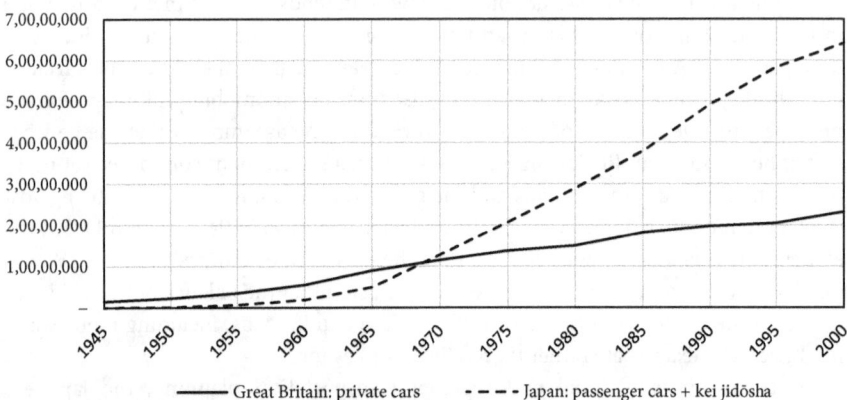

Graph 6.1 Personal transport vehicle ownership in Britain and Japan, 1945–2000

Source: *Historical Statistics of Japan*, http://www.stat.go.jp/english/data/chouki/; Department for Transport, *Household Car Availability: England*, Table NTS0205 (London: HMSO, 2017).

including Tokyo.[41] Traffic accidents in Nagoya peaked in 1964, just after the opening of the Meishin Expressway, at nearly 26,000 of which 2,000 involved pedestrians. While the number of casualties began to fall in subsequent years, the figures for pedestrians stubbornly remained at the same level. In 1971 there were still 15,000 traffic accident casualties in the city.[42] Initiated in 1972, the pilot-scheme was projected to cost $25 million (around £10 million) and was the first in Japan to put into operation citywide, interrelated traffic control and transportation measures. A Traffic Management Committee, comprising engineers and local government representatives, proposed a seven-point, four-year plan designed specifically to shift the emphasis from private cars to public transportation.[43]

The first priority was to remove as much through-traffic from the city centre and residential areas as possible by redesigning the existing Nagoya inner loop-road. The idea was to relieve congestion in the city itself and reduce the number of accidents. The old loop-road had a huge number of intersections. These not only increased the potential for accidents as traffic entered or exited the road but also, since there were no traffic controls, there was no means of controlling the flow of traffic on to it. Most of the 384 intersections were closed leaving just forty-six which were now controlled by an automated traffic control system to regulate the flow of traffic. The initial results were promising. Reducing the number of intersections actually increased the volume of traffic while at the same time decreasing travel time for drivers by nearly 20 per cent. With a smoother flow of traffic more vehicles were able to enter the loop-road and, with a decrease in congestion, were less likely to exit onto surrounding roads and streets. The strategy was initially successful in decreasing accidents on or around the inner loop-road by one-third.[44]

The promise of containing through-traffic on designated routes soon turned to disappointment. As in Birmingham, the architects of the Nagoya inner loop-road improvement scheme soon ran into the perennial problem of 'induced traffic': when roads are improved and capacity increased the number of vehicles will simply expand to fill it. By 1974, within just two years of the road improvements, the inner loop-road had once again reached maximum capacity; congestion was rising, and the invasion of the city centre and residential areas appeared imminent. In an attempt to pre-empt the dangers of exiting traffic entering these areas, stringent access and exit controls had also been placed on surrounding arterial road networks in the hope of preventing through-traffic invasion into neighbouring residential areas. In addition, a new computerized, area-wide signal control system was installed to secure optimum traffic flow on main roads. Maintaining optimum traffic flow was also considered to reduce the impact on the urban environment since congestion was linked to high levels of vehicle-exhaust pollution.[45]

If containing the car on routes in and out of the city was difficult enough, encouraging drivers to use public transport at a local level proved even more elusive. A ban on roadside parking in the commercial and business district (CBD) of the city aimed to discourage the use of private cars and restrict parking in streets as a garage substitute. In what was considered 'compensation' for the parking ban, the introduction of bus lanes and bus priority signals would, it was hoped, encourage more use of public transport.[46] Consequently between December 1972 and September 1973 roadside parking in the CBD was banned during daytime, apart from temporary stops for loading and unloading of up to five minutes. This was followed in December 1974 (perhaps rather belatedly) by the introduction of nineteen bus lanes on congested routes during the rush hour. Bus frequency was increased and bus priority signals had already been installed on an experimental basis on four suburban routes. In addition, the expansion of pedestrian streets and cycle paths aimed to facilitate better safety and access to workplaces and encourage walkers and cyclists. In the government office area of the CBD, some government employees who previously used cars for commuting did convert to public transport.[47] Whether this was because of the extra availability of public transport is not stated in the report, but other factors have to be taken into account, such as national government policies.

From 1970 pro-public transport and anti-car measures were already being implemented nationally by the Japanese government, mostly through increasing various costs associated with car ownership and car use. The government attempted to slow down the number of new drivers by escalating the costs of applying for a licence, as well as learning to drive through insisting on a minimum number of hours classroom and in-car tuition. The written and practical driving examinations became much more rigorous.[48] Taxes on gasoline and vehicle licencing also rose steeply after 1970. After 1969 not only did fines for parking and driving violations increase, but offenders were pursued more assiduously and risked losing their hard-won and expensive driving licence if they did not pay fines. Ticket issuance for driving violations increased by 200 per cent between 1969 and 1977. The government relied on ensuring detection through better law enforcement rather than draconian punishments and most fines, around 96 per cent, were paid promptly.[49]

The work place was also targeted to reduce commuting by car. Employees using public transport were rewarded with fringe-benefit reimbursement of fares, the number of parking spaces near workplaces was reduced in major cities and private parking was very expensive. Local governments and national government appealed to their employees to leave their cars at home on a voluntary basis by extensive use of propaganda and anti-commuting posters. In 1980 the government prohibited all its employees from using private cars for commuting to work as part of an energy saving campaign, but not all employees respected the ban.[50] Car ownership statistics indicate that government attempts to constrain the car in the 1970s were destined to fail. But, as Koshi Masaki and his co-authors pointed out: 'If the government had not undertaken policies to restrain the use of the car, the situation could have been worse.'[51]

The pilot-scheme enacted in Nagoya, therefore, broadly followed the aims of the national government, with the same results. Government employees in the CBD had already been subjected to anti-commuting propaganda by the national government, so it would be difficult to attribute a switch to commuting by public transport entirely to the pilot-scheme. This argument is strengthened by the fact that elsewhere in the city car drivers were generally not persuaded to switch to public transport. In terms of numbers of bus passengers, the net gain from the local CBD schemes was reported to amount to a mere 3 per cent increase or less. Presenting these results to a conference in Paris in 1975, Miyazaki Tadashi, Associate Director of the Traffic Planning Division in Tokyo, rather gloomily pointed out:

> The reason for this small demand for bus service was too simple; the bus journey times were still far outweighed by the short travel time of automobiles. For the average customer, 10 minutes gain on the lanes was insufficient to evoke the potential demand for mass transit that has a number of deficiencies in reliability, availability and pricing.[52]

In addition, the attempt at coercion merely exacerbated existing problems. For example, a side effect of the parking restrictions was a mushrooming of off-street parking facilities provided by private companies sensing profit. In terms of the volume of traffic coming into the city centre, these new parking spaces effectively offset the potential gains of on-road parking bans. More seriously, the general failure of this scheme tended to compromise the initial aim of reducing through-traffic in residential areas by improving the Nagoya inner loop-road. When car drivers experienced delays on the approaches to the CBD area because of the installation of new bus-lanes, they quickly found a way around the congestion by using other, sometimes residential, roads.

As part of the pilot-scheme, a system of 'unit cell control' targeted residential areas plagued by accidents, noise, and other traffic problems. Typically consisting of one-way systems, speed limits, parking bans, turning restrictions and the exclusion of commercial vehicles, the cells were designed to make them less car-friendly, preventing their use as 'rat-runs'. The one-way system in the cell was usually arranged in an 'L' or 'U' shape so as to deter vehicles entering the cell zone. Pedestrian streets were restricted to car owners with permits. All streets under 3.5 meters wide were restricted to pedestrian use and, in wider streets, traffic was limited to certain hours. By September 1974, ninety-two cells had been implemented. According to a survey of sixty-four of these cells, there was a net reduction of 43 per cent in traffic fatalities, and nearly 40 per cent in severe injury accidents. This was compared to streets outside the cell system itself where, despite some improvements being made, there was a less than 17 per cent reduction in fatalities. While the reduction of accident rates appeared to indicate a measure of success, the scheme was not without its problems. Traffic restrictions within the cells were enforced only by advisory signage and residents found that there was a heavy, albeit worthwhile, sacrifice to pay in as much as the proliferation of road signs destroyed the aesthetic appearance of the streets. Even so residents campaigned for more physical barriers such as concrete bollards or trees to be installed, indicating that lack of enforcement was a problem.

Despite these difficulties, Miyazaki was optimistic: 'It is expected that the unit cell control will pave the way for complete redesigning of the community living environment.'[53] The relatively high costs of the Nagoya scheme and the fact that the zones had only limited, localized success in restricting the car did not prevent similar schemes being introduced in other cities in Japan. Indeed by 1980, largely because of demand from residents, around 10,000 unit cell control zones had been introduced with some being converted into fully landscaped zones with pedestrianized streets and shopping arcades. Residents' Surveys conducted in Fukuoka and Abeno, Osaka revealed that the schemes were very popular, not least because of the reduction in traffic noise and fumes as well as in traffic accidents involving pedestrians. Residents in Abeno also believed that new landscaping and pedestrianized areas had made walking much more pleasurable and improved the aesthetics of the zone.[54] While claiming some success with schemes in residential areas by the 1980s, cities everywhere continued to be blighted by roads construction and, as in Nagoya, attempts to contain the car had only limited success.

In both countries, new roads were objected to on the grounds of their damaging effects for the environment. What 'environment' meant in the 1970s, however, was circumscribed by comparison with how it would come to be understood a decade later. In Britain the concept was pervasive in public discourse while remaining defined largely within the terms of the Buchanan report and the perception of the danger posed by mass automobility to 'civilized living'. 'Environment', declared the transport planner Michael Thomson in his authoritative study, *Great Cities and Their Traffic* (1977), 'means the quality, as distinct from the utility, of one's surroundings'. Motor vehicles were the greatest threat of all transport modes to the urban environment, a threat Thomson related to air pollution, noise and loss of amenity.[55] The case of Gravelly Hill, with the harm caused by carbon monoxide and lead poisoning from vehicle emissions, alongside constant traffic noise, was highlighted by the SOCEM report on Newcastle. The report also noted the problem of 'blight' in Birmingham, citing the view of the city's health authorities that the environmental deterioration caused by urban motorways meant houses adjoining them might have to be demolished.[56]

The environmental question surrounding automobiles underwent subtle changes in the 1970s at both governmental level and among the general public. But conservation of both the built and natural environment was as much an issue in

Figure 6.1 Historic Tokyo dwarfed by the Metropolitan Expressway: The Meiji Nihonbashi Bridge. Source: Wikipedia Commons [public domain] https://ja.wikipedia.org/wiki/%E3%83%95%E3%82%A1%E3%82%A4%E3%83%AB:Nihonbashi_1114.jpg

Japan as it was in Britain (Figure 6.1). As early as 1966 the Special Measures for the Preservation of Historic Landscape in Ancient Capitals Act was passed to preserve the cultural centres of cities such as Nara, Kyoto and Kamakura.[57] There were a few indigenous environmental NGOs founded in Japan such as the Citizen's Alliance for Saving the Atmosphere and the Earth (CASA) which arose from a campaign for air pollution regulation in Osaka in the 1960s and 1970s, and a Japanese branch of the World Wildlife Fund opened in 1971.[58] What changed after 1973 was the terminology associated with 'environment' which gave it new meaning. In Britain also conservation of natural resources had become a larger concern voiced by the early 1970s, under the influence of the early environmentalist movement: the British branch of Friends of the Earth was founded in 1970 and the first issue of Edward Goldsmith's journal the *Ecologist* was launched in the same year. Resource depletion, specifically related to oil, was a problem seemingly emphasized by the oil shock of 1973 with its threat of petrol rationing and the reality of the three-day week. A Friends of the Earth report in 1974 linked the various threats, noting that a quarter of the oil used in Britain went into transport while one-third of the country's population were suffering from air pollution and excessive road noise.[59] Others went even further in their prognoses. In a 'state of the nation' debate in parliament in November 1974, the Labour MP Bruce Douglas-Mann blamed the oil crisis on the economic model of advanced industrial states. 'We have developed an entire economic system which appears to depend for its survival on using more of the world's resources in an increasingly wasteful fashion'. Even the roads lobby was forced to accept the terms of debate after 1973, arguing, somewhat counter-intuitively, that roads were one of the ways of preserving the environment by taking traffic away from urban areas and reducing emission-generating congestion.[60]

In the twenty years after 1970 the environmental debate in Britain mutated. It began to encompass conservationism, both urban and rural, and to take a more militant form. Building on the success of protests in London, Newcastle and elsewhere roads protest became widespread in the 1980s and 1990s, garnering considerable attention from a startled media. Protestors used ever more imaginative tactics to outwit government and road contractors, and to halt construction if only temporarily. At Otmoor, an area of natural wetland near Oxford through which the M40 motorway was scheduled to run, a local Friends of the Earth organizer hit on the idea of buying an acre of land from a farmer and selling it off in tiny parcels to thousands of new landowners. Since government was legally required to consult with landowners prior to compulsory purchase, the planning process became impossible and the government eventually decided in 1985 to re-route the road away from Otmoor. At Leytonstone in east London where the M11 motorway had long been planned, protestors barricaded houses and chained themselves to trees and washing machines filled with cement.[61] By the 1990s, Joe Moran suggests, campaigns had turned a 'protest against a specific road to one of symbolic resistance against road culture in general'.[62] The change was epitomized by the 'Reclaim the Streets' movement in which cars were symbolically dismantled and tarmac dug with drills, all to the sound of high energy rave and hip hop.[63]

As this implies, the protests of the 1980s worked to expand the concept of environment and redefine its relationship to automobility. In Britain, conservation of the historic and the natural environment had been a focus for opposition since the campaign to stop the inner ring road being built across Christ Church Meadows in Oxford in the mid-1950s. But now opposition was not only more militant but had also expanded its goal to protect the whole urban and natural environment, not just buildings or sites deemed to be exceptional. An unlikely coalition of conservationists, new age travellers and community activists began to challenge the 'car system' itself.[64]

This enlarged ambition was underpinned by the 'discovery' of global warming and climate change, occurring at the same period. Meteorologists gathered at a conference in Austria in 1985 were the first to predict a 'rise of global mean temperature ... greater than any in man's history', while British scientists in the same year discovered a hole in the ozone layer above Antarctica. At Vienna in 1987 governments agreed to protect the ozone layer by restricting damaging emissions, and by the late 1980s the threat of climate change was taken up as a cause by the environmental movement internationally.[65] Although chlorofluorocarbons (CFCs) from aerosols and refrigerators were first to be identified as causes of ozone depletion, carbon emissions from motor vehicles soon followed as major contributors to greenhouse gases. In Britain motor vehicles were estimated to be responsible for between a fifth and a quarter of all CO_2 emissions, a proportion that proved stubbornly resistant to efforts at reduction. Between 1990 and 2015 emissions from transport (made up overwhelmingly of motor transport) fell by only 2 per cent, whereas those from domestic energy supply reduced by 48 per cent.[66] By the late twentieth century, in effect, cars appeared to be a threat not just to the urban environment but to the planet itself.

Road construction remained a focus of most citizens' groups in Japan throughout the 1970s and 1980s. In addition to the campaign against the Nagoya Urban Expressway, there were protests in Osaka against the Hanshin Expressway and road construction projects across the country. In some cases such disputes lasted between ten and twenty years. This did not, however, discourage public spending on roads in the 1970s or 1980s. For the first time in the post-war period, public spending on major construction projects, such as dams, hydro-electric plants and underground storage facilities for oil and water flat-lined in Japan in the 1980s. By contrast, public spending on roads effectively doubled.[67] With roads construction on the increase, the number of disputes escalated. In 1970, a system for resolving environmental disputes was instituted under the Law Concerning the Settlement of Environmental Disputes which focussed on saving costs through recommending extra-judicial methods of resolving disputes through mediation, conciliation, arbitration and adjudication. Between 1970 and 1986, 567 cases were brought before government adjudicators and 351 before prefectural commissions. The majority of these cases involved road construction projects. One example was the Tokyo Bay Area Artery Project, consisting of a six-lane expressway and national highway route 357 (originally planned with eight lanes and later reduced to four) which was approved by the Ministry of Construction in 1969. Local residents took on the Ministry of Construction, the Japan Highway Public Corporation and the Public Enterprise Agency of Chiba Prefecture. The case set a standard pattern of resolving disputes, including the dispute over the Nagoya Urban Expressway in the 1970s. While they might delay construction, sometimes for ten years or more, ultimately the most residents could hope for were changes in the planned route, adjustments to design which mitigated noise and air pollution, such as raising the height of soundproofing walls, and the installation of air pollution and vibration frequency monitoring.[68]

Kameyama Yasuko argued that few Japanese were aware of terms such as 'global warming' and 'climate change' until the late 1980s. A Japanese branch of Friends of the Earth opened in 1980 and a branch of Greenpeace in 1989, but enjoyed only limited support in local communities.[69] Japanese standards of living had improved significantly by the 1980s and the harrowing details of the Big Four pollution cases were becoming a distant memory. Environmental issues close to home did impinge on national consciousness such as waste management, and the ongoing issues of traffic congestion and air quality. But acid rain, desertification and the depletion of the ozone layer remained on the margins of public consciousness until the late 1980s. Japanese industry had, to a large extent, exported its pollution by establishing facilities in southeast Asia and elsewhere, but these operations came under increasing scrutiny and attracted unwanted criticism, largely from NGOs in the affected areas. This is one reason why it was external pressure, rather than internal opinion which finally galvanized the Japanese government into action. The government was compelled to take part in international conventions on climate change and start making financial contributions to global environmental agencies in the late 1980s, but it was reluctant to join other countries in setting targets for CO_2 emissions at the Noordwijk Ministerial conference in November 1989. Nevertheless there were signs that public attitudes were changing. When the government's attitude made headline news in Japanese newspapers, it brought condemnation from a Japanese public now awakened to the dangers of ignoring global environmental issues. A combination of public pressure and the international endorsement of a need for action on environmental issues finally caused Japanese ministers to relent and agree to the proposal to set CO_2 targets for 2000.[70] Responses to the larger environmental threats from automobility, such as global warming, were slower to take shape in Japan than in Britain, but by the end of the twentieth century they were very much on the agenda.

The persistence of automobility

In the decades that followed the 1960s, 'car dominance' came to be questioned by planners and scientists as much as by protesters. At the same time, the car system was far from undone. New roads continued to be opened, car ownership grew and automobility persisted at the expense of other modes of getting about. If societies in Britain and Japan have become less car dependent since 1970, it is a movement that has been ambiguous and uncertain.

In Britain in May 1970 the Ministry of Transport published a bold new programme entitled *Roads for the Future: The New Inter-Urban Plan for England*. Its tone was confident, even bullish. 'The aim', the document proclaimed, 'is to provide a comprehensive national system of trunk roads on which commercial traffic and private cars can move freely and safely and on which congestion and its economic costs will have been virtually eliminated'. Congestion, it predicted, could be banished within fifteen to twenty years. Urban roads would also be upgraded, although it was acknowledged in the shadow of Buchanan that British cities suffered from 'formidable and complex problems'. New roads, it was also acknowledged, might have implications for 'amenity' in some places, but overall, the document asserted, 'new roads ... improve the total environment'.[71] Just over a decade later the ebullient tone had gone, but in a further paper, *Policy for Roads in England* (1983), the government continued to insist on the 'environmental gains' derived from new roads by reducing 'the adverse effects of traffic on people's lives'. Furthermore, the 1983 paper insisted that policy had to be 'based on a thorough appreciation of why our society has come to depend upon road transport and of the benefits it has brought' in the form of economic growth and increased personal mobility; 'roads have improved the quality of our lives'.[72] While acknowledging costs, environmental and otherwise, therefore, government policy repeatedly affirmed both the necessity and desirability of mass automobility in justifying expenditure on new roads programmes.

A twin-track policy was also visible in Birmingham. In December 1973 the chair of the Public Works Committee, Harold Edwards, signalled the end of the city's commitment to the roads programme, a logical extension of its new *Structure Plan* prioritizing public transport. 'The time has come', Edwards declared, 'when we cannot afford to build any more big roads and expressways, not only because they generate traffic, but also because of the effects on the environment'. Yet on the same day, it was announced that, through the *Structure Plan*, the Corporation would commit itself to a further £68 million of spending on the Middle Ring Road.[73] In part, the apparent contradiction could be explained by the need to complete road projects once begun, as had been the case with the Inner Ring. Roads projects had their own momentum and logic; in the end Birmingham's Middle Ring would not be finished until 1998.[74] But while one voice appeared to place a veto on new schemes for major roads in Birmingham after 1973, other voices urged continued spending. Birmingham's Outer Ring, including a section of the M42 motorway linked to the National Exhibition Centre, opened in 1976, was another project which continued to attract large-scale investment into the next decade.

The most ambitious British roads programme, however, was reserved for the late 1980s. Despite the experience of almost twenty years of protest and the mounting evidence of global warming, in 1989 the Conservative government published a controversial white paper, *Roads for Prosperity*. Billed as 'the biggest road-building programme since the Romans', the paper proposed 2,700 miles of roads, exceeding in scale the grand expansion of the 1960s. It declared itself to represent a 'step-change' in roads policy to 'deal with growing and forecast inter-urban road congestion'.[75] The programme, costed at £12 billion, envisaged a profusion of new and upgraded motorways. It immediately aroused the ire of the conservation lobby, including the Council for the Protection for Rural England.[76] Predictably, too, the proposals were never fully implemented: some 60 per cent of the construction projects were shelved over the next five years and a further 77 motorway and trunk schemes abandoned in 1995.[77]

This stop-start approach to roads and infrastructure policy was a product not only of volatile fiscal conditions but also, in Britain, of high-profile protest. Set-piece confrontations between contractors, police and protesters, symbolized in the media by the new age Dongas, reached their climax at Twyford Down on the path of one of the extended motorways, the M3 between London and south-west England in December 1992.[78] But stop/start also reflected deeper conflicts within government and the state about the value and effects of expanding the road system. Motorways in particular were seen – sometimes by different people, sometimes by the same people – as simultaneously economically desirable and environmentally destructive. Congestion remained a hot political issue for ordinary drivers as well as for manufacturing and logistics companies, whatever the views of experts that new roads added to rather than subtracted from traffic. Under these pressures government policy was unsurprisingly schizophrenic, alternating between the demand to provide for mass motorization and the need to control it. In political terms, turning ones back on the car was not a practicable option.

A further reason for governmental uncertainty was that the demand to own and drive vehicles showed no sign of diminishing. Between 1970 and 2000 the number of licensed private cars rose steadily from just under 10 million to just over 23 million, with only a brief hiatus around the 1973 oil shock. Motor vehicles as a whole rose from 13 million to 28 million over the period, heavy good vehicles slightly declining to fewer than half a million while light goods vehicles expanded in numbers from 1.4 to 2.4 million, reflecting the economic shift away from heavy industry to services.[79] A key element in the changing picture in Britain was the increase in the number of women drivers. In the 1960s less than a fifth of adult women held a driving licence compared to half of all men. In 1975/6 the proportion of women able to drive was still only 29 per cent. But thereafter the numbers took off, reaching 41 per cent by 1986 and 55 per cent in the early 1990s. By 2005 over two-thirds of women held a driving licence. Among men the proportion of drivers has been static at 80 per cent since the late 1980s, so that while a gender gap remains, it is narrowing.[80] The 'no-car folk' similarly shrank as a group, from 48 per cent of all households in 1971 to 32 per cent twenty years later; by 2005 only a quarter of households in England were estimated to be without a car or van.[81]

The success of the new 'mini-car' explains why the rate of car ownership increased more rapidly during the 1990s in Japan, with the addition of another 16.5 million vehicles compared to around 9 million added during the 1980s. The mini-car was thought to be responsible for the increase in multi-vehicle families which rose from virtually none in 1965 to 12 per cent of families in 1980.[82] In 1990 the maximum cubic capacity of the light car class was raised to 660cc and its maximum dimensions and kerb-weight increased to allow slightly larger vehicles. Better design and engineering improved both the looks and performance of the mini-car, giving it wider appeal. It was much cheaper to tax and insure than larger cars and owners enjoyed favourable parking rates in cities and reduced toll-road charges. In the 1960s owning a mini- or light-car was seen as 'Hobson's choice', a cheap car for the financially embarrassed middle-class *salariman*, but in the increasingly eco-conscious 1990s it became a favourite with fashionable young women and practical housewives alike.[83]

The Japan Automobile Manufacturers Association's survey of the 'entry generation' (18–24-year-olds) in 2008 confirmed that, in 2007, the use of private passenger cars among 18- to 24-year-olds declined from a peak in 2001 (from around 73 per cent to 68 per cent for males and from 70 per cent to 63 per cent for females) but it also showed that the gap between men and women drivers was relatively narrow in this generation, in contrast to much of the twentieth century. Indeed, the number of passenger car users in the male population actually fell from around 55 per cent in 1999 to 51 per cent in 2007, while the number of female car users rose very slightly from 48.2 per cent to 48.4 per cent of the total female population in the same period.[84]

One aim of the survey was to examine how attitudes to work and life had changed since the 1990s. Importantly, this generation had been born in the 1990s when Japan entered a period of declining economic growth and stagnating incomes. They were more pessimistic about the future than their forebears born in the High Growth Era. Fears about access to education and employment opportunities made them cautious as consumers and they stayed closer to their families. These circumstances had greatly influenced their attitudes towards the car. Most importantly, among 70 per cent of respondents there was an acute consciousness of environmental issues such as global warming and air pollution from exhaust gases, leading to a desire to recycle and use less energy. Yet their attitudes towards the 'image' of the car were ambiguous, demonstrating the persistence of the ME dilemma. On the one hand the car was seen as a burden, expensive to maintain, generally unaffordable to buy and prone to accidents. On the other hand, the allure and pleasure of driving, freedom of movement and privacy were still present, with 90 per cent of respondents either owning or aspiring to car ownership. Among women in particular, the car afforded privacy and security in a country where sexual harassment (*sekuhara*) was known to be a problem on public transport, until recent initiatives to introduce women-only carriages.

Other changes were also indicated offering a contrast to twentieth-century patterns of car ownership and car use. There was an increase in shared family use of the car, often with the family going out together, as well as an emphasis on groups of friends of the same sex going out in the car. Rather than commuting to work, cars were increasingly used for shopping, especially (and rather unexpectedly) for men. As well as for shopping women used the car for leisure and travel. Eighteen- to 24-year-olds were also buying cheaper and more second-hand cars, and keeping them for longer, demonstrating the pressure of rising rents and higher costs of living compared to the twentieth century. However, the survey also showed that women (nearly 62 per cent) were more inclined to buy new cars than men (52 per cent). Indeed, as was evident in the twentieth century to a large degree, women made crucial decisions about which car to buy in around 70 per cent of all car sales.[85]

In Britain too, since 2000 a more complex picture has begun to emerge. In a similar pattern to Japan, while the number of licensed vehicles continued to rise in the first decade of the twenty-first century, new car registrations showed a year-on-year decline, reflecting a number of factors, including changes in company car use and a general fall in use in urban areas.[86] A decline in car use has been observable among young adults since the mid-1990s, the reasons for which are largely financial. Costs of insurance and car purchase are high among a group who are achieving financial independence later than previous generations. There is also evidence, however, that like their counterparts in Japan, young people in Britain are less attracted to the car than their parents or grandparents, whether for environmental or more pragmatic reasons. Automobility appears to have lost some of its symbolic lustre, becoming simply one transport mode among others.[87] The revival of the railways in Britain since privatization in the early 1990s with passenger numbers doubling between 1995 and 2010 has also done something to blunt the inevitable progress of the car.[88] Meanwhile, there are signs of a definite shift within automobility itself towards low emission, low impact vehicles especially in high-density urban areas. As in Japan, sales of electric and hybrid cars have grown rapidly since the early 2000s, while Oxford City Council has threatened to ban all petrol and diesel vehicles from its city centre by 2020.[89] Connected and autonomous vehicles (CAVs), developed in Japan after 1977, are predicted to represent the next phase of vehicular transport, although experts suggest that the point at which the majority of new cars are CAVs is unlikely to arrive before the mid-twenty first century.[90] In both Britain and Japan, the car may be here to stay, it would seem, but its future form is uncertain.

Conclusion

So if the car system remains with us, what exactly has changed since the onset of mass automobility in the 1960s? Growing recognition of the environmental effects of mass motorization, in air pollution and climate change, has begun to moderate the celebratory aspects of car culture and inserted a troubling question mark in public discussion of roads and transport policy. This represents a significant departure from the eras of Manzoni and *Mai-kā* when the car appeared intimately aligned with the vision of freedom and the future. The expansion of mobility in the later twentieth century, too, of travel by rail, air or bicycle, means that use of the private car is increasingly viewed by people as one option among many rather than necessarily the privileged mode.[91]

The evidence is that in both Birmingham and Nagoya there has been at most a change, or at least a rebalancing of the relationship between the city and the automobile in the latter half of the twentieth century. In Japan, as in Britain, change was prompted as much by economic restructuring as changing attitudes towards the automobile. In Japan in the 1980s there was fear of the 'hollowing out' evident in the industrially developed nations as they moved production facilities to the developing nations. As welfare spending rose, this fear led to speculation that the 'English disease,' as it was widely referred to in the press, would reach Japan, beginning the cycle of economic decline, social conflict and inner-city decay.[92] In the 1980s, therefore, national, regional and city planning emphasized the importance of internationalization, technological innovation and improving the quality of life in Japan's major cities which had begun to lose population. Only Nagoya managed to buck the trend of population decline, taken by some observers to be a measure of its success in reinventing itself.[93] Crucially the city was able to weather the storms of globalization and industrial restructuring when it lost 35 per cent (roughly 130,000) of manufacturing jobs mostly between 1969 and 1981. Many of these jobs were in textiles and ceramics which were largely transferred to the developing economics of China and Southeast Asia to save labour costs. However, Nagoya made up for that loss with employment growth in the retail and service sectors.[94]

Since the 1980s, there has been a determination to improve Nagoya's image as a dull and lacklustre place dominated by the 100-metre-wide roads. Driven by Motoyama Masao, the same reforming mayor who presided over the Nagoya Urban Expressway conflict in the 1970s, the city's hopes were raised in 1984 when it became the Japanese candidate to host the 1988 Olympic Games, but it was struck a blow when it lost out to Los Angeles, ironically one of its sister cities. Turning away from its 'motor city' reputation, Nagoya adopted a 'Design City Declaration' after the successful hosting of the World Design Exposition in 1989 in the hope of promoting development that placed a high value on good urban design. The emphasis was on the upgrading of infrastructure, but focused on expanding the subway system and investing in buses and new terminals rather than roads.[95] At the centre of the plan was the new station complex which opened in 1999 and the construction of Chūbu Centrair International Airport which opened in 2005 to replace the outdated Nagoya Airport. A massive upgrade of the Nagoya Port area facilities, both in terms of cargo handling and as a place of leisure and entertainment, turned it into the most successful port in Japan. Parks and green spaces were not forgotten. Overall, fifteen additional parks were completed between 1985 and 1997 almost doubling green spaces per capita within the city itself.[96] Instead of building more shopping malls, the 100-metre-wide road Hisaya Ōdōri was reinvented as a 'Cultural Mall' with the creation of facilities such as the Aichi Arts Centre which opened in 1992 and an International Design Centre in Sakae.[97]

The Highbury Initiative and its implementation confirmed in very visible and physical terms the retreat from the idea of the motor city in Britain. In this respect places like Birmingham have indeed turned away from the car since the late twentieth century. Motorization no longer guides the vision of planners but a version of the 'walking city' across different ambient spaces, with controlled use of other modes of mobility from travelator to taxi. In the early 2000s the largest infrastructure project in Birmingham was not an urban motorway but a railway station, New Street Station, redeveloped between 2009 and 2015 at a cost of £600 million to accommodate, among other things, the new high-speed rail link, HS2. What this suggests is that while we are happy to rely on the car for certain of our travel needs, we no longer wish to have it in other parts of our urban lives. From the congestion charge to sleeping policemen, the private car has become ever more highly regulated in cities so that its imminent removal from city centres no longer seems as improbable as it did at the start of the twenty-first century. In urbanized societies like Japan and Britain, a large proportion of the population still relies on the car for shopping, commuting and ferrying. But from a historical viewpoint, the romance is over.

Yet ambiguity towards the automobile has not gone away. In 2005 Nagoya and Aichi hosted the World Expo. Its central message 'Nature's Wisdom' sums up the ME dilemma of the twentieth century:

> Thanks to rapid technological development, the 20th Century was characterized by mass-production and mass consumption, which in turn led to material improvements in our daily lives. At the same time, these trends resulted in various global issues such as desertification, global warming, and a shortage of natural resources. As these issues cannot be resolved by any one nation, the international community needs to unite in confronting them: we must come together and share our experience and wisdom, in order to create a new direction for humanity which is both sustainable and harmonious with nature.[98]

Lest we imagine this statement indicates a turning away from the car, the Expo was sponsored by Toyota Motor Corporation, an irony seemingly lost on those dazzled by the shiny futuristic vision of 'personal mobility' on display in the Toyota Group Pavilion.[99]

Conclusion

It is a historical commonplace to speak of the twentieth century as the 'century of the car' but it is a hyperbole that also conceals as much as it reveals.[1] After all, it was not the case everywhere or for everyone. Many parts of the world remained relatively untouched by automobility for the large part of the twentieth century and even in the developed West, the majority of households were car-less before the 1970s. In transport, the bicycle remained the principal means of getting about for millions and in technology, the internal combustion engine would have to compete for significance with other scientific breakthroughs such as the jet engine.[2] Moreover, where it took hold it was not so much the car as a commodity which transformed twentieth-century societies as automobility as a system. It was automobility involving all kinds of motorized transport and its infrastructure – roads, garages, car parks, oil refineries and so on – that was the moving force behind change.

But we have argued in this book that the car and automobility deserve a central place in the histories of twentieth-century Japan and Britain. When a 34-year-old Japanese male IT executive complained in *Newsweek* that the car was 'so 20th century',[3] that is because, in the words of Kristin Ross, it was 'the central vehicle of all twentieth-century modernization'.[4] The reasons are multiple. First, during the mid-twentieth century the motor industry developed as the major manufacturing industry in both countries, employing millions. It became the single most important export industry, driving Britain out of austerity in the 1950s and helped to fuel the Japanese economic miracle in the 1970s; at these successive historical moments Britain and Japan became, for a time, the world's leading exporters of cars. As a result, governments in both countries saw the motor industry as the barometer of national economic activity. Secondly, once automobility took hold it dominated transportation. While road freight supplanted rail in the carriage of goods between the wars in Britain, the private car won out over all other modes of transport in the second half of the twentieth century; only air travel could compare in terms of the exponential growth of passengers. In Japan rail continued to represent a rival to the car in some domains, such as commuting, but for Japanese drivers the private car came to represent the mode of choice for shopping, recreation and many other uses. Thirdly, automobility was a significant factor in helping to reshape everyday life in cities like Nagoya and Birmingham as we have shown. One of the reasons for the invisibility of automobility in so much of societal change in the twentieth century was that it rarely operated alone. Automobility was a key factor in the expansion of urban consumerism as shops and streets were recast to make them accessible to buses and cars, most notable in Birmingham. It equally helped to refashion the home as the car was brought into or under the home as in the Japanese carport and *doma jūtaku* (earth-floor house). In these ways automobility became knitted into the fabric of everyday life of households and whole societies in the developed world during the last quarter of the twentieth century. Fourthly, automobility had significant repercussions for the way the environment was understood as something increasingly to be protected from the effects of mass motorization, whether through the greening of the city or, ultimately, through measures to counteract global warming as the effects of CO_2 emissions on the ozone layer became evident from the mid-1980s. Finally – and of central importance here – our book has shown how automobility served to refigure the modern city itself, whether deliberately, as in the design of motorways and expressways, or indirectly, through the creation of urban 'blight', smog and pollution. As the British planner Colin Buchanan noted in his celebrated report, by the 1960s cities and cars could no longer be thought about separately; they had to be thought together.

As this implies, in certain respects Japan and Britain experienced the onset of automobility similarly. Mass motorization in both societies was underpinned if not directed by a sizeable motor industry. Both countries were highly urbanized which meant that planners and urban populations confronted similar sets of problems of congestion and pollution in the third quarter of the twentieth century. Both were late to create a motorway network between and within major urban centres. More surprising, perhaps, the polluting effects of mass motorization gave rise to effective protest movements at the same historical moment around 1970.

But these comparisons do not mean that the advent of urban automobility occurred everywhere in the same fashion or – more pertinently in the light of recent historiography – that countries like Britain and Japan followed the example of North America. It is the value of comparative history of the type we have undertaken in this study that the differences in the adoption of a transnational phenomenon – automobility – become visible and open to analysis. One key difference between Japan and Britain was in chronology. Britain's transition to mass automobility was drawn out. A national trunk road system was in place by the 1920s and there were already more than 2 million private cars on British roads by the outbreak of the Second World War in 1939. While the main phase of mass motorization occurred in Britain between 1950 and 1970 when cars increased five-fold, this was still notably less sharp and concentrated than in Japan where, as we have seen, numbers of passenger cars were negligible before 1960, and outnumbered by 'light vehicles' (*keijidōsha*) until the 1970s. Roads in post-war Japan likewise remained in a rudimentary state before the late 1950s when construction of the Meishin Expressway and the 100-metre-wide roads in Nagoya began. But in the 1960s car ownership accelerated in extraordinary fashion, rapidly surpassing the number of vehicles on Britain's roads, while a national expressway network, connecting the main hubs in Japan's Megalopolitan belt, was implemented in the same decade. The 'shock' of mass automobility in urban Japan was more acute than in urban Britain partly because it occurred so rapidly and on such a massive scale. Differences were spatial as well as temporal. Population density, much lower and more stable in Birmingham than

Nagoya, had implications for roads planning. In Nagoya, roads aligned with generous walkways for pedestrians and greenery were means of creating space in otherwise congested districts. The example of the Parisian Champs-Élysées as a locus both for traffic and for strollers loomed large in the imagination of planners in urban Japan but hardly at all in urban Britain.

There were also significant differences in the ways motorization occurred in the two societies as well as its timing, as we shall see. This dialectic of similarity and difference is valuable because it reminds us that while the coming of automobility was transnational it was far from uniform. The technics, planning and meanings of automobility were distinct in, say, socialist Eastern Europe, the 'global Middle East' and suburban Australia in ways of which we are only beginning to be made aware.[5] At the same time, automobility was an inexorably global process as historians are beginning to recognize.[6] How, then, do these themes play out in relation to the objectives which structure the research behind the present book? In our concluding remarks, we return to each of the three objectives in turn to assess how far our findings provide answers to the tasks we originally set.

Meeting the objectives

The first objective of the study was to compare the relationship between motor vehicles, the urban environment and planning in two major centres, Nagoya and Birmingham, and analyse their reconstruction as 'motor cities'. In particular we wanted to examine the place of roads and the associated infrastructure of automobility – underpasses, flyovers, car parks and so on – in the reconstruction of the two cities in the decades after 1945. What priority if any was given to the car in the planning of the post-war city and how did this compare with other priorities such as mass housing and consumer demand?

Both Birmingham and Nagoya can be defined as 'motor cities' in several senses. They were both major centres of motor production. In the case of Nagoya this applied less to the city itself than to the Chūkyō 'Auto Region' of which the city was an integral part; the main site of manufacturing, Toyota City, was over 18 miles (30 kilometres) from central Nagoya and the motor industry was spread over a region containing some 10 million people. The motor industry was more concentrated in the Birmingham area itself, considered as the headquarters of Britain's motor industry, but it too had important regional outposts, at Coventry and elsewhere in the West Midlands. Although in neither city did the motor industry have a direct influence over urban planning, planners in both cities saw their environs as profoundly shaped by the advent of mass motorization. This was, again, most strongly the case in Birmingham where the guiding influence of Herbert Manzoni as City Engineer between the mid-1930s and the early 1960s meant that the vision of Birmingham as the 'city of the motor car' remained remarkably constant over this period. Birmingham's network of arterial and ring roads was laid down between the wars and only altered to accommodate the links to the national motorway system via the Aston Expressway and Gravelly Hill in the later 1960s. The relationship of the chief architect of post-war Nagoya, Tabuchi Jurō, to the planning of the city's major roads was less straightforward. He was almost certainly influenced by his experience of working in China during the Japanese occupation where a lack of consensus and popular support had prevented the implementation of ambitious colonial urban planning. While Ishikawa Hideaki's 1920s blueprint for roads building in Nagoya was an important legacy, after 1945 the building of major urban and national roads was deemed essential for reasons of economic recovery. The relatively late expansion of car ownership in Japan also meant that factors other than accommodating the private motorist were uppermost before the 1960s. Such factors included the need for firebreaks to mitigate the effects of natural disasters like earthquakes and typhoons and the desire to increase the area of green space in what were densely populated metropolitan areas by British standards.

Yet automobility and roads drove the reconstruction of cities like Nagoya and Birmingham in the middle third of the twentieth century to a much greater extent than planning and architectural historians, concerned as they are with buildings rather than infrastructure, have been prepared to acknowledge. The Inner Ring Road was the centrepiece of Manzoni's 'new Birmingham', conjoined with slum clearance, renewal of utilities like gas and water, and the revitalization of the city centre. Equally, the five 'new towns' in central Birmingham which rehoused populations from the old back-to-backs in new tower blocks were linked to a new type of road in Britain, the 'parkway', itself conceived as part of the Middle Ring. The imperative for new roads was less trumpeted in Nagoya but scarcely less marked. In the city centre the proportion of land accounted for by roads expanded from 17 per cent in the early 1950s to around 41 per cent twenty years later. Nagoya's underground shopping areas or *sakariba* were developed as an escape from the so-called white streets, reflecting the dominance of motor vehicles in the grid-pattern streets above. Here was a form of 'vertical integration' on a scale that proponents of 'traffic architecture' in 1960s Britain could only dream of. Almost every new development in built form, from tower block housing to shopping mall, was attached to networks that emphasized the priority given to automobility. The only rival to the car was the train, the underground pedestrian and shopping areas in Nagoya being designed originally around the city's railway stations. But even here the car became increasingly indispensable, some nine underground car parks being built between 1965 and 1978 to give access to the 'white streets'.

The second aim was to examine what we termed the ME or motorization/environment dilemma at the point of its historical emergence. The ME dilemma encapsulated the contradiction between the desire for freedom and mobility that the car (and to a lesser extent, the motorcycle) stood for, on the one hand, and, on the other, the dawning recognition among politicians and citizens of the damage to the environment caused by mass automobility. This was not a contradiction that was automatically evident to contemporaries in either Britain or Japan. Those who enthusiastically embraced the opportunities of the 'My Car Era' in early 1960s Japan saw the car as a central component of the consumer-driven modernity that economic prosperity was opening up; it was, in all senses, a 'good'. Politicians of both main political parties in Britain similarly welcomed private car ownership as an extension of home ownership, something to which every family and household could aspire and which, in conditions of continuous growth, could gradually be brought within the reach of all.

Furthermore, in the eyes of planners like Manzoni, the infrastructure of automobility, above all new and expanded roads, could be used to solve urban problems: to help clear slum housing, renew utilities and even provide new green spaces between roads and tower blocks. The vision of the 'motor city', articulated most clearly in Birmingham, was of a city made legible, modern and mobile.

It was only gradually that the ME dilemma came to the forefront of public attention. Air pollution from motor traffic in the United States, Los Angeles especially, was noted internationally in the 1950s but in Japan and Britain 'smog' was attributed to other sources, such as industry and (in Britain) smoke from coal-fuelled household fires.[7] In both countries, too, concerns about the impact of increasing levels of automobility tended to be couched in terms of sense perception: motor vehicles were associated by 1960 with 'visual pollution', cluttering up city streets, with noise, and above all with the problems of traffic congestion and road casualties, neither of which were new but which were deemed to be reaching unacceptably high levels. 'All the indications are', wrote the British traffic planner Colin Buchanan in 1963, 'that given its head the motor vehicle would wreck our towns within a decade'.[8] What Buchanan referred to as the urban 'environment' needed protection from the ravages of automobility no less than did the countryside. Similarly, concerns about traffic and smog voiced in Tokyo at the time of the Olympic Games in 1964 focused on the obliteration by smog of the classical views of Mount Fuji, altering the perceptual relationship between the city and its surroundings.

The tipping point for the ME dilemma, however, was only reached in the years around 1970 and it was triggered in the first instance by invisible rather than visible pollution. Japan led the way. By 1968 there was evidence from Tokyo of asthma conditions related to emissions from traffic on the urban expressway. In December 1968 the first anti-roads group was formed in Nagoya in opposition to the city's Expressway Plan, announced the previous year. In Birmingham, similar protests were ignited by the concerns about noise and lead pollution caused by the opening of the Gravelly Hill Interchange – Spaghetti Junction – in 1972. In both Nagoya and Birmingham it was the public health effects of emissions from motor traffic that fuelled debates about the negative externalities of urban roads, particularly motorways, throughout the 1970s. One result was to add a significant new layer to local political activism, involving women and children, the latter being seen as especially vulnerable to the epidemiological and physical effects of urban traffic. While fears about health remained at the forefront of public concern in the two cities, they were joined by other issues: 'blight' in areas through which major roads passed, 'smog', noise and vibration. By the mid-1970s the process of urban road construction had become mired in political, legal and financial issues which slowed the process of construction or in some cases, such as London's Motorway Box, brought it to a halt altogether. The civic celebration which accompanied the opening of Birmingham's Inner Ring Road in 1972 was almost certainly the last of its kind, in Britain or Japan. The Ring Road's subsequent history, first as the object of investigation for corrosion and corruption, and then in 1988 its identification at the Highbury workshop as an obstacle to Birmingham's urban renewal, provides a graphic illustration of the multiple ways in which automobility itself came into question in the two decades after 1970. All this occurred against the global backdrop of successive oil crises and, from the mid-1980s, the 'discovery' of ozone depletion and the threat of global warming to which transport in general and automobility in particular were found to be significant contributors. By the late twentieth century it was impossible to think of mass motorization as an unalloyed good; the age of innocence was over.

Our third aim was to examine how automobility and environment, the car and 'urban nature', were thought about in the process of planning 'motor cities' like Nagoya and Birmingham. Were there significant differences in the ways they were conceptualized? Did the allegedly non-dualistic view of self and nature that infuses much Japanese thought mean that the car and the city were conjoined in a different fashion from Britain where a fundamental division between human society and the physical world could be seen to have structured the way in which the 'motor city' was envisaged?

We remain sceptical about the idea that Japanese modernity was somehow singular (or, indeed, that Britain's modernity was) – or that these could be reduced to differences between 'East' and 'West', group-orientated and individualistic societies.[9] Both Japan and Britain were cultures which exhibited a relatively high degree of reverence for aesthetic and social tradition while also pioneering and embracing new, modern forms of urban living. Automobility was as much part of Japanese consumerism in the My Car Era as it was in 1960s Britain; shopping was no less integrated with Nagoya's underground malls than Birmingham's Inner Ring was with the neon glitter of Smallbrook Ringway and the walk-in world of the Bull Ring. Nor did the two motoring nations afford a strict contrast in attitudes to eco-consciousness and conservation. While the ever-present threat of natural disasters meant that Japanese town planners like Tabuchi Jurō and Ishikawa Hideaki had always to be alert to environmental considerations, conserving the urban environment was of paramount importance to many 1960s British planners like Konrad Smigielski at Leicester and Wilfred Burns at Newcastle upon Tyne who also preached large-scale road-building.[10] This commitment to preserving the urban fabric where possible was paralleled in Nagoya by the practice of moving thousands of individual buildings to enable road widening. While Herbert Manzoni at Birmingham was largely antipathetic to conservation, his engineering-led view of roads and town planning was not the sole or dominant perspective, in Britain or in planning circles abroad.

Differences of approach there were though. One of the most fundamental – and conceptual – was the stress on scale and space in Japanese approaches to urban design. This was true of Nagoya especially. Tabuchi's plan for roads in central Nagoya emphasized not only breadth, enabling multiple lanes of traffic, but also space in the form of green parkland between carriage-ways and wide tree-lined pavements at the sides. The intention, as Tabuchi himself made clear, was to create a vista from which to view the TV Tower as well as a site for strolling and sitting; Tabuchi's analogy of Hisaya Ōdōri with Paris's Champs Élysées caught something of the scale and purpose of the road but underplayed its distinctively Japanese, multi-level form of combining motion and vision, automobile and pedestrian mobilities (Figure 7.1).

By comparison Manzoni's road designs were more linear, emphasizing speed and flow of motor vehicles. Only in the 'parkways' that bisected the central tower block estates was green space fully integrated into the newly created townscape. The

Figure 7.1 Space and vista: Hisaya Ōdōri seen from the TV tower. Photo by Susan Townsend.

small numbers of pedestrian islands at Colmore Circus and Manzoni Gardens were overshadowed by the roads that surrounded them. In Manzoni's Birmingham, speed – and thus time – was of the essence. When it was proposed in 1960, the extended Skyway flyover on the Coventry Road was justified by the fact that it would allegedly connect the expanding Birmingham airport with the city centre by car in only ten minutes. Traffic flow, not space or vista, was the imperative that underpinned road layout and design in post-1945 Birmingham. Other non-motorized types of mobility, such as bicycles, were deliberately excluded from the ring roads while pedestrians were separated by rails and subways.

Consequently, while the infrastructure of automobility in both Nagoya and Birmingham was constructed according to an engineering vision of the city, this vision was implemented in different combinations that prioritized space or speed, aesthetic coherence or functional efficiency. In envisaging the Japanese 'motor city' in 1960, Tange Kenzo spoke of a 'flowing mobility' that gave 'the open organisation of the city its organic life'. While they might have shared Tange's aspirations, these were not terms that his counterparts in Birmingham, Manzoni and his successor Neville Borg, would have recognized as meaningful.

In certain respects, then, the relationship between the car and the city was understood differently in Japan and Britain; even the narrower idea of the 'motor city' did not denote the same thing to the planners and policymakers involved in shaping Nagoya and Birmingham. Yet the histories of this relationship in the two places were remarkably similar in many ways. Planning for expanding road traffic began in Birmingham and Nagoya from the 1920s; it was part of the larger town planning movement itself and in Birmingham, in particular, the idea of the 'motor city' was installed as a guiding principle from the mid-1930s. In other words, the notion of the city as organized importantly around power-driven mobility preceded the advent of mass motorization in Britain and Japan by over a generation. Major new roads were also a long time in the making. The plan for Birmingham's Inner Ring was outlined in the 1930s; it gained parliamentary approval in 1946 but construction did not begin till over a decade later and it was only fully opened to traffic in 1972. In Nagoya the Urban Expressway, first planned from 1961, was less protracted in its design and construction but still took almost two decades from conception to completion. Protests in the two cities arose in the wake of these major roads projects and centred on the same issue, air pollution at broadly the same historical moment around 1970. Finally, automobility came under pressure in both cities during the last decades of the twentieth century, urban motorways coming to be seen as a corollary of economic decline and a block to urban renewal in Birmingham, while in Nagoya and Japan a more general 'turning away from the car' (*kuruma banare*) was observable. Japanese commentators noted that in the early twenty-first century the domestic car market had reached saturation and young people, in particular, were shunning the car for environmental and other reasons. Yet even here the car remained an object of desire. In effect, within the long-term trajectory of the mid- and later twentieth century, urbanized countries like Japan and Britain underwent broadly similar processes of planning for the car and experiences of resistance to it.

In the early decades of the twenty-first century we have arrived at a point where the 'car system' as it was known over the previous hundred or more years is in question. Sociologists such as Kingsley Dennis and John Urry have suggested that 'the car as a complete system may have been surpassed', by which they mean a system of steel-bodied automobiles, fuelled by petrol, powered by the internal combustion engine, and personally owned. Kingsley and Dennis argue that simultaneously 'a new system is coming into being'. Our current condition, they propose, 'is a bit like the period around 1900 when the current car system was being formed; it was emergent although no one at the time could imagine exactly what it was going to be like'. Governments in Japan, Britain and elsewhere have followed a similar line of thinking as have the major automobile manufacturers. They talk of electric cars, CAVs (connected autonomous vehicles), of car sharing and of 'disrupters' to the old dispensation such as Uber. Experts and policy advisers attempt to peer into the future in order to estimate the infrastructure necessary to support this new emergent system and the timescales involved.[11] Crucial decisions will need to be made involving massive expenditure, no less significant than those which accompanied the advent of mass motorization in the mid-twentieth century. Equally, changes will be made to cities to accommodate the results of governmental decisions; it is likely that more cities will follow the example of

Oxford in excluding petrol and diesel cars from its city centre. In the developed world the form of cities may not itself change dramatically but the ways of getting about them are likely to alter substantially over the next generation. All the signs are that the age of private car dominance is giving way to plural mobilities, to walking, skateboarding, cycling, tram-riding and more.

Yet even as this new future has begun to open up, so it enables historians to examine the contours of the twentieth-century car system which for so long went largely unremarked. If the twentieth century was the century of the car, the rule of automobility became normalized to the point of invisibility. The car seemed inevitable, timeless, permanent, even as resource depletion, roads protest and global warming increasingly came to pervade public discussion of automobility after 1970. It was equally unimaginable for most of the twentieth century to envisage cities without cars, so powerfully, it seemed, had the urban environment been shaped around them.

One effect of the critical questioning of the future of automobility, therefore, is to throw into relief the features of the car system as it evolved over the previous century. This book is a product of that moment of questioning. In it, we have examined how automobility and the city began, through planning, to be thought together as an ensemble embodied in the concept of the motor city. From the comparative study of Japan and Britain, automobility emerges as a global process with recognizable features across countries in different parts of the world but one which adapted to distinct historical conditions and cultural patterns. It was never a process that possessed a singular logic or centre, important as the example of North America may have been. For those countries, like India and China, that are only now entering the age of mass motorization, as well as those societies which see themselves as turning away from the car, the message is clear: automobility shares many features across societies, but it is also indelibly marked by its encounter with the physical and cultural environment in which it is embedded – and which it, in turn, transforms.

Notes

Note on Text and Translation

1   *Motor Cities: Automobility and the Urban Environment in Nagoya and Birmingham, c. 1955–1973* (RA15GO175, 2011–2015).

Introduction

1   *Tokyo Nagaremono* (1966), [Film] Dir. Suzuki Seijun, accessed 8 May 2018, https://archive.org/details/TokyoDrifter.
2   Le Corbusier, *The City of Tomorrow and Its Planning* (New York: Dover Press, 1987), xxiii.
3   Ibid., xxiv.
4   Japan Automobile Manufacturers Association (JAMA), 'Motor Vehicle Statistics of Japan 2009', http://www.jama.english.jp; British Road Federation, *Basic Road Statistics* (London: British Road Federation, 1975).
5   Peter R. White, 'Trends in Transport: Japan and Britain Compared', *Transportation Planning and Technology* 10 (1985): 44.
6   The literature on automobility is massive but for a useful summary of current debates, see Kingsley Dennis and John Urry, *After the Car* (Cambridge: Polity, 2009); Brian Ladd, 'Cities on Wheels: Cars and Public Space', in *New Blackwell Companion to the City*, ed. Gary Bridge and Sophie Watson (Chichester: John Wiley, 2011), 265–274; Matthew Paterson, *Automobile Politics: Ecology and Cultural Political Economy* (Cambridge: Cambridge University Press, 2007).
7   Dennis and Urry, *After the Car*, 10, 38.
8   Jeffrey Broadbent, *Environmental Politics in Japan* (Cambridge: Cambridge University Press, 2010), refers to the 'Growth Environment dilemma', but the motorization/environment dilemma is a more targeted feature of our book.
9   The classic early indictment of the safety record of the American automobile industry is Ralph Nader, *Unsafe at Any Speed* (New York: Grossman Publishers, 1965).
10 Peter D. Norton, *Fighting Traffic: The Dawn of the Motor Age in the American City* (Cambridge, MA: MIT Press, 2008); D. W. Jones, *Mass Motorization and Mass Transit: An American History and Policy Analysis* (Bloomington: Indiana University Press, 2008). Both these authors eschew the conspiracy theory that the removal of streetcars was the result of a deliberate policy by automobile manufacturers, notably General Motors, to buy up streetcar companies and create an effective transport monopoly.
11 Stephen L. Bottles, *Los Angeles and the Automobile: The Making of the Modern City* (Berkeley: University of California Press, 1987); Tom Lewis, *Divided Highways: Building the Interstate Highways, Transforming American Life*, 2nd edn. (Ithaca: Cornell University Press, 2013).

12 Cotton Seiler, *Republic of Drivers: A Cultural History of Automobility in America* (Chicago: Chicago University Press, 2008), 9.
13 J. M. Diefendorf, 'Artery: Urban Reconstruction and Traffic Planning in Postwar Germany', *Journal of Urban History* 15, no. 2 (1989): 131–158.
14 Jonathan Mantle, *Car Wars* (New York: Little, Brown and Co., 1995), 102–103.
15 Roy Church, *The Rise and Decline of the British Motor Industry* (Cambridge: Cambridge University Press, 1994), 44; JAMA, 'Motor Vehicle Statistics'.
16 For a fascinating account of Britain's first national motorway, see Peter Merriman, *Driving Spaces: A Cultural-Historical Geography of England's M1 Motorway* (Chichester: John Wiley, 2007).
17 Cited in T. Fujino, 'Expressway in Japan: Toll Road System and Status', East Nippon Expressway Co., Ltd. (NEXCO East), last modified, 4 November 2002, http://www.carecprogram.org/uploads/events/2009/Road-Development-Seminar-Tajikistan/JICA-Expressway-in-Japan-Toll-Road-System.pdf.
18 On bombing and its legacy, see Nicholas Tiratsoo, Jun'ichi Hasegawa, Tony Mason and Takao Matsumura, *Urban Reconstruction in Britain and Japan, 1945–1955* (Luton: University of Luton Press, 2002).
19 An earlier attempt to understand the history of automobility across Western Europe and North America is Gijs Mom, *Atlantic Automobilism: Emergence and Persistence of the Car 1895–1940* (New York: Berghan, 2014). Urban history itself has recently undergone a transnational turn, often assumed to supplant an older comparative history but which can also undervalue the insights to be derived from the latter approach. For a useful overview of recent thinking, see the collection edited by Nicolas Kenny and Rebecca Madgin, *Cities beyond Borders: Comparative and Transnational Approaches to Urban History* (Abingdon: Routledge, 2015).
20 Toyoda Ki'ichiro, regarded as the founder of Toyota Motor Corporation, had already made an important contribution to automatic loom technology in the 1920s after visiting Platt Brothers in Oldham while working in the Toyoda textile business. Legend has it that the money he made in selling the rights to manufacture and sell the technology back to Platt Brothers in 1929 (around £100,000) was re-invested in the development of his prototype automobile. However, for a more accurate account of Toyota's founding, see Wada Kazuo, 'The Fable of the Birth of the Japanese Automobile Industry: A Reconsideration of the Toyota-Platt Agreement of 1929', *Business History* 48, no. 1 (2006): 90–118.
21 The name 'Toyota' was chosen after a public competition was held in 1936. There is some debate about why the name was chosen. See 'Why Is the Car Giant Toyota Not Toyoda?', BBC News, accessed 4 December 2014, http://news.bbc.co.uk/1/hi/world/asia-pacific/8534294.stm, 24 February 2010. But the most likely explanation is that while it retains its root, it also differentiates itself and the name 'Toyota' cannot be confused with any other Japanese word since it is, so to speak, 'empty' of meaning.
22 A. J. Jacobs, 'Embedded Autonomy and Uneven Metropolitan Development: A Comparison of the Detroit and Nagoya Auto Regions, 1969–2000', *Urban Studies*, 40, no. 2 (2003): 335–360.
23 Gordon Cherry, *Birmingham: A Study in Geography, History and Planning* (Chichester: John Wiley, 1994), 65. For the early years of Austin, see also Roy Church, *Herbert Austin: The British Motor Car Industry to 1941* (London: Europa, 1979).
24 D. J. Norton, 'Inside the Inner Ring Road', accessed 14 January 2015, http://www.photobydjnorton.com/InsideTheInnerRingRoad.html.

25 H. Mönnich, *Die Autostadt* (Munich: Wilhelm Andermann Verlag, 1951); A. Harth et al., *Wolfsburg: Stadt am Wendepunkt* (Opleden: Kesje und Bundrich, 2000); Martina Hessler, 'Crisis in Automotive Cities: The Ambivalent Role of the Car Industry in the "Autostadt" Wolfsburg and the "Motor Town" Detroit', in *Industrial Cities: History and Future*, ed. Clemens Zimmerman (Frankfurt: Campus Verlag, 2013).

26 The literature on Detroit is large but see Scott Martelle, *Detroit: A Biography* (Chicago: Chicago Review Press, 2014). The classic work is Thomas Sugrue, *The Origins of the Urban Crisis: Race and Inequality in Post-War Detroit* (Princeton: Princeton University Press, 1996).

27 Tabuchi Jurō, *Aru Dobokugishi no Hanjijoden* (Nagoya: Chūbu Keizai Rengōkai, 1962).

28 Norton, 'Inside the Inner Ring'.

29 Only one other 100-metre-wide road was eventually built as part of Hiroshima's memorialization as the first atomic bomb site. Hasegawa Jun'ichi, 'The 100-metre-road in the Reconstruction of Bombed Cities in Japan', *Planning History* 28, nos. 2&3 (2006): 13.

30 André Sorensen, *The Making of Urban Japan: Cities and Planning from Edo to the Twenty-First Century* (Abingdon: Routledge, 2002), 162.

31 Michael Hebbert, '*Sen-biki* amidst *Desakota*: Urban Sprawl and Urban Planning in Japan', in *Planning for Cities and Regions in Japan*, ed. P. Shapira, I. Masser and D. W. Edgington (Liverpool: Liverpool University Press, 1994), 70.

32 See Anthony Sutcliffe and Roger Smith, *History of Birmingham, Vol. 3: Birmingham 1939–1970* (London: Oxford University Press, 1974), ch. 5 and pp. 489–490.

33 In Japan, modern urban planning began in 1869 with the new Meiji government's designation of regional authorities to replace the feudal domains (*han*) of the Tokugawa period. Thus, the former feudal area of Owari-han became Nagoya-han. Then, in 1871, the 274 independent domains were abolished and replaced by 72 normal prefectures (*ken*) and 3 special prefectures (Kyoto, Osaka and Tokyo). Nagoya-han became Nagoya-ku, or Nagoya-ward. After further rationalization in 1890 there were just forty-six prefectures. In the massive upheavals of this period, it took a while for the regions and cities to settle into their modern form. Initially, in 1872 Nagoya and Aichi (covering the rest of the Owari domain) both became prefectures, but in 1889, after several more re-designations Nagoya became Nagoya-shi (Nagoya City), the capital city of Aichi prefecture. *Nagoya-shi: Naka-ku seishikō 100 shūnen kinen*, (Nagoya: Nagoya Central Ward Office, 2010), 30.

34 The Chūkyō Metropolitan Area is one of seven such areas designated after the 1995 Population Census of Japan. Each metropolitan area consists of a central city, in this case Nagoya and the surrounding area (cities, towns and villages). 'Statistics Bureau of Japan Home Page: Explanation of Terms for the 1999 Census', accessed 22 August 2017, http://www.stat.go.jp/english/data/jigyou/yougo.htm.

35 The 1971 figure for Birmingham was 1,013,000, Sutcliffe and Smith, *Birmingham*, 179. *Nagoya My Town* (Nagoya: Nagoya City Hall, 2008), 39.

36 According to the 2001 Population Census, Birmingham is around 268 square km with a population density of 3,649 people per square km (compared with 377.2 per square km for England). Nagoya covers a larger area of nearly 327 square km with a population density of 6,818 per square km (Japan's population density is 340 people per square km).

37 For recent economic statistics on Nagoya, see 'Nagoya Industry – Introduction to Companies Established in Nagoya', accessed 23 August 2017, http://www.city.nagoya.jp/en/cmsfiles/contents/0000032/32724/9_Nagoya_Industry.pdf.

38 Joseph McKenna, *Birmingham: The Building of a City* (Stroud: Tempus, 2005), 9.

39 The most authoritative history of Birmingham remains the three-volume study under the general editorship of Asa Briggs: Volume 1, Conrad Gill, *Manor to Borough to 1865*

(London: Oxford University Press, 1952); Volume 2: Asa Briggs, *Borough and City, 1865–1938* (London: Oxford University Press, 1952); the reference for Volume 3 by Anthony Sutcliffe and Roger Smith is cited above in fn.25. See also Eric Hopkins, *Birmingham: The First Manufacturing Town in the World* (London: Weidenfeld and Nicholson, 1989).

40   Bournville Village Trust, *When We Build Again* (Birmingham: Bournville Trust, 1941), 52.
41   Sutcliffe and Smith, *Birmingham*, 168.
42   John D. Eyre, *Nagoya: The Changing Geography of a Japanese Regional Metropolis* (Chapel Hill: University of North Carolina Press, 1982), 1, 22.
43   *Nagoya My Town*, 37.
44   Eyre, *Nagoya*, 32.
45   Jacobs, 'Embedded Autonomy', 336–337.
46   Carola Hein, 'Rebuilding Japanese Cities after 1945', in *Rebuilding Urban Japan after 1945*, ed. Carola Hein, Jeffry Diefendorf and Yorifusa Ishida (London: Palgrave Macmillan, 2003), 9.
47   Ibid.
48   The process of land readjustment is explained more fully in Chapter 1.
49   West Midland Group, *Conurbation: A Planning Survey of Birmingham and the Black Country by the West Midland Group* (London: The Architectural Press, 1948), 209.
50   Eyre, *Nagoya*, 34.
51   Estimates for the destruction in Nagoya vary. According to Nagoya City Planning Office, 23 per cent of Nagoya's urban area was destroyed. *Fukkō Tochikukaku Seiri Jigyō no Aramashi* (Nagoya: Nagoya City Planning Office, 1991), 5. However, the United States Strategic Bombing Survey estimated that 31 per cent of the city's area (12.4 square miles) was destroyed out of 40 square miles. 'United States Strategic Bombing Survey (USSBS): The Effects of the Air Attack on Nagoya, (June, 1947), 8', accessed 28 August 2016, https://babel.hathitrust.org/cgi/pt?id=mdp.39015002274325; view=1up;seq=3. See also Eyre, *Nagoya*.
52   Cherry, *Birmingham*, 134–136.
53   Carl Chinn *Brum Undaunted: Birmingham during the Blitz*, 2nd edn. (Brewin: Studley, Warks, 2005), 132.
54   The literature on urban devastation and reconstruction after the Second World War is substantial. A selective sample might include Tiratsoo, Hasegawa, Mason and Matsumura, *Urban Reconstruction in Britain and Japan, 1945–1955*; Carola Hein, Jeffry Diefendorf and Yorifusa Ishida, eds., *Rebuilding Urban Japan after 1945* (London: Palgrave Macmillan, 2003); Jeffry Diefendorf, *In the Wake of War. The Reconstruction of Germany's Bombed Cities After World War II* (Oxford: Oxford University Press, 1993); Mark Clapson and Peter Larkham, eds., *The Blitz and Its Legacy' Wartime Destruction to Post-War Reconstruction* (Aldershot: Ashgate, 2013).
55   The foundational work here of course is Edward Said, *Orientalism* (Harmondsworth: Penguin, 1985 [1978]). See Simon Gunn, *History and Cultural Theory* (London: Longman, 2006), ch. 7 for a critical survey of postcolonialism and historical writing.
56   For historians, the most interesting statement on this is Dipesh Chakrabarty, *Provincialising Europe* (Princeton: Princeton University Press, 2000).
57   For specific examples relating to Japanese urbanism, see Gideon S. Golany et al., *Japanese Urban Environment* (Oxford: Pergamon, 1998) and to some extent Barrie Shelton, *Learning from the Japanese City: West Meets East in Urban Design* (London: E&FN Spon, 1999); Karel van Wolferen, *The Enigma of Japanese Power: People and Politics in a Stateless Nation* (London: Macmillan, 1989) provides a standard *Nihonjinron* analysis of Japan's economic miracle. For a critique of

Nihonjinron literature, see Peter N. Dale *The Myth of Japanese Uniqueness* (London: Routledge, 1988).
58 Conrad Totman, *A History of Japan* (Oxford: Blackwell, 2005), 2–3.
59 Henry D. Smith, 'Tokyo as an Idea: An Exploration of Japanese Urban Thought until 1945', *Journal of Japanese Studies* 4, no. 1 (Winter 1978): 46.
60 Golany et al., *Japanese Urban Environment*, xxxiii. See also, Carola Hein, 'Machi: Neighborhood and Small Town. The Foundation for Urban Transformation in Japan', *Journal of Urban History* 35, no. 1 (2008): 75–107.
61 Chakrabarty, *Provincialising Europe*, 20.
62 The literature on the mid-later twentieth century is only just evolving. For comments on the circulation of traffic engineering, see Brian Ladd, *Autophobia: Love and Hate in the Automotive Age* (Chicago: Chicago University Press, 2008), 126. P. Lundin, 'Mediating Modernity: Planning Experts and the Making of the "Car-Friendly" City in Europe', in *Urban Machinery: Inside European Cities*, ed. M. Hård and T. J. Misa. (Cambridge, MA: MIT Press, 2008), 257–280. On 'transnational municipalism', see Shane Ewen, 'Transnational Municipalism in a Europe of Second Cities: Rebuilding Birmingham with Municipal Networks', in *Another Global City: Historical Explorations into the Transnational Municipal Moment, 1850–2000*, ed. Pierre-Yves Saunier and Shane Ewen (Basingstoke: Palgrave Macmillan, 2008), 101–117 and Jeffrey Hanes, 'Pacific Crossings? Urban Progressivism in Modern Japan', 51–68 in the same volume.
63 Although there are signs that this may be changing – see Nancy Kwak, 'Research in Urban History: Recent Theses on International and Comparative Urban History', *Urban History* 35, no. 2 (2008): 316–325.
64 For Britain, see John Gold, *The Practice of Modernism: Modern Architects and Urban Transformation, 1954–1972* (London: Routledge, 2007); Otto Saumarez Smith, 'Central Government and Town Centre Redevelopment in Britain 1959–1966', *Historical Journal* 58, no. 1 (2015): 217–244; Patrick Dunleavy, *The Politics of Mass Housing, 1945–1975* (Oxford: Oxford University Press, 1981). For Japan, Hein et al., *Rebuilding Urban Japan*; Sorensen, *The Making of Urban Japan*.
65 Stephen Graham and Simon Marvin, *Splintering Urbanism: Networked Infrastructures, Technological Mobilities and the Urban Condition* (London: Routledge, 2001), also Ash Amin and Nigel Thrift, *Cities: Reimagining the Urban* (Cambridge: Polity, 2002).
66 Dennis and Urry, *After the Car*, 63. For a further elaboration of the 'car system', see also John Urry, *Mobilities* (Cambridge: Polity, 2007), 115ff.
67 Ministry of Transport, *Traffic in Towns. A Study of the Long-Term Problems of Traffic in Urban Areas*. Reports of the Working and Steering Group (London: HMSO, 1963). On the historical context see Simon Gunn, 'The Buchanan Report, Environment and the Problem of Traffic in 1960s Britain', *Twentieth Century British History* 22, no. 4 (2011): 521–542; on the international context see Gunn, 'Introduction' to *Traffic in Towns* (Oxford: Routledge, 2015), xi–xii.
68 Golany et al., *Japanese Urban Environment*, xlvii.
69 Richard A. Johnson, *Six Men Who Built the Modern Auto Industry* (St. Paul, MN: Motorbooks, 2005), 54–55.
70 Gunn, 'Buchanan Report'; John Pendlebury, *Conservation in the Age of Consensus* (London: Routledge, 2009), 50–52.
71 F. Rosenbluth and M. F. Thies, 'The Political Economy of Japanese Pollution Regulation', Paper prepared for presentation at the annual meeting of the American Political Science Association, 2–5 September, Atlanta, Georgia (1999), 20–21, www.yale-university.com/leitner/resources/docs/1999-01.Pdf.

Chapter 1

1. 'City of Birmingham Rebuilds', *Architect and Building News*, 15 April 1959, 480.
2. Nagoya-shi Keikaku Kyoku, *Nagoya Toshi Keikaku-shi: Taishō 8 – Shōwa 44* (Nagoya: Nagoya-shi Keikaku Kyoku, 1999), 215.
3. For the details of the story prior to the Second World War see Sutcliffe and Smith, *Birmingham*, 400–401.
4. Nagoya Toshi Kenkyūkai, 'Sensai Fukkō Keikaku ni tomonau Nagoya no Toshi Kōzo no Henyō ni kansuru Kenkyū', *Chi'iki Mondai Kenkyū*, no. 52 (1996): 9–10.
5. The full story is told at some length in Justine Cook, 'Constructing Britain's Road Network: The Scientific Governance of British Roads and Their Users, 1900–1963' (University of Kent PhD, 2018), chs. 1–3.
6. H. G. Wells, paper to the Fabian Society published as Appendix 1 to *Mankind in the Making* (London: Chapman and Hall, 1903), 415–416.
7. See Lucy E. Hewitt, 'Towards a Greater Urban Geography: Regional Planning and Associational Networks in London in the Early Twentieth Century', *Planning Perspectives* 26, no. 4 (2011): 551–568.
8. Sorensen, *The Making of Urban Japan*, 63.
9. Yazaki Takeo, *Social Change and the City in Japan* (Tokyo: Japan Publications, 1968), 355.
10. Tristan R. Grunow, 'Paving Power: Western Urban Planning and Imperial Space from the Streets of Meiji Tokyo to Colonial Seoul', *Journal of Urban History* 42, no. 3 (2016): 509, 513, 523.
11. Susan C. Townsend, 'The Great War and Urban Crisis: Conceptualizing the Industrial Metropolis in Japan and Britain in the 1910s', in *The Decade of the Great War: Japan and the Wider World in the 1910s*, ed. Tosh Minohara, Evan Dawley and Tze-ki Hon (Leiden: Brill, 2014), 305.
12. Grunow, 'Paving Power', 512–513.
13. For further information, see Carola Hein, 'Visionary Plans and Planners: Japanese Traditions and Western Influence', in *Japanese Capitals in Historical Perspective: Place, Power and Memory in Kyoto, Edo and Tokyo*, ed. Nicolas Fieve and Paul Waley (Abingdon: Routledge, 2003), 567–632.
14. The so-called 'long Taishō period' (1905–1931) in Japan has been traditionally associated with the term 'modernity' and the influx of Western ideas of liberalism and democracy, although the nature and extent of these influences are hotly debated. See: Germaine Hoston, 'The State, Modernity, and the Fate of Liberalism in Prewar Japan', *Journal of Asian Studies* 51, no. 2 (May 1992): 287–316.
15. Itō Norio, *Nagoya no Machi: Sensai fukkō no kiroku* (Nagoya: Chūnichi Shimbun Honsha, 1988), 99.
16. Nagoya-shi Keikaku Kyoku, *Sensai Fukkōshi: Nagoya* (Nagoya: Nagoya-shi Keikaku Kyoku, 1984), 31.
17. Kashiwagi Hiroshi, 'On Rationalization and the National Lifestyle: Japanese Design in the 1920s and 1930s', in *Being Modern in Japan: Culture and Society from the 1910s to the 1930s*, ed. Elise K. Tipton and John Clark (Honolulu: University of Hawai'i Press, 2000), 63.
18. Keikaku Kyoku, *Sensai Fukkōshi*, 31–32.
19. Hiroshi, 'On Rationalization', 66–67.
20. Keikaku Kyoku, *Nagoya toshi keikaku shi*, 210 and 215.

21 Hein, 'Machi', 85.
22 Birmingham Archives (BA): BCC/TPS/1/1/1. Its sponsor, J. S. Nettlefold, was a member of a prominent Birmingham manufacturing family and first chair of the city's Housing Committee who had been active in the passing of the first Town Planning Act in 1909 – see Stephen Ward, *Planning and Urban Change* (London: Sage, 2004), 26–30.
23 *Birmingham Post*, 10 April 1971: Sutcliffe and Smith, *Birmingham*, 400; Cherry, *Birmingham*, 148.
24 *A History of the County of Warwick: Volume 7, the City of Birmingham*, ed. W. B. Stephens (London: Victorian County History, 1964), 1–3.
25 André Sorensen, 'Subcentres and Satellite Cities: Tokyo's 20th Century Experience of Planned Polycentrism', *International Planning Studies* 6, no. 1 (2001): 13.
26 Mark Pendleton and Jamie Coates, 'Thinking from the Yamanote: Space, Place and Mobility in Tokyo's Past and Present', *Japan Forum* 30, no. 2 (2018): 152.
27 Colin G. Pooley and Jean Turnbull, 'Coping with Congestion: Responses to Urban Traffic Problems in British Cities c.1920–1960', *Journal of Historical Geography*, 31 (2005): 85–86.
28 Alker Tripp, *Road Traffic and Its Control* (London: Edward Arnold, 1938).
29 On driving in Britain between the wars, see Sean O'Connell, *The Car in British Society: Class, Gender and Motoring, 1896–1939* (Manchester: Manchester University Press, 1998).
30 TNA: Letter, C. S. Bridges, Ministry of Transport to J. D. Rae, Treasury, 12 December 1955, MT 122/3; BCA: H. J. Manzoni, Central City Planning: Preliminary Report, Presented to the Public Works Committee, 16 October 1941, 7.
31 There were 160,000 bicycles, while jinrikisha had been reduced to 54 and there were just 3 ox-carts remaining. *Nagoya-shi Hyakunen no Nenrin: chōki tōkei deeta shū* (Nagoya: Nagoya-shi, 1989), 189–190.
32 The history of trams internationally can be traced through the British journal, *Tramways and Urban Transit* (Welling: LRTA Publishing, 1938–).
33 Pooley and Turnbull, 'Coping with Congestion', 78–93; Asa Briggs, *History of Birmingham, Volume II: Borough and City, 1865–1938* (London: Oxford University Press, 1952), 255–256.
34 *Traffic Engineering and Control*, June 1960 in Birmingham Archives, Records of Sir Herbert Manzoni, MS/543/1.
35 Keikaku Kyoku, *Nagoya toshi keikaku shi*, 208.
36 Hein, 'Visionary Plans and Planners', 578.
37 Hayashi Kitotaka. 'Land Readjustment in Nagoya', in *Land Readjustment*, ed. William A. Doebele (Lexington, MA, Toronto: Lexington Books, 1982), 110, 116–117, 119.
38 Sorensen, *Making of Urban Japan*, 122.
39 Ibid., 123.
40 André Sorensen, 'Conflict, Consensus or Consent: Implications of Japanese Land Readjustment Practice for Developing Countries', *Habitat International* 24, no. 1 (2000): 52.
41 Andrew J. Jacobs, 'Planning for a Vibrant Central City: The Case of Nagoya, Japan', *International Urban Planning Settings: Lessons of Success*, 12 (January 2001): 47. https://www.researchgate.net/publication/304377387.
42 J. B. Cullingworth and V. Nadin, *Town and Country Planning in the UK* (London: Taylor and Francis, 2006), 208.

43 Ward, *Planning and Urban Change*, ch. 4.
44 For an account, see Gordon Cherry, *The Evolution of British Town Planning* (Leighton Buzzard: Leonard Hill, 1974).
45 Ian Masser and Takahiro Yorisaki, 'The Institutional Context of Japanese Planning: Professional Associations and Planning Education', in *Planning for Cities and Regions in Japan*, ed. Philip Shapira, Ian Masser and David W. Edgington (Liverpool: Liverpool University Press, 1994), 117–118.
46 The Institution of Municipal and County Engineers was founded in 1913 although an association had run since 1873. To our knowledge there is no scholarly study either of this institution or as municipal engineers as a group despite their importance in urban development, including planning, in the late nineteenth and early twentieth centuries.
47 Keikaku Kyoku, *Nagoya toshi keikaku shi*, 215.
48 For details of the career of another significant City Engineer, Stanley Wardley, at Leicester, Wakefield and Bradford over the same period, see Simon Gunn, 'The Rise and Fall of British Urban Modernism: Planning Bradford, c.1945–1970', *Journal of British Studies* 49, no. 4 (2010): 849–869.
49 See his lecture at Birmingham University on 4 February 1936, 'City Planning: Some Problems of the Future', BCA: Records of Sir Herbert Manzoni, MS/543/1. For his career, Tom Caulcott, 'Manzoni, Sir Herbert John Baptista', in *Oxford Dictionary of Biography Online*, accessed 19 February 2015.
50 Jurō, *Aru Dobokugishi*, 146.
51 Aaron Stephen Moore, *Constructing East Asia: Technology, Ideology, and Empire in Japan's Wartime Era, 1931–1945* (Stanford, CA: Stanford University Press, 2013), 123.
52 Ibid., 107.
53 Ibid., 125, 133.
54 Tabuchi, *Aru Dobokugishi*, 163–164.
55 On the political support for Manzoni and Birmingham's planning process see Cherry, *Birmingham*, ch. 7 and Sutcliffe and Smith, *Birmingham*, ch. 3.
56 Yazaki Takeo, *The Japanese City: A Sociological Analysis*, trans. David L. Swain (Rutland: Vt. Japan Publications Trading Co., 1964), 50.
57 Tabuchi, *Aru Dobokugishi*, 167.
58 United States Strategic Bombing Survey (USSBS), 'The Effects of the Air Attack on Nagoya', (June, 1947), 1, accessed 28 August 2016, https://babel.hathitrust.org/cgi/pt?id=mdp.39015002274325;view=1up;seq=3.
59 Ibid., 9.
60 Statistics for Birmingham are from Sutcliffe and Smith, *Birmingham*, 33–35, 56.
61 Hasegawa, 'The 100-metre-road', 14.
62 Tabuchi Jurō, 'Eidan ga Unda Shin Nagoya – Hōka toshi no senbō no moto to natta Nagoya no toshi keikaku no seikō wa shiseisha no daieidan ni atta', *Bungei Shunjū* 39, no. 4 (April 1961): 144–145.
63 A general argument made in relation to British technology and manufacturing in David Edgerton's *Warfare State: Britain 1920–1970* (Cambridge: Cambridge University Press, 2006).
64 See *inter alia* Matthieu Flonneau, *Paris et L'Automobile: Un Siècle de Passions* (Paris: Hachette, 2005); Clay McShane, *Down the Asphalt Path: The Automobile and the American City* (New York: Columbia University Press, 1998).

65 The 1944 Act was officially the Town and Country Planning Act. According to Manzoni, 'the city was waiting for just this very Act' – 'Redevelopment of blighted areas', 24.
66 Cherry, *Birmingham*, 145.
67 Peter Hall, *Urban and Regional Planning* (London: Routledge, 1975), ch. 4.
68 See for example the classic handbook, J. B. Cullingworth, *Town and Country Planning in the UK*, 13th edn. (London: Routledge, 2000), 19–22.
69 Hotta Yoshihiro, *Jidōsha to kenchiku: Mōtarizeeshun jidai no kankyō dezain* (Tokyo: Kawade Shobo, 2011), 15–16.
70 Lawrence H. Odell, 'Hostilities Inspire and Hinder Port Development in Japan', *Far Eastern Survey* 8, no. 25 (1939): 300–301.
71 Eyre, *Nagoya*, 103, 105.
72 The detailed description of this phase of the development of the Inner Ring Road is to be found in the minutes of the Council and Public Works Committee and summarized by Alderman R. S. Thomas, 'Birmingham Inner Ring Road – Costs, Savings and Benefits', paper to the People and Cities conference, London, 11 December 1963, BCA: HLG 131/65.
73 The national statistics were staggering. Sixty-six cities had been bombed, destroying 40 per cent of the urban area and making 30 per cent of the population homeless. Fifty-one per cent of total urban residences (65 per cent in Tokyo) were destroyed in air raids and a further 15 per cent were levelled to make firebreaks. As well as the loss of almost 40 per cent of automobiles, over 80 per cent of shipping was destroyed. John Dower, *Japan in War and Peace: Essays on History, Culture and Race* (London: Fontana, 1996), 12.
74 This number included around 40 per cent of industrial facilities and 47 per cent of homes. Keikaku Kyoku, *Fukkō Tochikukaku Seiri Jigyō no Aramashi*, 5; USSBS, 'Nagoya City', 8.
75 Figures from H. J. Manzoni, 'Redevelopment of Blighted Areas in Birmingham', *Journal of the Town Planning Institute* (1955): 92.
76 Ishida Yorifusa, 'Japanese Cities and Planning in the Reconstruction Period', in *Rebuilding Urban Japan after 1945*, ed. Carola Hein, Jeffry H. Diefendorf and Ishida Yorifusa (London: Palgrave Macmillan, 2003), 24–25.
77 Eyre, *Nagoya*, 54.
78 Calculated at the historical exchange rate for 1960.
79 Keikaku Kyoku, *Sensai Fukkōshi*, 13.
80 Moto Nagoya Taimuzu, eds., *Nagoya Jōnetsu Jidai* (Nagoya: Ju'rin-sha, 2009), 255.
81 TNA: Letter from R. J. F. Sansome, West Midlands Division Road Engineer to the Town Clerk of Birmingham, 24 April 1967, HLG 131/65.
82 West Midland Group, *Conurbation*, ; Patrick Abercrombie and Herbert Jackson, *West Midlands Plan* (London: Ministry of Town and Country Planning, 1948).
83 For an account of debates and actions, see Sutcliffe and Smith, *Birmingham*, 130–132; Cherry, *Birmingham*, 194–195.
84 TNA: memo from Mr Willoughby, 19 July 1955, MT 122/3.
85 Sutcliffe and Smith, *Birmingham*, 225–226.
86 Sorensen, *The Making of Urban Japan*, 159.
87 Hasegawa, 'The 100-metre-road', 13–16.
88 Cited in the International Association of Traffic and Safety Sciences (ITS), eds., *Kuruma Shakai wa Dō Kawaru ka: ITS - kankyō - toshibunka no kanten kara mita kōtsū shakai* (Tokyo: Bungeisha, 2014), 130.

89 Ishida does reference another Japanese secondary source, F. Hayakawa, 'Toshi keikaku no kiki', *Kenchiku Zasshi* (October-November, 1954). Ishida, 'Japanese Cities in the Reconstruction Period', 19; Ichikawa Hiroo, 'Tokyo: The Attempt to Transform the Metropolis', in *Rebuilding Urban Japan after 1945*, ed. Carola Hein, Jeffry H. Diefendorf and Ishida Yorifusa (London: Palgrave Macmillan, 2003), 53.
90 Hasegawa, 'The 100-metre-road', 16.
91 BCA: BCC, Tramway and Omnibus Committee, reports to the City Council, 7 July 1936, 10 January 1939. See also P. L. Hardy and P. Jacques, *A Short Review of Birmingham Corporation Tramways* (St Albans: HJ Publications, 1971).
92 *Birmingham Mail*, 1 February 1949.
93 TNA: MT 122/3 City of Birmingham Inner Ring Road scheme, deputation to Ministry of Transport and Civil Aviation, 21 November 1955, 10. For an overview of Birmingham's public transport from the 1950s, see West Midlands Transport Study Technical Committee, *West Midlands Transport Study* (Birmingham: Freeman, Fox and Miller Smith and Associates, 1968).
94 BCA: BCC Public Works Committee proceedings, 27 July 1948; City of Birmingham, 'Visit to America, 26 March to 6 April 1956; report of the delegation to the Public Works Committee', 17 April 1956.
95 Keikaku Kyoku, *Nagoya Toshi Keikaku-shi*, 77.
96 Keikaku Kyoku, *Sensai Fukkōshi*, 36–37.
97 Tabuchi Jurō, *Aru Dobokugishi no Hanjijoden* (Nagoya: Chūbu Keizai Rengōkai, 1962), 163.
98 Review Article: Tiratsoo et al., *Urban Reconstruction in Britain and Japan, 1945–1955* in *Planning History* 24, no. 1 (2003): 29–33, 33.
99 Tabuchi, *Aru Dobokugishi*, 164.
100 Roads classed as 'prefectural roads' declined from just over 183 kilometres to around 170.5 km, but some of these roads would have been reclassified as either 'national' or 'urban'. *Nagoya-shi Hyakunen no Nenrin*, 185–187.
101 Historical Statistics of Japan, 'Length of Roads and Paved Roads, 1936–2004', accessed 8 August 2010, http://www.stat.go.jp; T. Demizu, 'The Motorization of Japan', in *A Social History of Science and Technology in Contemporary Japan*, vol. III, ed. Nakayama Shigeru and Gotō Kunio (Melbourne: Trans Pacific Press, 2006), 302.
102 Robert Millward, 'Industrial and Commercial Performance Since 1950', in *The Economic History of Britain since 1700*, ed. Roderick Floud and Deirdre McCloskey (Cambridge: Cambridge University Press, 1994), 41.
103 BCA: MT 122/3 City of Birmingham Inner Ring Road scheme, deputation to Ministry of Transport and Civil Aviation, appendix.
104 For a contemporary view of the emergence of the car industry as the mainstay of the British economy, see Graham Turner, *The Car Makers* (Harmondsworth: Penguin, 1964).
105 Phyllis A. Genther, *A History of Japan's Government-Business Relationship: The Passenger Car Industry* (Ann Arbor, MI: University of Michigan, 1990), 72.
106 An economic stabilization plan implemented at the end of 1948 to tackle rampant inflation, so called because it was to be monitored by Joseph Dodge, president of the Bank of Detroit.
107 Shimokawa Kō'ichi, *The Japanese Automobile Industry: A Business History* (London: Athlone, 1994), 33–34.
108 Eyre, *Nagoya*, 153.

109 TNA: MT 122/3, City of Birmingham Inner Ring Road scheme: appendix: notes on population, employment and industries of Birmingham and Midlands, Table 2. The exact figures were 100,049 in the three sectors indicated out of a total insured population of 622,081.
110 'The Industrial Structure of Birmingham', *Times*, 8 May 1958.
111 Figures on the industrial structure of Birmingham between 1961 and 1971 can be found in Sutcliffe and Smith, *Birmingham*, 160–161 and 486–487.
112 Nishimura Yuichiro and Okamoto Kohei, 'Yesterday and Today: Changes in Worker's Lives in Toyota City Japan', in *Japan in the Bluegrass*, ed. Pradyumna Karan (Lexington: University of Kentucky Press, 2001), 100.
113 Eyre, *Nagoya*, 152.
114 Of these 16,000 workers, around 17 per cent were white-collar workers. Okayama Reiko, 'Industrial Relations in the Japanese Automobile Industry 1945-70: The Case of Toyota', in *Between Fordism and Flexibility*, ed. Steven Tolliday and Jonathan Zeitlin (Oxford: Berg, 1992), 179–180.
115 Oliver Marriott, *The Property Boom* (London: Hamish Hamilton, 1967), 80, 136; 'Britain's Changing Cities 1: Building Fever in Birmingham', *Financial Times*, 31 May 1961.
116 Department of Employment, *Family Expenditure Survey* (London: Office of Population Censuses and Surveys, 1963).
117 The literature responds of course to the famous 'affluent worker' debate of the 1960s in political sociology. For the recent literature, see Ben Jones, *The Working Class in Mid-Twentieth Century England* (Manchester: Manchester University Press, 2012); Mike Savage, 'Working-Class Identities in the 1960s: Revisiting the *Affluent Worker* Study', *Sociology* 39, no. 5 (2005): 929–946.
118 City of Birmingham Central Statistics Office, *Abstract of Statistics* (Birmingham: Birmingham Corporation, 1974); Department of the Environment, *Transport Statistics: Great Britain 1964–1974* (London: HMSO 1974).
119 Rory Parsons and Geoff Vigar, '"Resistance was Futile": Cycling's Discourses of Resistance to UK Automobile Modernism, 1950–1970', *Planning Perspectives* (online publication 16 July 2017).
120 In 1949, these vehicles were restricted to a maximum length of 2.8 metres, a width of 1 metre and height of 2 metres in dimension and a maximum displacement of 150 cc for a four-stroke engine and 100 cc for a two-stroke engine. In 1951, new regulations increased the size and displacement of these vehicles to 3 metres in length x 1.3 metres in width and a displacement of 360 cc for a four-stroke engine and 240 cc for a two-stroke engine.
121 In Nagoya, there were 63,783 *keijidōsha* in 1960, more than double the 1955 figure of 24,176. *Nagoya-shi Hyakunen no Nenrin*, 189–190.
122 City of Birmingham, *Development Plan: Report on the Survey* (Birmingham: Birmingham Corporation, 1952), 61; Manzoni, verbal response at a conference reported in *Institute of Municipal Engineers' Journal* 86, no. 12 (1959): 345.
123 *Nagoya-shi Hyakunen no Nenrin*, 106–109.
124 Yamamoto Satoshi, 'Nagoya Toshi Kōsoku Dōro Kensetsu no Hitsuyōsei', *Shintoshi* 24, no. 2 (February 1970), 55.
125 William Plowden, *The Motor Car and Politics 1896–1970* (London: Bodley Head, 1971), 341–342; M. Hamer, *Wheels Within Wheels: A Study of the Road Lobby* (London: Friends of the Earth, 1974), 4.

126 Peter Merriman, *Driving Spaces: A Cultural-Historical Geography of England's M1 Motorway* (Oxford: Blackwell, 2007), ch. 3.
127 Yoshida Shigeru, *The Yoshida Memoirs: The Story of Japan in Crisis*, trans. Yoshida Ken'ichi (London: Heinemann, 1961), 113.
128 Fujino, 'Expressway in Japan'.
129 The IBRD, from which the World Bank eventually grew, was founded in Washington in 1944 to facilitate post-war reconstruction and development, at first largely in Europe.
130 World Bank, *Japan – Report on the Proposed Expressway Project* (Technical operations projects series; no. TO 172) Washington, DC (24 April 1958), 2–3 http://documents.worldbank.org/curated/en/1958/04/1554606/japan-report-proposed-expressway-project.
131 In Britain, central government provided 75 per cent of the costs of building major trunk roads, such as the Inner Ring Road, the remainder being paid by local authorities through the rates or by other revenue means. The details of the financing of the Inner Ring Road are discussed in Chapter 2.
132 TNA: MT 122/3, B. E. Bellamy memo, 7 September 1955.
133 TNA: MT 122/3, City of Birmingham Inner Ring Road scheme, deputation to the Ministry of Transport and Civil Aviation, 21 November 1955, memorandum, 6–9, 15.
134 TNA: MT122/3, letter from B. E. Bellamy to DRE Midland and the Town Clerk of Birmingham, 21 February 1956; the first grant was actually made in January 1957.
135 'Stones and Rubble Shower on Minister and Council: A Spectacle that Misfired', *Guardian*, 9 March 1957, 12.

Chapter 2

1 In the 1960s, the officially designated Chūbu Economic Region covered the Chūkyō prefectures of Aichi, Mie and Gifu, as well as Nagano and Shizuoka prefectures in the east, to form an extended geographical area which was roughly the equivalent of the English 'Midlands'.
2 The official name of the Meishin Expressway is the rather long-winded Express National Highway Chūō Motorway Nishinomiya Line (*Kōsoku Jidōsha Kokudō Chūō Jidōshadō Nishinomiya-sen*). The shortened form 'Meishin' is made up by the first Chinese character (*kanji*) for Nagoya ('na', or in this case, due to the vagaries of Japanese pronunciation of characters, 'mei') and Kobe ('ko', or in this case 'shin').
3 In May 1969, the whole of the 350 kilometre- (218 mile-) long Tōmei Expressway (*Tōmei Kōsoku Dōro*) was also opened connecting Nagoya to Tokyo in the east, although some sections were opened in 1968.
4 Lynda Nead, *Victorian Babylon: People, Streets and Images in Nineteenth-Century London* (New Haven: Yale University Press, 2000); Merriman, *Driving Spaces*, ch. 4. The M6 motorway was built piecemeal in stretches from 1958, the last section being that between the Rugby intersection with the M1 and the A38 road north-east of Birmingham, opened in 1971.
5 The Tokyo Expressway was constructed by a private consortium and was toll-free. The Metropolitan Expressway network begun in 1962, in contrast, was built and operated as a toll-road by a government-affiliated corporation from 1959 until it was

privatized in 2005. Hasegawa Jun'ichi, 'Tokyo's Elevated Expressway in the 1950s: Protest and Politics', *Journal of Transport History* 36, no. 2 (2015): 228–229.
6 *Birmingham Post*, 6 October 1959.
7 *Birmingham Mail*, 12 November 1959.
8 *Traffic Engineering and Control*, June 1960.
9 Reported in the *Birmingham Post*, 23 September 1963.
10 Eyre, *Nagoya*, 35.
11 Review Article: Tiratsoo et al. *Urban Reconstruction in Britain and Japan, 1945–1955*, in *Planning History*, 29–33, 31.
12 Tabuchi, *Aru Dobokugishi*, 188–189.
13 See, for example, Ian Masser, 'Land Readjustment: An Overview', *Third World Planning Review* 9, no. 3 (1987): 205–210. In 1982, Nagoya City, together with the United Nations Centre for Regional Development, organized an international seminar on 'Urban Development Policies and Land Readjustment' to commemorate the completion of Nagoya's 'War Recovery Land Readjustment Project' the largest in the world. By 1979, almost 70 per cent of Nagoya' s territory had been transformed through L. R. Nagamine Haruo, 'The Land Readjustment Techniques of Japan', *Habitat International* 10, nos. 1–2 (1986): 52.
14 British Road Federation, *Basic Road Statistics*; Department of the Environment, *Transport Statistics*.
15 Department for Transport, *Transport Statistics Great Britain* (London: HMSO, 2007), 158.
16 Source for Japanese Figures: Statistics Bureau, Ministry of Internal Affairs and Communications, Japan, *Historical Statistics of Japan*, last modified, April 2012, http://www.stat.go.jp/english/data/chouki/.
17 Graham Turner, *The Car Makers* (London: Penguin, 1963), 9.
18 The figures for 1960 do not include the 'light' vehicle or *keijidōsha*. JAMA, 'Motor Vehicle Statistics'.
19 OICA, 'Vehicle Production Statistics'. http://www.oica.net/category/production-statistics/2016-statistics/.
20 British Road Federation, *Basic Road Statistics*, 23.
21 Figures for Japan: JAMA, 'Motor Vehicle Statistics'.
22 *Hansard*, HC, vol. 621, col. 917 (11 April 1960).
23 Mark Clapson, *Suburban Century: Social Change and Urban Growth in England and the United States* (Oxford: Berg, 2003), 46; *The Motorist Today* (London: Automobile Association, 1965).
24 John H. Goldthorpe et al., *The Affluent Worker in the Class Structure* (Cambridge: Cambridge University Press, 1969), 8.
25 Shinohata is located 25 miles from Sano City in Tochigi Prefecture to the north of Tokyo. When Dore arrived in 1955 the village was a 5-mile walk or 8-mile taxi ride from the nearest train station. When he revisited in the 1970s the village had been totally transformed into a car-owning society. Ronald Dore, *Shinohata: A Portrait of a Japanese Village* (London: Allen Lane, 1978), 16.
26 Ibid., 17.
27 TNA: CAB/129/1010, 25 March 1960, 1 and Appendix C.
28 Koyama Tōru, 'Construction of a Nationwide Network of Expressways', in *A Social History of Science and Technology in Contemporary Japan*, vol. III, ed. Nakayama Shigeru and Gotō Kunio (Melbourne: Trans Pacific Press, 2006), 347.
29 Reported in the *Guardian*, 8 May 1959, 2.

30 Ministry of Transport, *Road Accidents* (London: HMSO, 1961); Road Safety Bill, HC Deb, 10 February 1966, 655.
31 David Taylor and Keith Laybourn, *The Battle for the Roads of Britain* (Basingstoke: Palgrave Macmillan, 2015); Department for Transport, *Transport Statistics Great Britain*, 144.
32 Statistics Bureau, 'Road Traffic Accidents (1924–2005)', *Historical Statistics of Japan*. http://www.stat.go.jp/english/data/chouki/29.html.
33 In 1970, in Japan 16,765 people were killed and 981,096 injured, around 1 person for every 1,000 vehicles. However, although the numbers of accidents and casualties were rising, in terms of the ratio between the number of vehicles and the number of deaths, there had been a steady improvement after a high of 265 deaths per 10,000 vehicles in 1946. Ibid.
34 TNA: CAB 129/99, 15 December 1959.
35 J. M. Richards, *An Architectural Journey in Japan* (London: The Architectural Press, 1963), 90.
36 City of Birmingham Central Statistical Office, *City of Birmingham Abstract of Statistics* (Birmingham, 1974).
37 *Nagoya-shi Hyakunen no Nenrin*. In 1973 the total number of vehicles had reached nearly half a million at 543,169. Ibid.
38 Vehicles with licences current, per 1,000 population: London 187, West Midlands 186, South East Lancashire 164, Merseyside 153, West Yorkshire 172, Tyneside 148, Central Clydeside 87; Colin Buchanan and Partners, *The Conurbations* (London: British Road Federation, 1969), 96.
39 Exact figures for households per 1,000 without a motor car: Birmingham 577, Sheffield 610, Leeds 644, Liverpool 674, Manchester 684, Newcastle-upon-Tyne 700. Per cent of cars per household calculated by subtracting quoted figures from 1,000 to present number of households per 1,000 with car. Number then divided by 10 to give per cent; Office of Population Censuses and Surveys, *Census 1971: England and Wales* (London: HMSO, 1971).
40 *Times*, 6 February 1962.
41 World Bank, *Japan – Report on the Proposed Expressway Project*, 2–3.
42 For an account, see David Starkie, *The Motorway Age* (Oxford: Pergamon Press, 1982).
43 Plowden, *The Motor Car and Politics 1896–1970*, 479.
44 Figures are based on historical currency conversion rates in 1960 and 1970, respectively. Construction expenses include expenditure for road improvement, bridge improvement, pavement construction, surveys, etc. but does not include general employment measures or environmental controls. Statistics Bureau, 'Settled Accounts of Road Investment (F.Y. 1956–2003)', *Historical Statistics of Japan*.
45 Anthony Sutcliffe and Roger Smith, *History of Birmingham, Vol. III:1939–1970* (Oxford: Oxford University Press, 1974), 398.
46 Terence Bendixson, 'City of Men', *Spectator*, 6 December 1963, 16; Colin Buchanan, *Traffic in Towns* (London: HMSO, 1963). For an historical analysis of the report, see Gunn, 'The Buchanan Report, Environment and the Problem of Traffic in 1960s Britain', 521–542.
47 On the Smeed report and its limited influence at the time, see David Rooney, 'The Political Economy of Congestion: Road-Pricing and the Neo-Liberal Project, 1952–2003', *Twentieth Century British History* 25, no. 4 (2014): 628–650; British Road Federation, *People and Cities: Report of the 1963 London Conference* (London: British Road Federation, 1964).

48 TNA: MT 128/99, Steering Group for the Study of the Long-Term Problem of Traffic in Towns, memo by Colin Buchanan, 12 September 1961.
49 Address to the AMC Conference reprinted in *Municipal Review*, November 1959.
50 Mark Metzler, *Capital and Will and Imagination: Schumpeter's Guide to the Postwar Japanese Miracle* (Ithaca and London: Cornell University Press, 2013), 201.
51 See Minami Ryoshin, 'Income Distribution of Japan: Historical Perspective and its Implications', *Japan Labor Review* 5, no. 4 (Autumn 2008): 5–20.
52 See Susan C. Townsend, 'The Miracle of Car Ownership in Japan's "Era of High Growth," 1955–1973', *Business History* 55, no. 3, (2013): 498–523.
53 Statistics Bureau, 'Average of Monthly Income and Expenditures per Household – All Japan (1955–2010)', *Historical Statistics of Japan*. April 2012. http://www.stat.go.jp/english/data/chouki/20.html.
54 Sheldon Garon, 'The Transnational Promotion of Saving in Asia: "Asian Values" or the "Japanese Model"?' in *The Ambivalent Consumer: Questioning Consumption in East Asia and the West*, ed. Sheldon Garon and Patricia L. Maclachlan (Ithaca; London: Cornell University Press, 2006), 168–169.
55 Koshi Masaki et al., 'Japanese National Policy toward the Automobile', *Transport Reviews* 3, no. 1 (1 January 1983): 2.
56 TNA: MT 122/77, Thomas, 'Birmingham Inner Ring Road – Costs, Savings and Benefits'; Sutcliffe and Smith, *History of Birmingham*, 401. This financial model was also deployed, of course, by Baron Haussmann in the rebuilding of central Paris between 1850 and 1870.
57 The figures and arguments in this section are from Alderman Thomas' paper, 'Birmingham Inner Ring Road'. It is not clear whether the income from the road claimed in 1963 was in fact forthcoming by the time the road was finally opened in 1971.
58 Hayashi, 'Land Readjustment in Nagoya', 107.
59 Sorensen, *The Making of Urban Japan*, 159.
60 Miyazawa Michio, 'Land Readjustment in Japan', in *Land Readjustment*, ed. William A. Doebele (Lexington, MA, Toronto: Lexington Books, 1982), 91–92.
61 Sorensen, 'Conflict, Consensus or Consent', 53.
62 Nagoya-shi Keikaku Kyoku, *Fukkō Tochikukaku*, 7.
63 Nagoya-shi Keikaku Kyoku, *Sensai Fukkō-shi* (Nagoya: Nagoya-shi Keikaku Kyoku, 1984), 111.
64 Nagoya Kōsokudōro Kōsha 40 Nenshi Henshū I'inkai, eds. *Nagoya Kōsokudōro Kōsha 40 Nenshi* (Nagoya: Nagoya Expressway Corporation, October 2012), 6.
65 Ibid., 7.
66 *Birmingham Mail*, 6 April 1971.
67 Cited in *Birmingham Evening Despatch*, 5 February 1960.
68 Media Archive of Central England, *Regenerating Birmingham 1955–1975*, DVD (Lincoln: University of Lincoln, n.d.).
69 T. Bendixson, 'Las Vegas of the Midlands', *Guardian*, 20 December 1969.
70 TNA: MT 128/99, Steering Group for the Study of the Long-term Problem of Traffic in Towns, Draft Paper by Colin Buchanan to Steering Group, 22 June 1962, 16.
71 See Thomas, 'Birmingham Inner Ring Road', 167; *Birmingham Post*, 7 April 1971, 4.
72 Hasegawa, 'Tokyo's Elevated Expressway', 228–229.
73 Nagoya-shi Keikaku Kyoku, *Fukkō Tochikukaku*, 7–8.
74 Tabuchi, *Aru Dobokugishi*, 188.
75 Nagoya-shi Keikaku Kyoku, *Sensai Fukkō-shi*, 111.

76 Ibid., 192.
77 Buildings continued to be moved in large numbers, over a thousand a year, until 1971 when numbers began to reduce to several hundred per year, but the technique is still used today. *Fukkō Tochikukaku*, 17.
78 These included the buildings of major companies such as the Nagoya Branch Nippon Life Insurance, Fukoku Mutual Life Insurance, Nagoya Branch Bank of Japan, the Asahi Shimbun Offices, Shizuoka Bank and the Sakae Branch of the Tokai Bank. Sawai Suzu'ichi, 'Nagoya Hirokōji Monogatari', accessed 7 April 2014, http://network2010.org/article/1036.
79 Buchanan, *Traffic in Towns*, 36.
80 Originally published in 1941, the updated second edition of 1950 was published by Institute of Traffic Engineers and Association of Casualty and Surety Companies, New York. Its purpose was 'to collate in one volume basic traffic engineering data as a guide to best practice in those portions of the field in which well-accepted principles have been established.' The full text is available at http://archive.org/stream/trafficengineeri00instrich/trafficengineeri00instrich_djvu.txt.
81 On the importance of this work, see W. K. Kittelson, 'Historical Overview of the Committee on Highway Capacity and Quality of Service', in *Transportation Research Circular E-CO18: 4th International Sumposium on Highway Capacity*, 2000, 5–16.
82 Kōtsū Kogaku Kenkyūkai, *Kōtsū Kogaku Handobukku* (Tokyo: Kōtsū Kogaku Kenkyūkai,1984), 274.
83 Herbert Manzoni, 'Structural Engineering and the Urban Motorways', *Surveyor and Municipal and County Engineer* 118, no. 3482 (17 January 1959), 57.
84 UA 16/6, Birmingham University Special Collections, Birmingham Department of Transport and Highway Engineering, correspondence and reports.
85 'Driver's Eye-View to Guide You Along the Aston Expressway', *Birmingham Mail*, 27 April 1972.
86 Koyama, 'Construction of Nationwide Network', 347–348.
87 John A. Black and Peter J. Rimmer, 'Japanese Highway Planning: A Western Interpretation', *Transportation* 11, no. 1 (1982): 33.
88 Hotta Yoshihiro, *Jidōsha to kenchiku: Mōtarizēshun jidai no kankyō dezain* (Tokyo: Kawade Shobo Shinsha, 2013), 30; Koyama, 'Construction of a Nationwide Network', 352–353.
89 Koyama, 'Construction of a Nationwide Network', 352–353.
90 Cook, 'Constructing Britain's Road Network', ch. 3.
91 *Birmingham Mail*, 6 April 1971; 'Lighting the Inner Ring Road', *Engineering*, 13 February 1959; *Birmingham Post*, 9 December 1958; Birmingham City Council Public Works Committee, *Ringway* (1963).
92 Sutcliffe and Smith, *History of Birmingham*, 409.
93 According to Manzoni in 1959, excluding cars from the central area would be an 'ostrich act' and the view continued to be echoed by Corporation officials in the 1960s, *Birmingham Post*, 8 April 1959.
94 TNA: MT 122/3, minute from E. R. Raworth, Divisional Road Engineer, 24 September 1956; Birmingham City Council Public Works Committee, *Ringway*.
95 Black and Rimmer, 'Japanese Highway Planning', 36.
96 Kōtsū Kogaku Kenkyūkai, *Kōtsū Kogaku Handobukku*, 278.
97 Black and Rimmer, 'Japanese Highway Planning', 38, 40.
98 Buchanan, *Traffic in Towns*, 68.
99 City of Birmingham, *Development Plan*, 62.

100 Paul Long and David Parker, 'The Mistakes of the Past? Visual Narratives of Urban Decline and Regeneration', *Visual Culture in Britain* 5, no. 1 (2004): 44.
101 Ministry of Transport, *Design and Layout of Roads in Built-Up Areas: Report of the Departmental Committee Set Up by the Minister of War Transport* (London, 1946), 31.
102 Bendixson, 'Las Vegas of the Midlands', 8.
103 City of Birmingham PWC, *Inner Ring Road Scheme* (Birmingham: Birmingham Corporation, 1957).
104 Fujikawa Hisayo *Nagoya Chikagai Tanjō Monogatari* (Nagoya: C & D Shuppan, 2007), 10–12.
105 Nagoya-shi Keikaku Kyoku, *Sensai Fukkōshi*, 49 and 383.
106 On the concept of 'megastructure' in 1960s Britain, see John Gold, 'The Making of a Megastructure: Architectural Modernism, Town Planning and Cumbernauld's Central Area, 1955–1975', *Planning Perspectives* 21 (April 2006), 109–131. They are also discussed in relation to Birmingham in Gold, *The Practice of Modernism*.
107 For a description, see Oliver Marriott, *The Property Boom* (London: Hamish Hamilton, 1969), 222–233.
108 MACE: *The Bull Ring Shopping Centre Birmingham* [film] (Laing Development Company Limited, 1965).
109 LBA: BCC/1/AG/37/1/32, CDSc, Report from Madin, J. M., and Maudsley, J. A., Civic Centre Redevelopment – Paradise Circus: Report on Central Library Scheme Design, July 1966.
110 Fujikawa, *Nagoya Chikagai*, 8. The song is still a great favourite and can be heard at https://www.youtube.com/watch?v=e36nXq-0RPg.
111 MACE: *Bull Ring Shopping Centre*; for a vision of the 'drive-in' city of the future, see the speech by Clive Bossom MP, HC Deb, 11 April 1960, vol. 621, 923–925.
112 Recollections of Peter Walker, http://www.photobydjnorton.com/InsideTheInnerRingRoad.html, accessed 12 April 2015. On the ideas behind the subways, see also *Birmingham Post*, 8 April 1959.
113 I. Nairn, 'Keeping the Pedestrians Down', *Observer*, 30 January 1966.
114 Ibid.
115 Todokoro Takashi, 'Nagoya ni Okeru Chikagai no Keisei: Toshin Rittaika no Ichi Keitai toshite', *Jimbun Chiri* 31, no. 3 (1979): 199. https://doi.org/10.4200/jjhg1948.31.193.
116 Ibid., 197, 211.
117 Marriott, *Property Boom*, 230–231; Diana Rowntree, 'Undercover Shopping', *Guardian*, 29 May 1964; MACE, *Regenerating Birmingham*. On the targeting of women as shoppers in 1960s Birmingham, see Peter Larkham and David Adams, 'Bold Planning, Mixed Experiences: The Diverse Fortunes of Post-War Birmingham', in *The Blitz and Its Legacy: Wartime Destruction to Post-War Reconstruction*, ed. Mark Clapson and Peter Larkham (Farnham: Ashgate, 2013), 145–147.
118 *Birmingham Sketch*, vol. 9: 68, January 1963.
119 TNA: HLG 131/65 City Centre Redevelopment; 'Big Plan for Birmingham', BBC Light programme, radio newsreel, broadcast 7pm, 25 May 1965.
120 *Birmingham Sketch*, vol. 9: 66, November 1962.
121 Richards, *An Architectural Journey*, 116, 120.
122 Tabuchi, *Aru Dobokugishi*, 188–189.

123 Günter Nitschke, *From Shinto to Ando: Studies in Architectural Anthropology in Japan* (London: Academy Editions, Ernst & Sohn, 1993), 34–35.
124 *Birmingham Mail*, 6 April 1971; see also the special edition of the *Birmingham Post*, 7 April 1971.
125 Simon Gunn, 'The Rites of Civic Culture in English Provincial Cities, 1830–1914', in *Urban Governance: Britain and beyond since 1750*, ed. R. J. Morris and R. H. Trainor (Aldershot: Ashgate, 2000), 226–241.
126 *Birmingham Post*, 9 April 1971.
127 *Birmingham Post*, 12 October 1971.
128 Ian Nairn, 'Birmingham', in *Nairn's Towns*, ed. O. Hatherley (London: Notting Hill Editions, 2013), 9; *Birmingham Post*, 12 October 1971.
129 McKenna, *Birmingham*, 127; 'Complete Rebuilding of Our Cities Envisaged', *Birmingham Post*, 21 May 1954.
130 Herbert Manzoni as quoted in A. Foster, *Birmingham: Pevsner Architectural Guides* (London: Architectural Press, 2005), 197.
131 Simon Gunn, 'Between Conservation and Modernism: Konrad Smigielski and the Planning of 1960s Leicester', in *Leicester: A Modern History*, ed. Richard Rodger and Rebecca Madgin (Lancaster: Carnegie Press, 2015); John Pendlebury, 'Alas Smith and Burns? Conservation in Newcastle upon Tyne City Centre 1959-1968', *Planning Perspectives* 16, no. 2 (2001): 115–141.
132 http://www.photobydjnorton.com/InsideTheInnerRingRoad.html, accessed 14 April 2015.
133 Cited in Larkham and Adams, 'Bold Planning',145.
134 *Birmingham Mail*, 30 October 1969; Harold Dawson of the Birmingham Market Hall Tenants Association, *Birmingham Mail*, 26 March 1971.
135 Hein, 'Rebuilding Japanese Cities after 1945', 9, 13.
136 Edward Seidensticker *Tokyo Rising: The City Since the Great Earthquake* (Cambridge, MA: Harvard University Press, 1991), 147.
137 It is not entirely clear where the term '*waito rōdo*' came from, but at least one anecdote from a Nagoya native suggested that it was because in the 1970 and 1980s, Japanese cars were largely white.
138 Eyre, *Nagoya*, 132.
139 Pradyumna P. Karan, *Japan in the 21st Century: Environment, Economy and Society* (Lexington: University Press of Kentucky, 2005), 95.
140 Nitschke, *From Shinto to Ando*, 35.
141 Sutcliffe and Smith, *Birmingham*, 441, 447.
142 Photographs from its construction in 1964/5 show Manzoni Gardens as rather desolate, and indeed it is described in this way by Marriott, *Property Boom*, 227, but Birmingham residents recall it fondly as a peaceful spot on websites, e.g http://www.birminghamforum.co.uk/index.php?topic=4688.0, accessed 14 April 2015; *Birmingham Mail*, 20 June 1969.
143 'Life-Wish', *Guardian*, 15 August 1963, 7.

Chapter 3

1 Lewis Mumford, *The City in History* (New York: Harcourt Brace, 1961), 577.
2 Ibid., 573–574; Kenneth T. Jackson, *Crabgrass Frontier: The Suburbanization of the United States* (Oxford: Oxford University Press, 1985); Sam Bass Warner, Jr, *Streetcar*

Suburbs: *The Process of Growth in Boston 1870–1900* (Cambridge, MA: Harvard University Press, 1962); Norton, *Fighting Traffic*.
3   David Cannadine, *Lords and Landlords: The Aristocracy and the Towns 1774–1967* (Leicester: Leicester University Press, 1980) has a substantial account of the development of Edgbaston by the Calthorpes.
4   Sorensen, *The Making of Urban Japan*, 124.
5   Gary D. Allinson, *Suburban Tokyo: A Comparative Study in Politics and Social Change* (Berkeley: University of California Press, 1979), 61.
6   Hayashi Takashi, 'Kōtsu no Hatten to tomoni Keishiki Saretekita Nagoya no Toshi Kōzō', in *Nagoya-shi Naka-ku Shi*, ed. Naka-ku sei 100 shūnen kinen jigyō jikkō iinkai, 172–183 (Nagoya: Naka-ku Yakusho, 2010), 175–179.
7   Piper Gaubatz, 'Community, Modernity, and Urban Change in Japan and the USA', in *Suburban Form: An International Perspective*, ed. Brenda Case Sheer and Kiril Stanilov (New York and London: Routledge, 2004), 28.
8   'The Growth of the City', in *A History of the County of Warwick: Volume 7, the City of Birmingham*, ed. W. B Stephens (London: Victoria County History,1964), 4–25. *British History Online* http://www.british-history.ac.uk/vch/warks/vol7/pp4-25 [accessed 22 September 2017]; Gill and Briggs, *History of Birmingham*, 305.
9   Clapson, *Suburban Century*, 46; Colin Pooley, 'Landscapes without the Car: A Counterfactual Historical Geography of Twentieth-Century Britain', *Journal of Historical Geography* 36, no. 3 (2010): 273.
10 Nagoya-shi Keikaku Kyoku, *Nagoya Toshi Keikak-shi: Taishō 8 – Shōwa 44, Toshūhen* (Nagoya: Zaidan Hōjin, Nagoya Toshi Sentā, 1999), 25.
11 Ibid., 33.
12 Ibid., 37.
13 Ibid., 35–37.
14 Ann Waswo, *Housing in Postwar Japan: A Social History* (London: RoutledgeCurzon, 2002), 45.
15 H. J. Manzoni, *The Production of Fifty Thousand Municipal Houses* (Birmingham: Birmingham Corporation, 1939); Briggs, *History of Birmingham*.
16 Birmingham only formally adopted such a policy in 1975. M. Elson, *Green Belts: Conflict Mediation on the Urban Fringe* (London: Architectural Press, 1986), 37.
17 City of Birmingham, *Development Plan*; Abercrombie and Jackson, *West Midlands Plan*; West Midlands Group, *Conurbation*.
18 Peter Hall et al., *The Containment of Urban England: Vol. I* (London: George Allen & Unwin, 1973), 527.
19 West Midlands Group, *Conurbation*, 150.
20 Jilly Traganou, 'The Transit Destinations of Japanese Public Space: The Case of Nagoya Station', in *Suburbanizing the Masses: Public Transport and Urban Development in Historical Perspective*, ed. Colin Divall and Winstan Bond (Aldershot: Ashgate, 2003), 292.
21 Ōtobashi and Jōshin also served commuter traffic in southwestern and northwestern areas respectively and Ōmon to the west of the main station is a pleasure quarter for the western side of the city. Eyre, *Nagoya*, 127–129.
22 Gill and Briggs, *History of Birmingham*, 305.
23 West Midlands Group, *Conurbation*, 184; on urban sprawl between the wars, see David Matless, *Landscape and Englishness* (London: Reaktion Books, 1998), ch. 1.
24 Manzoni, *The Production of Fifty Thousand Municipal Houses*, 67–68.
25 Ishida, 'Planning in the Reconstruction Period', 20–21.

26 Ibid., 41.
27 Nagoya-shi Keikaku Kyoku, *Fukkō Tochikukaku Seiri Jigyō no Aramashi*, 7.
28 Kitotaka, 'Land Readjustment in Nagoya', 107–108.
29 Ibid., 121.
30 *Nagoya-shi Hyakunen no Nenrin*, 190.
31 Japanese Ministry of Land Infrastructure and Transport, 'Introduction of Urban Land Use Planning System of Japan', http://www.mlit.go.jp/common/000234477.pdf [accessed 28 August 2015].
32 Nagoya-shi Keikaku Kyoku, *Nagoya Toshi Keikaku-shi, Toshūhen*, 41–42, 49–50.
33 Eyre, *Nagoya*, 44–45.
34 Richards, *An Architectural Journey*, 120.
35 Ibid., 127.
36 Hayakawa Fumio *Seikatsu, Jūtaku, Kankyō: Nagoya Daitoshien no Toshi-Jūtaku Kenkyū* (Nagoya: Nagoya University, E & S Shuppan-bu, 1975), 95. In 1973, 52 per cent of households in the three largest metropolitan areas owned their own home with 34 per cent renting from private landlords and 8 per cent from the JHC. Waswo, *Housing in Postwar Japan*, 59.
37 Sorensen, *The Making of Urban Japan*, 39.
38 Eyre, *Nagoya*, 67.
39 It now has a population 87,000. See Itō Shigeru, 'The Outline of Kozoji Newtown', *Ekistics* 19, no. 99 (February, 1964): 115–120.
40 Kiuchi Shinzo and Inouchi Noboru, 'New Towns in Japan', *Geoforum* 7, no. 1 (1976): 1–12, 2.
41 Efforts are now being made to renovate Kozoji Newtown and entice younger people back. See Harada Yoko, 'Sengo Nihon no Shoki Nyūtaun ni okeru Jūkankyō Hyōka to Sumikae ikō ni Kansuru Hikaku Kenkyū', *Journal of the Architectural Institute of Japan*, no. 629 (September 2007): 9–16.
42 However, in the 1990s this area was redeveloped and when JR Central Towers was opened in 1999, the total floor area of the station and its two 254-metre towers made it the largest station building in the world. It has a throughput of 1 million passengers a day and is a 'befitting gateway', according to the publicity, for one of Japan's biggest cities. City of Nagoya, *Nagoya: My Town* (2008), 4.
43 Traganou, 'Transit Destinations', 300.
44 Ibid., 301.
45 Eyre, *Nagoya*, 142–144.
46 Ibid., 71, 75.
47 *Nagoya-shi Hyakunen no Nenrin*, 193.
48 Jacobs, 'Planning for a Vibrant Central City', 31.
49 Tonouchi Hiroshi, ed. *Kōsha Setsuritsu 40 Shūnen Kinen Zadankai: Nagoya Kōsoku Dōro no Kensetsu no Rekishi o Furikaette*, 15 July 2012, 150. http://www.nagoya-expressway.or.jp/kosya/pdf/08.pdf.
50 These would radiate out to the Meishin Expressway, Nagoya Interchange, General Route 41 to Komaki, General Route 22 to Ichinomiya (the Higashi-Meihan Expressway to Yokkaichi, and the West Chita Industrial Road to Chita direction) and the road to Okazaki. *Nagoya Kōsokudōro Kōsha 40 Nenshi*, 14.
51 Tonouchi, *Kōsha Setsuritsu*, 56.
52 Car journeys were taken into account for the first time in government statistics in 1969.
53 Compiled from 'Historical Statistics of Japan, Domestic Passenger Transportation by Mode of Transportation (F.Y. 1950–2004)'.

54 Eyre, *Nagoya*, 81.
55 The area measured was within a 70 kilometre radius of Tokyo centre and 50 kilometres in the case of Osaka and Kyoto. 'Historical Statistics of Japan, Population by Sex, Area and Population Density (1970–2005)'.
56 See, for example, the study of mega-city Shenzhen, Liu Qian et al., 'How Does Parking Interplay with the Built Environment and Affect Automobile Commuting in High-Density Cities? A Case Study in China', *Urban Studies* 54, no. 14 (2017): 3299–3317.
57 Chauncy D. Harris, 'The Urban and Industrial Transformation of Japan', *Geographic Review* 72, no. 1 (January 1982): 77.
58 Edward Seidensticker, *Tokyo Rising: The City since the Great Earthquake* (Tokyo: Charles E. Tuttle, 1990), 147.
59 Ishida, 'Planning in the Reconstruction Period', 45.
60 In 1954, the numbers of vehicle per mile were estimated at 22.3 in Great Britain, 14.2 in West Germany, 17.0 in the United States and 8.2 in France, British Road Federation, *Basic Road Statistics*.
61 H. Manzoni, 'Verbal Response at Conference on Urban Traffic Congestion', *Institute of Municipal Engineers Journal* 86, no. 12 (December 1959), 345; TNA: CAB/129/1010, 25 March 1960, 1 and Appendix C.
62 Gunn, 'The Buchanan Report, Environment and the Problem of Traffic in 1960s Britain', 521–542; Saumarez Smith, 'Central Government and Town Centre Redevelopment in Britain, 1959–1966', 217–244.
63 For historical contextualization, see Colin Pooley and Jean Turnbull, 'Commuting, Transport and Urban Form: Manchester and Glasgow in the Mid-Twentieth Century', *Urban History* 27, no. 3 (2000): 360–383.
64 Freeman, Fox, Wilbur Smith and Associates, *West Midlands Transport Study*, 38.
65 The figure was 49.7 per cent. The figures for Birmingham, Manchester, Liverpool, Leeds, Sheffield and Newcastle are given in Table I.2, Matthew Parker, 'Making the City Mobile: The Place of the Motor Car in the Planning of Post-War Birmingham' (University of Leicester PhD, 2015), 7.
66 West Midlands Economic Planning Council, *The West Midlands: Patterns of Growth* (London: HMSO, 1967), 26.
67 Hall, *Containment of Urban England*, 509. This was approximately one-twelfth of the workforce at the time.
68 City of Birmingham, *Development Plan*.
69 William Plowden, *The Motor Car and Politics in Britain* (Harmondsworth: Penguin, 1971), 479.
70 Sutcliffe and Smith, *History of Birmingham*, 399.
71 Hayakawa, *Seikatsu, Jūtaku, Kankyō*, 109.
72 Physical and medical analogies with the city have a long history in Western thought, of course. In a large literature, see especially Richard Sennett, *Flesh and Stone: The Body and the City in Western Civilization* (London: Faber School of Economics, 1994).
73 TNA: HLG 81/17, Ministry of Town and Country Planning, Note on Deputation from Birmingham City Council received by the Minister on 21 July 1943; Manzoni, 'Redevelopment of Blighted Areas in Birmingham', 91. The formal title of the 'Blitz and Blight Act' was the Town and Country Planning Act, 1944. For an account of the episode, see Parker, 'Making the City Mobile', 90–91.
74 Manzoni, 'Redevelopment of Blighted Areas in Birmingham', 97.

75 LBA: BCC/1/AO/1/1/86, PWC, Manzoni, H. J., Duddeston and Nechells Redevelopment Area, Report to PWC, 11 November 1937. The Summer Lane area was significantly renamed 'Newtown'.
76 LBA: BCC/1/AO/1/1/95, PWC, Manzoni, H. J., Duddeston and Nechells Redevelopment Area, Report to PWC, 27 May 1943, 4.
77 TNA: HLG 79/35, Ministry of Town and Country Planning, City of Birmingham Duddeston and Nechells Redevelopment Area, Internal Memo, 3 May 1949.
78 Lynsey Hanley, *Estates: An Intimate History* (London: Granta, 2012), 25.
79 Cited in ibid., 16.
80 Ibid., 22.
81 City of Birmingham, *Development Plan*, 61; City of Birmingham Central Statistical Office, *City of Birmingham Abstract of Statistics* (Birmingham, 1952, 1962, 1972); Hall, *Containment of Urban England*, 350.
82 Ibid., 550.
83 City of Birmingham, *Development Plan*, 23.
84 Office of Population Censuses and Surveys, *Census 1971*.
85 Alison Ravetz, *The Government of Space* (London: Routledge, 1986), 75–82.
86 TNA: MT 122/48, Ministry of Transport, Note on the Proposal to Construct an Elevated Road in Coventry Road, Birmingham, 1.
87 TNA: MT 122/48, Ministry of Transport, Note on the Proposal to Construct an Elevated Road in Coventry Road, Birmingham, 20.
88 'City Skyway Again Rejected', *Birmingham Post*, 13 April 1965.
89 City of Birmingham, *Structure Plan* (Birmingham, 1973), 88. The Skyways episode is discussed in more detail in Parker, 'Making the City Mobile', 103–107.
90 *Birmingham Post*, 23 February 1971.
91 City of Birmingham Central Statistical Office, *City of Birmingham Abstract of Statistics* (Birmingham, 1966).
92 Michael Young and Peter Wilmott, *Family and Kinship in East London* (London: Penguin, 1957), 158. For a larger discussion of this topic, see Simon Gunn, 'People and the Car: The Expansion of Automobility in Urban Britain, c.1955–1970', *Social History* 38, no. 2 (2013): 220–237.
93 Goldthorpe et al., *The Affluent Worker in the Class Structure*. For interesting recent reflections on the attitudes of the researchers and interviewers in the study, see Jon Lawrence, 'Social Science Encounters and the Negotiation of Difference in Early 1960s England', *History Workshop Journal*, 77, no. 1 (2013): 215–239.
94 Papers to the People and Cities Conference, 11 December 1963, London, TNA, MT 122/77, Part 1.
95 *Birmingham Mail*, 26 March 1971; David Adams, 'Walking in the Modern City: Pedestrian Experiences of Post-War Birmingham', *Birmingham City University Centre for Environment and Society Research Working Paper Series*, 22 (2013).
96 Pooley and Turnbull, 'Commuting, Transport and Urban Form', 379.
97 Parsons and Vigar, 'Resistance Was Futile'.
98 Parker, 'Making the City Mobile', 110–111 on evidence of the 1940s; Phil Jones, 'Performing the City: A Body and a Bicycle Take on Birmingham, UK', *Social and Cultural Geography* 6, no. 6 (2005): 813–830.
99 See City of Birmingham Central Statistical Office, *City of Birmingham Abstract of Statistics* (Birmingham, 1955) for figures for passenger journeys. Trolley buses also operated but carried relatively small numbers of passengers.

100 *Birmingham Mail*, 1 February 1949; Pooley and Turnbull, 'Coping with Congestion', 78–93; Briggs, *History of Birmingham*, 249.
101 Joan Bakewell, *Stop the Clocks: Thoughts on What I Leave Behind* (London: Virago, 2016), 8–11; *Birmingham Mail*, 4 July 1953; Pooley and Turnbull, 'Coping with Congestion', 84.
102 Passenger figures from City of Birmingham Central Statistical Office, *City of Birmingham Abstract of Statistics* (Birmingham, 1970). See also Parker, 'Making the City Mobile', 140–141.
103 British Railways Board, *The Reshaping of British Railways – Part 1: Report* (London, 1963), 15.
104 TNA: MT 97/536, Brief for the Minister about Rail Closures and Area Transport Surveys in the West Midlands, 27 July 1962. The Ministry did, however, agree the setting up of a West Midlands Area Transport Survey in 1963, which was to prove influential.
105 LBA: BCC/1/AO/1/1/115, PWC, Minutes, 27 July 1950; *Birmingham Post*, 1 November 1952.
106 Tange Kenzo, 'A Plan for Tokyo', cited in *Kenzo Tange 1946–1969: Architcture and Urban Design*, ed. Udo Kultermann (London: Pall Mall Press, 1970), 120.
107 Ibid., 118–119.
108 Dennis and Urry, *After the Car*, 28.
109 Peter Freund and George Martin, *The Ecology of the Automobile* (Montreal: Black Rose Books, 1994), 27.
110 Kōtsu Kogaku Kenyūkai, eds. *Kōtsu Kogaku Handobukku*, 543.

Chapter 4

1 David Lodge, *Changing Places* (London: Secker and Warburg, 1975), 210.
2 Reyner Banham, *Los Angeles: The Architecture of Four Ecologies* (London: Allen Lane, 1971), 213–214.
3 See, for example, Marshall Berman, *All That Is Solid Melts into Air: The Experience of Modernity* (London: Verso, 1983), 164–171, 290–329; James Donald, *Imagining the Modern City* (London: Athlone, 1999); Paul Virilio, *Speed and Politics* (Los Angeles: Semiotexte, 2006).
4 On the motoring 'sublime', see Kristin Ross, *Fast Cars, Clean Bodies: Decolonization and the Reordering of French Culture* (Cambridge, MA: MIT Press, 1996), 22ff.
5 Road Traffic and Roads Improvement Bill, *HC Deb*, 11 April 1960, vol. 621, 969.
6 Roy Church, *The Rise and Decline of the British Motor Industry* (Basingstoke: Macmillan, 1994), 45; AA, *The Motorist Today*.
7 For a fuller discussion, see Gunn, 'People and the Car', 226–228.
8 Freeman, Fox, Wilbur Smith and Associates, *West Midlands Transport Study*, 38.
9 Speech to the Royal Institute of British Architects reported in the *Birmingham Mail*, 22 January 1958; see also Manzoni's comments on the same lines reported in *Municipal Engineering*, 22 November 1957.
10 Road Traffic and Roads Improvement Bill, 923–925.
11 The name 'Publica', from 'public' and 'car', was adopted after a competition to name the new model. Japan Automobile Manufacturers' Association (JAMA), 'The Tokyo Motor Show: History' (2011), http://www.tokyo-motorshow.com.

12 Calculated from Statistics Bureau of Japan, 'Annual Average of Monthly Receipts and Disbursements per Household for Cities with Prefectural Government (Workers' Households) – (1953–2004) – All Japan', *Historical Statistics of Japan*, http://www.stat.go.jp /english/data/chouki/20.htm [accessed 17 April 2012].
13 Ibid.
14 Motor Manufacturing Economic Development Council, *Japan: Its Motor Industry and Market* (London: HMSO, 1971), 10–14.
15 In 1985, for example, an article in the *New York Times* commented on a Japanese 'rich list', published by Japan's National Tax Administration Agency, which suggested that the number of individuals paying higher taxes had increased exponentially between 1972 and 1983. To Western reporters viewing the Japanese through culturally specific lenses, this seemed strange since it was well-known that wealthy Japanese, 'shunned conspicuous consumption, not only as vulgar but as insensitive to the economic struggles of most Japanese in the postwar years.' Susan Chira, 'Japan List Shows Growing Affluence: But Tax-Cut Pleas Increase', *New York Times*, 6 May 1985, D12.
16 Andrew Gordon, 'Consumption, Leisure and the Middle Class in Transwar Japan', *Social Science Japan Journal* 10, no. 1 (2007): 1.
17 William W. Kelly, 'Finding a Place in Metropolitan Japan: Ideologies, Institutions, and Everyday Life', in *Postwar Japan as History*, ed. Andrew Gordon (Berkeley: University of California Press, 1993), 189–292, 195. For a criticism of the '90 per cent' myth, see Aoki Shigeru, 'Debunking the 90%-Middle-Class-Myth', *Japan Echo* 6, no. 2 (1979): 29–33.
18 Gordon, 'Consumption, Leisure and the Middle Class', 18–19.
19 Generally speaking, the idea of the 'affluent society' in Britain in the later 1950s and 1960s has been treated with critical caution by recent historians. See, for example, Hugh Pemberton and Lawrence Black, eds., *An Affluent Society: Britain's Post-War 'Golden Age' Revisited* (London: Routledge, 2004); Selina Todd, 'Affluence, Class and Crown Street: Reinventing the Post-War British Working Class', *Contemporary British History* 22, no. 4 (2008): 501–518.
20 The estimated annual wage of such workers was £581 in 1960, G. Routh, *Occupation and Pay in Great Britain 1906–1987* (London: Macmillan,1980), 120–121.
21 S. C. H. Davis, *Car Driving as an Art* (Coventry: Iliffe and Sons,1952); Mike Savage, *Identities and Social Change in Britain since 1940* (Oxford: Oxford University Press, 2010), 75; *Daily Express*, 5 October 1963.
22 To view these, visit the official Tokyo Motor Show website at http://www.tokyo-motorshow.com/en/history/01.html.
23 *Japanese Motor Vehicles Guide Book (Jidōsha Gaidobukku)*, vol. 3, 1956 and vol. 4, 1957.
24 Masatoshi Takada, 'The Japanese Meet the Automobile', *The Wheel Extended*, 17 (1987): 23.
25 Koshimidzu Isamu, 'Parking in Tokyo', *Traffic Quarterly* 18, no. 2 (1964): 173.
26 Ibid., 174.
27 Urry, *Mobilities*, 124–130.
28 *Autocar*, 5 January, 1967; *Motoring*, January 1965.
29 Williams was referring to the capacity of television to transport the viewer beyond the home but the car also enabled drivers to surround themselves with elements of the home. Raymond Williams, *Television: Technology and Cultural Form* (London: Fontana, 1974), 19–21.

30 In 1949, these vehicles were restricted to a maximum length of 2.8 metres, a width of 1 metre and height of 2 metres in dimension, and a maximum displacement of 150 cc for a four-stroke engine and 100 cc for a two-stroke engine. In 1951, new regulations increased the size and displacement of light vehicles to 3 metres in length × 1.3 metres in width and a displacement of 360 cc for a four-stroke engine and 240 cc for a two-stroke engine. JAMA, 'Japan's Auto Industry', *About JAMA*, accessed 4 June 2010, http://www.jama-english.jp/about/index.html.
31 *The Motor* CV, no. 2734 (23 June 1954), 869–870.
32 Bowen C. Dees, *The Allied Occupation & Japan's Economic Miracle: Building the Foundations of Japanese Science and Technology 1945–52* (Richmond, Surrey: Japan Library, 1997), 225. For further details about car ownership in Japan, see Townsend, 'The Miracle of Car Ownership in Japan's "Era of High Growth," 1955–1973', 498–523.
33 Genther, *The Passenger Car Industry*, 73.
34 Any proposed car would have to weigh less than 400 kilograms, have an engine capacity of between 350 and 500 cc, fuel efficiency of 30 kilometres per litre, and be big enough to carry two to four persons. It also had to be capable of speeds up to 100 kilometres an hour and enduring for over 100,000 kilometres. Ibid., 100–101.
35 Statistics Bureau of Japan, 'Annual Average of Monthly Receipts and Disbursements', *Historical Statistics of Japan*. April 2012. http://www.stat.go.jp/english/data/chouki/20.html
36 Genther, *The Passenger Car Industry*, 103–104.
37 JAMA, 'The Tokyo Motor Show'.
38 Kobayashi Shotarō, '1964 Tokyo Motor Show', *Autocar* (1964): 8.
39 Quoted in Plowden, *The Motor Car and Politics*, 381–382.
40 Colin Atkins, *People and the Motor Car* (Birmingham: University of Birmingham, 1964), 47.
41 James Greenhalgh, 'Consuming Communities: The Neighbourhood Unit and the Role of Retail Spaces on British Housing Estates, 1944–1958', *Urban History* 43, no. 1, (2016): 158–174; Alistair Kefford, 'Constructing the Affluent Citizen: State, Space and the Individual in Post-war Britain, 1945–1979' (PhD thesis, Manchester, 2015).
42 'The New Birmingham', *Birmingham Sketch*, September 1965.
43 *Birmingham Evening Despatch*, 5 February 1960.
44 *Birmingham Post*, 8 April 1959; *Guardian*, 20 December 1969.
45 Marriott, *Property Boom*, 230–231; MACE, *Regenerating Birmingham*.
46 Jacques Gravereau, *Le Japon l'ère de Hirohito* (Paris: Imprimerie nationale, 1988), 380.
47 Traganou, 'The Transit Destinations of Japanese Public Space', 204.
48 See Chapter 3 for a fuller discussion.
49 Mimi Sheller and John Urry, 'The City and the Car', *International Journal of Urban and Regional Research* 24, no. 4 (2000): 746.
50 Michael Young and Peter Wilmott, *Family and Kinship in East London* (Harmondsworth: Penguin, 1962 [1957]), 158.
51 University of Birmingham, 'People and the Motor Car', 19, 34, 50.
52 Ferdynand Zweig, *The Worker in an Affluent Society* (London: Heinemann, 1961), 107; Goldthorpe et al., *The Affluent Worker*, 50.
53 These points are discussed more extensively in Gunn, 'People and the Car', 232ff.
54 Gravereau, *Le Japon l'ère de Hirohito*, 379.
55 Kelly, 'Finding a Place', 195.
56 Waswo, *Housing in Postwar Japan*, 96.

57 See Takahashi Tomoko and Ihara Satoshi, '"Jidōsha Shakai" wa Ikani Ronjiraretekita ka: 1. Gendai gijutsu-ron no kadai to kakawatte', *Ibaraki Daigaku Kyōyōbu Kiyō* 24 (1992): 135–155. http://hdl.handle.net/10109/9951
58 Hotta Yoshihiro, '"Mai kā" to "mai hōmu" o meguru jūtakuchi dezain nitsuite', 59–67 (Nagoya University Research Papers, 2014), no. 59, www.lij.jp/html/jli/jli_2014/2014winter_p059.pdf.
59 Kamei Yosuko et al., 'Kōgai ōkibo kodatejūtaku danchi no jūko dasai to gairo keikan ni kansuru kenkyū',*Nihonkenchiku gakkai keikaku-kei ronbun-shū* 70, no. 590 (April 2005), 9–10.
60 Hotta, 'Mai kā to mai hōmu', 65.
61 Inge Daniels, 'Japanese Homes Inside Out', *Home Cultures* 5, no. 2 (2008), 119.
62 Ibid., 123.
63 Ibid., 117.
64 Joe Moran, 'Crossing the Road in Britain, 1931–1976', *Historical Journal* 49, no. 2 (2006): 477–496; Alker Tripp, *Town Planning and Road Traffic* (London: Edward Arnold, 1942).
65 A. C. Durie, 'Motoring into the 1980s', paper to the Insurance Institute, London, 22 January 1968, 5, Automobile Association Archive, Hampshire Record Office, 73 M94/H14/8/14; Department for Transport, *Reported Road Casualties Great Britain 2013 Annual Report* (London: HMSO, 2014), 166.
66 *Birmingham Post*, 14 February 1974.
67 Bureau, 'Road Traffic Accidents (1924–2005)', *Historical Statistics of Japan*. British figures from Department of the Environment, *Transport Statistics*.
68 Although the British system decreed that people should walk on the right, facing the traffic.
69 Saitō Toshihiko, *Kurumatachi no Shakaishi* (Tokyo: Chuko Shinsho, 1997), 263–264.
70 *Nagoya-shi Hyakunen no Nenrin*, 106–109.
71 Road Safety Bill, HC Deb, 10 February 1966, *Hansard*, vol. 724, cc 655.
72 'The Traffic War Intensifies', *Japan Quarterly* 15, no. 1 (1 January 1968): 10.
73 'Death Unlimited', *Japan Quarterly* 13, no. 3 (1July1966): 288–289.
74 Ibid., 290.
75 *Birmingham Mail*, 2 November 1959.
76 'Automobile Society', *Japan Quarterly* 21, no. 2 (1 April 1974): 134.
77 Merriman, *Driving Spaces*, 141–161.
78 Traffic regulation in Japan has been determined by the updated 1965 Road Traffic Enforcement Order which can be found at http://elaws.e-gov.go.jp/search/elawsSearch/elaws_search/lsg0500/detail?lawId=335CO0000000270&openerCode=1#1534.
79 TNA: MT 112/322, article by James Clayton, 26 August 1971.
80 Birmingham Mail, 27 April 1972.
81 Banham, *Los Angeles*, 217, 220.
82 Plowden, *The Motor Car and Politics*, 376.
83 Opposition can be traced through the annual reports of the RAC held in the Churchill College archives, University of Cambridge. See also Piers Brendon, *The Motoring Century: The Story of the Royal Automobile Club* (London: Bloomsbury, 1997). For road safety, see the special issue, '(Auto)mobility, Accidents and Danger', ed. M. Esbester and J. Wetmore, *Technology and Culture* 56, no. 2 (2015), 307–497.
84 'Interview at the Top', *Autocar*, 13 July 1967.

85 See Joshua H. Roth, 'Heartfelt Driving: Discourses on Manners, Safety, and Emotion in Japan's Era of Mass Motorization', *Journal of Asian Studies* 71, no. 1 (February 2012): 171–192.
86 For Britain, see Krista Cowman, 'Play Streets: Women, Children and the Problem of Traffic, 1930–1970', *Social History* 42, no. 2 (2017): 233–256.
87 Joshua H. Roth, 'Harmonizing Cars and Humans in Japan's Era of Mass Automobility', *The Asia-Pacific Journal: Japan Focus* 45, no. 3 (November 2011). http://apjjf.org/2011/9/45/Joshua-Roth/3643/article.html.
88 Figures for Britain can be found in Department for Transport, *Reported Road Casualties*, 2–3.
89 'The Traffic War Intensifies', 10.
90 Ibid.
91 Ministry of Transport, *Traffic in Towns*, foreword and 32; Standing Advisory Committee on Trunk Road Assessment, *Trunk Roads and the Generation of Traffic* (London: HMSO, 1994), 31–32.
92 'Buchanan on Birmingham', *Birmingham Post*, 12 October 1971.
93 Koshimidzu, 'Parking in Tokyo', 174–176.
94 Ibid., 186.
95 Yoshino Tsuyoshi, Sasaki Tsuna and Hasegawa Toshiharu, 'The Traffic-Control System on the Hanshin Expressway', *Interfaces* 25, no. 1 (January–February, 1995): 94–96.
96 Nagoya Kōsokudōro Kōsha 40 Nenshi Henshū I'inkai, *Nagoya Kōsokudōro Kōsha 40 Nenshi*, 190.
97 Yoshino et al. 'Traffic Control System', 100.
98 Peter Popham, *Tokyo: The City at the Edge of the World* (Kodansha: Japan, 1985), 24.
99 AA, *The Motorist Today*; figures for breakdowns can be followed in the AA annual reports located at the Automobile Association archive, Hampshire Record Office.
100 Yoshino et al. 'Traffic-Control System', 97.
101 'A Hard Shoulder to Cry On', in *Drive*, XXIV (Basingstoke: Automobile Association, 1973), 24; 'Car Costs Double in Two Years', *Guardian*, 23 January 1976, 6.
102 See, for example, 'Driving into Birmingham', *ATV Today*, 27 April 1966.
103 'Spaghetti Junction', *ATV 45* (n.d.1972), Media Archive for Central England, University of Lincoln.
104 *Guardian*, 10 May 1973, 16.
105 Brian Goodey, Alan Duffett, John Gold and David Spencer, *City Scene: An Exploration into the Image of Central Birmingham as Seen by Area Residents* (Birmingham: University of Birmingham, 1971); Kevin Lynch, *The Image of the City* (Boston, MA: MIT Press, 1960), 3.
106 Goodey et al., *City Scene*, 46; Matthew Parker, 'Making the City Mobile: The Place of the Motor Car in the Planning of Post-War Birmingham, c.1945–1973' (University of Leicester PhD, 2015), 206.
107 Goodey et al., *City Scene*, 48, 125; *Birmingham Post*, 25 May 1968.
108 Shelton, *Learning from the Japanese City*, 9.
109 Popham, *Tokyo*, 41–42.
110 Ibid., 48.
111 For a full explanation and guide in English, visit the website 'Road Signs in Japan'. https://en.wikipedia.org/wiki/Road_signs_in_Japan.
112 The sub-committee comprised a number of government and police agencies, including the Ministry of Construction, MITI and the Public Works Research

Notes   211

Institute, as well as experts from the Japan Highway Public Corporation and various police agencies.

113 Murashige Yoshiyasu, 'Kōsoku dōrohyōji no reiauto henkō ni yoru shinin-sei kōjō', *International Association of Traffic and Safety Sciences (IATSS) Review* 40 no. 3, (February 2016): 199–205, 199–200. The International Association of Traffic and Safety Sciences was founded in 1974 as Japan's first research institute in the field of transportation sciences. For further information and publications, see http://www.iatss.or.jp/.

114 Robert Trumbull, 'Japan Road Signs Confuse Drivers: New Traffic Instructions, Written in "Japlish," Cause Linguistic Bewilderment', *New York Times (1923-Current File)*. Retrieved from http://Ezproxy.Nottingham.Ac.Uk/Login?url=https://search-proquest-com.ezproxy.nottingham.ac.uk/docview/115091422?accountid=8018

115 Shelton, *Learning from the Japanese City*, 28.

116 Takahashi and Ihara, 'Jidōsha shakai', 136.

117 Ibid., 139–140.

118 Office of Population Census and Surveys, *Census 1971*.

119 Statistics extrapolated from Statistics Bureau, 'Motor Vehicles Owned by Kind (F.Y. 1936–2004)', *Historical Statistics of Japan*, http://www.stat.go.jp/english/data/chouki/20.htm; *Nagoya-shi Hyakunen no Nenrin*, 190.

120 Joshua H. Roth, 'Is Female to Male as Lightweight Cars Are to Sports Cars?: Gender Metaphors and Cognitive Schemes in Recessionary Japan', in *Vehicles: Cars, Canoes and Other Metaphors or Moral Imagination*, ed. David Lipset and Richard Hander (New York: Berghahn, 2014), 94; Department for Transport, 'Driving Licence Holding and Vehicle Availability', in *National Travel Survey: 2010* (London: HMSO, 2010), 1.

121 *Nagoya-shi Hyakunen no Nenrin*, 193.

122 F. D. Hobbs, M. B. A. Walker and I. Johnson, *A Survey of Travel Characteristics in Birmingham* (Birmingham: University of Birmingham, 1974), 42, 50.

123 Data for this is from Hobbs, Walker and Johnson, *A Survey of Travel Characteristics in Birmingham*.

124 City of Birmingham Central Statistical Office, *City of Birmingham Abstract of Statistics* (Birmingham, 1967).

125 Pooley and Turnbull, 'Coping with Congestion', 79.

126 The phrase is that of Ladd, 'Cities on Wheels', 270.

127 *Birmingham Post*, 23 August 1971; Jeremy Bugler, 'The Ringway to Ruin', *Observer*, 25 February 1973.

128 *Birmingham Mail*, 30 September 1970. Ten per cent of people asked were undecided.

129 *Birmingham Mail*, 26 March 1971.

130 'Road Traffic Accidents (1924–2005)', *Historical Statistics of Japan*; Statistics Bureau, Ministry of Internal Affairs and Communications, Japan. http://www.stat.go.jp/english/data/chouki/29.html. [accessed 26 January 2011].

131 'Traffic War', 11.

132 Philip Shabecoff, 'Japanese Drivers Face New Curbs', *New York Times* 25 August 1969, 9.

133 'Traffic War Intensifies', 12.

134 Network 2010, 'Time Travel in Nagoya', http://timetravel.network2010.org/article/129 [accessed 20 July 2018].

135 'Automobile Society'; In Britain too, the steady decline of cycling from the 1950s began to stabilize in the 1970s, although there was no compensatory 'craze' as in Japan.

Chapter 5

1. *Sunday Times*, 29 May 1977; 'The Depths of Despair', *Birmingham Post*, 28 June 1977.
2. Report of the Study Group, *Traffic in Towns* (London: HMSO, 1963), conclusion.
3. See, for instance, John Pendlebury, *Conservation in the Age of Consensus* (London: Routledge, 2008); Lionel Esher, *A Broken Wave: The Rebuilding of England 1940–1980* (London: Allen Lane, 1981); Gunn, 'The Rise and Fall of British Urban Modernism', 849–869.
4. Key works include John Sheail, *An Environmental History of Twentieth-Century Britain* (Basingstoke: Palgrave, 2002); John Sheail, '"Torrey Canyon": The Political Dimension', *Journal of Contemporary History* 42, no. 3 (July 2007): 485–504; John McCormick, *The Global Environmental Movement* (Chichester: John Wiley, 1995); Derek Wall, *Earth First! And the Anti-Roads Movement* (London: Routledge, 1999), ch. 2; Gunn, 'The Buchanan Report, Environment and the Problem of Traffic in 1960s Britain', 521–542.
5. See, for example Peter Thorsheim, *Inventing Pollution: Coal Smoke and Culture in Britain since 1800* (Athens, Ohio: Ohio University Press, 2006); Stephen Mosley, '"A Network of Trust": Measuring and Monitoring Air Pollution in British Cities, 1912–1960', *Environment and History* 15 (2009): 273–302. A more determinedly urban environmental history has been prominent in the United States – among many important studies, see Martin Melosi, *Effluent America: Cities, Industry, Energy and the Environment* (Pittsburgh: Pittsburgh University Press, 2001); Joel Tarr, *The Search for the Ultimate Sink: Urban Pollution in Historical Perspective* (Akron: University of Akron Press, 1996); Frank Uekotter, *The Age of Smoke: Environmental Policy in Germany and the United States 1880–1970* (Pittsburgh: University of Pittsburgh Press, 2009).
6. For example, Jeffrey Broadbent, *Environmental Politics in Japan: Networks of Power and Protest* (Cambridge: Cambridge University Press, 1998); Timothy S. George, *Minamata: Pollution and the Struggle for Democracy in Postwar Japan* (Cambridge, MA: Harvard University Asia Centre, 2001).
7. For example, Pamela J. Asquith and Arne Kalland, *Japanese Images of Nature: Cultural Perspectives* (Richmond: Curzon, 1997); W. Puck Brecher, *An Investigation of Japan's Relationship to Nature and Environment* (Lampeter: Edwin Mellen Press, 2000).
8. 'Negative Impact of Tokyo Olympics Profound', *Japan Times*, 24 October 2014, http://www.japantimes.co.jp/sports/2014/10/24/olympics/negative-impact-1964-olympics-profound/#.VFJcbxYnaAQ.
9. For example, S. Ichikawa and N. Yamada published a series of papers in 1959 entitled 'Air Pollution by Exhaust Gas' in the *Bulletin of National Hygiene Laboratory* in Tokyo.
10. Rodney R. Beard et al. 'Observations on Tokyo-Yokohama Asthma and Air Pollution in Japan', *Public Health Reports (1896–1970)* 79, no. 5 (May 1964): 442.
11. Ibid., 442.
12. Wakamatsu Shinji, Morikawa Tazuko and Ito Akiyoshi, 'Air Pollution Trends in Japan between 1970 and 2012 and Impact of Urban Air Pollution Countermeasures', *Asian Journal of Atmospheric Environment* 7, no. 4 (2013): 177, doi: http://dx.doi.org/10.5572/ajae.2013.7.4.177.
13. Norie Huddle and Michael Reich, *Island of Dreams: Environmental Crisis in Japan* (New York: Autumn Press Inc. 1975), 51.
14. Shigeto Tsuru, 'Kōgai', UNESCO *Courier*, July 1971, cited in Huddle and Reich, *Island of Dreams*, 51.

15 Huddle and Reich, *Island of Dreams*, 56.
16 Ibid., 59–60.
17 Ibid., 61–65.
18 Ibid., 73–75.
19 Simon Avenell, *Transnational Japan in the Global Environmental Movement* (Honolulu: University of Hawaii Press, 2017), 28. Other 'Big Four' cases involved cadmium poisoning in Toyama Prefecture, and another case of methyl mercury poising in Niigata.
20 Ibid., 2.
21 Broadbent, *Environmental Politics*, 14.
22 Avenell, *Transnational Japan*, 2.
23 Justin Jesty, 'Tokyo 1960: Days of Rage & Grief', MIT Visualizing Cultures, https://ocw.mit.edu/ans7870/21f/21f.027/tokyo_1960/anp2_essay01.html. [accessed 5 July 2018].
24 The Japanese term 'kōgai', which Ui does not refer to in the text under discussion, was also translated by Ui in a later work as 'destruction of the public domain' and was in common parlance by the 1960s. Ui Jun, *Industrial Pollution in Japan* (Tokyo: United Nations University Press, 1992) open access, http://archive.unu.edu/unupress/unupbooks/uu35ie/uu35ie02.htm#i.%20environmental%20pollution:%20basic%20precepts.
25 Ui Jun, 'The Singularities of Japanese Pollution', *Japan Quarterly* 19, no. 3 (1 July 1972), 282.
26 Ibid., 286.
27 Ibid.
28 However, this experience proved seminal since, in his work in urban engineering, Ui became increasingly involved in pollution issues, setting up a forum series called Independent Symposia on Pollution (*Kōgai Jishu Kōza*). Much to Ui's surprise, the first series attracted over 800 attendees from all over the world. In 1972, Ui's group produced a hard-hitting report, *Polluted Japan,* in time for the Stockholm Conference on the Human Environment. Not only did it embarrass the government, but it made Ui well-known in international activist circles. Simon A. Avenell, *Making Japanese Citizens: Civil Society and the Mythology of the Shimin in Postwar Japan* (Berkeley: University of California Press, 2010), 163.
29 Ui, 'Singularities of Japanese Pollution', 291.
30 Ellis S. Krauss and Bradford L. Simcock, 'Citizens' Movements: The Growth and Impact of Environmental Protest in Japan', in *Political Opposition and Local Politics in Japan*, ed. Kurt Steiner, Ellis S. Krauss and Scott C. Flanagan (Princeton, NJ: Princeton University Press, 1980), 195.
31 Huddle and Reich, *Island of Dreams*, 56.
32 Johnson, *Six Men Who Built the Modern Auto Industry*, 54–55.
33 Parker, 'Making the City Mobile', ch. 6.
34 Genther, *The Passenger Car Industry,* 173.
35 Report of the Study Group, *Traffic in Towns*, 32 and conclusion.
36 Nader, *Unsafe at Any Speed*, 147, 151.
37 Jane Jacobs, *The Death and Life of American Cities* (New York: Random House, 1961); Rachel Carson, *Silent Spring* (Boston, MA: Houghton Mifflin, 1962).
38 Committee on the Problem of Noise, *Noise: Final Report* (London: HMSO, 1963), 133.
39 'Worse Noise Pollution in Japan', *Observer-Reporter*, Washington, 8 January 1983.

40 Miyazaki Tadashi, 'Case Study Nagoya (Japan)', in *Proceedings of the Better Towns with Less Traffic Conference 14–16 April 1975* (Paris: OECD, 1975), 132.
41 Ibid., 139.
42 'Olympic Construction Transformed Tokyo', *Japan Times*.
43 Miranda A. Schreurs, *Environmental Politics in Japan, Germany, and the United States* (Cambridge: Cambridge University Press, 2004), 43.
44 C. Johnson, *MITI and the Japanese Miracle: The Growth of Industrial Policy* (Stanford, CA: Stanford University Press, 1982), 284.
45 K. A. Oye and J. H. Maxwell, 'Self-interest and Environmental Management', in *Local Commons and Global Interdependence*, ed. R. O. Keohane and E. Ostrom (London: Sage, 1995), 191–221, 209 and 213.
46 Rosenbluth and Thies, 'The Political Economy of Japanese Pollution Regulation'.
47 Central Unit on Environmental Pollution, *The Protection of the Environment: The Fight against Pollution* (London: HMSO, 1969), 11–12.
48 'Spaghetti Junction Compensation Plea', *Times*, 13 July 1972.
49 TNA: AT 67/214, D. J. Fisk, A. C. Salvidge and J. W. Sargent, 'Traffic Noise Propagation from the M6 Motorway – Perry Bar, Birmingham', Building Research Station, January 1973.
50 'Noise Protest by Ringway Residents', *Birmingham Mercury*, 3 December 1972.
51 Peter Snape, *HC Debs*, 29 July 1974, 878, cols. 151–186; I. D. Jones, *Road Traffic Noise* (London: Pergamon Press, 1976), 138.
52 TNA: HLG 156/749, Joint Working Party on Lead Pollution around Gravelly Hill, *First Report*, December 1974.
53 Sydney Chapman, *HC Debs*, 17 May 1972, 837, cols. 517–519.
54 Joint Working Party, *First Report*; 'Brain Injury Threat from Lead in Big Cities', *Times*, 24 November 1972.
55 J. O. Nriagu, 'The Rise and Fall of Leaded Gasoline', *Science of the Total Environment* 92 (1990), 21–23. For Britain, see also Des Wilson, *The Lead Scandal* (London: Ashgate, 1983).
56 J. W. Rooker, *HC Deb*, 5 April 1974, vol. 871, 1692–1694.
57 Joint Working Party, *First Report*, summary.
58 Joint Working Party on Lead Pollution around Gravelly Hill, *Final Report* (London: HMSO, 1978); *New Scientist*, 13 July 1978, 118–119.
59 *Financial Times*, 6 January 1979.
60 TNA: HLG 156/749 Lead pollution in Birmingham Steering Committee, flyer produced by Birmingham Environmental Health Department, November 1979.
61 Media Archive for Central England (MACE) 'Spaghetti Junction', *ATV Today*, 14 March 1974.
62 *Birmingham Mail*, 30 March 1973.
63 'Rapid Transit System Forecast for 1980s', *Times*, 8 June 1972.
64 The best account of the issue and campaigns remains Peter Hall, 'London's Motorways', in his *Great Planning Disasters* (Berkeley: University of California Press, 1980), 56–86.
65 *Birmingham Post*, 24 May 1973.
66 *Birmingham Post*, 3 May 1977; *Birmingham Post*, 5 June 1973.
67 *Birmingham Post*, 24 May 1973; 3 July 1974; 30 March 1973.
68 *Birmingham Mail*, 25 May 1977.
69 *Birmingham Mercury*, 3 December 1972; *Birmingham Mail*, 14 June 1974 and 26 November 1974.

70 'Do It Yourself Crossing', *Birmingham Mail*, 26 June 1969. For the role of women in roads protest more generally, see Cowman, 'Play Streets', 233–256.
71 *Birmingham Post*, 14 February 1974.
72 *Birmingham Mail*, 13 April 1970.
73 *Birmingham Post*, 26 June 1975; *Birmingham Mail*, 25 July 1973.
74 'Red for Danger', *Birmingham Post*, 25 and 26 August 1971; letter from James Clayton, 11 November 1971. The whole debate can be found in TNA: MT 112/322, Motorways – Traffic Regulations Policy, Aston Expressway.
75 *Birmingham Mercury*, 29 March 1970.
76 Quoted in the *Birmingham Evening Despatch*, 26 February 1959. See also Alderman Thomas speaking in 1963; 'We have not reached the conclusion in Birmingham that the motor car should be excluded from the city centre; I personally hope we never shall'. TNA: MT122/77, Part 1, 'Papers to the People and Cities conference, 11 December 1963, London'.
77 *Birmingham Mail*, 18 February and 6 October 1974.
78 'Jam Tomorrow', *Birmingham Post*, 3 January 1974.
79 *Birmingham Mail*, 7 April 1977.
80 'City's Ring Road Falling Apart, Says Engineer', *Sunday Times*, 29 May 1977; Bernard I. Clark, 'General Report on Structural State of Birmingham Queensway', commissioned by the *Sunday Times*, 27 May 1977.
81 *Birmingham Mail*, 31 May 1977; *Birmingham Post*, 2 June 1977.
82 *Guardian*, 4 June 1977.
83 *Birmingham Mail*, 1 June and 17 June 1977; *Times*, 31 May 1977.
84 *Birmingham Mercury*, 17 July 1977.
85 TNA: AT 63/33, Local Transportation, Birmingham Inner Ring Road, 1997/8, report of Department of the Environment, 11 November 1977.
86 *Birmingham Post*, 21 and 24 June 1977.
87 *Birmingham Post*, 28 June 1977.
88 *Sunday Times*, 24 July 1977; see also 'Borg Too Far', *Private Eye* [n.d.] in TNA: AT 63/33 Local Transportation.
89 *The Times*, 5 April 1978; 'The Moral Flaws behind Birmingham's Modern Face', *The Times*, 18 May 1978; *Guardian*, 26 September 1978. This last article indicates that the directors had their sentences cut.
90 *The Times*, 20 and 25 March 1978; *Birmingham Post*, 20 May 1978.
91 *Birmingham Mail*, 7 and 13 July 1978; TNA: AT 63/33, letter from West Midlands County Council to Birmingham District Council, 12 July 1978 and internal memos, DoE, 26 July 1978.
92 *Asahi Shimbun*, 11 January 1968.
93 *Nagoya Kōsokudōro Kōsha 40 Nenshi*, 236.
94 *Asahi Shimbun*, 13 May 1970.
95 *Nagoya Kōsokudōro Kōsha 40 Nenshi*, 236.
96 Jeffrey Broadbent, *Environmental Politics in Japan: Networks of Power and Protest* (Cambridge: Cambridge University Press, 1998), 11.
97 Ibid., 19.
98 Ibid., 14.
99 Wakamatsu et al., 'Air Pollution Trends in Japan between 1970 and 2012', 178.
100 Broadbent, *Environmental Politics*, 14–15.
101 *Nagoya Kōsokudōro Kōsha 40 Nenshi*, 453.
102 *Chūnichi Shimbun*, 13 June 1970.

103 Waswo, *Housing in Postwar Japan*, 37.
104 Schreurs, *Environmental Politics*, 42.
105 *Chūnichi Shimbun*, 10 July 1970.
106 *Chūnichi Shimbun*, 4 August 1971.
107 *Nagoya Kōsokudōro Kōsha 40 Nenshi*, 251.
108 Huddle and Reich, *Island of Dreams*, 99.
109 Tonouchi, *Kōsha Setsuritsu 40 Shūnen Kinen Zadankai*, 159.
110 Ibid., 158.
111 Ibid., 161.
112 Ibid., 162; 'Leftist's Victory Is a Setback for Tanaka', *The New York Times*, 23 April 1973. https://www.nytimes.com/1973/04/23/archives/leftistss-victory-in-japan-is-a-setback-for-tanaka.html. Proquest.
113 Huddle and Reich, *Island of Dreams*, 286.
114 The Japanese term '*kakushin*' often translated as 'progressive', means literally 'reform' or 'innovation' relating to social and other organizations. Originally supported by socialist or communist groups and espousing anti-conservative, leftist or radical policies, in the post-war period 'new progressive' politicians were specifically concerned with the problems of economic growth and urbanization. Alan G. Rix, 'Tokyo's Governor Minobe and Progressive Local Politics in Japan', *Asian Survey* 15, no. 6 (July 1975): 530.
115 Ibid., 531.
116 *Chūnichi Shimbun*, 19 May 1973.
117 Ibid., 31 May 1973.
118 Miyazaki, 'Case Study Nagoya', 133.
119 Kamata Satoshi, *Japan in the Passing Lane: An Insider's Account of Life in a Japanese Auto Factory* (London: Allen and Unwin, 1984), 46–47.
120 *Chūnichi Shimbun*, 11 June 1973; *Asahi Shimbun* 11 June 1973.
121 Hayakawa, *Seikatsu, Jūtaku, Kankyō*, 193.
122 *Chūnichi Shimbun*, 25 June 1973.
123 *Nagoya Kōsokudōro Kōsha 40 Nenshi*, 455.
124 *Chūnichi Shimbun*, 29 June 1973.
125 Ibid., 20 September 1973.
126 Ibid., 11 October 1973.
127 *Nagoya Kōsokudōro Kōsha 40 Nenshi*, 240.
128 Ibid., 249.
129 'Nagoya Minami-bu Taisa Osen Kogai Saiban', nihon-taikiosen.erca.go.jp/taiki/nagoya/ 06/08/2015.
130 Examples might include David Starkie, *Motorway Age: Road Traffic Policies in Post-War Britain* (London: Pergamon Press, 1982); Wall, *Earth First! And the Anti-Roads Movement*; Dennis and Urry, *After the Car*.
131 These concerns extended back further than the Buchanan and Wilson reports of the early 1960s, of course; they dogged the history of motoring throughout the twentieth century – see for instance Michael John Law, 'Speed and Blood on the Bypass: The New Automobilities of Inter-War London', *Urban History* 39, no. 3 (August 2012): 490–509.
132 British Road Federation, *Road Needs in the Midlands* (London: BRF, 1970).
133 For a national account, see Andy Beckett, *When the Lights Went Out* (London: Faber, 2009).
134 Adams and Larkham, 'Bold planning', 137.

135 Cherry, *Birmingham*, 161–162.
136 'Birmingham Inner City Construction Plan Agreed', *The Times*, 13 August 1977.
137 See Thomas Sugrue, *The Origins of the Urban Crisis: Race and Inequality in Postwar Detroit* (Princeton, NJ: Princeton University Press, 2005).

Chapter 6

1 Kashiwagi Akiko, 'A Post-Car Society', *Newsweek*, 2 February 2008, http://www.newsweek.com/post-car-society-94133. The *Newsweek* report presented figures suggesting that 'new car sales' fell from 7.8 million in 1990 to 5.4 million in 2007. However, these figures referred to total new vehicle registrations, including trucks and buses. In fact new car sales fell only 6.6 per cent between 1990 and 2007 to 4.8 million, while truck sales fell 64.6 per cent and sales of new buses declined by 37.3 per cent during the same period. JAMA, 'Motor Vehicle Statistics'.
2 JAMA, *Jōyōsha shijō dōkō chōsa 2008: Kuruma shijō ni okeru entorii sedai no kuruma ishiki* (Tokyo: JAMA, 2009).
3 Terry Grimley, 'Birmingham's Long Road to Renewal', *Birmingham Post*, 31 March 2008. Grimley had been the newspaper's arts editor since 1973 and was a participant in the Highbury symposium of 1988.
4 Kieran Connell, 'A Micro-history of "Black Handsworth": Towards a Social History of Race in Britain' (University of Birmingham, PhD thesis, 2012).
5 Llewelyn Davis, Weeks, Forestier-Walker and Bor, *Unequal City: Final Report of the Birmingham Inner Area Study* (London: HMSO, 1978).
6 Austin Barber and Stephen Hall, 'Birmingham: Whose Urban Renaissance? Regeneration as a Response to Economic Restructuring', *Policy Studies* 29, no. 3 (2008): 283–284; M. Carley, I. Christie, M. Fogarty and R. Legard, *Profitable Partnerships: A Report on Business Investment in the Community* (London: Policy Studies Institute, 1991).
7 For Detroit, see Thomas Sugrue, *The Origins of the Urban Crisis: Race and Inequality in Postwar Detroit* (Princeton: Princeton University Press, 2014). For the comparison with Birmingham, see Alan Digaetano and John S. Klemanski, 'Urban Regime Capacity: A Comparison between Birmingham, England and Detroit, Michigan', *Journal of Urban Affairs* 15, no. 4 (1993): 367–384.
8 Cited in Grimley, *Birmingham Post*.
9 P. Jones, 'The City as Artwork: The Dismemberment of Modern Birmingham', The City in Art conference, September 2004, Krakow, Jagellonian University.
10 Roy Licklider, *Political Power and the Arab Oil Weapon* (Berkeley: University of California Press, 1988) provides a study of the international relations dimension of the 1973/4 oil crisis. For a stimulating analysis of the politics of oil more widely, see Timothy Mitchell, *Carbon Democracy* (London: Verso, 2011).
11 The narrative is recounted in Dominic Sandbrook, *State of Emergency* (London: Allen Lane, 2010).
12 Miyoshi Shūichi, 'Oil Shock', *Japan Quarterly* 21, no. 2 (1 April 1974): 144–147.
13 Shibata Hirofumi, 'The Energy Crises and Japanese Response', *Resources and Energy* 5, no. 2 (June 1983): 144. https://doi.org/10.1016/0165-0572(83)90010-5
14 Ibid., 136.
15 JAMA, 'Motor Vehicle Statistics'.

16 Daitō Eisuke, 'Automation and Organization of Production in the Japanese Automobile Industry: Nissan and Toyota in the 1950s', *Enterprise & Society: The International Journal of Business History* 1, no. 1 (2000): 139.
17 Kameyama Yasuko, *Climate Change Policy in Japan from the 1980s to 2015* (London and New York: Routledge, 2016), 26.
18 Department for Transport, *Transport Statistics Great Britain: 2011* (London: HMSO, 2012); Automobile Association, *Living with the Car* (Basingstoke: Automobile Association, 1977).
19 Peter Hall, *Great Planning Disasters* (London: Weidenfeld and Nicholson, 1980); John Davis, 'Simple Solutions to Complex Problems: The GLC and the GLDP 1965-1973', in *Civil Society and British History*, ed. José Harris (Oxford: Oxford University Press, 2003); Michael Dnes, 'Ringways: Planning the Rise and Fall of London's Primary Network', University of Cambridge, MA dissertation, 2004.
20 Miyoshi Shūichi, 'Mutual Dependence in the Castle Built on Oil', *Japan Quarterly* 26, no. 4 (1 October 1979): 466.
21 Ibid., 463.
22 These figures do not include light cars (*keijidōsha*) cars. Statistics Bureau, Ministry of Internal Affairs and Communications, Japan, 'Motor Vehicles Owned by Kind, 1936-2004', *Historical Statistics of Japan*, last modified, 20 April 2012, http://www.stat.go.jp/english/data/chouki/.
23 Ministry of Transport, *Cars for Cities* (London: HMSO, 1967).
24 Ministry of Transport, *Roads in England* (London: HMSO, 1970).
25 Peter Hall and Carmen Hass-Klau, *Can Rail Save the City?* (Aldershot: Gower, 1985), 3.
26 *Times*, 26 September 1974.
27 David Parish, *The 1973-1975 Energy Crisis and Its Impact on Transport* (London: RAC Foundation, 2009), 6, 7.
28 City of Birmingham, *Structure Plan*, 39.
29 Ibid., 66.
30 For a discussion of this, see Parker, 'Making the City Mobile', 135.
31 City of Birmingham, *Structure Plan*, 55. The reference in the 1960 *Development Plan* was to New Street station.
32 *Hansard*, Greater London Plan, HC Deb 19 February 1973, vol. 851, c. 31.
33 Mary Cooper/SOCEM, *Motorways and Transport Planning in Newcastle upon Tyne* (Manchester: Moss Side Press, 1974).
34 'The City Centre's Hollow Ring', *Guardian*, 10 May 1973, 16ff.
35 Cooper, *Motorways*, 7; Stephen Plowden, *Towns against Traffic* (London: Deutsch, 1972); Bugler, 'The Ringway to Ruin'; Peter Headicar, *Transport Policy and Planning in Great Britain* (London: Routledge, 2009), 90-92.
36 Cited in Standing Advisory Committee on Trunk Road Assessment, *Trunk Roads and the Generation of Traffic*, 31.
37 Ibid., ii.
38 Roderick A. Smith, 'The Japanese Shinkansen: Catalyst for the Renaissance of Rail', *Journal of Transport History* 24, no. 2 (2003): 226.
39 Ibid., 230-231.
40 *Historical Statistics of Japan*, 'Passengers Carried within 3 Largest Cities Traffic Range by Type of Transportation (F.Y. 1965-2003)'.
41 Miyazaki, 'Case Study Nagoya', 134.
42 *Nagoya-shi Hyakunen no Nenrin*, 106-107.

43 Miyazaki, 'Case Study Nagoya', 134.
44 Ibid., 136.
45 Ibid. Although at the time there was little research into the connection between traffic congestion and pollution, from the 1980s scientific research has verified the link. For an overview of the research, see Kai Zhang and Stuart Batterman, 'Air Pollution and Health Risks Due to Vehicle Traffic', *Science of the Total Environment* 450–451 (15 April 2003): 307–316, https://doi.org/10.1016/j.scitotenv.2013.01.074.
46 Miyazaki, 'Case Study Nagoya', 134.
47 Ibid., 143.
48 Mary P. McShane, Koshi Masaki and Oluf Lundin, 'Public Policy toward the Automobile: A Comparative Look at Japan and Sweden', Transportation Reports – A 18A, no. 2 (1984): 109; Masaki, et al., 'Japanese National Policy toward the Automobile', 4.
49 McShane et al., 'Public Policy toward the Automobile', 100–101.
50 Masaki et al., 'Japanese National Policy toward the Automobile', 1–32.
51 Ibid., 3.
52 Miyazaki, 'Case Study Nagoya', 144.
53 Ibid., 140.
54 Koshi et al., 'Japanese National Policy towards the Automobile', 6.
55 J. Michael Thomson, *Great Cities and Their Traffic* (London: Penguin, 1978 [1977]), 53–55.
56 Cooper, *Motorways*, 14.
57 McShane et al., 'Public Policy', 101, 77–109.
58 Kameyama, *Climate Change Policy*, 41.
59 Hamer, *Wheels within Wheels*, 1.
60 Bruce Douglas-Mann, HC Deb 5 November 1974, *Hansard*, vol. 880, c. 972; Alan Fitch, HC Deb, 31 July 1974, vol. 878, c. 866.
61 Aufheben, 'The Politics of Anti-Road Struggle and the Struggles of Anti-Road Politics: The Case of the No M11 Link Road Campaign', in *DiY Culture: Party and Protest in Nineties Britain*, ed. George McKay (London: Verso, 1998), 100–128.
62 Joe Moran, *On Roads* (London: Profile, 2009), 217.
63 John Jordan, 'The Art of Necessity: The Subversive Imagination of Anti-Road Protest and Reclaim the Streets', in McKay, *DiY Culture*, 129–151.
64 Joe Moran describes the protests and their protagonists well in *On Roads*, ch. 7.
65 Spencer R. Weart, *The Discovery of Global Warming* (Cambridge, MA: Harvard University Press, 2008), 146–151.
66 Committee on Climate Change, *Factsheet: Transport* (London: HMSO, 2015); Office for National Statistics, https://www.gov.uk/government/uploads/system/uploads/attachment_data/file/589602/2015_Final_Emissions_Statistics_one_page_summary.pdf.
67 Bureau, 'Settled Accounts of Road Investment (F.Y. 1956–2003)'.
68 Harashina Sachiko, 'Environmental Dispute Resolution in Road Construction Projects in Japan', *Environmental Impact Assessment Review* 8, no. 1 (March 1988): 31, 37, https://doi.org/10.1016/0195-9255(88)90058-3.
69 Kameyama, *Climate Change Policy*, 41.
70 Ibid., 26–27.
71 Ministry of Transport, *Roads for the Future: The New Inter-Urban Plan for England* (London: HMSO, 1970).
72 Department of Transport, *Policy for Roads in England: 1983* (London: HMSO, 1983).
73 *Birmingham Mercury*, 11 February 1973.

74 Maureen Alcott and Brian Pearce, *A Ring of Change* (Birmingham: published by authors, 2001), v.
75 Moran, *On Roads*, 211; Department of Transport, *Roads for Prosperity* (London: HMSO, 1989).
76 *Independent*, 19 May, 1989.
77 'The Wrong Road', *Economist*, 2 December 1995.
78 Wall, *Earth First! And the Anti-Roads Movement*, ch. 4.
79 Department for Transport, *Licensed Vehicles by Tax Class, Great Britain*, Table VEH0103 (London: HMSO, 2016).
80 Department for Transport, *Full Licence Holders by Age and Gender: England*, Table NTS0201 (London: HMSO, 2017).
81 Department for Transport, *Household Car Availability: England*, Table NTS0205 (London: HMSO, 2017).
82 McShane et al., 'Public Policy', 101.
83 JAMA, *Jōyōsha shijō dōkō chōsa*, 5.
84 Ibid., 8.
85 Ibid., 6–8.
86 Office for National Statistics, *Social Trends 41. Transport* (London: HMSO, 2011); S. Le Vine and P. Jones, *On the Move. Making Sense of Car and Travel Trends in Britain* (London: RAC Foundation, 2012).
87 Judith Green et al., 'Automobility Reconfigured? Ironic Seductions and Mundane Freedoms in 16–21 year Olds' Accounts of Car Driving and Ownership', *Mobilities* 13, no. 1 (2008): 14–28.
88 Terry Gourvish, *Britain's Railway, 1997–2005* (Oxford: Oxford University Press, 2008).
89 Office for National Statistics, *Social Trends 41*, 1.
90 Adam Stocker and Susan Shaheen, *Shared Automated Vehicles: Review of Business Models* (Berkeley: University of California Press, 2016).
91 For an overview of mobility trends in Britain in the recent past, see Simon Gunn, 'Review of the History of Transport Systems in the UK', *Future of Mobility* (London: Government Office for Science and Foresight, 2018).
92 Sorensen, *The Making of Urban Japan*, 273–274.
93 Nagoya's increase in population of around 6 per cent between 1970 and 1995 is in contrast to Tokyo's decline by nearly 10 per cent and Osaka's of over 12 per cent following trends in the United States (New York's population declined by 7 per cent, Chicago by 17 per cent and one of Nagoya's twin cities, the motor city *sine qua non* Detroit declined by a massive 33.5 per cent in the same period). Jacobs, 'Planning for Vibrant Central City', 32.
94 Jacobs, 'Planning for Vibrant Central City'.
95 Two more routes of the Nagoya Urban Expressway, No. 3 and No. 1, were opened in 1985 and 1986, respectively.
96 In the suburbs, however, there was a loss of green space with the total ratio decreasing from 29.8 per cent in 1990 to 24.8 per cent in 2005. Murayama Akito, 'Urban Design Solutions to Environmental Issues', *Sustainable Urban Regeneration*, 23 (November 2012), 54.
97 *Nagoya: My Town*, (Public Relations Department of the Mayor City of Nagoya, March 2008), 27.
98 'Message from Japan: "Nature's Wisdom"', Expo 2005 Aichi Japan, accessed 25 July 2018. http://www.expo2005.or.jp/en/whatexpo/message_00.html.

99 See, for example, Jeff L. Brown, *Civil Engineering* (May 2005), 1, accessed 25 July 2018. http://web.b.ebscohost.com.ezproxy.nottingham.ac.uk/ehost/pdfviewer/pdfviewer?vid=1&sid=ced68b79-f839-4850-be67-c77e7587863b%40sessionmgr102. For a critique of the 'Showa nostalgia' of World Expo 2005 and similar mega events hosted by Japan, see David Murakami Wood and Kiyoshi Abe, 'The Aesthetic of Control: Mega Events and Transformations in Japanese Urban Order', *Urban Studies* 48, no. 15 (2011): 3241–3257.

Conclusion

1 Dennis and Urry, *After the Car*, ch. 2.
2 David Edgerton emphasizes the persistence of older forms of technology across the twentieth century over and alongside the new – *The Shock of the Old: Technology and Global History Since 1900* (London: Profile, 2008).
3 Kashiwagi, 'A Post-Car Society'.
4 Ross, *Fast Cars, Clean Bodies*, 19.
5 Lewis H. Siegelbaum, ed. *The Socialist Car: Automobility in the Eastern Bloc* (Ithaca, NY: Cornell University Press, 2011); Simon Jackson, '(Auto)mobility in the Global Middle East, Part 1' (2016), http://www.jadaliyya.com/Details/32961/Auto-Mobility-in-the-Global-Middle-East-Part-1 [accessed 12 March 2018]; Graeme Davison and Sheryl Yelland, *Car Wars: How the Car Won Our Hearts and Conquered Our Cities* (Crows Nest, New South Wales: Allen and Unwin, 2004).
6 See, for example, Bernhard Rieger, 'The Automobile', in *Cambridge World History*, vol. 7, part 2, ed. J. R. McNeil and K. Pomeranz (Cambridge: Cambridge University Press, 2017), 467–489; Marcos Chamon, Paolo Maoro and Yohei Okawa, 'Cars: The Implications of Mass Car Ownership in the Emerging Market Giants', *Economic Policy* 23 no. 54 (2008): 243–296, and the recent call for papers on a special issue of the *Journal of World History* on global automobilities.
7 Huddle and Reich, *Island of Dreams*; Christine L. Corton, *London Fog* (Cambridge, MA: Harvard University Press, 2015).
8 Report of the Steering Group, *Traffic in Towns* (London: HMSO, 1963), 32.
9 For Britain, see Simon Gunn and James Vernon, eds. *The Peculiarities of Liberal Modernity in Imperial Britain* (Berkeley, CA: University of California Press, 2011). For Japan, see Dale, *The Myth of Japanese Uniqueness*; Griseldis Kirsch, Dolores P. Martinez and Merry White, eds. *Assembling Japan: Modernity, Technology and Global Culture* (Bern: Peter Lang GmbH, Internationaler Verlag der Wissenschaften, 2015).
10 Simon Gunn, 'Between Conservation and Modernism: Konrad Smigielski and the Planning of Post-War Leicester', in *Leicester: A Modern History*, ed. R. Rodger and R. Madgin (Lancaster: Carnegie Press, 2016), 267–291; Pendlebury, 'Alas Smith and Burns?', 115–141.
11 For Britain see the Government Office for Science, *Foresight Future of Mobility* launched in 2017 https://www.gov.uk/government/collections/future-of-mobility accessed 21 July 2018.

Bibliography

Archives and Collections – Japan

Japanese Automobile Manufacturers Association Library, Tokyo
Ministry of Land, Information, Transport and Tourism (MLIT) Library
Nagoya City Archive
Nagoya Urban Institute
National Diet Library, Tokyo
NHK Archives, Saitama
Toyota Museum of Science and Technology Library, Nagoya

Archives and Collections – Britain

Automobile Association, Winchester
British Library, London
City of Birmingham Archives
City of Birmingham Local Studies Collection
Heritage Motor Centre Archive, Gaydon
Institution of Civil Engineers, London
Media Archive for Central England (MACE), University of Lincoln
National Archives, London
Royal Automobile Club, Churchill College, Cambridge
University of Birmingham Special Collections

Newspapers and Journals – Japan

Asahi Shimbun (Tokyo and Nagoya Versions)
Autocar
Chūnichi Shimbun
Japan Times
Japan Quarterly
Mainichi Shimbun
The Motor
New York Times
Newsweek
Observer-Reporter Traffic Quarterly

Newspapers and Journals – Britain

Architect and Building News
Autocar
Birmingham Evening Despatch Birmingham Gazette
Birmingham Mail
Birmingham Mercury
Birmingham Post
Birmingham Sketch
Daily Express
Drive
Economist
Engineering
Financial Times
Guardian
Hansard
Institute of Municipal Engineers' Journal
Journal of the Town Planning Institute
Motoring
Municipal Engineering
Municipal Review
New Scientist
Observer
Private Eye
Spectator
Sunday Mercury
Sunday Times
Surveyor and Municipal and County Engineer
Traffic Engineering and Control
The Times

Published Primary Sources – Japan

Aichi-ken Doboku-bu. *Nagoya Toshi Kōsokudōro Keikaku*. Nagoya: Aichi-ken Doboku-bu, 1969.

Aichi-ken Kikaku-bu Kōtsū Taisaku-shitsu, ed. *Kuruma Shakai: Sono Genjo, Sui'i, Hikaku*. Nagoya: Aichi-ken Kikaku-bu Kōtsū Taisaku-shitsu, 1975.

Beard, Rodney R., Robert J. M. Horton and Roy O. McCaldin. 'Observations on Tokyo-Yokohama Asthma and Air Pollution in Japan'. *Public Health Reports* (1896–1970) 79, no. 5 (May 1964): 439–444.

Dore, Ronald. *Shinohata. A Portrait of a Japanese Village*. London: Allen Lane, 1978.

Japan Automobile Manufacturers Association. *Jōyōsha shijō dōkō chōsa 2008: Kuruma shijō ni okeru entorii sedai no kuruma ishiki*. Tokyo: JAMA, 2009.

Kamata Satoshi. *Japan in the Passing Lane: An Insider's Account of Life in a Japanese Auto Factory*. London: Unwin, 1984.

Miyazaki Tadashi. 'Case Study Nagoya (Japan)'. In *Proceedings of the Better Towns with Less Traffic Conference 14–16 April 1975*, 133–145. Paris: OECD, 1975.

Miyoshi Nobuyoshi and Oka Tadao, eds. *Furusato no Omoide – Shashinshu, Meiji/Taisho/ Showa Nagoya.* Tokyo: Kokusho Kanko-kai, 1979.
Moto Nagoya Taimuzu, ed. *Nagoya Jōnetsu Jidai.* Nagoya: Ju'rin-sha, 2009.
Motor Manufacturing Economic Development Council. *Japan: Its Motor Industry and Market.* London: HMSO, 1971.
Nagoya Kōsokudōro Kōsha 40 Nenshi Henshū I'inkai, ed. *Nagoya Kōsokudōro Kōsha 40 Nenshi.* Nagoya: Nagoya Expressway Corporation, 2012.
Nagoya My Town. Nagoya: Public Relations Department of the Mayor. March 2008.
Nagoya-shi Hyakunen no Nenrin: chōki tōkei deeta shū. Nagoya: Nagoya-shi, 1989.
Nagoya-shi Keikaku Kyoku, ed. *Nagoya toshi keikaku shi: Taishō 8 – Shōwa 44.* Nagoya: Zaidan Hōjin, Nagoya Toshi Sentā, 1999.
Nagoya-shi Kensetsu Kyoku, ed. *Nagoya Toshi Keikaku-shi.* Nagoya: Nagoya-shi Kensetsu Kyoku, 1957.
Nikkan Jidōsha Shimbunsha, ed. *Tokyo Mōtā Shō no 50 Nen.* Tokyo: Nihon Jidōsha Kogyokai, 2005.
Odell, Lawrence H. 'Hostilities Inspire and Hinder Port Development in Japan'. *Far Eastern Survey* 8, no. 25 (1939): 300–301.
Richards, J. M. *An Architectural Journey in Japan.* London: The Architectural Press, 1963.
Rix, Alan G. 'Tokyo's Governor Minobe and Progressive Local Politics in Japan'. *Asian Survey* 15, no. 6 (July 1975): 530–542.
Tange Kenzo. 'A Plan for Tokyo'. In *Kenzo Tange: Archtecture and Urban Design 1946– 1969,* edited by Udo Kultermann. London: Pall Mall Press, 1970.
Tabuchi Jurō. *Aru Dobokugishi no Hanjijoden.* Nagoya: Chūbu Keizai Rengōkai, 1962.
Tabuchi Jurō. 'Eidan ga Unda Shin Nagoya – Hōka toshi no senbō no moto to natta Nagoya no toshi keikaku no seikō wa shiseisha no daieidan ni atta'. *Bungei Shunjū* 39, no. 4 (April 1961): 142–148.
Toyota Jidōsha Kabushiki Kaisha. '*Wakamono no Kuruma Banare*', *ni tsuite.* 26 July 2010.
World Car Catalogue 1970. New York: Herald Books, 1970.
Yoshida Shigeru. *The Yoshida Memoirs: The Story of Japan in Crisis.* Translated by Yoshida Ken'ichi. London: Heinemann, 1961.

Electronic Primary Sources – Japan

Beyond the Tokyo Motor Show History and Records, accessed 4 March 2017, https://www.tokyo-motorshow.com/en/history/.
Japan Automobile Manufacturers Association. 'Motor Vehicle Statistics of Japan'. http://www.jama-english.jp.
Statistics Bureau, Ministry of Internal Affairs and Communications, Japan. *Historical Statistics of Japan.* Last modified April 2012. http://www.stat.go.jp/english/data/chouki/.
Tokyo Nagaremono (1966), [Film] Dir. Suzuki Seijun, Japan, accessed 8 May 2018, https://archive.org/details/TokyoDrifter.
United States Strategic Bombing Survey. 'The Effects of the Air Attack on Nagoya' (June, 1947). https://babel.hathitrust.org/cgi/pt?id=mdp.39015002274325;view=1up;seq=3.
World Bank. *Japan – Report on the Proposed Expressway Project* (Technical operations projects series; no. TO 172) Washington, DC (24 April 1958). http://documents.worldbank.org/curated/en/1958/04/1554606/japan-report-proposed-expressway-project.

Published Primary Sources – Britain

Abercrombie, Patrick and Herbert Jackson. *West Midlands Plan*. London: Ministry of Town and Country Planning, 1948.

Automobile Association. *The Motorist Today*. London: Automobile Association, 1965.

Automobile Association. *Living with the Car*. Basingstoke: Automobile Association, 1977.

Banham, Reyner. *Los Angeles: The Architecture of Four Ecologies*. London: Allen Lane, 1971.

Birmingham Corporation Public Health Committee. *Report by the Medical Officer of Health on the Housing Survey 1946*. Birmingham, 1947.

Borg, N. 'City Planning and Engineering: Energy, Communications and the Environment'. *Proceedings of the Institution of Mechanical Engineers*, 185 (1970).

Borg, N. 'The Public Works Department, City of Birmingham'. *Institute of Civil Engineers Proceedings*, 40, no. 1 (1968).

Bournville Village Trust. *When We Build Again*. Birmingham: Bournville Trust, 1941.

British Road Federation. *Basic Road Statistics*. London: British Road Federation, 1975.

British Road Federation. *People and Cities: Report of the 1963 London Conference*. London: British Road Federation, 1964.

British Road Federation. *Road Needs in the Midlands*. London: BRF, 1970.

British Railways Board. *The Reshaping of British Railways – Part 1: Report*. London, 1963.

Buchanan, Colin. *The Conurbations*. London: British Road Federation, 1969.

Buchanan, Colin. *Traffic in Towns: A Study of the Long-Term Problems of Traffic in Urban Areas*. London: HMSO, 1963.

Carson, Rachel. *Silent Spring*. Boston, MA: Houghton Mifflin, 1962.

Central Unit on Environmental Pollution. *The Protection of the Environment: The Fight against Pollution*. London: HMSO, 1969.

City of Birmingham Central Statistical Office. *City of Birmingham Abstract of Statistics*. Birmingham, 1952–1975.

City of Birmingham Public Works Committee. *Inner Ring Road Scheme*. Birmingham, 1957.

City of Birmingham. *Development Plan: Report on the Survey*. Birmingham, 1952.

City of Birmingham. *Development Plan: Statement*. Birmingham, 1960.

City of Birmingham. *Structure Plan: Written Statement*. Birmingham, 1973.

Committee of Privy Council for Medical Research. *Report of the Medical Research Council for the Year 1960–1961*. London, 1962.

Committee on Air Pollution. *Interim Report*. London, 1953.

Committee on the Problem of Noise. *Noise: Final Report*. London: HMSO, 1963.

Cooper, Mary/SOCEM. *Motorways and Transport Planning in Newcastle upon Tyne*. Manchester: Moss Side Press, 1974.

Corbusier, Charles-Édouard, Le. *The City of Tomorrow and Its Planning*. New York: Dover Press, 1987.

Davis, S. C. H. *Car Driving as an Art*. Coventry: Iliffe and Sons, 1952.

De Leuw, Chadwick and O hEocha. *Birmingham Rapid Transit Study: Commissioned by the City of Birmingham and the Department of the Environment*. London, 1971.

Department of Economic Affairs. *The West Midlands: A Regional Study*. London, 1965.

Department of Employment. *Family Expenditure Survey*. London: Office of Population Censuses and Surveys, 1963.

Department of the Environment Central Unit on Environmental Pollution. *Lead Pollution: A Report of the Joint Working Party on Lead Pollution around Gravelly Hill – Pollution Paper No. 14*. London, 1978.
Department of the Environment. *Development and Compensation – Putting People First*. London, 1972.
Department of the Environment. *Inner Area Study: Birmingham – Small Heath Birmingham: A Social Survey*. London, 1975.
Department of the Environment. *Pollution: Nuisance or Nemesis?* London, 1972.
Department of the Environment. *Transport Statistics Great Britain 1964–1974*. London, 1974.
Department of Transport. *Policy for Roads in England: 1983*. London: HMSO, 1983.
Department of Transport. *Roads for Prosperity*. London: HMSO, 1989.
Fitton, A. 'Vehicle Exhaust Fumes'. In *Air Pollution: Based on Papers Given at a Conference Held at the University of Sheffield, 1956*, edited by Meredith Thring. London, 1957.
Freeman, Fox, Wilbur Smith and Associates. *West Midlands Transport Study*. Birmingham, 1968.
Friends of the Earth. *Getting Nowhere Fast: A Response to the Consultation Document on Transport Policy*. London, 1976.
General Register Office. *Census 1951: England and Wales*. London, 1951.
General Register Office. *Census 1961: England and Wales*. London: HMSO, 1961.
General Register Office. *Sample Census 1966: England and Wales*. London: HMSO, 1966.
Goldthorpe, John et al. *The Affluent Worker in the Class Structure*. Cambridge: Cambridge University Press, 1969.
Goodey, B., A. Duffett, J. Gold and D. Spencer. *City-Scene: An Exploration into the Image of Central Birmingham as Seen by Area Residents*. Birmingham, 1971.
Grant, B. E. and W. J. Russell. *Opportunities in Automated Urban Transport*. London, 1973.
Halliday, E. J. 'A Historical Review of Atmospheric Pollution'. In *Air Pollution*, edited by World Health Organization. Geneva, 1961.
Hobbs, F. D., M. B. A Walker and I. Johnson. *A Survey of Travel Characteristics in Birmingham*. Birmingham, 1974.
Jacobs, Jane. *The Death and Life of Great American Cities: The Failure of Town Planning*. New York: Random House, 1961.
Jones, I. D. *Road Traffic Noise*. Oxford: Pergamon Press, 1976.
Llewelyn-Davies, Weeks, Forestier-Walker & Bor. *Unequal City: Final Report of the Birmingham Inner Area Study*. London: HMSO, 1977.
Macmorran, J. L. *Municipal Public Works and Planning in Birmingham: A Record of the Administration and Achievements of the Public Works Committee and Department of the Borough and City of Birmingham 1852–1972*. Birmingham, 1973.
Manzoni, H. J. 'The Inner Ring Road, Birmingham'. *Institution of Civil Engineers Proceedings* 18, no. 3 (1961).
Manzoni, H. J. 'Redevelopment of Blighted Areas in Birmingham', *Journal of the Town Planning Institute*, (1955).
Manzoni, H. J. 'Urban Traffic Control'. In *Roads and Their Traffic*, edited by E. Davies. London, 1960.
Manzoni, H. J. *The Production of Fifty Thousand Municipal Houses*. Birmingham, 1939.
Marriott, Oliver. *The Property Boom*. London: Hamish Hamilton, 1967.
Ministry of Town and Country Planning. *The Redevelopment of Central Areas*. London: HMSO, 1947.

Ministry of Transport. *Road Accidents*. London: HMSO, 1961.
Ministry of Transport. *Cars for Cities: A Study of Trends in the Design of Vehicles with Particular Reference to Their Use in Towns*. London: HMSO, 1967.
Ministry of Transport. *Design and Layout of Roads in Built-Up Areas: Report of the Departmental Committee set up by the Minister of War Transport*. London: HMSO, 1946.
Ministry of Transport. *Roads in England*. London: HMSO, 1970.
Ministry of Transport. *Roads for the Future: The New Inter-Urban Plan for England*. London: HMSO 1970.
Nader, R. *Unsafe at Any Speed: The Designed-In Dangers of the American Automobile* New York: Grossman, 1965.
Norris, J. *Human Aspects of Redevelopment*. Birmingham, 1960.
Office of Population Censuses and Surveys. *Census 1971: England and Wales*. London: HMSO, 1971.
Office of Population Censuses and Surveys, *Census 1981: England and Wales*. London: HMSO, 1981.
Plowden, Stephen. *Towns against Traffic*. London: Deutsch, 1972.
Power, N. *The Forgotten People: A Challenge to a Caring Community*. Evesham, 1965.
Price, F. *Being There*. Leicestershire, 2002.
Rex, J. and R. Moore. *Race, Community and Conflict: A Study of Sparkbrook*. London: Oxford University Press, 1967.
Reynolds, F. 'pollution of Air'. *The Journal of the Royal Society for the Promotion of Health* 92 (1972).
Royal Commission on Environmental Pollution. *First Report*. London, 1971.
Royal Commission on Environmental Pollution. *Fourth Report – Pollution Control: Progress and Problems*. London, 1975.
Royal Commission on Environmental Pollution. *Fifth Report – Air Pollution: An Integrated Approach*. London, 1976.
Sheppard-Fidler, A. G., 'Post-War Housing in Birmingham'. *Town Planning Review* 26, no. 1 (1955).
Smith, R. 'Housing in Birmingham Immediately after the End of the Second World War'. In *History of Birmingham Project – Research Paper No. 4 (The Housing Environment – No. 1), University of Birmingham School of History*. Birmingham, no date given, likely approx. 1966/7.
Sutcliffe, A. R. 'The Production of Municipal Houses in Birmingham 1939–1966'. In *History of Birmingham Project – Research Paper No. 5, University of Birmingham School of History*. Birmingham, no date given – likely to be around 1966/7.
Thomson, J. M. *Great Cities and Their Traffic*. London: Penguin, 1978.
Townsend, Peter. *Poverty in the United Kingdom: A Survey of Household Resources and Standards of Living*. Harmondsworth: Allen Lane, 1979.
Tripp, Alker. *Town Planning and Road Traffic*. London: Edward Arnold, 1942.
Turner, Graham. *The Car Makers*. Harmondsworth: Penguin, 1964.
University of Birmingham. *People and the Motor Car*. Birmingham: University of Birmingham, 1964.
West Midlands Economic Planning Council. *The West Midlands: An Economic Appraisal*. London, 1971.
West Midlands Economic Planning Council. *The West Midlands: Patterns of Growth*. London, 1967.

West Midlands Group on Post-War Reconstruction and Planning. *Conurbation: A Planning Survey of Birmingham and the Black Country*. London, 1948.

West Midlands Transport Study Technical Committee. *West Midlands Transport Study*. Birmingham: Freeman, Fox and Miller Smith and Associates, 1968.

Zweig, Ferdynand. *The Worker in an Affluent Society*. London: Heinemann, 1961.

Electronic Primary Sources – Britain

ATV, 'Spaghetti Junction', *ATV* 45 (n.d. 1972), Media Archive for Central England.

ATV, 'Driving into Birmingham', *ATV Today*, 27 April 1966, Media Archive for Central England.

'Big Plan for Birmingham', BBC Light Programme, Radio Newsreel, Broadcast 7pm, 25 May 1965.

Birmingham City Council Public Works Committee, *Ringway* (film, 1963).

Jackson, Simon '(Auto)mobility in the Global Middle East, Part 1' (2016). http://www.jadaliyya.com/Details/32961/Auto-Mobility-in-the-Global-Middle-East-Part-1 [accessed 12 March 2018].

Media Archive for Central England, *The Bull Ring Shopping Centre Birmingham* [film] (Laing Development Company Limited, 1965).

Media Archive of Central England, *Regenerating Birmingham 1955–1975*, DVD (University of Lincoln: Lincoln, no date).

Norton, D. J. 'Inside the Inner Ring Road'. http://www.photobydjnorton.com/InsideTheInnerRingRoad.html.

Office for National Statistics. 2015 UK Greenhouse Gas Emissions. https://www.gov.uk/government/uploads/system/uploads/attachment_data/file/589602/2015_Final_Emissions_Statistics_one_page_summary.pdf.

Secondary Sources

Adams, David. 'Bold Planning, Mixed Experiences: The Diverse Fortunes of Post-War Birmingham'. In *The Blitz and Its Legacy: Wartime Destruction to Post-War Reconstruction*, edited by Mark Clapson and Peter Larkham. Farnham: Ashgate, 2013.

Adams, David. 'Everyday Experiences of the Modern City: Remembering the Post-War Reconstruction of Birmingham'. *Planning Perspectives* 26, no. 2 (2011): 237–260.

Adams, David. 'Stories from the "Big Heart of England": Architects' Narratives of the Post-War Reconstruction of Birmingham'. *Centre for Environment and Society Research Working Paper* 9 (2012).

Adams, David. 'Walking in the Modern City: Pedestrian Experiences of Post-War Birmingham'. *Birmingham City University Centre for Environment and Society Research Working Paper Series* 22 (2013).

Alcott, Maureen and Brian Pearce. *A Ring of Change*. Birmingham: Published by authors, 2001.

Alexander, Jeffrey W. *Japan's Motorcycle War: An Industry History*. Vancouver: University of British Columbia, 2008.

Allinson, Gary D. *Suburban Tokyo: A Comparative Study in Politics and Social Change*. Berkeley, LA: University of California Press, 1979.

Amin, Ash and Nigel Thrift. *Cities: Reimagining the Urban*. Cambridge: Polity, 2002.
Appleyard, Donald with Sue Gerson and Mark Lintell. *Livable Streets*. Berkeley, LA and London: University of California Press, 1981.
Ashihara Yoshinobu. 'Chaos and Order in the Japanese City'. *Japan Echo*, no. 14 (1987): 64–68.
Asquith, Pamela J. and Arne Kalland. *Japanese Images of Nature: Cultural Perspectives*. Richmond: Curzon, 1997.
Aufheben. 'The Politics of Anti-Road Struggle and the Struggles of Anti-Road Politics: The Case of the No M11 Link Road Campaign'. In *DiY Culture: Party and Protest in Nineties Britain*, edited by George McKay, 100–128. London: Verso, 1998.
Avenell, Simon A. *Making Japanese Citizens: Civil Society and the Mythology of the Shimin in Postwar Japan*. Berkeley, LA: University of California Press, 2010.
Avenell, Simon. *Transnational Japan in the Global Environmental Movement*. Honolulu: University of Hawai'i Press, 2017.
Bakewell, Joan. *Stop the Clocks: Thoughts on What I Leave Behind*. London: Virago, 2016.
Barber, Austin and Stephen Hall. 'Birmingham: Whose Urban Renaissance? Regeneration as a Response to Economic Restructuring'. *Policy Studies* 29, no. 3 (2008): 283–284.
Beckett, Andy. *When the Lights Went Out: Britain in the Seventies*. London: Faber, 2009.
Berman, Marshall. *All That Is Solid Melts into Air: The Experience of Modernity*. London: Verso, 1983.
Black, John A. and Peter J. Rimmer. 'Japanese Highway Planning: A Western Interpretation'. *Transportation* 11, no. 1 (1982): 29–49.
Bognár, Botond. *Contemporary Japanese Architecture: Its Development and Challenge*. New York: Van Nostrand Reinhold, 1985.
Bohm, Stephen, Campbell Jones, Chris Land and Matthew Paterson, eds. *Against Automobility*. Oxford: Wiley-Blackwell, 2006.
Bottles, Stephen L. *Los Angeles and the Automobile: The Making of the Modern City*. Berkeley: University of California Press, 1987.
Brecher, W. Puck. *An Investigation of Japan's Relationship to Nature and Environment*. Lampeter: Edwin Mellen Press, 2000.
Brendon, Piers. *The Motoring Century: The Story of the Royal Automobile Club*. London: Bloomsbury, 1997.
Briggs, Asa. *History of Birmingham: Vol. II – Borough and City, 1865–1938*. London: Oxford University Press, 1952.
Broadbent, Jeffrey. *Environmental Politics in Japan: Networks of Power and Protest*. Cambridge: Cambridge University Press, 1999.
Bull, Michael. 'Automobility and the Power of Sound'. *Theory, Culture and Society* 21, nos. 4/5 (2004): 245–260.
Calder, Kent E. *Crisis and Compensation: Public Policy and Political Stability in Japan, 1949–1986*. Princeton, NJ: Princeton University Press, 1988.
Cannadine, David. *Lords and Landlords: The Aristocracy and the Towns 1774–1967*. Leicester: Leicester University Press, 1980.
Carley, M., I. Christie, M. Fogarty and R. Legard. *Profitable Partnerships: A Report on Business Investment in the Community*. London: Policy Studies Institute, 1991.
Caulcott, Tom. 'Manzoni, Sir Herbert John Baptista'. In *Oxford Dictionary of Biography Online*, accessed 19 February 2015.
Chakrabarty, Dipesh. *Provincialising Europe*. Princeton: Princeton University Press, 2000.

Chamon, Marcos, Paolo Maoro and Okawa Yohei. 'Cars: The Implications of Mass Car Ownership in the Emerging Market Giants'. *Economic Policy* 23, no. 54 (2008): 243–296.

Cherry, Gordon. *Birmingham: A Study in Geography, History and Planning*. Chichester: John Wiley, 1994.

Cherry, Gordon. *The Evolution of British Town Planning*. Leighton Buzzard: Leonard Hill, 1974.

Chinn, Carl. *Brum Undaunted: Birmingham during the Blitz*. 2nd edn. Brewin: Studley, Warks, 2005.

Church, Roy. *Herbert Austin: The British Motor Car Industry to 1941*. London: Europa, 1979.

Church, Roy. *The Rise and Decline of the British Motor Industry*. Cambridge: Cambridge University Press, 1994.

Clapson, Mark. *Suburban Century: Social Change and Urban Growth in England and the United States*. Oxford: Berg, 2003.

Clapson, Mark and Peter Larkham, eds. *The Blitz and Its Legacy' Wartime Destruction to Post-War Reconstruction*. Aldershot: Ashgate, 2013.

Committee on Climate Change. *Factsheet: Transport*. London: HMSO, 2015.

Connell, Kieran. 'A Micro-History of "Black Handsworth": Towards a Social History of Race in Britain'. PhD thesis, University of Birmingham, Birmingham, 2012.

Cook, Justine. 'Constructing Britain's Road Network: The Scientific Governance of British Roads and the Uses, 1900–1963'. PhD thesis, University of Kent, Canterbury, 2018.

Corton, Christine L. *London Fog*. Cambridge, MA: Harvard University Press, 2015.

Cowman, Krista. 'Play Streets: Women, Children and the Problem of Traffic, 1930–1970'. *Social History* 42, no. 2 (2017): 233–256.

Cross, Andrew. 'Driving the American Landscape'. In *Autopia: Cars and Culture*, edited by Peter Wollen and Joe Kerr, 249–258. London: Reaktion, 2002.

Cullingworth, Barry and Vincent Nadin. *Town and Country Planning in the UK*. London: Taylor and Francis, 2006.

Daitō Eisuke. 'Automation and Organization of Production in the Japanese Automobile Industry: Nissan and Toyota in the 1950s'. *Enterprise & Society: The International Journal of Business History* 1, no. 1 (2000): 139–178.

Dale, Peter N. *The Myth of Japanese Uniqueness*. London: Routledge, 1988.

Daniels, Inge. 'Japanese Homes Inside Out'. *Home Cultures* 5, no. 2 (2008): 115–139.

Dargay, Joyce and Dermot Gately. 'Income's Effect on Car and Vehicle Ownership, Worldwide: 1960–2015'. *Transportation Research Part A* 33, no. 2 (1999): 101–138.

Dargay, Joyce, Dermot Gately and Martin Sommer. 'Vehicle Ownership and Income Growth'. *The Energy Journal* 28, no. 4 (2007): 143–170.

Davis, John. 'Simple Solutions to Complex Problems: The GLC and the GLDP 1965–1973'. In *Civil Society and British History*, edited by José Harris. Oxford: Oxford University Press, 2003.

Davison, Graeme and Sheryl Yelland. *Car Wars: How the Car Won Our Hearts and Conquered Our Cities*. Crows Nest, New South Wales: Allen and Unwin, 2004.

Dees, Bowen C. *The Allied Occupation & Japan's Economic Miracle: Building the Foundations of Japanese Science and Technology 1945–52*. Richmond, Surrey: Japan Library, 1997.

Demizu T. 'The Motorization of Japan'. In *A Social History of Science and Technology in Contemporary Japan*, vol. III, edited by Nakayama Shigeru and Gotō Kunio, 298–310. Melbourne: Trans Pacific Press, 2006.

Dennis, Kingsley and John Urry. *After the Car*. Cambridge: Polity, 2009.
Department for Transport. *Full License Holders by Age and Gender: England*, Table NTS0201. London: HMSO, 2017.
Department for Transport. *Household Car Availability: England*, Table NTS0205. London: HMSO, 2017.
Department for Transport. *Licensed Vehicles by Tax Class, Great Britain*, Table VEH0103. London: HMSO, 2016.
Department for Transport. *Reported Road Casualties Great Britain 2013*. London: HMSO, 2014.
Department for Transport. *Transport Statistics Great Britain*. London: HMSO, 2007.
Department for Transport. *Transport Statistics Great Britain: 2011*. London: HMSO, 2012.
Diefendorf, Jeffry. 'Artery: Urban Reconstruction and Traffic Planning in Postwar Germany'. *Journal of Urban History* 15, no. 2 (1989): 131–158.
Diefendorf, Jeffry. *In the Wake of War. The Reconstruction of Germany's Bombed Cities after World War II*. Oxford: Oxford University Press, 1993.
Digaetano, Alan and John Klemanski. 'Urban Regime Capacity: A Comparison between Birmingham, England and Detroit, Michigan'. *Journal of Urban Affairs*, 15, no. 4 (1993): 367–384.
Dnes, Michael. 'Ringways: Planning the Rise and Fall of London's Primary Network', MA dissertation, University of Cambridge, Cambridge, 2004.
Domench, Antonio. 'Tramways Revisited: An Analysis of the Role of Tramways in Urban Transportation during the Twentieth Century'. *Geography* 92, no. 2 (2007): 107–117.
Donald, James. *Imagining the Modern City*. Minneapolis: Minnesota University Press, 1999.
Dower, John. *Japan in War and Peace: Essays on History, Culture and Race*. London: Fontana, 1996.
Dunleavy, Patrick. *The Politics of Mass Housing in Britain, 1945–1975: A Study of Corporate Power and Professional Influence in the Welfare State*. Oxford: Oxford University Press, 1981.
Edgerton, David. *The Shock of the Old: Technology and Global History since 1900*. London: Profile, 2008.
Edgerton, David. *Warfare State: Britain 1920–1970*. Cambridge: Cambridge University Press, 2006.
Elson, Martin. *Green Belts: Conflict Mediation in the Urban Fringe*. London: Architectural Press, 1976.
English, John, Ruth Madigan and Peter Norman. *Slum Clearance: The Social and Administrative Context in England and Wales*. London: Croom Helm, 1976.
Esbester, Mike and Jameson Wetmore, eds. '(Auto)mobility, Accidents and Danger'. *Technology and Culture*, special issue 56, no. 2 (2015): 307–497.
Esher, Lionel. *A Broken Wave: The Rebuilding of England 1940–1980*. London: Allen Lane, 1981.
Essex, Stephen and Mark Brayshaw. 'Vision, Vested Interest and Pragmatism: Who Remade Britain's Blitzed Cities'. *Planning Perspectives* 22, no. 4 (2007): 417–441.
Eyre, John D. *Nagoya: The Changing Geography of a Japanese Regional Metropolis*. Chapel Hill: University of North Carolina Press, 1982.
Fairhurst, M. H. 'The Influence of Public Transport on Car Ownership in London'. *Journal of Transport Economics and Policy* 9, no. 3 (1975): 93–208.
Featherstone, Mike. 'Automobilities: An Introduction'. *Theory, Culture and Society* 21, nos. 4/5 (2004): 1–24.

Finer, Samuel. *Anonymous Empire: A Study of the Lobby in Great Britain*. London: Pall Mall Press, 1966.
Fishman, Leslie and J. Stuart Wabe. 'Restructuring the Form of Car Ownership: A Proposed Solution to the Problem of the Motor Car in the United Kingdom'. *Transportation Research* 3, no. 4 (1969): 429–442.
Flatman, Ben. *Birmingham: Shaping the City*. London, 2008.
Flink, James. *The Automobile Age*. Cambridge, 1990.
Flinn, Catherine. '"The City of Our Dreams"? The Political and Economic Realities of Rebuilding Britain's Blitzed Cities, 1945–54'. *Twentieth Century British History* 23, no. 2 (2012): 221–245.
Foster, Andy. *Birmingham: Pevsner Architectural Guides*. London: Architectural Press, 2005.
Freund, Peter and George Martin. *The Ecology of the Automobile*. Montreal: Black Rose Books, 1994.
Fujikawa Hisao. *Nagoya Chikagai Tanjō Monogatari*. Nagoya: C & D Shuppan, 2007.
Fujino Tomoyuki. 'Expressway in Japan: Toll Road System and Status'. East Nippon Expressway Co., Ltd. (NEXCO East). Last modified 4 November 2002. http://www.carecprogram.org/uploads/events/2009/Road-Development-Seminar-Tajikistan/JICA-Expressway-in-Japan-Toll-Road-System.pdf.
Garon, Sheldon. 'The Transnational Promotion of Saving in Asia "Asian Values" or the "Japanese Model"?' In *The Ambivalent Consumer: Questioning Consumption in East Asia and the West*, edited by Sheldon Garon and Patricia L. Maclachlan, 163–187. Ithaca and London: Cornell University Press, 2006.
Gaubatz, Piper. 'Community, Modernity, and Urban Change in Japan and the USA'. In *Suburban Form: An International Perspective*, edited by Brenda Case Sheer and Kiril Stanilov, 17–37. New York and London: Routledge, 2004.
Geeson, A. and C. Rodgers. 'Comprehensive Redevelopment in Birmingham'. In *Region and Renaissance: Reflections on Planning and Development in the West Midlands 1950–2000*, edited by D. Chapman, C. Harridge, J. Harrison, G. Harrison, and B. Stokes, 26–41. Studley: Brewin Books, 2000.
Genther, Phyllis A. *A History of Japan's Government-Business Relationship: The Passenger Car Industry*. Ann Arbor, Michigan: University of Michigan, 1990.
George, Timothy S. *Minamata: Pollution and the Struggle for Democracy in Postwar Japan*. Campbridge, MA: Harvard University Asia Centre, 2001.
Gill, Conrad. *History of Birmingham: Manor to Borough to 1865*, vol. 1. London: Oxford University Press, 1952.
Golany, Gideon S., Hanaki Keisuke and Koide Osamu, eds. *Japanese Urban Environment*. Oxford: Pergamon, 1998.
Gold, John. 'A SPUR to Action?: The Society for the Promotion of Urban Renewal, 'Anti-Scatter' and the Crisis of City Reconstruction, 1957–1963'. *Planning Perspectives* 27, no. 2 (2012): 199–223.
Gold, John. 'The Making of a Megastructure: Architectural Modernism, Town Planning and Cumbernauld's Central Area, 1955–1975'. *Planning Perspectives* 21 (April 2006): 109–131.
Gold, John. *The Practice of Modernism: Modern Architects and Urban Transformation, 1954–1972*. Abingdon: Routledge, 2007.
Gordon, Andrew. 'Consumption, Leisure and the Middle Class in Transwar Japan'. *Social Science Japan Journal* 10, no. 1 (2007): 1–21.
Gourvish, Terry. *Britain's Railway, 1997–2005*. Oxford: Oxford University Press, 2008.

Graham, Stephen and Simon Marvin. *Splintering Urbanism: Networked Infrastructures, Technological Mobilities and the Urban Condition*. London: Routledge, 2001.

Gravereau, Jacques. *Le Japan l'ère de Hirohito*. Paris: Imprimerie nationale, 1988.

Green, Judith et al. 'Automobility Reconfigured? Ironic Seductions and Mundane Freedoms in 16–21 Year Olds' Accounts of Car Driving and Ownership'. *Mobilities* 13, no. 1 (2008): 14–28.

Greenhalgh, James. 'Consuming Communities: The Neighbourhood Unit and the Role of Retail Spaces on British Housing Estates, 1944–1958', *Urban History* 43, no. 1 (2016): 158–174.

Gregory, David. *Green Belts and Development Control: A Case Study in the West Midlands*. Birmingham: Research Publications Services, 1970.

Griffiths, Clare and Anita Brock. 'Twentieth Century Mortality Trends in England and Wales'. *Health Statistics Quarterly* 18 (2003): 5–17.

Griseldis Kirsch, Dolores P. Martinez and Merry White, eds. *Assembling Japan: Modernity, Technology and Global Culture*. Bern: Peter Lang GmbH, Internationaler Verlag der Wissenschaften, 2015.

Gunn, Simon. 'Between Conservation and Modernism: Konrad Smigielski and the Planning of 1960s Leicester'. In *Leicester: A Modern History*, edited by Richard Rodger and Rebecca Madgin, 267–291. Lancaster: Carnegie Press, 2016.

Gunn, Simon. *History and Cultural Theory*. London: Longman, 2006.

Gunn, Simon. 'Introduction' to *Traffic in Towns*. Oxford: Routledge, 2015.

Gunn, Simon. 'People and the Car: The Expansion of Automobility in Urban Britain, c. 1955–1970'. *Social History* 38, no. 2 (2013): 226–228.

Gunn, Simon. 'Review of the History of Transport Systems in the UK', Government Office for Science and Foresight, *Future of Mobility*. London: Government Office for Science, 2018.

Gunn, Simon. 'The Buchanan Report, Environment and the Problem of Traffic in 1960s Britain'. *Twentieth Century History* 22, no. 4 (2011): 521–542.

Gunn, Simon. 'The Rise and Fall of British Urban Modernism: Planning Bradford, circa 1945–1970'. *Journal of British Studies* 49, no. 4 (2010): 849–869.

Gunn, Simon and James Vernon eds. *The Peculiarities of Liberal Modernity in Imperial Britain*. Berkeley, CA: University of California Press, 2011.

Hall, Peter. *Great Planning Disasters*. London, 1980.

Hall, Peter. *Urban and Regional Planning*. London: Routledge, 1992.

Hall, Peter and Carmen Hass-Klau. *Can Rail Save the City? The Impacts of Rail Rapid Transit and Pedestrianisation on British and German Cities*. Aldershot: Ashgate, 1985.

Hall, Peter, Ray Thomas, Harry Gracey and Roy Drewett. *The Containment of Urban England: Volume I – Urban and Metropolitan Growth Processes or Megalopolis Denied*. London: Allen and Unwin, 1973.

Hall, Peter, Ray Thomas, Harry Gracey and Roy Drewett. *The Containment of Urban England: Volume II – The Planning System*. London: Allen and Unwin, 1973.

Halsey, A. H. and Josephine Webb. *Twentieth-Century British Social Trends*. Basingstoke: Palgrave Macmillan, 2000.

Hamer, Mike. *Wheels within Wheels: A Study of the Road Lobby*. London: Friends of the Earth, 1974.

Hanley, Lynsey. *Estates: An Intimate History*. London: Granta, 2012.

Hanna, Erika. 'Seeing Like a Cyclist: Visibility and Mobility in Modern Dublin, c. 1930–1980'. *Urban History* 42, no. 2 (2015): 273–289.

Harada Yoko. 'Sengo Nihon no Shoki Nyūtaun ni okeru Jūkankyō Hyōka to Sumikae ikō ni Kansuru Hikaku Kenkyū'. *Journal of the Architectural Institute of Japan*, no. 619, (September 2007): 9–16.

Harashina Sachiko. 'Environmental Dispute Resolution in Road Construction Projects in Japan'. *Environmental Impact Assessment Review* 8, no. 1 (March 1988): 29–41. https://doi.org/10.1016/0195-9255(88)90058-3.

Hardy, P. L. and P. Jacques *A Short Review of Birmingham Corporation Tramways*. St Albans: HJ Publications, 1974.

Harris, Chauncy D. 'The Urban and Industrial Transformation of Japan'. *Geographic Review* 72, no. 1 (January 1982): 50–89.

Harth, A, et al. *Wolfsburg: Stadt am Wendepunkt*. Opleden: Kesje und Bundrich, 2000.

Hasegawa Jun'ichi. 'The 100-Metre-Road in the Reconstruction of Bombed Cities in Japan'. *Planning History* 28, nos. 2&3 (2006): 13–16.

Hasegawa Jun'ichi. 'Tokyo's Elevated Expressway in the 1950s: Protest and Politics'. *Journal of Transport History* 36, no. 2 (2015): 228–247.

Hasegawa, Jun'ichi. 'The Rise and Fall of Radical Reconstruction in 1940s Britain'. *Twentieth Century History* 10, no. 2 (1999): 137–161.

Hasegawa, Jun'ichi. *Replanning the Blitzed City Centre*. Buckingham, 1992.

Hatherley, Owen, ed. *Nairn's Towns*. London: Notting Hill Editions, 2013.

Havens, Thomas R. *Parkscapes in Modern Japan*. Honolulu: University of Hawai'i Press, 2011.

Hayakawa Fumio. *Seikatsu, Jūtaku, Kankyō: Nagoya Daitoshien no Toshi-Jūtaku Kenkyū*. Nagoya: Nagoya University E & S Shuppan-bu, 1975.

Hayashi Kitotaka. 'Land Readjustment in Nagoya'. In *Land Readjustment*, edited by William A. Doebele, 107–126. Lexington, MA, Toronto: Lexington Books, 1982.

Hayashi Takashi. 'Kōtsu no Hatten to tomoni Keishiki-saretekita Nagoya no Toshi Kōzō'. In *Nagoya-shi Naka-ku Shi*, edited by Naka-ku sei 100 shūnen kinen jigyō jikkō iinkai, 172–183. Nagoya: Naka-ku Yakusho, 2010.

Haywood, Russ. *Railways, Urban Development and Town Planning in Britain: 1948–2008*. Abingdon: Routledge, 2009.

Headicar, Peter. *Transport Policy and Planning in Great Britain*. London: Routledge, 2009.

Hebbert, Michael. 'Sen-biki amidst Desakota: Urban Sprawl and Urban Planning in Japan'. In *Planning for Cities and Regions in Japan*, edited by P. Shapira, I. Masser and D. W. Edgington, 70–91. Liverpool: Liverpool University Press, 1994.

Hein, Carola. 'Machi: Neighborhood and Small Town. The Foundation for Urban Transformation in Japan'. *Journal of Urban History* 35, no. 1 (2008): 75–107.

Hein, Carola. 'Rebuilding Japanese Cities after 1945'. In *Rebuilding Urban Japan after 1945*, edited by Carola Hein, Jeffry H. Diefendorf and Ishida Yorifusa, 1–16. London: Palgrave Macmillan, 2003.

Hein, Carola. 'Visionary Plans and Planners: Japanese Traditions and Western Influence'. In *Japanese Capitals in Historical Perspective: Place, Power and Memory in Kyoto, Edo and Tokyo*, edited by Nicolas Fieve and Paul Waley, 567–632. Abingdon, OX: RoutledgeCurzon, 2003.

Hessler, Martina. 'Crisis in Automotive Cities: The Ambivalent Role of the Car Industry in the "Autostadt" Wolfsburg and the "Motor Town" Detroit'. In *Industrial Cities: History and Future*, edited by Clemens Zimmerman. Frankfurt: Campus Verlag, 2013.

Hewitt, Lucy. 'Towards a Greater Urban Geography: Regional Planning and Associational Networks in London in the Early Twentieth Century'. *Planning Perspectives* 26, no. 4 (2011): 551–568.

Higgott, Andrew. 'Birmingham: Building the Modern City'. In *The Modern City Revisited*, edited by Thomas Deckker, 150–166. London: Routledge, 2000.

Hoare, Tony. *The Location of Industry in Britain*. Cambridge: Cambridge University Press, 1983.

Holtz Kay, Jane. *The Asphalt Exodus: How the Automobile Took Over America and How We Can Take It Back*. New York: University of California Press, 1997.

Holyoak, Joe. 'Street, Subway and Mall: Spatial Politics in the Bull Ring'. In *Remaking Birmingham: The Visual Culture of Urban Regeneration*, edited by Lewis Kennedy, 13–24. London: Routledge, 2004.

Hopkins, Eric. *Birmingham: The First Manufacturing Town in the World*. London: Weidenfeld and Nicholson, 1989.

Hotta Yoshihiro. *Jidōsha to kenchiku: Mōtarizēshun jidai no kankyō dezain*. Tokyo: Kawade Shobo Shinsha, 2013.

Hotta Yoshihiro. '"Mai kā" to "mai hōmu" o meguru jūtakuchi dezain nitsuite'. *Nagoya University Research Papers* (2014): 59–67. www.lij.jp/html/jli/jli_2014/2014winter_p059.pdf

Huddle, Norie and Michael Reich. *Island of Dreams: Environmental Crisis in Japan*. New York: Autumn Press Inc., 1975.

Ichikawa, Hiroo. 'Tokyo: The Attempt to Transform the Metropolis'. In *Rebuilding Urban Japan after 1945*, edited by Carola Hein, Jeffry H. Diefendorf and Ishida Yorifusa, 50–67. London: Palgrave Macmillan, 2003.

International Association of Traffic and Safety Sciences (ITS), ed. *Kuruma Shakai wa Dō Kawaru ka: ITS – kankyō – toshibunka no kanten kara mita kōtsū shakai*. Bungeisha: Tokyo, 2014.

Ishida Yorifusa. 'Japanese Cities and Planning in the Reconstruction Period'. In *Rebuilding Urban Japan after 1945*, edited by Carola Hein, Jeffry H. Diefendorf and Ishida Yorifusa, 17–49. London: Palgrave Macmillan, 2003.

Itō Norio. *Nagoya no Machi: Sensai fukkō no kiroku*. Nagoya: Chūnichi Shimbun Honsha, 1988.

Itō Shigeru. 'The Outline of Kozoji Newtown'. *Ekistics* 19, no. 99 (February, 1964): 115–120.

Jackson, Kenneth. *Crabgrass Frontier: The Suburbanization of the United States*. Oxford: Oxford University Press, 1985.

Jacobs, Andrew J. 'Embedded Autonomy and Uneven Metropolitan Development: A Comparison of the Detroit and Nagoya Auto Regions, 1969–2000'. *Urban Studies* 40, no. 2 (2003): 335–360.

Jacobs, Andrew J. 'Planning for a Vibrant Central City: The Case of Nagoya, Japan'. *International Urban Planning Settings: Lessons of Success* 12 (January 2001): 21–59. https://www.researchgate.net/publication/304377387.

Jesty, Justin. 'Tokyo 1960: Days of Rage & Grief'. MIT Visualizing Cultures, accessed 5 July 2018. https://ocw.mit.edu/ans7870/21f/21f.027/tokyo_1960/anp2_essay01.html.

Johnson, Chalmers. *MITI and the Japanese Miracle: The Growth of Industrial Policy*. Stanford, CA: Stanford University Press, 1982.

Johnson, Richard A. *Six Men Who Built the Modern Auto Industry*. St. Paul, MN: Motorbooks, 2005.

Jones, Ben. *The Working Class in Mid-Twentieth Century England*. Manchester: Manchester University Press, 2012.

Jones, David. *Mass Motorization and Mass Transit: An American History and Policy Analysis*. Bloomington: Indiana University Press, 2008.

Jones, Phil. 'Historical Continuity and Post-1945 Urban Redevelopment: The Example of Lee Bank, Birmingham, UK'. *Planning Perspectives* 19, no. 4 (2004): 365–389.

Jones, Phil. 'Performing the City: A Body and a Bicycle Take on Birmingham, UK'. *Social and Cultural Geography* 6, no. 6 (2005): 813–830.

Jones, Phil. 'The City as Artwork: The Dismemberment of Modern Birmingham'. The City in Art conference, September 2004, Krakow, Jagellonian University.

Jordan, John. 'The Art of Necessity: The Subversive Imagination of Anti-Road Protest and Reclaim the Streets'. In *DiY Culture: Party and Protest in Nineties Britain*, edited by George MacKay, 129–151. London: Verso, 1998.

Joy, Stewart. *The Train That Ran Away: A Business History of British Railways 1948–1968*. London: Allan, 1973.

Kamei Yosuko, Sono Yoko, Ishii Satoko and Yokoyama Riho. 'Kōgai ōkibo kodatejūtaku danchi no jūko dasai to gairo keikan ni kansuru kenkyū'. *Nihonkenchiku Gakkai Keikaku-kei Ronbun-shū* 70, no. 590 (April 2005): 9–16.

Kameyama Yasuko. *Climate Change Policy in Japan from the 1980s to 2015*. London and New York: Routledge, 2016.

Karan, Pradyumna P. *Japan in the 21st Century: Environment, Economy and Society*. Lexington: University Press of Kentucky, 2005.

Kashiwagi Hiroshi. 'On Rationalization and the National Lifestyle: Japanese Design in the 1920s and 1930s'. In *Being Modern in Japan: Culture and Society from the 1910s to the 1930s*, edited by Elise K. Tipton and John Clark, 61–74. Honolulu: University of Hawai'i Press, 2000.

Keedy, Malcolm. *Birmingham City Transport: A History of its Buses and Trolleybuses*. Glossop, 1979.

Kefford, Alistair. 'Constructing the Affluent Citizen: State, Space and the Individual in Post-War Britain, 1945–1979'. PhD thesis, University of Manchester, Manchester, 2015.

Kelly, William W. 'Finding a Place in Metropolitan Japan: Ideologies, Institutions, and Everyday Life.' In *Postwar Japan as History*, edited by Andrew Gordon, 189–292. Berkeley, LA and London: University of California Press, 1993.

Kennedy, Liam, ed. *Remaking Birmingham: The Visual Culture of Urban Regeneration*. London: Routledge, 2004.

Kenny, Nicholas and Rebecca Madgin, eds. *Cities beyond Borders: Comparative and Transnational Approaches to Urban History*. Abingdon: Routledge, 2015.

Kiuchi Shinzo and Inouchi Noboru. 'New Towns in Japan'. *Geoforum* 7, no. 1 (1976): 1–12.

Koshi Masaki, Miyazaki Masao, Morichi Shigeru, Takahashi Yoji, Tsukio Yoshio, Honda Histochi and Hayashi Waichiro. 'Japanese National Policy toward the Automobile'. *Transport Reviews* 3, no. 1 (1 January 1983): 1–32.

Kōtsū Kogaku Kenkyūkai. *Kōtsū Kogaku Handobukku*. Tokyo: Gihodo Shuppan, 1984.

Koyama Tōru. 'Construction of a Nationwide Network of Expressways'. In *A Social History of Science and Technology in Contemporary Japan*, vol. III, edited by Nakayama Shigeru and Gotō Kunio, 347–361. Melbourne: Trans Pacific Press, 2006.

Krauss, Ellis S. and Bradford L. Simcock. 'Citizens' Movements: The Growth and Impact of Environmental Protest in Japan'. In *Political Opposition and Local Politics in Japan*, edited by Kurt Steiner, Ellis S. Krauss and Scott C. Flanagan, 187–227. Princeton, NJ: Princeton University Press, 1980.

Krebs, Stefan. 'Standardizing Car Sound – Integrating Europe? International Traffic Noise Abatement and the Emergence of a European Car Identity, 1950–1975'. *History and Technology* 28, no. 1 (2012): 25–47.

Krier, James and Edmund Ursin. *Pollution and Policy: A Case Essay on California and Federal Experience with Motor Vehicle Air Pollution 1940–1975*. London: University of California Press, 1977.

Kultermann, Udo. *Kenzo Tange: Archtecture and Urban Design 1946–1969*. London: Pall Mall Press, 1970.

Kwak, Nancy. 'Research in Urban History: Recent Theses on International and Comparative Urban History'. *Urban History* 35, no. 2 (2008): 316–325.

Kynaston, David. *Austerity Britain: 1945–51*. London: Bloomsbury, 2007.

Ladd, Brian. *Autophobia: Love and Hate in the Automotive Age*. Chicago: Chicago University Press, 2008.

Ladd, Brian. 'Cities on Wheels: Cars and Public Spaces'. In *The New Blackwell Companion to the City*, edited by Gary Bridge and Sophie Watson, 265–274. Chichester: John Wiley, 2011.

Larkham, Peter. 'Hostages to History? The Surprising Survival of Critical Comments about British Planning and Planners c. 1942–1955'. *Planning Perspectives* 26, no. 3 (2011): 487–491.

Larkham, Peter. 'Rebuilding the Industrial Town: Wartime Wolverhampton'. *Urban History* 29, no. 3 (2002): 388–409.

Larkham, Peter. 'The Place of Urban Conservation in the UK Reconstruction Plans of 1942–1952'. *Planning Perspectives* 18, no. 3 (2003): 295–324.

Larkham, Peter and David Adams, 'Bold Planning, Mixed Experiences: The Diverse Fortunes of Post-War Birmingham'. In *The Blitz and Its Legacy: Wartime Destruction to Post-War Reconstruction*, edited by Mark Clapson and Peter Larkham, 137–150. Farnham: Ashgate, 2013.

Larkham, Peter and Keith Lilley. 'Plans, Planners and City Images: Place Promotion and Civic Boosterism in British Reconstruction Planning'. *Urban History* 30, no. 2 (2003): 183–205.

Law, Michael. 'Speed and Blood on the Bypass: The New Automobilities of Inter-War London'. *Urban History* 39, no. 3 (2012): 490–509.

Lawrence, Jon. 'Social Science Encounters and the Negotiation of Difference in Early 1960s England'. *History Workshop Journal* 77, no. 1 (2013): 215–239.

Lee, Derek. *Regional Planning and the Location of Industry*. London: Heinemann Educational, 1980.

Lewis, Tow. *Divided Highways: Building the Interstate Highways, Transforming American Life*. Ithaca: Cornell University Press, 2013.

Licklider, Roy. *Political Power and the Arab Oil Weapon*. Berkeley, CA: University of California Press, 1988.

Liu Qian, James Wang, Peng Chen and Zuopeng Xiao. 'How Does Parking Interplay with the Built Environment and Affect Automobile Commuting in High-Density Cities? A Case Study in China'. *Urban Studies* 54, no. 14 (2017): 3299–3317.

Lodge, David. *Changing Places*. London: Secker and Warburg, 1975.

Lundin, Per. 'Mediating Modernity: Planning Experts and the Making of the "Car-friendly" City in Europe'. In *Urban Machinery: Inside European Cities*, edited by Mikael Hård and Thomas Misa, 257–280. Cambridge, MA: MIT Press, 2008.

Lynch, Kevin. *The Image of the City*. Boston, MA: MIT Press, 1960.

Maki Fumihiko. *Nurturing Dreams: Collected Essays on Architecture and the City*, edited by Mark Mulligan. Cambridge, MA: MIT Press, 2008.

Mandler, Peter. 'New Towns for Old: The Fate of the Town Centre'. In *Moments of Modernity: Reconstructing Britain, 1946–1964*, edited by Becky Conekin, Frank Mort and Chris Water, 208–227. London: Rivers Oram Press, 1999.

Mantle, Jonathan. *Car Wars*. New York: Little, Brown and Co., 1995.
Markowitz, Gerald and David Rosner. *Deceit and Denial: The Deadly Politics of Industrial Pollution*. London: University of California Press, 2003.
Marling, Karal. 'America's Love Affair with the Automobile in the Television Age'. In *Autopia: Cars and Culture*, edited by Peter Joe Wollen and Kerr, 354–362. London: University of Chicago Press, 2002.
Martelle, Scott. *Detroit: A Biography*. Chicago: Chicago Review Press, 2014.
Masayoshi Takada. 'The Japanese Meet the Automobile'. *The Wheel Extended* 17, no. 3 (1987): 20–24.
Masser, Ian. 'Land Readjustment: An Overview'. *Third World Planning Review* 9, no. 3, (1987): 205–210.
Masser, Ian and Yorisaki Takahiro. 'The Institutional Context of Japanese Planning: Professional Associations and Planning Education'. In *Planning for Cities and Regions in Japan*, edited by Philip Shapira, Ian Masser and David W. Edgington, 113–125. Liverpool: Liverpool University Press, 1994.
Matless, David. *Landscape and Englishness*. London: Reaktion Books, 1998.
McCarthy, Tom. *Auto Mania – Cars, Consumers and the Environment*. New Haven: Yale University Press, 2007.
McCormick, John. *The Global Environmental Movement*. Chichester: John Wiley, 1995.
McKenna, Joseph. *Birmingham: The Rebuilding of a City*. Stroud: Tempus, 2005.
McShane, Mary P., Masaki Koshi and Olof Lundin. 'Public Policy toward the Automobile: A Comparative Look at Japan and Sweden'. *Transportation Reports – A* 18A, no. 2 (1984): 97–109.
Meller, Helen. *Towns, Plans and Society in Modern Britain*. Cambridge: Cambridge University Press, 1997.
Melosi, Martin. *Effluent America: Cities, Industry, Energy and the Environment*. Pittsburgh: University of Pittsburgh Press, 2001.
Merriman, Peter. 'Driving Places: Marc Auge, Non-Places and the Geographies of England's M1 Motorway'. *Theory Culture and Society* 21, no. 4/5 (2004): 145–167.
Merriman, Peter. *Driving Spaces: A Cultural-Historical Geography of England's M1 Motorway*. Chichester: John Wiley, 2007.
Metzler, Mark. *Capital as Will and Imagination: Schumpeter's Guide to the Postwar Japanese Miracle*. Ithaca and London: Cornell University Press, 2013.
Middleton, Jennie. 'Walking in the City: The Geographies of Everyday Pedestrian Practices'. *Geography Compass* 5 (2011): 90–105.
Miller, Daniel, ed. *Car Cultures*. Oxford: Berg, 2001.
Millward, Robert, 'Industrial and Commercial Performance since 1950'. In *The Economic History of Britain since 1700*, edited by Roderick Floud and Deirdre McCloskey. Cambridge: Cambridge University Press, 1994.
Minami Ryoshin. 'Income Distribution of Japan: Historical Perspective and Its Implications'. *Japan Labor Review* 5, no. 4 (Autumn 2008): 5–20.
Ministry of Land, Infrastructure. 'Transport and Tourism. History of Road Construction', Roads in Japan. Last updated 2008. http://www.mlit.go.jp.
Mitchell, Timothy. *Carbon Democracy*. London: Verso, 2011.
Miyazawa Michio. 'Land Readjustment in Japan'. In *Land Readjustment*, edited by William A. Doebele, 91–106. Lexington, MA, Toronto: Lexington Books, 1982.
Mohl, Raymond. 'Stop the Road: Freeway Revolts in American Cities', *Journal of Urban History* 30, no. 5 (2004): 674–706.

Mom, Gijs. *Atlantic Automobilism: Emergence and Persistence of the Car 1895–1940*. New York: Berghan, 2014.

Mönnich, Horst. *Die Autostadt*. Munich: Wilhelm Andermann Verlag, 1951.

Moore, Aaron Stephen. *Constructing East Asia: Technology, Ideology, and Empire in Japan's Wartime Era, 1931–1945*. Stanford, CA: Stanford University Press, 2013.

Moran, Joe. 'Crossing the Road in Britain, 1931–1976'. *Historical Journal* 49, no. 2 (2006): 477–496.

Moran, Joe. *On Roads: A Hidden History*. London: Profile Books, 2009.

Mort, Frank. 'Fantasies of Metropolitan Life: Planning London in the 1940s'. *Journal of British Studies* 43, no. 1 (2004): 120–151.

Mosley, Stephen. '"A Network of Trust": Measuring and Monitoring Air Pollution in British Cities, 1912–1960'. *Environment and History* 15 (2009): 273–302.

Mumford, Lewis. *The City in History*. New York: Harcourt Brace, 1961.

Murashige Yoshiyasu. 'Kōsoku dōrohyōji no reiauto henkō ni yoru shinin-sei kōjō'. *International Association of Traffic and Safety Sciences (IATSS) Review* 40, no. 3 (February 2016): 199–205.

Murayama Akito. 'Urban Design Solutions to Environmental Issues'. *Lecture Note: Sustainable Urban Regeneration B*, no. 23, (November 2012): 54–59.

Nagamine Haruo. 'The Land Readjustment Techniques of Japan'. *Habitat International* 10, nos. 1–2 (1986): 51–58.

Nagoya Kōsokudōro Kōsha 40 Nenshi Henshū I'inkai, eds. *Nagoya Kōsokudōro Kōsha 40 Nenshi*. Nagoya: Nagoya Expressway Corporation, October 2012.

Nagoya Toshi Kenkyūkai. 'Sensai Fukkō Keikaku ni tomonau Nagoya no Toshi Kōzo no Henyō ni kansuru Kenkyū'. *Chi'iki Mondai Kenkyū*, no. 52 (1996): 9–15.

Nagoya-shi Keikaku Kyoku, ed. *Fukkō Tochikukaku Seiri Jigyō no Aramashi*. Nagoya: Nagoya-shi Keikaku Kyoku, 1991.

Nagoya-shi Keikaku Kyoku, ed. *Sensai Fukkō-shi*. Nagoya: Nagoya-shi Keikaku Kyoku, 1984.

Nead, Lynda. *Victorian Babylon: People, Streets and Images in Nineteenth-Century London*. New Haven: Yale University Press, 2000.

Nechyba, Thomas and Randall Walsh. 'Urban Sprawl'. *Journal of Economic Perspectives* 18, no. 4 (2004): 177–200.

Neumaier, Christopher. 'Eco-Friendly versus Cancer-Causing: Perceptions of Diesel Cars in West Germany and the United States, 1970–1990'. *Technology and Culture* 55, no. 2 (2014): 429–460.

Newton, Kenneth. *Second City Politics: Democratic Processes and Decision-Making in Birmingham*. Oxford: Oxford University Press, 1976.

Nishimura Yuichiro and Okamoto Kohei. 'Yesterday and Today: Changes in Worker's Lives in Toyota City Japan'. In *Japan in the Bluegrass*, edited by Pradyumna Karan, 98–122. Lexington: University of Kentucky Press, 2001.

Nitschke, Günter. *From Shinto to Ando: Studies in Architectural Anthropology in Japan*. London: Academy Editions, 1993.

Norton, Peter. *Fighting Traffic: The Dawn of the Motor Age in the American City*. Cambridge: MIT Press, 2008.

O'Hara, Glen. *From Dreams to Disillusionment: Economic and Social Planning in 1960s Britain*. Basingstoke: Palgrave Macmillan, 2007.

Office for National Statistics. *Social Trends 41: Transport*. London: HMSO, 2011.

Okayama Reiko. 'Industrial Relations in the Japanese Automobile Industry 1945–70: The Case of Toyota'. In *Between Fordism and Flexibility*, edited by Steven Tolliday and Jonathan Zeitlin, 168–190. Oxford: Berg, 1992.

Ortolano, Guy. 'Planning the Urban Future in 1960s Britain'. *Historical Journal* 54, no. 2 (2011): 477–507.
Oye, Kenneth A. and James H. Maxwell. 'Self-interest and Environmental Management'. In *Local Commons and Global Interdependence*, edited by Robert O. Keohane and Elinor Ostrom, 191–221. London: Sage, 1995.
Parish, David. *The 1973–1975 Energy Crisis and Its Impact on Transport*. London: RAC Foundation, 2009.
Parker, David and Paul Long. '"The Mistakes of the Past"? Visual Narratives of Urban Decline and Regeneration'. *Visual Culture in Britain* 5, no. 1 (2004): 37–58.
Parker, David and Paul Long. 'Reimagining Birmingham: Public History, Selective Memory and the Narration of Urban Change'. *European Journal of Cultural Studies* 6, no. 2 (2003): 157–178.
Parker, Matthew. 'Making the City Mobile: The Place of the Motor Car in the Planning of Post-War Birmingham'. PhD thesis, University of Leicester, Leicester, 2015.
Parsons, Rory and Geoff Vigar. '"Resistance Was Futile": Cycling's Discourses of Resistance to UK Automobile Modernism, 1950–1970'. *Planning Perspectives* (online publication 16 July 2017).
Paterson, Matthew. *Automobile Politics: Ecology and Cultural Political Economy*. Cambridge: Cambridge University Press, 2007.
Pemberton, Hugh and Lawrence Black, eds. *An Affluent Society: Britain's Post-War 'Golden Age' Revisited*. London: Routledge, 2004.
Pendlebury, John. 'Alas Smith and Burns? Conservation in Newcastle upon Tyne City Centre 1959–1968'. *Planning Perspectives* 16, no. 2 (2001): 115–141.
Pendlebury, John. *Conservation in the Age of Consensus*. London: Routledge, 2009.
Pendleton, Mark and Jamie Coates. 'Thinking from the Yamanote: Space, Place and Mobility in Tokyo's Past and Present'. *Japan Forum* 30, no. 2 (2018): 149–162. DOI: 10.1080/09555803.2017.1353532.
Plath, David W. 'My Car-isma: Motorizing the Showa Self'. In *Shōwa: The Japan of Hirohito*, edited by Carol Gluck and Stephen R. Graubard, 229–244. New York; London: W.W. Norton, 1992.
Plowden, William. *The Motor Car and Politics in Britain*. London: Bodley Head, 1971.
Pooley, Colin. 'Landscapes without the Car: A Counterfactual Historical Geography of Twentieth-Century Britain'. *Journal of Historical Geography* 36, no. 3 (2010): 266–275.
Pooley, C. G. and Turnbull, J. 'Modal Choice and Modal Change: The Journey to Work in Britain since 1890'. *Journal of Transport Geography* 8, no. 1 (2000): 11–24.
Pooley, Colin and Jean Turnbull. 'Commuting, Transport and Urban Form: Manchester and Glasgow in the Mid-Twentieth Century'. *Urban History* 27, no. 3 (2000): 360–383.
Pooley, Colin and Jean Turnbull. 'Coping with Congestion: Responses to Urban Traffic Problems in British Cities, c. 1920–1960'. *Journal of Historical Geography* 31, no. 1 (2005): 78–93.
Pooley, Colin, Jean Turnbull and Mags Adams. *A Mobile Century? Changes in Everyday Mobility in Britain in the Twentieth Century*. Aldershot: Ashgate, 2005.
Popham, Peter. *Tokyo: The City at the Edge of the World*. Tokyo: Kodansha, 1985.
Ravetz, Alison. *The Government of Space*. London: Routledge, 1986.
Rieger, Bernhard. 'The Automobile'. In *Cambridge World History*, vol. 7, part 2, edited by J. R. McNeil and K. Pomeranz, 467–489. Cambridge: Cambridge University Press, 2017.
Romao, Tico. 'Engines of Transformation: An Analytical History of the 1970s Car Chase Cycle'. *New Review of Film and Television Studies* 1, no. 1 (2003): 31–54.

Rooney, David. 'The Political Economy of Congestion: Road Pricing and the Neoliberal Project, 1952–2003'. *Twentieth Century History* 25, no. 4 (2014): 628–650.

Rosenbluth, Francis and Michael F. Thies, 'The Political Economy of Japanese Pollution Regulation'. Paper Prepared for Presentation at the Annual Meeting of the American Political Science Association, 2–5 September Atlanta, Georgia, 1999, 20–21. www.yale-university.com/leitner/resources/docs/1999-01.Pdf.

Ross, Kristin. *Fast Cars, Clean Bodies: Decolonization and the Reordering of French Culture*. Cambridge, MA: MIT Press, 1996.

Roth, Joshua H. 'Harmonising Cars and Humans in Japan's Era of Mass Automobility'. *The Asia-Pacific Journal: Japan Focus* 9, 45, 3 (November 2011). http://apjjf.org/2011/9/45/Joshua-Roth/3643/article.html.

Roth, Joshua H. 'Heartfelt Driving: Discourses on Manners, Safety, and Emotion in Japan's Era of Mass Motorization'. *Journal of Asian Studies* 71, no. 1 (February 2012): 171–192.

Roth, Joshua H. 'Is Female to Male as Lightweight Cars Are to Sports Cars?: Gender Metaphors and Cognitive Schemes in Recessionary Japan'. In *Vehicles: Cars, Canoes and Other Metaphors or Moral Imagination*, edited by David Lipset and Richard Hander, 88–108. New York and Oxford: Berghahn Books, 2014.

Routh, Guy. *Occupation and Pay in Great Britain 1906–1987*. London: Macmillan, 1980.

Ruiz, Marco. *The Complete History of the Japanese Car: 1907 to the Present*. Yeovil: Haynes, 1986.

Said, Edward. *Orientalism*. Harmondsworth: Penguin, 1985 [1978].

Saitō Toshihiko. *Kurumatachi no Shakaishi*. Tokyo: Chūko Shinsho, 1997.

Sandbrook, Dominic. *State of Emergency: The Way We Were: Britain, 1970–1974*. London: Penguin, 2011.

Sandbrook, Dominic. *White Heat: A History of Britain in the Swinging Sixties*. London: Abacus, 2006.

Saumarez Smith, Otto. 'Central Government and Town Centre Redevelopment in Britain 1959–1966'. *Historical Journal* 58, no. 1 (2015): 217–244.

Saunier, Pierre-Yves and Shane Ewen, eds. *Another Global City: Historical Explorations into the Transnational Municipal Moment, 1850–2000*. Basingstoke: Palgrave Macmillan, 2008.

Savage, Mike. 'Working-class Identities in the 1960s: Revisiting the *Affluent Worker* Study'. *Sociology* 39, no. 5 (2005): 929–946.

Savage, Mike. *Identities and Social Change in Britain since 1940*. Oxford: Oxford University Press, 2010.

Sawai Suzu'ichi. 'Nagoya Hirokōji Monogatari'. Accessed 7 April 2014. http://network2010.org/article/1036.

Schaller, Michael. *The American Occupation of Japan*. Oxford: Oxford University Press, 1985.

Schmucki, Barbara. '"If I Walked on my Own at Night I Stuck to Well Lit Areas." Gendered Spaces and Urban Transport in 20th Century Britain'. *Research in Transportation Economics* 34, no. 1 (2012): 74–85.

Schreurs, Miranda A. *Environmental Politics in Japan, Germany, and the United States*. Cambridge: Cambridge University Press, 2004.

Sealey, K. R. 'Road and Rail Transport in Britain'. *Geography* 49, no. 3 (1964): 293–304.

Seidensticker, Edward. *Tokyo Rising: The City since the Great Earthquake*. Cambridge, MA: Harvard University Press, 1991.

Seiler, Cotton. *Republic of Drivers: A Cultural History of Automobility in America*. Chicago: Chicago University Press, 2008.

Sennett, Richard. *Flesh and Stone: The Body and the City in Western Civilization*. London: Faber, 1994.

Sheail, John. *An Environmental History of Twentieth-Century Britain*. Basingstoke: Palgrave Macmillan, 2002.

Sheail, John. '"Torrey Canyon": The Political Dimension'. *Journal of Contemporary History* 42, no. 3 (2007): 485–504.

Sheller, Mimi. 'Automotive Emotions: Feeling the Car'. *Theory, Culture and Society* 21, nos. 4/5 (2004): 221–242.

Sheller, Mimi and John Urry. 'The City and the Car'. *International Journal of Urban and Regional Research* 24, no. 4 (2000): 737–757.

Shelton, Barrie. *Learning from the Japanese City: West Meets East in Urban Design*. London: E & FN Spon, 1999.

Shibata Hirofumi. 'The Energy Crises and Japanese Response'. *Resources and Energy* 5, no. 2 (June 1983): 129–154. https://doi.org/10.1016/0165-0572(83)90010-5

Shimokawa Kō'ichi. 'Marketing History in the Automobile Industry: The United States and Japan'. In *Development of Mass Marketing: The Automobile and Retailing Industries*, edited by Akio Okochi and Koichi Shimokawa, 3–30. Tokyo: Tokyo University Press, 1981.

Shimokawa Kō'ichi. *The Japanese Automobile Industry: A Business History*. London: Athlone, 1994.

Siegelbaum, Lewis, ed. *The Socialist Car: Automobility in the Eastern Bloc*. Ithaca, NY: Cornell University Press, 2011.

Smith, Henry D. 'Tokyo as an Idea: An Exploration of Japanese Urban Thought until 1945'. *Journal of Japanese Studies* 4, no. 1 (Winter 1978): 45–80.

Smith, Roderick A. 'The Japanese Shinkansen: Catalyst for the Renaissance of Rail'. *Journal of Transport History* 24, no. 2 (2003): 222–237.

Smith, Roger. 'Post-War Birmingham: Planning and Development'. *Town Planning Review* 45, no. 2 (1974): 189–206.

Sorensen, André. 'Conflict, Consensus or Consent: Implications of Japanese Land Readjustment Practice for Developing Countries'. *Habitat International* 24, no. 1 (2000): 51–73.

Sorensen, André. 'Subcentres and Satellite Cities: Tokyo's 20th Century Experience of Planned Polycentrism'. *International Planning Studies* 6, no. 1 (2001): 9–32. DOI: 10.1080/13563470120026505.

Sorensen, André. *The Making of Urban Japan: Cities and Planning from Edo to the Twenty-First Century*. Abingdon: Routledge, 2002.

Souter, I. A. 'An Analysis of the Development of the Tramway/Light Rail Concept in British Isles'. *Proceedings of the Institution of Mechanical Engineers, Part F: Journal of Rail and Rapid Transit* 215, no. 3 (2001): 157–166.

Sperling, Daniel and Deborah Gordon. *Two Billion Cars: Driving towards Sustainability*. New York: Oxford University Press, 2009.

Spinney, Justin. 'Cycling the City: Movement, Meaning and Method'. *Geography Compass* 3 (2009): 817–835.

Standing Advisory Committee on Trunk Road Assessment. *Trunk Roads and the Generation of Traffic*. London: HMSO, 1994.

Starkie, David. *The Motorway Age: Roads and Traffic Policies in Post-War Britain*. Oxford: Pergamon Press, 1982.

Stedman, M. B. and P. A. Wood. 'Urban Renewal in Birmingham: An Interim Report'. *Geography* 50, no. 1 (1965).

Stocker, Adam and Susan Shaheen. *Shared Automated Vehicles: Review of Business Models.* Berkeley, CA: OECD, 2016.

Stradling, David and Peter Thorsheim. 'The Smoke of Great Cities: British and American Efforts to Control Air Pollution, 1860–1914'. *Environmental History* 4, no. 1 (1999): 6–31.

Struthers, W. A. K. and M. J. Brindell. 'The West Midlands: From Reconstruction to Regeneration'. In *English Structure Planning: A Commentary on Procedure and Practice in the Seventies*, edited by D. T. Cross and M. R. Bristow, 58–85. London: Routledge Kegan and Paul, 1983.

Sugrue, Thomas. *The Origins of the Urban Crisis: Race and Inequality in Post-War Detroit.* Princeton: Princeton University Press, 1996.

Sutcliffe, Anthony. 'A Century of Flats in Birmingham'. In *Multi-Storey Living: The British Working Class Experience*, edited by Anthony Sutcliffe. London: Croom Helm, 1974.

Sutcliffe, Anthony and Roger Smith. *History of Birmingham Vol. III – Birmingham 1939–1970.* London: Oxford University Press, 1974.

Takahashi Tomoko and Ihara Satoshi. '"Jidōsha Shakai" wa Ikani Ronjiraretekita ka: 1. Gendai gijutsu-ron no kadai to kakawatte'. *Ibaraki Daigaku Kyōyōbu Kiyō* 24 (1992): 135–155. http://hdl.handle.net/10109/9951

Tarr, Joe. *The Search for the Ultimate Sink: Urban Pollution in Historical Perspective.* Akron: University of Akron, 1996.

Taylor, David and Keith Laybourn. *The Battle for the Roads of Britain.* Basingstoke: Palgrave Macmillan, 2015.

Tewdwr-Jones, Mark. '"Oh, the Planners Did Their Best": The Planning Films of John Betjeman'. *Planning Perspectives* 20, no. 4 (2005): 389–411.

Thomas, Julia Adeney. 'The Cage of Nature: Modernity's History in Japan'. *History and Theory* 40, no. 1 (February, 2001): 16–36.

Thorsheim, Peter. *Inventing Pollution: Coal Smoke and Culture in Britain since 1800.* Athens, Ohio: Ohio University Press, 2006.

Thrift, Nigel. 'Driving in the City'. *Theory, Culture and Society* 21, nos. 4/5 (2004): 41–59.

Tiratsoo, Nicholas, Hasegawa Jun'ichi, Tony Mason and Takao Matsumura. *Urban Reconstruction in Britain and Japan, 1945–1955.* Luton: University of Luton Press, 2002.

Tiratsoo, Nick. 'Popular Politics, Affluence and the Labour Party in the 1950s'. In *Contemporary British History – 1931–1961*, edited by Anthony Gorst, Lewis Johnman and W. Scott Lucas, 44–61. London: Pinter, 1991.

Tiratsoo, Nick. 'The Reconstruction of Blitzed British Cities, 1945–55: Myths and Reality'. *Contemporary British History* 14, no. 1 (2008): 27–44.

Tiratsoo, Nick. *Reconstruction, Affluence and Labour Politics: Coventry, 1945–1960.* London: Routledge, 1990.

Todd, Selina. 'Affluence, Class and Crown Street: Reinventing the Post-War British Working Class'. *Contemporary British History* 22, no. 4 (2008): 501–518.

Todokoro Takashi. 'Nagoya ni okeru Chikagai no Keisei: Toshin Rittaika no Ichi Keitai toshite'. *Jimbun Chiri* 31, no. 3 (1979): 193–213. https://doi.org/10.4200/jjhg1948.31.193

Tonouchi Hiroshi, ed. *Kōsha Setsuritsu 40 Shūnen Kinen Zadankai: Nagoya Kōsoku Dōro no Kensetsu no Rekishi o Furikaette*, 15 July 2012. http://www.nagoya-expressway.or.jp/kosya/pdf/08.pdf.

Totman, Conrad. *A History of Japan.* Oxford: Blackwell, 2005.

Townsend, Susan C. 'The Great War and Urban Crisis: Conceptualizing the Industrial Metropolis in Japan and Britain in the 1910s'. In *The Decade of the Great War: Japan and the Wider World in the 1910s*, edited by Tosh Minohara, Evan Dawley and Tze-ki Hon, 301–322. Leiden: Brill, 2014.

Townsend, Susan C. 'The Miracle of Car Ownership in Japan's "Era of High Growth", 1955–1973'. *Business History* 55, no. 3, (2013): 498–523.

Traganou, Jilly. 'The Transit Destinations of Japanese Public Space: The Case of Nagoya Station'. In *Suburbanizing the Masses: Public Transport and Urban Development in Historical Perspective*, edited by Colin Divall and Winstan Bond, 287–314. Aldershot: Ashgate, 2003.

Uekotter, Frank. *The Age of Smoke: Environmental Policy in Germany and the United States 1880–1970*. Pittsburgh: University of Pittsburgh Press, 2009.

Ui Jun. *Industrial Pollution in Japan*. Tokyo: United Nations University Press, 1992. Open access, http://archive.unu.edu/unupress/unupbooks/uu35ie/uu35ie02.htm#i.%20 environmental%20pollution:%20basic%20precepts.

Ui Jun, 'The Singularities of Japanese Pollution'. *Japan Quarterly* 9, no. 3 (1 July 1972): 281–291.

Urry, John. *Mobilities*. Cambridge: Polity, 2007.

Urry, John. 'The "System" of Automobility'. *Theory Culture & Society*. 21, nos. 4/5 (2004): 25–39.

Victoria County History. *A History of the County of Warwick: Volume 7, the City of Birmingham*, edited by W. B. Stephens. London: Victoria County History, 1964.

Vigar, Geoff. *The Politics of Mobility: Transport, the Environment and Public Policy*. London: Routledge, 2002.

Vine, Scott Le and Peter Jones. *On the Move: Making Sense of Car and Travel Trends in Britain*. London: RAC Foundation, 2012.

Virilio, Paul. *Speed and Politics*. Los Angeles: Semiotext(e), 2006.

Wada Kazuo. 'The Fable of the Birth of the Japanese Automobile Industry: A Reconsideration of the Toyota-Platt Agreement of 1929'. *Business History* 48, no. 1 (2006): 90–118.

Wakamatsu Shinji, Morikawa Tazuko and Ito Akiyoshi. 'Air Pollution Trends in Japan between 1970 and 2012 and Impact of Urban Air Pollution Countermeasures'. *Asian Journal of Atmospheric Environment* 7, no. 4 (2013): 177–190. doi: http://dx.doi.org/10.5572/ajae.2013.7.4.177.

Wall, Derek. *Earth First! And the Anti-Roads Movement*. London: Routledge, 1999.

Walsh, Margaret. 'Gendering Mobility: Women, Work and Automobility in the United States'. *History* 93, no. 311 (2008): 376–395.

Ward, Stephen. *Planning and Urban Change*. London: Sage, 2004.

Warner, Sam Bass, Jr. *Streetcar Suburbs: The Process of Growth in Boston 1870–1900*. Cambridge, MA: Harvard University Press, 1962.

Waswo, Ann. *Housing in Postwar Japan: A Social History*. London: RoutledgeCurzon, 2002.

Weart, Spencer R. *The Discovery of Global Warming*. Cambridge, MA: Harvard University Press, 2008.

Webman, J. A. *Reviving the Industrial City: The Politics of Urban Renewal in Lyon and Birmingham*. London: Rutgers University Press, 1982.

Wegener, Michael. 'Tokyo's Land Market and Its Impact on Housing and Urban Life'. In *Planning for Cities and Regions in Japan*, edited by Philip Shapira, Ian Masser and David W. Edgington, 92–112. Liverpool: Liverpool University Press, 1994.

Wells, S. J. *British Export Performance: A Comparative Study*. Cambridge: Cambridge University Press, 1964.

White, Peter R. 'Trends in Transport: Japan and Britain Compared'. *Transportation Planning and Technology* 10 (1985): 45–52.
Williams, Raymond. *Television: Technology and Cultural Form*. London: Fontana, 1974.
Wilson, Des. *The Lead Scandal*. London: Ashgate, 1983.
Wolferen, Karel van. *The Enigma of Japanese Power: People and Politics in a Stateless Nation*. London: Macmillan, 1989.
Wolmar, Christian. *Fire and Steam: A New History of the Railways in Britain*. London: Atlantic Books, 2007.
Wood, David Murakami and Kiyoshi Abe. 'The Aesthetic of Control: Mega Events and Transformations in Japanese Urban Order'. *Urban Studies* 48, no. 15 (2011): 3241–3257.
Wood, P. A. *Industrial Britain: The West Midlands*. London, 1976.
Yamaguchi, Jack K. 'The Motor Industry of Japan'. In *World Car Catalogue 1970*. New York: Herald Books, 1970.
Yamamoto Satoshi. 'Nagoya Toshi Kōsoku Dōro Kensetsu no Hitsuyōsei'. *Shintoshi* 24, no. 2 (February 1970): 54–60.
Yazaki Takeo. *Social Change and the City in Japan*. Tokyo: Japan Publications, 1968.
Yoshino Tsuyoshi, Sasaki Tsuna and Hasegawa Toshiharu. 'The Traffic-Control System on the Hanshin Expressway'. *Interfaces* 25, no. 1 (January–February, 1995): 94–108.
Young, Michael and Peter Wilmott. *Family and Kinship in East London*. London: Penguin, 1957.
Zhang Kai and Stuart Batterman. 'Air Pollution and Health Risks due to Vehicle Traffic'. *Science of the Total Environment* 450–451 (15 April 2003): 307–316. https://doi.org/10.1016/j.scitotenv.2013.01.074.

Index

Abercrombie, Patrick 23, 24, 31, 76
accidents 2, 39, 49, 63, 111–16, 123, 140–1. *See also* road casualties
　pedestrian accidents 112, 161–2, 165
advertising and marketing 3, 14, 55, 65, 66, 103–4, 109
affluence 13, 14, 37, 94, 101–3
Aichi Prefecture 21, 28, 40, 53, 54, 84, 145, 149, 152
Aichi World Expo 2005 174
Air Pollution Control Law, 1968 (Japan) 146
Aston Expressway (Birmingham) 43, 58, 90, 94, 114, 136, 137, 141, 151, 177
Atsuta 10, 77, 80
Austin 3, 5, 9, 27, 35, 89, 104, 156
　British Leyland (from 1968) 37, 140, 156
　British Motor Corporation (from 1952) 35, 39, 106, 133
Austin A40 3, 35
Austin, Herbert 5
Austin Mini 103
Austin Seven 5
Automobile Association (AA) 48, 114, 115, 118
automobile dependency 81, 108, 121, 169
automobility
　and 'freedom' 2, 3, 12, 13, 100, 111, 114, 116, 117, 118, 121, 124, 152, 171, 173, 178
　impact on transportation patterns (Japan) 86–7
　and population density 87
average speeds on roads 48, 152
Ayuchi-dōri-Kagamigaike Line Opposition Alliance 145

Banham, Reyner 99–100, 114
barakku (barrack-built housing) 30

Barlow Committee on the Distribution of Industrial Population 30, 76, 90
Basic Law for Environmental Pollution Control, 1967 (Japan) 135
Basic Principles of Reconstruction Planning for War Damaged Areas, 1945 (Japan) 32
Beijing 25
Bendixson, Terence 50, 55, 62, 107
bicycles 21, 36, 38, 40, 89, 95, 110, 124, 173, 175, 181. *See also* cycling
'Big Four' pollution cases (Japan) 131, 135, 145, 146, 168
Big Top 64
Birmingham
　boundaries 6, 20, 41, 74–6, 97
　early history 7
　employment also unemployment 37, 76, 92, 153, 156
　population 7–9, 21, 31, 76, 91–3
　population density 8, 176
Birmingham city centre 20, 25–7, 29, 31–2, 44, 53, 59, 61–2, 65–6, 68, 69, 72, 92, 95, 98, 107, 119, 122, 141, 143, 156–7, 178
Birmingham Corporation Act 1946 27, 31, 52, 61
Birmingham Development Plan (1952) 31–2, 38, 61–2, 76, 90, 91, 93
Birmingham Development Plan (1960) 160
Birmingham New Street and Station 96, 122, 174
'Blitz and Blight Act' (1944) 27, 90
Borg, Neville 50, 55, 137, 144, 181
breakdown (mechanical) 111, 118
British Leyland. *See under* Austin
British Motor Show 39
British Roads Federation 39, 152
Bryant Civil Engineering 55, 127, 142–4
BSA (British Small Arms Company) 5, 9, 27, 35

Buchanan, Colin 13, 49, 50–1, 55, 58, 61, 62, 64, 68–9, 88, 93, 95, 116, 127, 134, 159, 165, 169, 176, 179
  Traffic in Towns 1963 13, 49–51, 61, 68, 88, 116, 134
Bull Ring 64, 65–6, 72, 95, 107–8, 157, 180
buses 18, 21, 33, 40, 41, 64–5, 73, 74, 75, 78, 82, 86, 89, 91, 93, 95–6, 107, 122, 127, 157, 160, 163, 164, 173, 176
bus-lanes 149, 151, 163, 164

car culture 3, 4, 12, 13, 67, 98, 99, 108–9, 111–18, 121, 172
car exports, imports
  Britain 3, 35–6, 40, 47, 133, 175
  Japan 47, 50, 133–4, 158, 175
car ownership (Britain) 2, 37–8, 46–52, 88, 101–6, 121–2, 141–2, 170–1
  Birmingham 94
  costs 104–6, 118, 152, 158, 172
  income factors 37, 102–3, 156
  and social profile 88, 94, 121–2, 170–1, 172
car ownership (Japan) 2, 38, 46–52, 121–2
  costs 102, 104, 105, 152, 155, 163, 172
  income factors 38, 50–2, 102–3, 105, 109, 171
  and social profile 121–2, 155, 162–4, 171–2
'car-owning democracy' 3, 47, 101, 103, 122, 136
car parks, parking 1, 2, 14, 49, 55, 59, 62–5, 70, 87, 103–4, 106, 107, 110–11, 117, 118, 143, 149, 163–4, 171, 175, 178
carports 110, 176
car purchase. *See* car ownership
cars
  containment 13, 47, 51, 116, 121–4, 141, 161–5
  criticism 3, 51, 68–9, 71, 73, 87, 95, 110, 115, 121–4, 127–8, 134, 153, 155, 183
  and house design 75, 76, 78, 80, 91, 94, 102, 109–11, 176
  as status symbol 101, 103–4, 107, 111, 152
Carson, Rachel, *Silent Spring* 134

'car system' 12, 74, 121, 167, 169, 172, 182–3
car taxation 48, 52, 53, 104, 106, 163, 171
car use 51, 86, 163, 171–2
Castle, Barbara 49–50, 112, 114
Chakrabarty, Dipesh 11–12
Chamber of Commerce (Birmingham) 25, 40
Chamberlain, Joseph 10, 53, 155
Champs Élysées (Paris) 1–2, 33, 34, 67, 177, 180
Chauffeurs 103–4, 117
Chicago Area Transportation Study (CATS) 60–1
Chikusa Ward (Nagoya) 75, 145, 147–8
China 9, 19, 24–5, 28, 56, 75, 87, 173, 178, 183
Chūbu Economic Sphere 83
Chūgoku (Central) Highway 148
Chūkyō Auto Region (Japan) 5
Chūkyō-Detroit Plan, 1929 28
Chūkyō Metropolitan Area 7, 8, 83, 84
Chūkyō region 28, 34, 37, 130, 145, 161
City Beautiful movement 25, 56
City Planning and Urban Building Law, 1919 (Japan) 41
Civic Amenities Act 1967 13
civil engineering 17, 24–5, 43, 45, 51, 54, 56, 58, 142, 156
Clean Air Act, 1970 (United States) 131, 134
Committee on the Problem of Noise, 1960 (Britain) 134
commuting 38, 39, 48, 77, 84, 87
commuting by car 48, 79, 80, 88–9, 92, 93, 97, 109, 163, 164
commuting by rail 77, 82, 175
comparative history 4–15
compensation, financial 94, 133, 135, 137, 142, 145–51
compulsory purchase (Britain) 23, 27, 32, 52–3, 90–1, 140, 167
conservationism 13, 67, 128, 165–7, 170, 180
consumerism 14, 37, 51–2, 94, 102–5, 106–11, 136, 152, 178, 180
  ambivalence towards 52, 136, 171–2
Conurbation (1948) 31, 76–7, 88
Corbusier, Le 2

Coventry 5, 36, 59, 101, 177
Crossroads (British TV series) 108–9
cycling 18, 21, 38, 40, 89, 95, 109, 124–5, 157, 163, 173, 175, 181, 183. *See also* bicycles

Detroit 5, 9, 153, 156
disaster prevention 6, 14, 33, 42, 56, 76, 77, 178, 180
Dore, Ronald 48
driving behaviour 4, 40, 49, 58, 99–121, 124
driving licence 21, 122
driving schools 21
driving speeds 1–2, 21, 22, 48, 54, 67, 111, 113–15, 118, 152, 158, 181
Duddeston 30, 72, 90
Dunlop 5, 27, 35

earthquakes 6, 23, 56, 57, 111, 113, 118, 178. *See also* natural disasters
'economic miracle' (Japan) 11, 51, 102, 175
Edo Period. *See* Tokugawa Period
Emperor Hirohito 34
environment 3, 12–13, 15, 67–70, 127–53, 155, 157–72, 178–83. *See also* pollution; urban environment
  definition of 3
Environment, Department of (Britain) 114, 128, 135, 144
Environment Agency (Japan) 134, 151
environmental activism 127–51, 160, 165–9, 170
'environmental awakening' 129–36, 157–9
environmental NGOs (Japan) 166, 168
expressways. *See under* motorways

Fidler, Sheppard 25, 72
First World War 5, 17, 41, 73
Friends of the Earth 166, 167, 168
fuel (including petrol, diesel and gasoline) 12, 14, 138, 147, 151, 166, 172, 182
  gasoline tax (Japan) 52–3, 163
Fukuoka-Kitakyūshū Expressway Corporation 148

garden city 18, 20, 25
Garden City Movement (Ebenezer Howard) 18, 25

German autobahn 3, 28, 44
Germany 3, 10, 23, 27, 28, 44, 47, 88, 105, 111
government policy (Britain) 53, 135–6, 159
government policy (Japan) 13, 30, 33, 49, 51–2, 120, 161, 163, 168
Gravelly Hill Interchange (Spaghetti Junction) 58, 100, 114, 118
  pollution 128, 136–9, 152, 165, 177, 179
green belt 10, 32, 67, 75, 76, 78, 97
green spaces 18, 19–20, 32, 59, 72, 130, 173, 179. *See also* garden city
  Beijing 25
  disaster prevention 76, 178
gridlock 21, 49

Hall, Peter 6, 27, 93, 159
Hanshin Expressway 117, 118
  Hanshin Expressway Public Corporation 117, 148, 168
Higashiyama (Nagoya) 54, 63, 73, 145, 151
  rapid transit line (subway) 63, 86
Highbury Initiative (Birmingham) 155–7, 159, 174, 179
Hiroshima 19, 32, 33, 61, 78
Honda 133
  Honda Soichirō 13, 133
Hoshino Yoshirō 110, 120
  and *mai-kā* 121
housing (Birmingham) 9, 29–30, 31–2, 75, 90–1, 93
  house building and reconstruction 74
  housing estates 74, 78
housing (Nagoya and Japan) 20, 30, 75, 79–80, 81, 97
  home ownership 80, 110
  house building and reconstruction 30, 76
  Japan Housing Corporation 30, 76, 81
Housing and Town Planning Act, 1919 (Britain) 41

Ichinomiya Interchange 43, 84, 161
Ikeda Hayato, 'Income Doubling Plan' 52
Inner Ring Road (Birmingham) 6, 17, 20, 27, 29, 31, 32, 43, 44, 52–3, 54–5, 59, 61–4, 178, 179

Index

'concrete collar' 92, 157
corruption scandal (1977) 127–8, 142–4
financing 40–1
'legibility' 119
opening 68
International Bank for Reconstruction and Development (World Bank) 40
Ishikawa Hideaki 9, 17, 19–20, 24, 41–2
Iwakura Embassy 18–19

Japan Automobile Federation (JAF) 39, 115
Japan Automobile Manufacturers' Association (JAMA) 39, 155
Japan Highway Public Corporation 58, 168
jinrikisha (rickshaws) 21–2

Kanayama (Nagoya) 56, 73, 77, 82
keijidōsha (light vehicle) 38, 105, 106, 114, 171, 176
Kobe 28
Korea 19, 30
Korean War 36
Koromo 5, 36–7, 76. See also Toyota City
Kozoji Newtown. *See under* new towns, Japan
Kume Kunitake 19
kuruma banare (turning one's back on the car) 155, 182

Ladywood (Birmingham) 30, 90
land readjustment, LR (Nagoya) 10, 22–3, 26, 33–4, 44, 53, 61, 74, 78–9, 81, 87
Law Concerning the Settlement of Environmental Disputes (Japan) 168
Leeds 50, 54, 69, 93, 95
Liberal Democratic Party, LDP (Japan) 36, 51, 146, 149
Liverpool 10, 24, 50, 95, 96
Lodge, David, *Changing Places* 99
London xiv, 6, 8, 10, 18, 20, 21, 24, 37, 40, 43, 48, 49, 50, 76, 94–6, 109, 128, 134, 139–40, 144, 153, 156, 158, 160, 167, 179
Longbridge (Birmingham) 3, 5, 9, 35, 89, 133, 140, 153, 156

Los Angeles 5, 13, 99, 100, 133, 134, 173, 179
Lucas, Joseph (firm) 9, 27, 35
Lynch, Kevin, *The Image of the City* 119.
See also urban legibility

MacArthur, General Douglas (Supreme Commander Allied Powers) 26, 29, 112
Mai-kā Gannen. See 'my car'
manufacturing industry (Birmingham) 5, 6, 8–9, 31–2, 35–7, 40, 47, 74, 76, 88–9, 92–3, 141, 156, 157, 175
manufacturing industry (Nagoya) 4, 5, 6, 9, 36–7, 47, 75, 76, 79, 83, 84, 173, 175, 177
Manzoni, Herbert 5, 6, 21, 22, 24–6, 27, 29, 31, 39, 41–2, 44, 51, 52, 54–5, 58–9, 62–4, 69, 72, 75, 78, 88, 90–1, 93, 95–6, 98, 101–2, 107, 116, 139, 141, 157, 160, 173, 177–81
Manzoni Gardens 72, 116, 181
Marples, Ernest 49, 51, 113, 159
Masshouse Circus 142–3, 156
megalopolitan areas 6, 161, 176
megastructures 63–4
Meiji Period 11, 18–19, 21, 33, 71, 130, 166
Meishin Expressway 39, 43, 50, 52, 59–60, 84, 120, 161–2, 176
Metropolitan Urban Expressway (Japan) 54
Minamata mercury poisoning case 131–3
Ministry of Construction (Japan) 145, 151, 168
Ministry of Housing and Local Government (Britain) 27, 31, 91
Ministry of International Trade and Industry, MITI, (Japan) 105, 110, 135
  Peoples Car Plan 105
Ministry of Transport, later Department (Britain) 112, 113, 114–15, 128, 159, 161, 169
Minobe Ryōkichi 124, 149
modernism 1–2, 14, 98, 99–100, 128
modernity 61, 65, 108, 121, 180
  automotive modernity 43, 100, 178
  Taisho modernity 19
  urban modernity 13, 19, 43, 45, 71

'motor city' 25, 37, 43, 52, 72, 75, 152–3, 182
   Birmingham 34, 78, 95, 127–8, 129, 139, 142, 179
   definition 5–6
   Nagoya 29, 173
   Tange Kenzo 97, 181
motorcycles 37–8, 40, 48, 114, 134, 153, 178
'motordom' 3, 4, 99
motorization 6, 12, 18, 37–40, 46–8, 78, 90, 93–4, 97, 116, 174, 176, 182
   ambivalence towards 51, 100, 127, 170, 172
motorization/environment (ME) dilemma 3, 13, 136, 142, 152, 178
motor manufacturing (Britain and Birmingham) 27, 34–7, 40–1, 42, 141, 176, 177
   employment 37, 76, 91, 146
motor manufacturing (Japan and Nagoya) 27, 34–7, 42, 176, 177
   employment 37, 75
'motor revolution' (Britain) 4, 46–7, 49–51, 69, 121, 141
motorways, expressways 4, 20, 27, 29, 40, 61, 88, 93, 100, 113, 114, 118, 124, 159, 161, 165
   M1 43, 58, 93, 113
   M6 (M5) 43, 58, 91, 136–7
   construction 50, 116, 127, 170
   pollution 127, 128, 137–9, 160, 165, 176
   protest against 127–8, 129, 139–41, 148, 150, 152–3, 158, 167–8, 170
   urban motorways 43, 50, 54–5, 58, 65, 89, 92, 118, 172, 182
Motoyama Masao 149–50, 173
moving buildings (Nagoya) 57–8
'my car' (*mai-kā*) 1–2, 19, 121, 173
My Car Era (*mai-kā jidai*) 2, 13, 48

Nagoya
   early history 9
   employment also unemployment 79, 83, 84, 173
   expansion 75, 77, 79
   population 7, 9, 173
   population density 8, 77, 80, 86, 186 n.36

Nagoya City Council 145–6, 149, 152
   and the 'Three Conditions and Eight Clauses' 145–6, 148–9, 152
Nagoya Expressway Corporation 54, 128, 151
Nagoya Port (Meiko) 28–9
Nagoya Station 5, 22, 31, 63, 65, 77, 82, 86, 96–7
Nagoya Urban Expressway 17, 43, 54, 117, 128, 145, 151
   planning and 'Marusa Plan' 84–5, 85, 145
   protest against 127–8, 129, 148, 150
natural disasters 6, 23, 56, 57, 113, 118, 178
nature 3, 13, 21, 33, 65, 66, 98, 128, 146, 174, 180
Nechells (Birmingham) 30, 90, 140
'New Birmingham' 32, 44, 62, 72, 107, 152, 153, 178
new towns 30, 76, 80–1
   in Birmingham 30, 90, 98, 178
   Kozoji (Nagoya) 80, 81
   Senri (Osaka) 80
   Tama (Tokyo) 80
Nissan Datsun 3, 105
'no-car folk' 100, 121, 124, 125

Occupation of Japan (1945–1952) 26, 29, 36
   and reconstruction 30, 32, 74, 78
'oil shocks' (1973, 1979) 14, 124, 155, 157, 166
   Britain 158, 170
   Japan 153, 158, 159
Olympic Games 1, 49, 100, 120, 129, 145, 173, 179
100-metre-wide roads (Nagoya) 17, 26, 32, 33
   Beijing 25
   as firebreaks and refuges 42, 56
   Hisaya Ōdōri 6, 33, 34, 45, 56–7, 67, 78, 173
   Sutcliffe, Anthony on 34, 45
   Wakamiya Ōdōri 6, 30, 33, 67
Osaka 6, 32, 43, 61, 67, 78, 86, 147, 149, 161, 165, 166, 168
   pollution 147, 166
   road protests 148, 168
   urban expressway 117

Ōsu (Nagoya) 71, 73, 77
Oxford 36, 54, 167, 172, 182–3
Ōzone (Nagoya) 77, 82

Paradise Circus (Birmingham) 64
Paris 1–2, 19, 27, 177
　Paris Périphérique 27
pedestrian crossings 22
pedestrianization 21, 59, 67, 120, 122, 124, 141, 163, 165
pedestrians 3, 21, 87, 122, 181
　accidents 39, 112, 115, 122–3, 162
　Birmingham 29, 54, 64, 69, 91, 95, 119, 122
　Nagoya 21, 39, 70, 71, 88, 123, 162, 177
pedestrian subways (underpasses) 61, 64, 119, 157
pollution (Britain) 13, 124, 127, 128, 133, 134, 135, 136–9, 142, 152–3, 165, 166, 168, 172, 176, 179, 182
pollution (Japan) 13, 84, 127, 129, 130–3, 145–8, 150–1, 161, 163, 166, 168, 171, 172
pollution control 133–4, 135
population and vehicle density 48, 59, 76–80, 86–8, 95, 96, 121, 172, 176
post-colonial history 11–12
post-war reconstruction (Nagoya) 20, 29–30, 32–3, 34, 42
post-war urban redevelopment (Birmingham) 12, 17, 23, 25, 27, 29–37, 90–3, 143
Preston by-pass 39, 43
Price, Frank 40, 59, 107
protest (Britain) 13, 14, 93, 127, 128, 129–30, 137, 139–40, 142, 151–3, 167, 170, 176, 179, 183
protest (Japan) 13, 14, 34, 127–8, 129, 131–3, 145, 147–8, 150–3, 168, 182, 183
public transport (road) Birmingham 21, 33, 95, 96, 109, 122, 159, 160, 169
public transport (road) Nagoya 48, 63, 73, 80, 84, 117, 147, 149, 162, 163–4
　passengers carried by type of transport 86–7
Public Works Committee (Birmingham) 25, 29, 33, 40, 59, 62, 64, 68, 93, 95, 107, 140, 169

railways (Britain) 14, 33, 54, 73, 74–5, 96, 108, 140, 159–60, 172, 174, 175
　Beeching Report (1963) 33, 96, 108, 160
railways (Japan) 1, 20, 28, 50, 56–7, 61, 63, 65, 73, 75, 76–8, 81–2, 86–7, 97, 107, 112, 117, 130, 149, 150, 161, 175, 178
rapid transit 33, 61, 63, 81, 86, 96
reconstruction planning (Birmingham) 10, 27, 31–2, 44, 90–2, 178
reconstruction planning (Nagoya) 5, 10, 19–20, 25, 29, 30, 32–4, 44–5, 53, 56, 67, 78, 178
Regional Highways Public Corporation Law, 1970 (Japan) 54, 145
ribbon development 75, 77. *See also* sprawl
ring roads. *See also* Inner Ring Road
　Birmingham, middle and outer 6, 9, 17, 20, 25, 29, 30, 51, 55, 58, 89–92, 97–8, 137, 141, 167, 177, 181
　Japan 20, 54, 58, 149
　London 18
　Oxford 167
road casualties 2, 21, 26, 49, 111–15, 121–2, 124, 147, 161–2, 179. *See also* accidents
road safety 3, 33, 49, 111, 114–16, 122–3, 140–1, 163
Roads Campaign Council (Britain) 39
'road scene' 33, 67
roads construction (Britain) 10, 24, 40, 43–72
roads construction (Japan) 19, 30, 32–5, 42–73, 121, 161
road signs 2, 58, 61, 114, 115–16, 118–20, 165
roads investment (Britain) 4, 32, 39, 40–1, 44, 53, 64, 128, 142, 170
roads investment (Japan) 4, 50–1, 53–4, 58, 79
roads policy 30, 50–3, 76, 89–90, 145, 149, 157, 159–61, 169–70
　link to motor manufacturing 37
Royal Automobile Club (RAC) 39, 114

Sakae 124, 173
sakariba 107–8, 178. *See also* underground malls and streets

salariman (white collar worker) 109, 171
Sano City 48
Second World War (Birmingham) 4, 5, 10, 25, 26–35, 41, 111, 112, 176
Second World War (Nagoya) 10, 25, 26–35, 41, 78–9, 82, 112, 129, 130, 178
Senri Newtown 80. *See under* new towns, Japan
shanty town 30. *See barakku*
Shibusawa, Ei'ichi (Den'enchōfu) 18
shinkansen ('bullet train') 1, 28, 65, 100, 150
  Tōkaidō Shinkansen 28, 56, 82, 161
Shinohara Kazuo 110
Shinohata 48
shopping 12, 14, 29, 44, 49, 55, 59, 62–7, 69–70, 71, 77, 87–8, 92–5, 97, 102–3, 107–9, 119–20, 122–4, 141, 146, 157, 165, 172–8, 180. *See also* consumerism
'shopper motorist' 107
Skyway (Coventry Road Expressway) 93–4, 98, 181
slum clearance (Birmingham) 29, 30, 32, 90, 93, 178
Smallbrook Ringway (also Queensway) 54, 62, 66, 107–8, 119, 142, 156, 180
Spaghetti Junction, Birmingham. *See* Gravelly Hill Interchange
Special Measures for the Preservation of Historic Landscape in Ancient Capitals Act (1966) 166
speed limits 22, 111, 114–15, 158, 164
Stilgoe, Henry 17, 20, 41
Subaru 360 (Lady Beetle) 105–6
suburbs, suburbanization
  Birmingham 10, 20, 73–5, 79–80, 88, 94, 142, 160
  Nagoya 73–7, 79–80, 97, 105–6, 109–10, 121
subway, rail 28, 61, 63–4, 71, 77, 81–2, 86, 97, 107, 173. *See also* rapid transit
subways, underpasses 59, 64, 91, 95, 119, 122, 143–4, 157, 181. *See also* underground malls and streets
Sugito Kiyoshi 128, 149

Tabuchi Jurō 5, 24–6, 34, 40, 41–2, 45, 56, 67, 71–2, 177–8, 180

Taisho Period 19
Tama Newtown. *See under* new towns, Japan
Tange Kenzo 1, 19, 59, 97, 100, 181
taxis 49, 86, 103, 119, 157, 174
Tokugawa Period 9, 33, 71, 77
Tokyo xiv, 1, 6, 8, 18, 19, 20, 21, 23–5, 26, 28, 32, 43, 44, 48–9, 54–6, 58, 61, 65, 70, 73, 77–80, 86–7, 97, 100, 103–6, 115, 117–18, 120, 124, 129, 130–2, 135, 145, 147, 149, 161–2, 164, 166, 179
  Tokyo Bay Area Artery Project 168
  Tokyo City Improvement Ordinance, 1888 (TCIO) 18, 20
Tokyo Drifter, 1966 film (Dir. Suzuki Seijun) 1–2, 100
Tokyo Urban Expressway 54–6, 58
Tokyo Metropolitan Urban Expressway Corporation 54
Tokyo Motor Show 102, 103, 105, 115–16, 124
Tokyo Olympics, 1964. *See* Olympic Games
toll roads 50, 52, 54, 56, 59, 60, 61, 117, 171
Tōmei Expressway 60, 145, 161
Town and Country Planning Acts, 1944, 1947 (Britain) 23, 27, 31, 90
town planning. *See* urban planning
Toyoda Ki'ichirō 5, 9, 36
Toyopet Crown 37
Toyota City 5, 36, 37, 177. *See also* Koromo
Toyota Corolla 102, 105
Toyota Motor Corporation 5, 36–8, 43, 63, 76, 80, 102, 105, 133, 150, 174
Toyota Publica 102, 105
traffic architecture 14, 46, 61–5, 178
traffic congestion 21, 22, 38–9, 42, 48–9, 64, 67, 88, 117–18, 145, 149
traffic engineering 6, 22, 45, 61, 65, 67, 117, 145
  influence of United States 3, 58
traffic flow 1, 3, 18, 55, 58–61, 64, 67, 84, 91, 114, 116, 141, 162–3, 180–1
Traffic in Towns. See under Buchanan, Colin
traffic islands (roundabouts) 2, 21, 58, 136

traffic lights (controls) 3, 21, 136, 162
traffic management 49, 56, 72, 117, 162
traffic, mixed 17, 18, 21, 22, 33, 38, 40
traffic safety 111, 115, 123
trams, trolley buses 21, 32, 50–2, 54, 56, 59, 60, 61, 117, 171
Tripp, Alker 21, 111, 112
Turin 5

Ui Jun (activist) 132
underground shopping malls and streets
  Birmingham 65, 119, 142
  Nagoya 63–5, 70–1, 82, 87, 97, 107–8, 178, 180
Unit Cell Scheme (Nagoya) 135, 164–5
United States 3, 4, 5, 6, 13, 18, 21, 26, 27, 47, 57, 59, 67, 96, 104, 121, 129, 131, 132, 133–5, 136, 139, 157, 158, 179
Unwin, Raymond 19
urban 'blight' xv, 14, 27, 74, 84, 90, 93–4, 98, 131, 134, 140, 142, 152, 153, 165, 176, 179
urban environment xiv, 3, 5, 10, 12–13, 20, 43–72, 127, 149, 152–3, 156, 163, 165, 167, 177, 180, 183
urban form 8, 14, 20–1, 73–98
urban legibility 118–21. *See also* Lynch, Kevin
urban planning (Britain) 9–10, 18, 20–1, 23, 35, 41–2, 128, 177, 182
urban planning (Japan) 9–10, 18–20, 22–5, 26, 32–3, 35, 41–2, 90, 115, 120, 152, 177–8
urban renewal 1–2, 6, 24, 31–2, 44, 59, 68, 144, 152, 153, 157, 178, 179, 182

urban sprawl 6, 14, 18, 32, 73, 75, 77, 79, 84, 96. *See also* ribbon development
Urry, John 12, 104, 109, 182

vehicle ownership. *See* car ownership
vibration 104, 129, 133, 135, 147, 150–1, 153, 168, 179
Volkswagen 5, 105

Walker, Patrick Gordon 47
Walker, Peter 68, 69
Watkins, Ralph J. 4, 39
  Watkins Survey 39
Watkinson, Harold 41
West Midlands 7, 37, 88, 141, 153, 156, 177
West Midlands County Council 140, 143–4
West Midlands Plan (1948) 31, 76, 88–9
'white streets', (*waito rōdo*) 88, 97, 178. *See also* underground malls and streets
Wilson, Sir Alan (Wilson Committee) 134, 137
Wolfsburg (Germany) 5
women 1, 14, 37, 65, 84, 95, 109, 150, 179
  and automobility 69, 84, 106, 122, 135, 140, 170–2

Yagoto Hills (Nagoya) 73, 75, 79
Yamanote 'loop' railway (Tokyo) 20
Yamawaki Iwao 110
Yokkaichi asthma case 130–2, 145, 148, 152
Yokohama 20, 23, 32, 149
Yoshida Shigeru 39
Yugawa Toshikazu 121

www.ingramcontent.com/pod-product-compliance
Lightning Source LLC
Chambersburg PA
CBHW070025010526
44117CB00011B/1712